simoniacal entry

into religious life

from 1000 to 1260

Joseph H. Lynch

simoniacal entry into religious life from 1000 to 1260

a social, economic and legal study

Ohio State University Press : Columbus

Copyright © 1976 by the Ohio State University Press
All Rights Reserved.
Manufactured in the United States of America

Library of Congress Cataloguing in Publication Data
Lynch, Joseph H   1943-
    Simoniacal entry into religious life from 1000 to 1260.
    Bibliography: p.
    Includes index.
    1. Monasticism and religious orders—Middle Ages, 600-1500. 2. Simony—History
I. Title.
BX2470.L95   271   76-22670
ISBN 0-8142-0222-5

contents

	List of Abbreviations	vii
	Acknowledgments	ix
	Introduction	xi
I	Monastic Economic Problems and the Reception of New Members	3
II	Lay Needs and Entry into Religious Life	25
III	Gifts from Entrants: The Beginnings of Criticism	61
IV	Entry Payments as Simony	83
V	The Canonists and Simoniacal Reception	107
VI	Measures against Simoniacal Entry, 1163–1198	147
VII	Innocent III and Simoniacal Entry	179
VIII	The Aftermath of the Fourth Lateran Council	203
	Bibliography	231
	Index	261

Illustrations

The illustrations on the preceding pages are from illuminated manuscripts, and are reproduced here by permission.

Page i   A father, in company with kinsmen and friends, offers a son and a bag of money to a group of monks. Illumination of Gratian's *Decretum, causa I, questio 2*, Archives of Prague Castle, ms. XII, A12, fol. 80.

Page ii   A husband and wife offer their son, along with a bag of money, to a bishop and a monk. Illumination by Master Honoré, Bibliothèque Municipale of Tours, ms. 558, fol. 93.

Page v   A father, with a handful of coins at his breast, offers his son to two monks. Illumination of *Decretum, causa I, questio 2*, Staatsbibliothek Preussischer Kulturbesitz, Berlin, ms. Lat. Fol. 1, fol. 64^r.

Abbreviations

Cartularies are cited in abbreviated form by the name of the religious house's patron saint or location. Other frequently used abbreviations are:

AASS
Acta Sanctorum (Antwerp, 1643–), 70 vols. to date.

Auvray
Les Registres de Grégoire IX, ed. Lucien Auvray (Paris, 1890–1907), 3 vols. Bibliothèque des écoles françaises d'Athènes et de Rome.

Canivez, *Statuta*
Statuta capitulorum generalium ordinis cisterciensis, ed. Joseph Marie Canivez (Louvain, 1933–41), 8 vols. Bibliothèque de la Revue d'histoire ecclésiastique, fasc. 9–14b.

Capitularia
Monumenta Germaniae historica, *Leges*, II: *Capitularia regum francorum*, ed. A. Boretius and V. Krause (Hanover, 1883–97), 2 vols.

Charvin, *Statuts*
Statuts, chapitres généraux et visites de l'Ordre de Cluny, ed. Gaston Charvin (Paris, 1965–), 7 vols. to date.

Concilia
Monumenta Germaniae historica, *Leges*, III: *Concilia*, ed. F. Maassen and A. Werminghoff (Hanover, 1924), 2 vols.

DDC
Dictionnaire de droit canonique, ed. R. Naz (Paris, 1935–), 7 vols. to date.

DHGE
Dictionnaire d'histoire et de géographie ecclésiastiques, ed. A. Baudrillart et al. (Paris, 1912–).

JL

P. Jaffé, *Regesta Pontificum Romanorum ab condita ecclesia ad annum post Christum natum 1198*, 2d ed., ed. F. Kaltenbrunner (to A.D. 590); P. Ewald (590‒882); and S. Loewenfeld (882‒1198) (Leipzig, 1885‒88), 2 vols.

Mansi

Sacrorum conciliorum nova et amplissima collectio, ed. J. D. Mansi (Florence and Venice, 1759‒98), 31 vols.

MGH, *SS*

Monumenta Germaniae historica, *Scriptores* in folio (Hanover, 1826‒1934), 32 vols.

Migne

J. P. Migne, *Patrologiae cursus completus.* Series latina (Paris, 1844‒55), 221 vols. Index (Paris, 1862‒64), 4 vols.

Pott

A. Potthast, *Regesta Pontificum Romanorum inde ab anno 1198 ad annum 1304* (Berlin, 1874‒75), 2 vols.

Pressutti

Regesta Honorii papae III, ed. Pietro Pressutti (Rome, 1888‒95), 2 vols.

Rolls series

Rerum Britannicarum medii aevi scriptores, under the direction of the Master of the Rolls (London, 1858‒96), 99 vols.

Ronceray

"Cartularium monasterii beatae Mariae Caritatis Andegavensis," ed. Paul Marchegay, *Archives d'Anjou* (Angers, 1854), vol. 3.

Acknowledgements

The author of a book written over a long period of time owes many debts of gratitude. I apologize in advance for any that I may overlook. I wish first to thank Professor Giles Constable, Harvard University, for his advice and encouragement. I thank also Professor Anthony Melnikas, the Ohio State University, for his assistance in acquiring the book's illustrations. I wish to express gratitude to the libraries whose resources and generosity made my research possible: Harvard University Libraries; the Bibliothèque Nationale, Paris; the University of Illinois Library; the Ohio State University Library; the Institute of Medieval Canon Law, Berkeley. Finally, I thank my wife, Ann, for her patience and support.

Introduction

The century and a half from 1050 to 1200 was crucial for the development of both church and society in the Latin West. It was a complex period, and modern scholars have employed a wide variety of approaches and techniques in order to grasp that complexity. Economic historians have described the period as one of economic and demographic expansion. Historians of the church have characterized it as an age of religious ferment that generated both new religious orders and new heresies. Institutional historians have found in those decades the beginnings of centralization and rationalization of government, most evident in the rise of the papacy and of the feudal monarchies. Finally, historians of culture and intellectual life have described a major revival in art, literature, and education that has been called the "Renaissance of the Twelfth Century."

In this study I propose to treat the unfolding of a single issue, that of the propriety of obtaining membership in a religious house in return for a payment. The debate over gifts at entry into religion is an illuminating one for the general history of monasticism, and it is also significant because it offers insight into the genesis and spread during the twelfth century of new legal and moral concerns from the university-trained elite to other groups in the church. Put briefly, this is a study of the formulation and partial implementation of new, disapproving views of gifts at entry into religion, views that upset generations-old social and economic arrangements. An understanding of the origin and diffusion of those views sheds considerable light on the forces of rationalization at work in the church between 1050 and 1200.

The primary, though not exclusive, focus of this examination is Benedictine and French. It is based in good part upon some fifty monastic cartularies, which were examined for the information that they provided about traditional entry practices. The views gained from the charters were broadened and corrected by examining the legislation of religious orders, the writings of the canonists, the decrees of church councils, and documents issued by papal and episcopal chanceries. Virtually all religious houses, whatever their formal affiliation or rule, confronted analogous social and economic problems in the twelfth century, and virtually all found in the negotiations that preceded reception of a new member an opportunity to deal with some of those problems. One of the facts that emerged from this study was that, in spite of some differences from group to group, almost all varieties of religious communities in the twelfth century followed a similar pattern in that they received new members with gifts and under conditions.

Since the origins of Christian monasticism in fourth-century Egypt, the decision to join an ascetic community had been a complex phenomenon, not easily reduced to the formulaic treatment accorded it by hagiographers. When Benedict of Nursia (ca. 480–ca. 550) composed his *Rule* in the mid-sixth century, he drew upon a monastic tradition already more than two centuries old.[1] Benedict was aware of his debt to the past, and the *Rule* itself recommended to his followers the writings of John Cassian and Basil of Caesarea.[2] Modern scholarship has painstakingly ferreted out and identified the earlier writers upon whom Benedict drew.[3] In 1940 Dom Augustin Génestout suggested the revolutionary view that Benedict had drawn heavily upon one particular source, an anonymous rule known as the *Rule of the Master*, apparently written in Italy between 500 and 535.[4] Dom Génestout's hypothesis stimulated a generation of investigation into the relationship between the *Rule* of Benedict and that of the Master, which has generally confirmed the chronological priority of the latter and its extensive use by Benedict as a source. As a consequence of this revised view of Benedict's work, recent scholarship has modified the traditional estimate of Benedict's originality and has placed him more clearly in the tradition of late Roman monastic legislators.[5]

However, these brilliant discoveries have had remarkably little effect on the assessment of the *Rule*'s importance in the medieval West. The primary facts for medievalists are that during the seventh and early eighth centuries Benedict's *Rule* was one of several important pieces of monastic legislation and that during the late eighth and ninth centuries the combined efforts of Anglo-Saxon missionaries and the Carolingian monarchs made it the norm for monastic life in the West.[6] Although the *Rule of the Master* and other sources used by Benedict fell into oblivion, his *Rule* served as the framework of life for generations of monks and nuns.

Benedict's monastery was a celibate community, and it perpetuated itself by admitting outsiders, first to a probationary membership and then to permanent membership. Aside from the implicit requirements that all new members be male and Christian, the *Rule* excluded no group in society from membership. Slaves and freemen were admitted,[7] as well as children and adolescents.[8] The *Rule* also assumed that there would be sick and aged members of the community.[9] Rich, middling, and poor could be members.[10] Laymen provided most of the recruits, but priests and other clerics could join provided that they did not demand privileges because of their possession of holy orders.[11] Even a monk from another community could be received, but if he came from a known monastery, permission or a letter of recommendation was required from his abbot.[12]

Benedict's *Rule* contained some important silences about entrants. It laid down no minimum or maximum age for entry, no educational requirement, no specific arrangements about the state of health of the new member. In addition, it made no comment on his marital status. Indeed, the sole expressed requirements for entry were of a moral nature. The entrant had to be persistent, sincere, willing freely to give up his own will and to promise the observance of obedience to the abbot, lifelong stability in the monastery, and conversion of his life style.[13] The Benedictine abbot was a powerful figure—indeed, a monarch—and could no doubt exercise considerable discretion in admitting new members. But from the letter of the *Rule*, any male could join Benedict's monastery if the abbot found him acceptable on the grounds of sincerity and other personal moral qualities.

When a person chose to enter religious life, the disposition of his property was a socially important decision. Benedict's *Rule* demanded no contribution from the new member. Unlike some monastic rules that forbade any gift at all to the monastery,[14] it did, however, permit the recruit the choice of offering his property to the poor or to the monastery.[15] When a family offered a boy to the monastery, the *Rule* asked it to disinherit the child, and only if it wished to do so was a gift to be given along with the child.[16] Thus a gift at entry was a possibility, but by no means a requirement.

Because of its social importance, monasticism was not permitted to develop in a vacuum. Both secular rulers and the episcopate in the later Roman Empire and in the Middle Ages attempted to specify more clearly who could and who could not enter a monastery. Benedict's *Rule* was, of course, not rewritten; but on many matters, including that of recruits, legislation and custom modified significantly its provisions and filled in its silences. By the eleventh century the norms for entry were much developed and elaborated.

The right of an unfree person to enter religious life was a threat to the property rights of his owner. The Council of Chalcedon (451), legislating even before Benedict's lifetime, forbade the reception of a slave without the permission of his master.[17] Subsequent secular and canon law reconfirmed that prohibition in various forms, sometimes more favorable to the master and sometimes to the slave-religious. Serfs, who were not slaves in the Roman sense but were unfree because of the serious burdens upon them, were also affected by the prohibition of free entry. After the Carolingian period religious life was open only rarely to serfs and other unfree persons.[18]

In its attempts to guarantee essential services, the late Roman Empire had placed restrictions on certain groups of free persons, especially by fixing them permanently in their occupations. Soldiers, *curiales*, and others could enter a monastery only under restrictions that served to guard the state against any loss that might result. Merovingian and Carolingian rulers also attempted to check the entry of free men and nobles into religious life without permission. However, such attempts at control failed, and by the eleventh century the archaic restrictions on the freedom of those with public responsibilities to enter religious life had disappeared in practice.[19]

In the eleventh century marriage had developed into the most important restriction on the right of a free man to enter religion. If a married person with a living spouse sought to join a religious community, the status of the partner who remained in the world had to be decided. Justinian had been inclined to view the entry of one spouse as the equivalent of a divorce. His legislation allowed the person left in secular life to remarry after one year.[20] However, Pope Gregory I and the canon law after him had rejected Justinian's solution because it undermined the permanence of marriage. By the eleventh century both spouses had to agree to the separation, and refusal on the part of one was sufficient to prevent entry into religious life by the other. The bishop normally encouraged both spouses to enter religion. Failing that, he sought for a vow of chastity from the spouse remaining in the world. The sole situation in which a married person could enter religion without the consent of his spouse was when the spouse was guilty of adultery.[21]

Passage by a monk from one monastery to another, called *transitus*, was also marked by certain restrictions. Benedict's *Rule* had provided that if a monk from a "known" house sought to join his monastery, he was not to be received without permission from the monk's present abbot.[22] In the eleventh century that restriction still remained, though the law governing *transitus* evolved considerably in the twelfth century.[23]

Thus in the eleventh century Benedict's provisions for the reception of new members had been modified by subsequent legislation and custom so that slaves, serfs, married persons, and religious from other houses could be received only after legal requirements peculiar to their respective situations had been observed. Beyond these restrictions, in the eleventh century there were still no formal requirements about education, age, or state of health. Hence a considerable spectrum of individuals could and did enter religious life in that century.

One of the most important developments in the procedure for obtaining entry into religion had not been the subject of legislation, but had arisen out of custom. Benedict had offered his adult entrant the option of giving his property to the poor or to the monastery, and he had not specifically ruled out the possibility that the entrant would give it to his family.[24] In the case of children offered to the monastery, Benedict had recommended disinheritance of the child by his parents. If the parents were unwilling to go so far as to disinherit their child, Benedict permitted them to make any gift that they chose to the monastery.[25] Benedict's younger contemporary, the emperor Justinian, had included provisions in the civil law that were more favorable to the economic interests of religious houses. Before Justinian the Roman law had left to the individual religious the right to make a will and to exercise some control over his or her property.[26] Justinian's legislation diminished the religious' control of his property in favor of the religious house. According to Novella 5, issued in April 535, a person was free to dispose of his property up to his formal entry into a religious house. Thereafter, any property that he still possessed at the moment of entry passed automatically into the control of the religious house.[27] These provisions apparently appeared to do an injustice to the sons of the entrant. In Novellae 76 (538 A.D.) and 123 (546 A.D.), Justinian softened the provisions of Novella 5 so that the sons of a man entering religion could receive their share of his property, called the *legitima* in Roman law, even if he had entered religious life without giving it to them beforehand.[28] Any property over and above the portions due to children still passed into the control of the monastery. In spite of

Justinian's attribution to the religious house of any undisposed goods in the possession of an entrant, his legislation in no way demanded that an entrant give property to the house that he entered.

Thus both Benedict and Justinian treated the gift at entry as optional, according to the choice of the entrant. By the eleventh century the optional or voluntary nature of the gift at entry had virtually disappeared. With few exceptions an entrant was expected to bring a gift of some sort.[29] The gift was not a dowry in the post-Tridentine sense of a fixed sum required of all entrants.[30] Instead it could vary significantly in size and nature from one entrant to the next. There was no written legislation about the gift in the eleventh century, and the situation was very fluid. But if a family refused to give a gift or an acceptable gift, it risked rejection of its candidate. For most of the eleventh century there was no criticism of this practice as simoniacal, that is, as the buying or selling of a holy thing. Indeed, there was little criticism at all. The monastic charters and other texts repeated over and over again the admonition of Jehovah in Exodus 23:15: "You will not appear in my presence empty-handed."[31] The gift at entry, in fact, became the focus around which certain serious economic and social problems were worked out between a religious house and its neighbors.

1. T. P. McLaughlin, *Le très ancien droit monastique de l'occident*, Archives de la France monastique, no. 38 (Ligugé-Paris, 1935), pp. xi-xii.

2. *Sancti Benedicti Regula Monachorum*, ed. P. Schmitz, 2d ed. (Maredsous, 1955), chap. 73.

3. Benedict's sources are indicated in *Benedicti Regula Monasteriorum*, ed. C. Butler, 3d ed. (Freiburg im Breisgau, 1935), and in *La Règle de saint Benoît*, ed. A. de Vogüé and J. Neufville (Paris, 1972), Sources chrétiennes 181-82, Série des textes monastiques d'occident nos. 34-35.

4. A. Génestout, "La Règle du Maître et la Règle de S. Benoît," *Revue d'ascétique et de mystique* 21 (1940): 51-112. The *Rule of the Master* was edited with extensive commentary in *La Règle du Maître*, ed. A. de Vogüé (Paris, 1964), Sources chrétiennes 105-7, Série des textes monastiques d'occident, nos. 14-16.

5. For a review of the controversy see D. Knowles, "The *Regula Magistri* and the *Rule* of Saint Benedict*," in *Great Historical Enterprises* (London, 1963), pp. 135–95; or A. de Vogüé, *La Règle de saint Benoît*, 1:173–314.

6. McLaughlin, *Le très ancien droit*, pp. 3–33.

7. *Sancti Benedicti Regula*, chap. 2.

8. Infantes: *Sancti Benedicti Regula*, chaps. 31, 37, 45, 70; adulescentes: ibid., chaps. 22, 30, 63.

9. Infirmes: ibid., chaps. 27, 28, 31, 36, 40, 42, 48, 64; senes: ibid., chaps. 37 and 66.

10. Ibid., chap. 59.

11. Ibid., chap. 60.

12. Ibid., chap. 61.

13. Ibid., chap. 58.

14. John Cassian, *Institutions cénobitiques*, ed. J.-C. Guy (Paris, 1965), bk. 4, chaps. 3 and 4, pp. 124–26; *Regula monastica communis*, attributed to Fructuosus of Braga, Migne, vol. 87, chap. 18, col. 1125.

15. *Sancti Benedicti Regula*, chap. 58.

16. Ibid., chap. 59.

17. Mansi, vol. 7, col. 374, canon 4.

18. C. M. Figueras, *De impedimentis admissionis in religionem usque ad Decretum Gratiani* (Montserrat, 1957), pp. 1–28; McLaughlin, *Le très ancien droit*, pp. 59–60.

19. Figueras, *De impedimentis*, pp. 29–44; McLaughlin, *Le très ancien droit*, pp. 60–61.

20. *Corpus iuris civilis 3: Novellae*, ed. R. Schoell and W. Kroll (Berlin, 1895), Novella 123, chap. 40.

21. Figueras, *De impedimentis*, pp. 104–12; McLaughlin, *Le très ancien droit*, pp. 62–63.

22. *Sancti Benedicti Regula*, chap. 61.

23. M.-A. Dimier, "S. Bernard et le droit en matière de *transitus*," *Revue Mabillon* 43 (1953): 48–82; and K. Fina, "*Ovem Suam Require*. Eine Studie zur Geschichte des Ordenswechsels im 12. Jahrhundert," *Augustiniana* 7 (1957): 33–56.

24. *Sancti Benedicti Regula*, chap. 58.

25. Ibid., chap. 59.

26. R. Orestano, "Beni dei monachi e monasteri nella legislazione Giustinianea," in *Studi in onore di Pietro de Francisci* (Milan, 1956), 3:561–94; see also E. Chénon, *Histoire générale du droit français public et privé des origines à 1815*, ed. F. Olivier-Martin (Paris, 1929), 2:17–20.

27. "Ingredientem namque simul secuntur omnino res, licet non expressim quia introduxit eas dixerit, et non erit dominus earum ulterius ullo modo" (*Corpus iuris civilis 3*, Novella 5, chap. 5).

28. Ibid., Novella 76 and Novella 123, chap. 38.

29. The assumption that an entrant would make a gift was implicit in charters that specified that a particular gift would suffice for a future entry: *Aniane*, no. 293, 1060–1108; no. 219, 1115; *Gellone*, no. 288, 1103; *St. Sernin*, no. 349, 1140–41; *Vaux de Cernay*, p. 34, ca. 1162. At times a charter specified that a particular gift would not suffice for future reception, but had to be supplemented: *Gellone*, no. 471, 1103; *Conques*, no. 475, 1105; *St. Sernin*, no. 598, 1173–74.

30. On the post-Tridentine character of fixed dowries, see A. Leinz, *Die Simonie. Eine kanonistische Studie* (Freiburg im Breisgau, 1902), pp. 18–25; T. M. Kealy, *Dowry of Women Religious*, Catholic University of America Canon Law Studies no. 134 (Washington, D.C., 1941), pp. 4–38; R. Kowalski, *The Sustenance of Religious Houses of Regulars*, Catholic University of America Canon Law Studies no. 199 (Washington, D.C., 1944), pp. 1–37; J. Deshusses, "Chape (droit de)," *DDC*, vol. 3, col. 519–21; J. Deshusses and R. Naz, "Dot des religieuses," *DDC*, vol. 4, col. 1431–36.

31. "Non apparebis in conspectu meo vacuus." The admonition was cited as a proof-text in defense of gifts at the entry of oblates by Rudolph of Saint Trond: MGH, *SS*, 10: 321. *St. Victor*, vol. 1, no. 589, 1069, cited it in relation to entry gifts. *Redon*, no. 384, 1095, said that a man offered a gift because he was unwilling to enter the Lord's sanctuary with a closed hand and wished to enter with a gift to hand over. See also *Redon*, no. 371, 1114–39, and *St. Vaast*, p. 399.

simoniacal entry
into religious life
from 1000 to 1260

CHAPTER ONE

Monastic Economic Problems
And the Reception of New Members

The gift at entry served the straightforward purposes of increasing the wealth and income of a religious house and of defraying at least part of the expense that a new member would require for clothing, food, and other necessities. As in the case of modern colleges and universities, there were vast differences among the various institutions comprehended under the rubric "religious house." One of the chief differences lay in the size of the income available to a given house. Many monasteries and nunneries did not receive an adequate initial endowment or else did not maintain an equilibrium between income and the number of religious in the community. At least since Carolingian times there had been sporadic attempts to balance numbers against resources. In 787 King Pippin of Italy ordered his *missi* to investigate the resources available to religious houses in his kingdom.[1] In 811 Charlemagne met with some bishops and abbots to discuss problems, among which was the troublesome desire of some prelates to rule larger communities than was fitting or feasible.[2] On 12 November 826 a Roman council under Pope Eugene II recommended that the *modus discretionis* be observed in receiving clerics of any kind, lest more be admitted than resources could support.[3] Following initiatives taken by his ancestors, Charles the Bald in 853 ordered a financial inquest of canonries, monasteries, and nunneries, so as to fix the number of religious in each house relative to the resources of the house.[4] This plan, as with so many other Caroling-

3

ian attempts at reform, was aborted with the decline of the empire, and the problem of supporting religious houses remained. For many religious houses in the eleventh century, the gift normally received from new members was an important contribution to the maintenance of some proportion between numbers and resources.

However, the gift at entry served other less obvious purposes as well. Religious houses in the eleventh and twelfth centuries were endowed institutions that had their economic foundation in their status as possessors of men, of land, and of profitable rights. The religious houses were seigneuries, similar in many ways to their lay counterparts. In spite of certain obvious differences attributable to the contrast between an undying corporation on the one hand and a family with its dowries, inheritances, and pious donations on the other, these analogous seigneuries exercised similar practices over similar possessions for similar ends.[5]

One of the key traits of these seigneuries, especially the richer among them, was the complexity of their structure and of their sources of income. Most religious houses drew revenues and services from their rights over their men and over the tenants of their domains. They also derived income from the normal appendages to agricultural life, such as mills, pasture rights, hunting rights, and forest rights. Many religious houses also participated, in varying degrees, in the practice of holding proprietary churches. Like other lords, they had benefited from the general breakdown of diocesan structures during the troubled ninth and tenth centuries. They had gathered into their patrimonies ecclesiastical sources of income, such as churches and the accompanying tithes, burial fees, and other parochial dues.[6] The reform movements of the eleventh century increased significantly the share of ecclesiastical forms of revenue received by religious houses. The reformers placed pressure on lay possessors of ecclesiastical rights to give them up, but they generally allowed ecclesiastical possessors of parochial rights to retain them. The reform propaganda began to have a significant impact in the later eleventh and twelfth centuries.[7] For reasons rooted in contemporary piety, many of the laymen influenced by reform sentiment offered their illicitly held ecclesiastical property to religious houses rather than to the dioceses and parishes from which it was originally alienated. The monasteries were favored recipients of such restitutions because a man whose conscience troubled him normally valued the prayers of monks higher than he did those of bishops or parish priests.[8] Some bishops sought to reassert their general control over restored properties by insisting that a lay donor give the property to them, and they would hand it on to the monastery.[9] In spite of these episcopal efforts to regulate transactions, the later eleventh and early twelfth centuries saw much ecclesiastical property flow by gift and purchase into the possession of religious houses.[10]

In addition, the religious seigneury, like its lay counterpart, sought by purchase, by gift, and by usurpation to enrich its patrimony with various public rights, such as justice, tolls, and market dues.[11] The resulting conglomerate of real properties, rights, and exemptions that constituted the patrimony of many religious houses was not radically different from that which formed the economic base of many lay lordships of comparable size in eleventh-century France. Of course, in addition to the similarities, religious houses often had sources of income unavailable to a lay lord, such as pious donations, entry gifts, and pilgrim offerings.[12]

It is crucial to an understanding of the role that entry gifts played in the economy of most religious houses that this complexity of endowment be fully appreciated. Normally, the monastic patrimony was interspersed among the possessions of lay and ecclesiastical neighbors, and complexity meant that interaction with those neighbors was both common and necessary. It was a rare seigneury, ecclesiastical or lay, that held its properties and rights in a compact block. Scattered fields, divided rights, and shared revenues were the normal conditions of economic life.[13] Not only were properties and rights subdivided, but the processes that led to further division continued to function in the eleventh and twelfth centuries. There was, of course, no unified legal system in medieval France, and large differences were particularly evident between regions of written law and those of customary law. However, in spite of important variations, it was generally true that the property rights of an individual were limited seriously by the rights of his kin.[14] Exclusive ownership of property by individuals, as had existed to a degree in Roman law, did not prevail in eleventh- and twelfth-century society. In that society families of property experienced a series of recurring events that demanded the transfer and subdivision of property within the kin group and, less often, outside it. The most prominent of these social "crises" were marriage, with its need for dowries; death, with its need for prayers, burial, and division among heirs; entry into religion, with its demand for a gift; and financial emergencies, which led to sales of, and mortgages on, property. Property could be parceled out to a virtually unlimited number of individuals and institutions. Even when the custom of primogeniture developed, the process of fragmentation was merely slowed rather than ended.[15] Because there were no firm limits to the subdivision of property, the process could go very far. In a region where the rhythm of life had not been violently interrupted for three or four generations, the natural evolution toward subdivision in response to family needs normally produced a complicated mix of shared rights, properties, and revenues.[16]

Religious houses might seem relatively immune to these processes of subdivision, but in fact they participated actively in them, chiefly as buyers and sellers of properties, as mortgagers,[17] and as recipients and givers of gifts. In due course, they accumulated patrimonies that included many subdivided rights and properties. For example, in about 1100–1102 the monastery of Gellone received one-half of a church dedicated to Saint Julian, along with the one-fifteenth of the tithe and the entire fief of the priest. The nunnery of Ronceray at Angers received an eighth share of the altar of Saint George, which included one-eighth of the offerings of money, candles, bread, tithes, rents, and first fruits.[18] Secular properties too were subject to the social need for subdivision, and a religious house might come into possession of half a mill, a quarter of a toll, a quarter of an allodial field, or half a fief.[19] The monastic cartularies make it clear that in the eleventh century it became rarer for a religious house to receive gifts of land or of rights that were not shared or partitioned with others.[20]

A complex endowment entailed considerable inconvenience for a religious house. A great portion of the religious' interest and energy was devoted to economic affairs, and a large number of the religious held positions in the economic hierarchy of the house. It has been estimated that in English Black Monk houses during the twelfth and thirteenth centuries about half the community, including the aged and novices, held offices, frequently with revenues attached to them.[21] In addition, a complicated, scattered patrimony was difficult to manage. Considerable time and energy could be expended to collect relatively modest sums, e.g., one-eighth of the candle offerings of a distant church. Rather than attempt to collect such dues or to exploit distant possessions directly, religious houses often farmed them out, enfeoffed them to their men, and sold or exchanged them for more convenient possessions.[22]

There is evidence that contemporaries were aware of the difficulties and annoyances inherent in a complex endowment. In the twelfth century, English Black Monk houses preserved the economically inefficient system of farming out properties on long-term leases because it was a secure, relatively bother-free technique when compared with the burdens of direct management.[23] Many of the new religious orders of the late eleventh and early twelfth centuries were critical of the older monasticism because of its frequent contacts with secular persons and secular business. The new orders were apparently aware that complex endowments were a major cause of the imperfections of the older houses.[24] In an effort to avoid such difficulties for themselves, the most successful of the new orders, the Cistercians, initially sought to exploit by their own labor large compact blocks of hitherto uncultivated land. They sought to buy out, or in some other way to remove, all others who possessed property and rights within the block. They refused to retain the tithes of other men, burial rights, churches, mills, serfs, and most other forms of property that might

7

have involved them in contacts with the secular world.[25] In all of this the Cistercians were not unique; the Premonstratensians, Carthusians, and Grandmontines pursued comparable policies.[26] Indeed, the fear of litigation about gifts and property was the expressed motive for certain elements of Grandmontine and Trinitarian legislation.[27] If the Cistercians had adhered rigorously to this policy of economic isolation, they would have been spared the problems characteristic of the older, more complex patrimonies. However, the Cistercians began to accept forbidden forms of property in the second half of the twelfth century. The rapidity with which these forms of property were added to Cistercian patrimonies depended to a large degree on the zeal of abbots and the vigilance of visitors. By 1200 many Cistercian houses had endowments that included forbidden elements and fragmented properties. Although the proportion of such possessions might vary from house to house, it is nonetheless true that by the later twelfth century the White Monks faced problems in managing their patrimonies that were similar to those long familiar to the Black Monks.[28]

Complex patrimonies gave rise to at least one additional serious problem for religious houses, that of litigation. Shared or subdivided properties were properties precariously held and peculiarly subject to encroachment, usurpation, and dispute. One need only thumb through several cartularies to see how frequently monasteries were involved in litigation about their possessions and claims to possessions. Such litigation was so much a part of life that the religious often anticipated it and attempted to forestall it.[29]

Some of the reasons for the frequency of litigation are not difficult to discern. The rights of a seller or donor were limited by the legitimate claims of his kin or his feudal lord, and he could not with insouciance sell or give his property to a religious house. A charter from the monastery of the Holy Trinity at Vendôme, written about 1072, illustrated the difficulties inherent in transferring property. A married couple were impoverished, and they sought to trade their modest property for a life support.[30] Initially they approached relatives, who were unwilling to agree to the terms offered by the couple. Only then did the couple approach the monks of the Holy Trinity, who accepted the proposed arrangement. The woman declared explicitly that she did not want to offer any property that would be disputed after her death. Therefore, she gave or sold some property to relatives who had a claim on it, and "she gave to the Holy Trinity those allods of Listriaco which she received from her father, and which no relative or other person could legally claim."[31] This couple, and the monks of the Holy Trinity who drew up the charter, were not being overly cautious in their attempts to guarantee the stability of this arrangement. The relatives of the sellers had rights, and the charter made clear that proper procedures had been observed and that those rights had been forfeited by the refusal of the kinsmen to give the couple a life rent in return for their property.

Repeatedly the charters reflect the insecurity of acquisitions made without the consent of kin. Religious houses that received gifts or that made purchases were aware of the crucial need to secure the assent of as many of the relatives of the owner as possible. Not only adult relatives actually present at the transfer of property were to be induced to agree, but also absentees[32] and children under age[33] were to be asked or forced to agree at the proper time. To arrange for the assent of kin was sometimes as expensive and often more laborious than the gift or purchase itself. In addition to the spouse and children of the owner, a wide variety of other relatives might have to consent,[34] including in-laws,[35] bastards,[36] grandchildren,[37] uncles,[38] and cousins.[39] Careful planning did not always prevent frustration of a gift or purchase. It was not unusual for relatives to refuse to agree. Even when they had agreed, such arrangements were unstable. More often than was comfortable for the monks, some kin repudiated their assent, denied that they had in fact agreed, or simply laid claim to the property in question.

Once litigation began it could drag on for years or even decades. The final settlement in such disputes was seldom a clearcut victory for either party. The claims of kinship were very strong in the eyes of contemporaries, and ordinarily had to have some satisfaction. In the common course of events, the religious house was obliged to strike a bargain in order to vindicate its claims. Indeed, it was not unknown to pay more than once for the extinction of claims against a disputed possession.[40] A religious house could expect to be secure in its properties only after thirty or forty years of undisputed possession, if then.[41]

It was not merely the relatives of the donor or seller who could threaten the stability of a transaction. There were others who might be in a position to lay claims against the acquisitions of a religious house. Much of the property offered to the houses was held in some form of feudal tenure. The feudal lord had rights and claims to be settled before he would sanction his vassal's sale or gift. Since the monastery was an undying corporation, the lord effectively lost his rights of escheat, wardship, and marriage, and understandably he expected some *quid pro quo* for his assent. In the twelfth and thirteenth centuries, feudal lords sought to exploit this right of assent as a way to raise money.[42] A religious house might pay well for a feudal lord's assent, and even then it was not secure against further difficulties.[43] In some charters a contingency plan was offered by the seller or donor in the event that a feudal lord refused to cooperate.[44] On occasion religious houses received as a boon from a feudal lord the promise that he would allow it to accept freely any gift that his vassals might wish to make.[45] Without such a guarantee, or its equivalent, the house's new possession was menaced by the lord's rights.

Whether a property was allodial or feudal, it might be mortgaged or otherwise burdened when it came into the monastery's possession. It is evident from the charters that many laymen found it a convenient and relatively inexpensive gift to offer an indebted property, since religious houses often had the cash necessary to settle the debt and gain full use of the property. If the monastery accepted such a gift, it was responsible for settling claims against it, often at considerable expense.[46] Another common burden on property was a life interest in it guaranteed to some person, for example, the widow of the donor or seller. Only after the death of the favored party at some indeterminate time in the future did the house come into full possession of the property. Innocent III dealt with a dispute arising from the fact that a man had given himself and his possessions to a religious house under the condition that he retain use of the property for life. He had lived so long that no one alive had witnessed his gift, and it was disputed by other claimants after his death.[47] Such delayed gifts were a frequent source of litigation.[48]

In view of the myriad opportunities for dispute arising out of complicated patrimonies and the web of those who might be able to raise a claim against a property transfer, it is not surprising that there were few religious houses that did not have a series of active or potential property disputes at any given time. The religious protected what they perceived as their rights by litigation, arbitration, and compromises worked out with their opponents. However, the religious houses also used recruitment and the traditional gift at entry as an opportunity to deal with litigation about their property. The great monasteries, like Cluny or Cîteaux, might draw novices from far and wide, but most houses depended primarily on local families for new recruits.[49] The recruit and his family were expected to make a gift at entry, and often that was simply what happened. But from a study of entry charters, it emerges that many of the very families that wished to place someone in a monastery were potential or actual litigants with the house concerning its property. With the exception of very poor or troubled houses,[50] monasteries in the eleventh and twelfth centuries had a steady stream of applicants seeking admission; and consequently the religious houses were in a position to exercise choice and to reject recruits if they wished.[51] When the opportunity presented itself, negotiations about entry and the gift at entry were used to end litigation and to correct the deficiencies of a complex patrimony.[52]

Negotiations about Entry into Religion

In his commentary on *causa* I, *questio* II, of Gratian's *Decretum*, the canonist Rufinus, writing about 1157–59, faced the question,

11

"Whether for entrance to a monastery money ought to be demanded?", to which he replied in the negative. After citing authorities who condemned the insistence on money from those entering, he used the following case to illustrate one of the illicit forms of payment for entry:

Imagine that the Church of Saint Peter had a dispute with Scannabicus concerning a certain field, and when Scannabicus sought to have his son ordained in that Church the canons would not agree unless he offered ten pounds for his son or else gave up the dispute.[53]

Rufinus' creation of this example was not merely a school exercise. He was criticizing a widespread contemporary practice, which had fallen into disrepute in his day but which had borne no stigma a few generations earlier. The cartularies of religious houses reveal without equivocation that the reception of new members was frequently accompanied by conditions and agreements that were in intention and often in form similar to that criticized by Rufinus. When opportunity offered itself, the entry of a new member was perceived as an invitation to settle outstanding quarrels with him and his kin.[54]

A charter of Ronceray, dated about 1080, contains a full description of the negotiations that preceded the reception of the daughter of a local lord. At some time before 1080 Ascelina Cata entered the nunnery and gave as a gift the woods at Brain-sur-l'Authion and other forest rights. Her nephew Girorius of Beaupréau confirmed the donation. But such agreements were always unstable, and the nephew subsequently changed his mind and laid claim to the woods. The nuns settled with him for ten pounds. When Ascelina Cata died, her nephew renewed the claim. The charter makes it clear that the nuns believed he had revived the lawsuit in order to place a daughter in the house. He already had one daughter in the nunnery, and when the second was received, he returned the ten pounds, abandoned the claim on the woods, and added to the settlement ten *arpents* of meadow and the right for the nuns to buy things in the region without paying him any fees that they might otherwise owe him.[55] Thus the entry of a new member served to quiet claims against a piece of property that had itself been a gift at an earlier entry.

As the nuns of Ronceray implied about Girorius of Beaupréau, a person with a claim against the property of a religious house might seek a position in that particular house precisely because his claim was a reason for the house to consent and thereby extinguish the claim as part of the entry bargain. It was a common procedure, recorded in many charters, for one seeking a place for himself or for another person to make a gift and then to add to it a general renunciation of all claims that he might be able to raise. This was no idle gesture, since a potential claim was a threat that the religious house might be eager to end.[56]

The religious were of course in a favorable position with relation to someone who was seeking admission to their congregation. Contemporaries in the eleventh and twelfth centuries seldom criticized the use that the religious made of their position of strength to free themselves from litigation. Particularly when the reception was sought for a seriously ill person, *ad succurrendum*, the religious house could and would apply pressure for concessions. At Saint Aubin at Angers in the early twelfth century, Geoffrey de Carco asked that his dying father, Robert de Carco, be made a monk. Geoffrey was pursuing a claim against some vineyards belonging to the house, and in order to gain admission for his father he renounced his claim on the spot and subsequently made a modest gift for his father's reception *ad succurrendum*.[57]

Thus recruitment offered an opportunity, perceived as legitimate by contemporaries, to allay at least some of the insecurity of, and litigation about, property. The monastic charters also reveal that the reception of new members served other purposes as well. Important lay and ecclesiastical figures at every level of medieval society had dependents for whom to provide. Some of those dependents wished to enter religious houses, but it was a social reality of the eleventh and twelfth centuries that there were individuals who had difficulty in finding a place without the aid of a patron. Retired soldiers,[58] superannuated chaplains,[59] children,[60] and bastards were generally not perceived as attractive candidates for the religious habit. To some degree, the prestige of an important figure was bound up with his ability to gain for his protégés and servants positions in religious houses that they could not gain for themselves. From the perspective of the religious house, the favorable influence of a friend at court or at Rome was useful to its interests and was worth seeking by favors.

The letter collections of twelfth-century churchmen, including the popes, contain numerous examples of requests for the reception of individuals in religious houses. Although the letters of such persons almost never mentioned the prospect of money or property from the entrant, they did promise explicitly or implicitly that the patron would show his appreciation for the favor by aiding the religious house at some future time.[61] The reception of the recommended candidate was a sign of the friendship existing between his patron and the house. There was, of course, the implication that a failure to admit the person would be viewed as an insult to his patron.[62] Religious houses too requested one another to receive new members, as a sign of their mutual fraternity and protection. A refusal to accept a person at the request of another house was a threat to continued cordial relations.[63]

Many of the receptions made at the request of pope, bishop,[64] or king[65] were apparently tolerated without the clear assent of the monastic community, which might be more or less constrained to accept the nominee or else face unpleasant consequences. Far more illuminating for an understanding of the role that entry agreements played are the situations in which a religious house accepted the candidate of some locally powerful person. For when the two parties were more nearly equal in power, true negotiations about aid, favor, or property could take place. The monks of the Holy Trinity at Vendôme had a series of disagreements with a local feudal lord, Andreas of Alluyes. They came to a peaceful settlement in 1199 when Andreas offered the monks some revenues to compensate for others that he had seized and wished to retain. In addition he promised the monks full justice in his feudal court in a dispute over possession of a tithe. "The monks, as a recompense for this favor and because they have affection for me, created for me one monk whose name is Andreas Charrete."[66]

In circumstances such as these the new monk was a symbol of the agreement; his entry into the monastery was almost incidental to the settlement of issues between his patron and the religious. In many situations it was the reception of a child that served as the cement for an agreement and as the living guarantee of its endurance.[67] An early twelfth-century charter from the Breton monastery of Redon reenforces the impression that an individual's entry into religion could be one element of a larger agreement that brought to the religious house something it wanted.

> . . . Redoret, priest and lord of the church of Crossac, . . . came to Abbot Justin of Redon and to the other brethren. He handed over himself, all his possessions, his father, his mother, and his little son Restanet, with this agreement: they should take the religious habit, and he would retain the forenamed church by the leave of the monks until they ordered him to put on the habit. Thereafter the monks should possess all he owned. . . .[68]

In this transaction the monks of Redon received two older adults and a boy, none of whom had an obvious religious calling, and agreed to receive the priest at some future time, in order to obtain a valuable possession, a church.

A charter of Saint Aubin at Angers illustrated even more pointedly how a patron could aid a man, in this case a soldier, who might not otherwise have been able to enter religion. A lord named Adam was disputing with the monks about the church of Bousse and the *vicaria* of l'Aleu:

> It happened that a certain soldier of Adam, Hugo by name, who had served him well in secular subjection, wished to be a monk. Therefore Adam ordered Abbot Otbrannus and the congregation . . . for his sake to make of the aforementioned soldier a monk. By a friendly reciprocity he gave them the church and handed over the *vicaria*. It was agreed between the monks and lord Adam that the monks should satisfy him by receiving his soldier as a monk, and that lord Adam should do what he had promised before. . . .[69]

Thus the negotiations that normally preceded entry into religion on occasion served as a form of diplomacy, in which important men were bound to the religious house by ties created when their friends and protégés were received into the community.

15

In addition to the termination of litigation and to the winning of favor from influential men, there was yet a third broad category of conditions under which new members were received. The religious were apparently aware that the complex collection of properties and rights constituting their patrimony often needed consolidation and, to use a modern term, rationalization. It was easier and more profitable to collect the whole of a tithe than it was to collect one-eighth of it. Religious houses also sought self-sufficiency, and they might need a meadow or a mill or some other element to meet a specific requirement.[70] Some religious communities tried, as opportunity appeared, to round out their domains by purchase, exchange, and soliciting particular gifts. They also sought properties and rights that would complement their holdings and would meet their immediate or long-range needs.[71] The reception of a new member presented important opportunities for this work of consolidation. The potential monk's family expected to offer something for his reception, and it was in the religious house's interest to pressure for a gift that would be useful to it. Since the properties of the house and the local lay world interpenetrated or were often parts of a subdivided whole, the religious must have found on occasion that their new member, born of a family often of local origin, could bring something particular that they wanted.[72] If the family could not be induced to give outright a particular property, then at least it might agree to sell it to the religious, for there were rights and properties that might be difficult even to buy without some inducement.[73] Entrance gifts and purchases alternated over a period of years until a monastery had reconstituted a more or less consolidated possession.[74] A charter from the Cistercian house of Berdoues, dated 1181, reveals the details of one successful attempt at consolidation. Over a period of years the monks of Berdoues received a man as a monk, paid his niece and nephew 42 shillings, received both of them into the prayer confraternity of the house, and promised to receive the nephew if at some future time he wished to become a monk. The charter states clearly the net result of this mix of religious and secular payments:

And now the brethren of Berdoues possess in permanent right the entire *villa* of Lezian and the entire church, with all their appurtenances, both as a result of these donors and as a result of Arnald of Lezian, their uncle, a monk of Berdoues.[75]

Although this charter is more explicit than most, it reveals a result that is to be found in other charters as well:

Hugo Berlaius of Fay had a tithe in the parish of Saint Peter of Cetone, and the monks of Saint Denys of Nogent possessed a third part of the same tithe. He decided that he would make a monk of his little son who was a cleric, and he gave to the monks who received the boy as a monk two parts of the same tithe. . . .[76]

The monks also paid Hugo one hundred shillings and promised him an honorable burial. With this combination of a reception, cash, and spiritual benefits, the monks consolidated their possession of a tithe.

In most cases it is difficult to know with certainty whether such consolidations took place by accident and luck or by planning. The basic idea of consolidating property for the sake of spiritual isolation and economic convenience was well known in the twelfth century. The ascetic, separatist orders of that time, like the Cistercians and the Carthusians, sought as a matter of policy to own entire blocks of land. They systematically removed all outsiders possessing rights and properties within the boundaries of their blocks. They did this primarily for the sake of separation from worldly affairs, but there were economic advantages as well, for such consolidated territories could be exploited effectively by *conversi* and granges. Furthermore, a religious house that had exclusive possession of a property stood less chance of being involved in litigation about that property.[77] It seems clear that even in some of the houses of the older tradition, the entry of a new monk was seen as an opportunity to acquire in a rather non-systematic way needed or complementary additions to the monastic patrimony.

The conclusion is inescapable that in the eleventh and twelfth centuries reception of new members into religious houses had a significance far beyond that of perpetuating a celibate community. Undoubtedly, many new members brought with them a modest, uncomplicated gift of land, money, or rights. But the monastic cartularies make clear that the negotiations about entry and the entry gift were used by the religious to protect or to advance their interests. Such negotiations about reception were expected, respectable, and legitimate in the eyes of contemporaries, and only in the 1120s and thereafter were serious questions raised about their propriety.

1. *Pippini capitulare papiense*, chap. 11, *Capitularia regum francorum*, vol. 1, ed. A. Boretius, MGH, *Legum sectio* 2 (Hanover, 1883), p. 199.

2. *Capitula de causis*, chap. 11, *Capitularia* 1:164. See also *Capitulare missorum in Theodonis villa datum* (805), chap. 12, *Capitularia* 1:122; Council of Arles (813), chap. 8, *Concilia aevi Karolini*, ed. A. Werminghoff, MGH, *Legum sectio* 3 (Hanover, 1908), vol. 2, pt. 1, p. 251; and Council of Reims (813), chap. 27, ibid., p. 256.

3. Chap. 9, *Capitularia* 1:373.

4. "Numerum etiam canonicorum et monachorum sive sanctimonialium uniuscuiusque loci describant, et nobis referant, ut secundum qualitatem et quantitatem loci cum consilio episcoporum et fidelium nostrorum, ubi minor numerus fuerit, nostra auctoritate addamus; ubi vero indiscretione praelatorum superfuerit, ad mensuram redigamus . . ." (chap. 1, *Capitularia* 2:267–68).

5. G. Duby, *Rural Economy and Country Life in the Medieval West*, trans. C. Postan (Columbia, S.C., 1968), pp. 173–86.

6. G. Constable, *Monastic Tithes from Their Origins to the Twelfth Century* (Cambridge, 1964), pp. 63–66, 75–83.

7. G. Mollat, "La Restitution des églises privées au patrimoine ecclésiastique en France du ixᵉ au xiᵉ siècle," *Revue historique de droit français et étranger*, 4th ser., 27 (1949): 399 ff., notes that restitution began in the ninth century, but increased in extent because of the eleventh-century reform movements. For some accounts of regional differences in the degree of restitution, see M. Dillay, "Le Régime de l'église privée du xiᵉ au xiiiᵉ siècle dans l'Anjou, le Maine, la Touraine," *Revue historique de droit français et étranger*, 4th ser., 4 (1925): 253–94; and G. Devailly, "Une Enquête en cours: l'application de la réforme grégorienne en Bretagne," *Annales de Bretagne* 75 (1968): 293–316. Monastic charters alluded to guilt feelings aroused in some lay holders of ecclesiastical properties: see *Assé-le-Riboul*, no. 5, ca. 1100; no. 1, before 20 June 1097; and *Saint Aubin*, vol. 2, no. 910, 1104.

8. Mollat, "La Restitution," pp. 400–407.

9. Council of Melfi (1089), canons 5 and 6, Mansi, vol. 20, col. 723. Some charters specified that this procedure had been observed: *St. Père*, vol. 2, no. 26, 1113–39; no. 45, 119–24; *St. Stephan*, no. 71, 1098–99.

10. Constable, *Monastic Tithes*, p. 98, points out that episcopal attempts at control were generally a formality.

11. Justice: *St. Victor*, vol. 2, no. 1092, 1097; tolls: *St. Père*, vol. 2, no. 172, 1130–50. See R. H. Snape, *English Monastic Finances in the Later Middle Ages* (Cambridge, 1926), p. 92.

12. Rudolph, abbot of Saint Trond, reported that when the popularity of the shrine of Saint Trond was at its height in the eleventh century, it produced more revenue than all the rest of the monastery's income combined (*Chronique de l'abbaye de Saint Trond*, ed. C. de Borman [Liège, 1872], 1:18).

13. Monastic cartularies often contain inventories of income, particularly of revenues marked for support of the individual officials of the house. Such inventories reveal how diverse and scattered sources of income could be: see *Conques*, nos. 87, 372, 386, 457, 478, 529; *St. Vaast*, pp. 205, 215, 217.

14. E. Chénon, *Histoire générale du droit français public et privé des origines à 1815*, ed. F. Olivier-Martin (Paris, 1929), 2:17 ff. See also Duby, *Rural Economy*, p. 182. F. L. Ganshof, *Qu'est-ce que la féodalité?*, 3d ed. (Brussels, 1957), pp. 134, 181–82, traces the "realization" of fiefs, i.e., the stress on fiefs as property, to the pressure of kin claims to turn temporary grants into hereditary ones. Religious houses frequently dealt with a kin group rather than with an individual: *Gellone*, no. 239, 1093; *St. Père*, vol. 2, no. 26, 1113–39; no. 53, 1119–28; *Vaux de Cernay*, pp. 55–56, 1170–96; *St. Aubin*, vol. 2, no. 663, 1151.

15. M. Bloch, *Feudal Society*, trans. L. Manyon (London, 1961), 1:203–6. Duby, *Rural Economy*, p. 182, says that lay lands were in a state of flux and dissolution as a result of socially demanded division, as in *St. Sernin*, no. 7, 1158, a charter that records a family's sale of a portion of an *honor* in order to use the sale price to make a daughter a nun.

16. *Paraclet*, vol. 2, no. 84, 1194; *Gellone*, no. 261, 1077–99.

17. F. L. Ganshof and A. Verhulst, "Medieval Agrarian Society in Its Prime: France, the Low Countries, and Western Germany," *The Cambridge Economic History*, 2d ed. (Cambridge, 1966), 1:299–300, describe how religious houses used mortgages and money-lending to bring properties into their possession. On the role of mortgages in the economy of Norman religious houses, see R. Génestal, *Rôle des monastères comme établissements de crédit* (Paris, 1901).

18. *Gellone*, no. 300, 1100–1102; *Ronceray*, no. 271, ca. 1100. See also *Redon*, no. 387, 1148: one-seventh of the tithe of half a *villa*; *St. Maur*, no. 18, ca. 1066: one-third of the income from five church feast days; *Ronceray*, no. 397, ca. 1105: one-twelfth of an altar and a tithe.

19. *Ronceray*, no. 343, before 1100: half of one mill and one-quarter of another; *St. Aubin*, vol. 1, no. 170, 1082–1106: one-quarter of certain fishing rights; *St. Stephan*, no. 240, 1083–98: one-half of a field; *St. Père*, vol. 1, no. 61, 1035–63: one-quarter of a *villa*, a woods, a mill, and a meadow.

20. L. Genicot, "L'Evolution des dons aux abbayes dans le comté de Namur du xᵉ au xivᵉ siècle," *XXXᵉ congrès de la fédération archéologique et historique de Belgique: annales* (Brussels, 1936), pp. 139–42, traces the increasingly fragmented and condition-laden character of gifts to religious houses after the eleventh century. Genicot attributed the decline in number and size of gifts to the financial distress of the nobility. Duby, *Rural Economy*, pp. 182–86, notes that a decline in gifts was merely one of several steps taken by the nobility to protect its position. M.-J. LeCacheux, *Histoire de l'abbaye de Saint-Amand de Rouen des origines à la fin du xviᵉ siècle* (Caen, 1937), p. 140, detects a similar decline in number and size of gifts to Saint Amand in the thirteenth century. See also Ganshof and Verhulst, "Medieval Agrarian Society," in *Cambridge Economic History*, 1:300–301.

21. D. Knowles, *The Monastic Order in England*, 2d ed. (Cambridge, 1963), pp. 427-31. See also A. Hansay, *Etude sur la formation et l'organisation économique du domaine de l'abbaye de Saint-Trond depuis les origines jusqu'à la fin du xiiie siècle* (Ghent, 1899), pp. 74-79; and Snape, *English Monastic Finances*, pp. 30-32.

22. Duby, *Rural Economy*, pp. 175-76, 182, notes that distant or superfluous possessions were customarily granted out in various forms of tenure to powerful "friends" of a monastery to bind them more closely to it. *Aniane*, no. 46, 1097: the house regranted most of a gift to the giver, but retained control of a church; *Vaux de Cernay*, no. 37, 1170-96: a woman's gift was traded back to her son in return for some marl-bearing lands. When a property of Saint Trond had been reintegrated into the house's possession at great cost and then proved unmanageable, abbot Rudolph exchanged it for a more useful possession (*Gesta abbatum Trudonensium*, bk. 10, chap. 4, ed. R. Koepke, MGH, SS, vol. 10 [Hanover, 1852], p. 292).

23. E. Miller, "England in the Twelfth and Thirteenth Centuries: An Economic Contrast?", *Economic History Review*, 2d ser., 24 (1971): 1-14.

24. J. Leclercq, "La Crise du monachisme aux xie et xiie siècles," *Bulletino dell'Istituto Storico Italiano per il Medio Evo e Archivio Muratoriano* 70 (1958): 19-41, finds that the recurring themes in the criticism of monasticism from 1050 to 1150 were the wealth and worldliness of the Benedictine houses.

25. Idungus of Prufening, *Dialogus duorum monachorum*, ed. R. B. C. Huygens, "Le moine Idung et ses deux ouvrages: *Argumentum super quatuor questionibus* et *Dialogus duorum monachorum*," *Studi medievali*, 3d ser., 13 (1972):400. J. B. Mahn, *L'ordre cistercien et son gouvernement des origines au milieu du xiii^e siecle*, 2d ed. (Paris, 1951), pp. 48-51.

26. The Premonstratensian statutes of 1131-34 specified: "Hec sunt que proposuimus ammodo non recipere: telonium, vectigalia, servos, ancillas, advocatias secularium, altaria ad que cura animarum pertinet, nisi possit esse abbatia" (R. van Waefelghem, "Les premiers statuts de l'ordre de Prémontré: le clm 17.174 (xiie siècle)," *Analectes de l'ordre de Prémontré* 9 [1913]: 45). The Grandmontines also took measures to ensure their separation from worldly business (J. Becquet, "La Règle de Grandmont," *Bulletin de la société archéologique et historique du Limousin* 87 [1958]: 20-22). For Carthusian attempts to avoid excessive wealth and its problems, see *Die ältesten Consuetudines der Kärtauser*, ed. J. Hogg (Berlin, 1970), the *capitulum generale Basilii secundum* (1156), chaps. 5 and 9, pp. 138-40; *capitulum generale Basilii tertium* (1157-58?), chap. 1, p. 141; and *Consuetudines Basilii* (ca. 1170), chap. 48, par. 12, p. 216.

27. *Scriptores ordinis Grandimontensis*, ed. J. Becquet, Corpus Christianorum, Continuatio Mediaevalis, vol. 8 (Turnhout, 1968), *Regula sancti Stephani Grandimontensis*, chap. 19, p. 80; chap. 21, pp. 80-81; chap. 24, p. 82; chap. 31, p. 84; see also pp. 183, 485, 488. The Rule of the Order of the Holy Trinity, founded at Paris by John of Matha, forbade novices to give gifts that might cause litigation: chap. 7, Migne, vol. 214, col. 448.

28. Leclercq, "La Crise," pp. 34-36; Mahn, *L'Ordre cistercien*, pp. 48-49, n. 3, lists instances of the acceptance by Cistercian houses of forbidden revenues, to which may be added *Ourscamp*, no. 303, 1140, and *Berdoues*, no. 266, 1155.

29. *St. Père*, vol. 2, no. 32, 1101-29: the family of a monk *ad succurrendum* was forced to agree that if its gift was not secure and free from litigation within two years, it would give another gift of comparable value; *St. Aubin*, vol. 1, no. 55, date uncertain: a man was promised entry if he settled all claims against his dwelling place and gave it as a gift; *La Chronique de Saint-Hubert dite Cantatorium*, ed. K. Hanquet (Brussels, 1906), pp. 58-65.

30. For a study of arrangements with religious houses to obtain life rents, see E. Lesne, "Une Source de la fortune monastique: les donations à charge de pension alimen-

taire du viiie au xe siècle," *Mémoires et travaux* . . . *des facultés catholiques de Lille* 32 (1927):33–47; or H. M. Stuckert, *Corrodies in the English Monasteries: A Study in English Social History of the Middle Ages* (Philadelphia, 1923).

31. *St. Trinité*, vol. 1, no. 233, ca. 1072.

32. If a relative was absent, the charter might record that fact: *St. Trinité*, vol. 1, no. 134, 1060; *St. Père*, vol. 2, no. 24, 1109: an absent daughter was sought out for her consent, and the unexpected return of another absent relative threw the situation into turmoil. J.-G. Bulliot, *Essai historique sur l'abbaye de Saint-Martin d'Autun* (Autun, 1849), vol. 2, no. 34, 1218: a father promised to force his absent son to agree to a gift.

33. *St. Denys*, no. 67, 1100: donors promised explicitly that when an infant grew up, he would confirm a gift.

34. *Redon*, no. 363, 1095: a gift was made "cum consensu suorum aliorum filiorum et parentum."

35. *Vigeois*, no. 338, 1165–71.

36. *St. Père*, vol. 2, no. 26, 1113–39: a bastard son contested a gift and received one-half of it in return for his consent.

37. *Redon*, no. 295, 1081–83.

38. *Gellone*, no. 465, 1077–99.

39. *St. Stephan*, no. 164, 1075–80: a charter recording attempts to reestablish the unity of an allod that had been fragmented among a maze of cousins and others belonging to a *parentela*, i.e., an extended kin group.

40. *Berdoues*, nos. 787, 788, 1199 and 1210: a man was paid twice in eleven years to assent to his father's gift at entry.

41. In theory, prescription should have given security to possessors: see R. Naz, "Prescription," *DDC*, vol. 7, cols. 178–94; but claims of kin could not be dismissed easily: E. Durtelle de Saint-Sauveur, *Recherches sur l'histoire de la théorie de la mort civile des religieux* (Rennes, 1910), pp. 78 ff. *Vigeois*, nos. 118, 122, 306, 1092–1137: a dispute of forty-five years' duration was settled by a compromise favorable to the lay disputant; *Vigeois*, no. 322, 1147–64: an entrant confirmed a gift that had been made fifty years earlier; *Redon*, no. 295, 1081–83: a deathbed entrant confirmed gifts of his father and grandfather, which he had refused to confirm earlier; *St. Victor*, vol. 1, no. 449, 1079, and vol. 2, no. 702, 1156: the monks paid claimants who disputed a gift made seventy-five years before.

42. Duby, *Rural Economy*, pp. 232–42; Génestal, *Rôle des monastères*, pp. 121–24; Genicot, "L'Evolution des dons," p. 147.

43. *St. Père*, vol. 2, no. 53, 1119–28: a lord was paid for his assent. On other occasions full or partial payment for a lord's assent included admission of some dependent to the monastery: *St. Père*, vol. 1, no. 3, 1079–88; *Ronceray*, no. 354, 1120.

44. *St. Maur*, no. 58, ca. 1140.

45. *St. Père*, vol. 1, no. 20, 1033–69; no. 23, 1086; vol. 2, no. 108, 1120–50.

46. Génestal, *Rôle des monastères*, pp 73–81, notes that Norman monasteries used mortgages as a preferred way to obtain property in the twelfth century. Monasteries frequently received indebted properties as entry gifts: *Conques*, no. 572, 1060; *Redon*, no. 352, 1104; *Berdoues*, no. 135, 1208; no. 682, date uncertain; *Vigeois*, no. 338, 1165–71: in order to regain direct possession of one of its fiefs, the monastery received four male members of a family, gave a life rent to a wife, and paid large debts on the property in question.

47. Pott 252.

48. *Gellone*, no. 206, 1082: a donor's mother retained lifetime use of part of a gift;

St. Père, vol. 2, no. 172, 1130–50: a donor retained half of the revenue from a gift for his lifetime, and after his death a cousin litigated successfully for the donor's half; *Vigeois*, no. 169, 1096: a gift would pass to the monastery after the deaths of the donor's children; *Cîteaux*, no. 158, ca. 1160: a priest offered a gift but retained usufruct for life.

49. For the far-flung recruitment efforts of Bernard of Clairvaux, see M.-A. Dimier, "Saint Bernard et le recrutement de Clairvaux," *Revue Mabillon* 42 (1952): 17–30, 56–78. On Cluny's recruitment in the eleventh and twelfth centuries, see J. Fechter, *Cluny, Adel und Volk. Studien über das Verhältnis des Klosters zu den Ständen (910–1156)* (Stuttgart, 1966), pp. 1–49. Knowles, *Monastic Order*, pp. 422–25, holds that in the later twelfth century Black Monk houses in England recruited locally, though they received a few men of more distant origins.

50. Saint Trond near Liège had suffered from disputed abbacies and the enmity of some neighbors who usurped its property. In order to increase its numbers, the house was compelled to receive some unsavory and unstable monks: *Gesta abbatum Trudonensium*, MGH, SS, 10:257. From 1098 to 1112 Cîteaux could attract no recruits because of its poverty: *Exordium parvum*, chap. 17, in J. Turk, "Cistercii statuta antiquissima," *Analecta sacri ordinis cisterciensis* 4 (1948): 34.

51. In twelfth- and early thirteenth-century sources, complaints about overpopulation in religious houses are common, and complaints about a shortage of recruits are rare: *Statuts, chapitres généraux et visites de l'ordre de Cluny*, ed. G. Charvin (Paris, 1965), vol. 1, no. 3, p. 55, 1205–6; no. 8, p. 43, 1200; and *Statuta capitulorum generalium ordinis cisterciensis*, ed. J. M. Canivez (Louvain, 1933), vol. 1, no. 2, p. 118, 1190; no. 9, p. 225, 1198; no. 5, pp. 306–7, 1205; no. 12, p. 359, 1209. Charters confirm the view that the religious could and did refuse entry to some: *St. Aubin*, vol. 1, no. 328, 1060–67; no. 294, 1070; no. 45, 1082–1106. Caesarius of Heisterbach, *Dialogus miraculorum*, ed. J. Strange (Cologne, 1851), 1:43, 45–46, 224, indicates that in the first third of the thirteenth century the Cistercian houses with which he was familiar could afford to turn away recruits.

52. The frequency with which entry charters contained a renunciation of claims against monastic possessions is a sign that entry negotiations played a key role in stabilizing monastic possessions: *St. Père*, vol. 2, no. 29, 1101–29; *Ronceray*, nos. 93, 95, 96, ca. 1080; *St. Aubin*, vol. 2, no. 432, 1107–20; *Gimont*, vol. 1, no. 59, 1179; vol. 6, no. 61, 1173; *Gellone*, no. 206, 1082.

53. Rufinus, *Summa decretorum*, in *Die summa decretorum des Magister Rufinus*, ed. H. Singer (Paderborn, 1902), p. 224: "Puta ecclesia beati Petri habebat cum Scannabico causam de quodam predio, cumque Scannabicus filium suum in eadem ecclesia peteret ordinari, non aliter annuunt canonici, nisi ipse vel X libras pro filio offerat vel liti cedat." The same example was used by John of Faenza in his commentary on Gratian (BN lat. 14606, fol. 111ʳ). In a twelfth-century collection of canonistic *quaestiones*, it was asked whether it was permissible for a child to be received as a canon on the condition that his father cease to seize and harass the property of the canonry (G. Fransen, "Les 'questiones' des canonistes: essai de dépouillement et de classement," *Traditio* 12 [1956]: no. 32, p. 576).

54. *St. Aubin*, vol. 2, no. 675, 1195: the monks and a priest named Robert disputed over certain properties and debts. An amicable agreement was worked out, which included: "Rursus, abbas monacabit nepotem Roberti, Johannem nomine, et vestiet eum in ingressu monasterii; exinde Robertus vestiet eum omnibus diebus vite sue et habebit eum secum in predicta domo, etiam statim monachatum."

55. *Ronceray*, no. 95, ca. 1080. See also *Aniane*, no. 121, 1110: a man relinquished a claim against a tithe in order to be received *ad succurrendum*; *Aniane*, no. 327, 1204: a man compensated for the depredations of his parents, uncles, and other relatives in order to have a son received; *St. Trinité*, vol. 2, no. 586, 1188: a family dropped claims against a vineyard in order to have a member received.

56. *St. Aubin*, vol. 2, no. 432, 1107–20; *Gimont*, pt. 6, no. 3, 1162; no. 61, 1173.

57. *St. Aubin*, vol. 2, no. 432, 1107-20. *St. Trinité*, vol. 3, no. 671, 1227: the monks flatly refused to bury a dead man until his sons renounced a claim against the monastery.

58. *St. Aubin*, vol. 1, no. 328, 1060-67; vol. 2, no. 873, 1114; *St. Trinité*, vol. 2, no. 487, ca. 1140; no. 528, ca. 1150; no. 619, 1199; no. 640, 1203.

59. *St. Père*, vol. 2, no. 6, ca. 1095.

60. Children almost invariably needed a patron or a gift, or both, to be received: *St. Trinité*, vol. 2, no. 335, 1091; vol. 3, no. 649, 1207; *St. Aubin*, vol. 2, no. 659, 1096; *Ronceray*, no. 405, 1111-20; *St. Père*, vol. 2, no. 82, 1130-50; Odo Rigaud, *Registrum*, pp. 207, 310, 338.

61. Letter of Bishop Marbod to Vitalis of Savigny, Migne, vol. 171, cols. 1474-75: if Vitalis would receive a poor girl at Marbod's request, the bishop promised he would "gladly favor you if you think something should be sought from my humility."

62. From the twelfth to the fourteenth centuries, the papacy perfected a system of appointing to benefices (G. Barraclough, *Papal Provisions* [Oxford, 1935]). An analogous though less-developed movement went on with relation to religious houses (U. Berlière, *Le Recrutement dans les monastères bénédictins aux xiiie et xive siècles*, Académie royale de Belgique, Classe des lettres et des sciences morales et politiques: Mémoires in 8⁰, vol. 18, fasc. 6 [1924], pp. 34-35). See JL 11316 and 13135; by 1196 papal letters requesting entry were common enough to be obtained under false pretenses (JL 17426a).

63. *St. Trinité*, vol. 2, no. 335, 1091: the monastery was given a gift on condition that the monks negotiate entry to a nunnery for the donor's sister; *Ronceray*, no. 405, 1111-20: the cathedral chapter of Le Mans asked for the reception of a girl, the chapter gave the nunnery some revenues, and each house received the other in *beneficium* and *fraternitas*.

64. *St. Trinité*, vol. 2, no. 479, ca. 1137: a monk was received at the request of the bishop of Angers and of a subdeacon of Orleans. Innocent III ordered the bishop of Norwich to stop forcing the prior of the cathedral monastery to accept his nominees (*The Letters of Pope Innocent III (1198-1216) concerning England and Wales*, ed. C. and M. Cheney [Oxford, 1967], no. 205, 1200).

65. J. M. Besse, "Du droit d'oblat dans les anciens monastères français," *Revue Mabillon* 3 (1907): 1-21, 116-33, esp. 8-11. J. Marchal, *Le Droit d'oblat: essai sur une variété de pensionnés monastiques* (Poitiers, 1955), pp. 57-59. Some royal agents attempted to exercise such a right as well, and Louis IX forbade his *baillis* to place their sons, daughters, or dependents in religious houses within their jurisdiction (Jean de Joinville, *Histoire de Saint Louis*, ed. Natalis de Wailly [Paris, 1868], p. 252). For Germany see H. Bauer, *Das Recht der Ersten Bitte bei den deutschen Königen bis auf Karl IV*, Kirchenrechtlichen Abhandlungen, vol. 94 (1919), pp. 37-39, 57.

66. *St. Trinité*, vol. 2, no. 619, 1199: "Monachi vero pro hujus recompensatione beneficii et dilectione quam erga me habent, faciunt mihi unum monachum, Andream scilicet Charrete." Cf. *St. Aubin*, vol. 2, no. 881, 1163-70.

67. *St. Père*, vol. 2, no. 35, 1101-29: a child was offered as a *pignus* and *testimonium* of a gift; *Ronceray*, no. 304, 1075: a man offered the house *auxilium necessaribus rebus* if it accepted his daughter; *Redon*, no. 358, 1086-91: the monks actively solicited the offer of a child in order to end enmity between the house and a local family; *St. Stephan*, no. 71, 1098-99: a child was offered *in testimonio* of the restitution of a church; *St. Denys*, no. 70, ca. 1190: a knight offered *auxilium* and *consilium* in return for a son's reception. The Paris theologian Peter the Chanter defended such receptions to promote a public good, like peace (*Summa de sacramentis*, ed. J.-A. Dugauquier [Louvain, 1963], vol. 3, part 2a, p. 25: "Esto enim quod ecclesia desiderat favorem principis propter liberationem ecclesie, propter ejus tuitionem, et canonicat filium eius hac intentione. Videtur hoc licitum esse").

68. *Redon*, no. 374, 1104(?): " . . . Redoret, presbyter et dominus ecclesie Chroachac, . . . ad ecclesie rothonensis abbatem nomine Justinum venerit, et ad reliquos fratres, et se et omnia sua necnon et patrem et matrem et parvulum filium suum Restanet

tradiderit, hoc tamen pacto ut illi habitum religionis sumerent, et ipse ecclesiam predictam, licentia monachorum, donec pannos sumere ammonerent, teneret, ita ut monachi . . . post hoc omnia sua, . . . possideret."

69. *St. Aubin*, vol. 1, no. 328, 1060-67: "Contigit autem ut quidam miles Adam, nomine Hugo, qui eı de servitio seculari strenue servierat, monachus fieri vellet. Mandavit ergo Adam abbati Otbranno et congregationi . . . , ut pro amore suo facerent monachum ,de milite supradicto, et ille eis amica vicissitudine et ecclesiam concederet et vicariam perdonaret. Convenit igitur ita inter monachos et dominum Adam quod monachi satisfecerent ei de milite suo recipiendo in monachitatem, et dominus Adam exequutus est eis quod⁺ proloquutus erat. . . . "

70. *Sancti Benedicti Regula*, chap. 66.

71. Genicot, "L'Evolution des dons," pp. 141-42, discusses examples of reconstitution of fragmented properties. W. Kurze, "Der Adel und das Kloster S. Salvatore all'Isola im 11. und 12. Jahrhundert," *Quellen und Forschungen aus italienischen Archiven und Bibliotheken* 47 (1967): 518-20, discusses the economic policy of Abbot Hugh (1154-95), who consciously sought to increase and to round out the abbey's holdings by shrewd purchases. Some houses brought back into direct control properties that had been given out on feudal tenure and that had become hereditary in the family of the lay holder: *Gesta abbatum Trudonensium*, MGH, SS, 10:292; *St. Aubin*, vol. 2, no. 884, 1127; *Vigeois*, no. 338, 1165-71.

72. In reaction against precisely such calculation, the Grandmontines forbade their members to choose or to ask for particular properties from patrons or entrants (*Regula*, chaps. 19, 21, in Becquet, *Scriptores*, pp. 80-81).

73. *St. Aubin*, vol. 2, no. 884, 1127: a sick man was received *ad succurrendum* in return for a modest gift. The monks sought for a mill from his wife, and when she balked at donating it, they purchased it from her.

74. *Gellone*, no. 293, 1079; *St. Stephan*, no. 296, 1084; *Ronceray*, no. 273, ca 1100; *St. Trinité*, vol. 2, no 386, ca. 1100. Charters often noted when a new acquisition was near other possessions of the house: *St. Père*, vol. 2, no. 24, ca. 1109; *Cîteaux*, no. 158, ca. 1160. Charters likewise noted when claims against properties of the house were extinguished: *St. Trinité*, vol. 2, no. 487, ca. 1140; vol. 3, no. 649, 1207; *St. Père*, vol. 2, no. 108, 1120-50.

75. *Berdoues*, no. 197, 1181: "Et nunc fratres de Berdonis possident omnem villam de Leziano et omnem ecclesiam cum omnibus pertinentiis eorum jure perpetuo tam ab ipsis donatoribus quam ab Arnaldo de Leziano, avunculo eorum, monacho Berdonarum."

76. *St. Denys*, no. 67, ca. 1100: "Hugo Berlaius de Faieto habebat decimam in parrochia Beati-Petri de Cetone, tertiam partem cujus decime habebant monachi Beati-Dionisii de Nogento, et placuit ei quod faceret monachum de quodam clericulo filio suo, et dedit monachis duas partes supradicte decime, qui puerum susceperunt in monachum. . . . " For other charters that record the use of cash, spiritual benefits, and receptions to consolidate fragmented property in the hands of the religious, see *Conques*, no. 284, 1060; no. 45, 1081; no. 356, 1060-1108; no. 559, 1183; *St. Stephan*, no. 164, 1075-80; no. 240, 1083-98; no. 520, 1141-49; *St. Père*, vol. 2, no. 6, ca. 1095; *Ronceray*, no. 343, before 1100; *Redon*, no. 368, 1101; *Perseigne*, no. 342, 1166-67; *Clairvaux*, p. 37, 1147; *St. Croix*, no. 85, 1082.

77. Mahn, *L'Ordre cistercien*, pp. 48-51. Grandmontine *Regula*, chap. 4, in Becquet, *Scriptores*, pp. 71-72. A Grandmontine commentator, Gerard, writing in the late 1190s stressed the spiritual reasons for the order's land policy (ibid., p. 485): " . . . In hoc maxime capitulo iustitia eius declaratur qua se suosque discipulos praemunire dinoscitur, ut decimas et reditus, possessionesque terrarum permaximas rehabere non permittit, timens ne cum saecularibus frequenter conflictum haberent, unde contigeret eos multotiens egredi de heremi solitudine et dulcedinem divinae inspirationis, vellent nollent, amitterent."

CHAPTER TWO

Lay Needs and
Entry into Religious Life

Reception of new members under conditions and after negotiation served the interest of religious communities by helping to perpetuate the group while at the same time contributing to the management of serious economic problems. But why did those who sought reception, primarily laymen and their families, cooperate in the functioning of this social institution? Certainly laymen valued religious houses for their prayers and their asceticisms, which were thought to promote good fortune in this world and salvation in the next. But the answers to that question are also to be sought in the useful functions that religious houses performed for the lay world when they received new members.

Places in religious houses were a moderately scarce commodity. The medieval monastery did not usually have a large population of religious. There were variations in size that the history of a given house and its wealth would go far to explain. There were, of course, houses with very large numbers; but these were few and favored places, the aristocracy of the monastic world.[1] In spite of the fragmentary and relatively late nature of the evidence, it is possible to make certain generalizations about the size of houses, at least in France. Dom Philibert Schmitz has pointed out that though Cluny at its height had about four hundred monks, the Cluniac priories of La Charité and Moissac had about eighty monks, and most of the hundreds of other Cluniac priories had no more than twenty monks.[2] Similarly, Dom Ursmer Berlière has gathered the admittedly imperfect statistics on French Benedictine houses, and his work suggests that in the twelfth and thirteenth centuries a house with sixty monks was large, whereas a figure in the thirties was more normal.[3] The visitation register of Odo Rigaud, archbishop of Rouen, reveals that for his ecclesiastical province in the years 1248 to 1269, the 162 religious houses subject to his visitation had an average of 11.4 members, whereas the eighteen nunneries visited had about forty-four members each.[4] For purposes of comparison, John Moorman estimated in his *Church Life in England in the Thirteenth Century* that few English Benedictine houses had a population of fifty, but that forty was rather common.[5]

From these figures it is clear that even though the death rate in medieval religious houses is unknown, one can be relatively certain that the number of new members that needed to be admitted annually in order to keep the house's population in equilibrium was rather small. Consequently, positions in any given house were relatively scarce. Contemporary piety and social institutions cooperated to exert a certain pressure on the supply of available places and to make positions objects of value, indeed, of competition.

There were three groups of people who sought entry to religious houses in the eleventh and early twelfth centuries. First, adults in good health sought to enter monastic life for a variety of personal, social, and religious reasons. Second, adults in danger of death took the religious habit as an act of piety and as a form of spiritual insurance. This was the entry *ad succurrendum*. Third, children were offered to religious houses by their parents or relatives to be raised there as monks or nuns. The effect of these practices was to create a steady and relatively large pool of people who sought admission to religious houses.[6]

Adult Conversion

The decision of an adult in good health to join a monastic community for religious reasons constitutes the classic paradigm of conversion. Hagiographers and the drafters of charters described such an adult convert as inspired,[7] or remorseful for sin,[8] or yearning for a more satisfying way of life.[9] In the eleventh and twelfth centuries adult converts constituted a modest but significant portion of those who entered religious life. The religious community provided a framework for a life of prayer and asceticism, and the grateful convert normally arranged that some portion of his possessions went as a gift to the support of the group.[10]

Entry ad succurrendum

Medieval spiritual writers were well aware that many adult converts were driven by circumstances rather than by religious conviction to seek entry into religion.[11] In a letter of the mid-twelfth century, attributed to a regular canon of Saint Victor at Paris, those who entered religious life were divided into three categories: those who sought God and abandoned the world, that is, converts in the classic sense; those who were drawn by a certain sort of society; and those who were moved by the force of disease.[12] Disease, injury, and the ravages of old age were catalysts, personal crises, that frequently aroused in medieval men a desire for entry into religious life. Most spiritual writers saw nothing wrong with such a motive, since they were convinced that Divine Providence could bring a person to a better life as well by the goad as by love. Anselm of Canterbury pointed out to a monk who regretted that he had converted because he feared he was dying that Saint Paul himself had been forced to conversion on the road to Damascus.[13]

Popular piety, fostered by the religious, saw in the religious habit a talisman powerful enough to forgive sins and to ease the transition to the next world. The entry into religious life was a second baptism, which left the soul as pure and sinless as the first baptism had. A saying in the popular *Vitae Patrum*, a record of early Egyptian monasticism, was one of the sources for this view: "There was a certain one who was great among the seers; he declared, saying: I saw over the clothing of the monk, when he took the spiritual habit, the virtue which I saw standing over baptism."[14] It was commonly believed that a sincere reception of the religious habit would save a person from damnation, no matter how evil his prior life had been.[15] Indeed, there were those who held that even a reception marked by fear and self-interest would, or at least could, save a man from perdition.[16] The monks of the twelfth and thirteenth centuries were willing to make very strong claims about the efficacy of their particular habit to save its wearer. Gerald of Wales, who was, of course, no friend to monks, recorded the following tale about the Cistercians, which is, however, paralleled by other sources:

> It happened however that the said rich abbot, that he might be richer, approached with two or three monks a certain matron in the city of Dublin who was gravely ill, whom he knew to be rich. And filling her with dire tales, he then promised her the kingdom of heaven with an assured guarantee putting forth himself and the whole Order as sponsors. . . .[17]

Although Gerald saw in such bold promises a thing to be ridiculed,[18] many members of the secular clergy felt that they would prefer to die as monks and arranged to take the habit at the end of life. In a letter written about 1150, Odo, a monk of Canterbury, described, with only modest exaggeration, one of the major streams of contemporary feeling about the monastic habit:

> Hence it is that all peoples, nations, tribes, and tongues run to him [Saint Benedict] to receive his blessings; so much so that those mockers who in their lifetime attack this form of religious life do not dare to be secure in death without the habit of this religion, i.e., the hood, finally taken on their deathbed.[19]

Likewise, in his defense of deathbed receptions, the Anglo-Norman monk Ralph stressed that no one in danger of death says "Make me a bishop, make me a cleric or a regular canon or anything of that sort; but they say 'Make me a monk'."[20]

There is considerable sober documentary support for these views in the cartularies of religious houses, in which transactions centering on reception at death or *ad succurrendum* are common. There was no mention of deathbed reception in Benedict's *Rule*, but its development as a regular feature of Benedictine monasticism is readily comprehensible. The concept justifying such receptions is relatively simple. A person in imminent danger of death was as free as any other man to convert to the religious life. A sincere conversion, no matter how late, was preferable to no conversion at all.[21]

When a seriously ill person sought to become a religious, he or his representatives petitioned for reception and for clothing in the habit, which was the crucial event in the popular imagination. Caesarius of Heisterbach told of a *tyrannus* who ordered his friends to clothe him in a habit as soon as he had died, "but be very careful that you do not do it while I am alive." The religious habit did him no good in the next world because he had donned it too late.[22] The race against death to complete the ritual and clothe the new monk in the habit was noted in many texts. An abbreviated ritual was permitted when death seemed imminent.[23] In an emergency any monk, acting as the abbot's delegate, could clothe an ill person in the habit, even in the sick man's home, and arrangements would be made to move him to the monastery.[24] It was a canonical precondition for reception *ad succurrendum* that the person be in grave danger of death, and it was frankly anticipated that the new religious would die soon.[25] In the meantime he was cared for in the monastic infirmary[26] and was buried in the monastic cemetery after he had expired.

The individual so received was truly and, in theory, permanently a religious, with the spiritual privileges and duties of a religious. If the entrant had possession of his mental faculties and if his spouse had consented to the reception, it was legally impossible to escape from the obligation to remain, even if he unexpectedly recovered from his illness.[27]

In this study the category of religious received *ad succurrendum* will be broadened to include not only the sick and injured but also those whom the regular canon of Saint Victor described as drawn by a certain sort of society, i.e., the old and tired. It was not uncommon for a man who was old but not actually in imminent danger of death to seek to spend his last years in a religious house. The following charter, dated to about 1150, concerns such a man:

. . . A certain knight of Vendôme, Joscelin by name, of the Rue des
Vasseleurs, decided to finish his life in the monastic habit. For he had
now almost reached decrepitude, and he wanted to leave behind him
the world and worldly affairs. Therefore Joscelin sent his two sons
and other friends to the lord abbot of Vendôme, Robert, so that he
might request humbly that he [the abbot] might make him a monk
for the love of God. The lord abbot, acknowledging the result of
Joscelin's good intentions, gave assent to his prayers and to the peti-
tions of his friends, and he made him a monk. Before Joscelin was
made a monk he gave an offering to God and to the monks who
served God, so that he might win heavenly goods by means of his
earthly goods.[28]

Alongside those like Joscelin, who became religious in order to
retire from worldly affairs or were pushed by their sons to retire,[29]
there were others who were driven to the habit by more vigorous
goads. Fighting, a favored occupation of the knightly class, had
its dangers and disasters that could force an injured man to seek
refuge in the cloister. Even modest wounds were often fatal. The
frequent wars, feuds, and tournaments of the eleventh and twelfth
centuries left in their wake injured men who sought to expiate
their sins in a monastic conversion.

Norman, the son of Drogo of Montoire, was captured by Geoffrey of
Mayenne and was gravely wounded. He vowed himself to God and
he promised that he would be a monk at the Holy Trinity if G[eof-
frey], his captor, would allow it. At the request of the monks the
latter agreed to it. The monks therefore came and clothed him with
the habit in the porch of the prison in which he was being held. He
gave one half of the church of Martaizé, with all its revenues.[30]

But of course it was not merely for the aged or the injured that
the habit *ad succurrendum* was sought. Disease struck youths and
men in their prime, and they were often disposed to die as religious.

At length the same young man fell into sickness and being fearful of
death, he sent for the monks to come to him. When they were present he gave to them all that he held at Boisseau. . . . Then he asked
that the brethren receive him as a monk in their community, but his
mother objected, lest she be left alone and deprived of the solace of a
son. . . . [His condition grew worse.] Then he begged in every way

30

that they make him a monk. . . . And so the monks blessed him a monk. He then left to us whatever he had at Oucques from his father, [which we would get] after the death of his mother. . . . After these events the monks were taking him to the monastery, but he died *en route*, and his corpse was transported to the monastery.[31]

Thus when old age, serious injury, or disease raised the specter of death, many persons saw in the reception of the religious habit that "second baptism" which would atone for their sins and would give them spiritual comfort. The religious shared the belief of their society that their prayers and habit did in fact benefit the man who was accorded them. Many of those whom they received *ad succurrendum* had been friends and patrons of the house. The *Deeds of the Abbots of St. Trond* told of a man who helped over the years to defray building costs at Saint Trond. In return he and his wife received membership in the prayer confraternity; they were given a monk's portion of food daily for life; their son was received as an oblate; and when the wife died, she was buried within the monastery, before the chapter room. The man obtained permission from his third wife to become a monk, and he spent several years in the habit, died, and was buried in the monastic cemetery. Thus a close association of many years' duration was capped by reception in old age.[32] It is also no accident that all of the charters quoted in this chapter reveal the monastery as recipient of gifts on the occasion of the reception of a member *ad succurrendum*. The new monk and his family virtually always accompanied his entry with gifts. Thus the reception of a religious *ad succurrendum* was for the house an act of piety, a gesture of good public relations, and an economic benefit.

Many laymen wanted sincerely, indeed desperately, to die in a religious habit, for the sake of the assurances of salvation that it provided. The ability to influence the salvation of men at the critical period of a last illness was a useful economic tool in the hands of the religious. Lay families expected to offer something in return for the great benefit given them. Since time was on the side of the religious in negotiating entry *ad succurrendum*, they could afford to drive a hard bargain when necessary. A charter from

Saint Maur-sur-Loire, dated about 1040–45, exposed the hard, venal aspect of one such reception. Stabulus gave one *borderia* of land to the monastery, but his son Peter laid a claim against it. Stabulus fell ill and asked to be made a monk, but the monks responded that "they were in no way going to receive him since his son was claiming that land from the monks and from the saint." The son begged the mercy of the monks, gave up his claim, and confirmed his father's earlier gift, after which his father was received.[33] In situations such as these, it must have been possible for the religious to go too far in their demands and provoke criticism, but I have found no instance of it. Negotiation, with the advantage on the side of the religious, was simply in the nature of the transaction.

However, the institution of receiving monks *ad succurrendum* was not without its frictions and problems, arising chiefly out of legal considerations. To seek reception *ad succurrendum* was not a step to be taken lightly, because if the sick man recovered, he was bound by law to remain a religious.[34] The charters make clear that, if there was any hope for recovery, the sick person and his relatives were reluctant to receive the habit.

> Geoffrey of Oudon was gravely wounded at Chantoceaux while serving in the army of the Count of Anjou, and he was brought to death's door. He had himself carried to the house of the monks of Oudon, and he humbly sought the monastic habit there. His friends however were opposed to his wishes. Since they thought he might live, they advised him not to become a monk. At length, however, seeing himself very close to death . . . he gave the site of one mill on the river Loire, and one fishing weir . . . , and his share in the vineyard of Guihenocus Burellus, and all his meadows at La Vieille-Cour.[35]

Not only laymen feared a premature reception to the habit. The ecclesiastical hierarchy was reluctant to permit too easy an entry to those seeking reception *ad succurrendum* because of the scandals, disorders, and disputes that arose when those who recovered attempted to leave.[36] Peter Damian attacked vigorously the opinion of a bishop who held that those who took the religious habit in sickness might abandon it freely when they recovered. Damian cited an impressive series of canon law texts to prove that once a person was formally received as a religious *ad succurrendum*, he could abandon the habit only if his spouse's permission had not been granted. Mere recovery was no justification for leaving.[37] Damian clearly upheld the traditional view that saw such persons as apostates from their vows, who should be forced to return to the monastery.

In addition to problems occasioned by the recovery of the dying man, religious houses found in the gifts given for reception *ad succurrendum* a frequent source of litigation. In the emotional period of sickness and death, the new religious could often induce his family to give gifts, which, in sober afterthought, they regretted. In his last illness Duke Godfrey of Lorraine (d. 1069) made a generous gift to found a religious house. The gift consisted in large part of properties supporting soldiers, who complained among themselves about what they perceived as an injustice to them. The duke's son and heir also resented the gift because it would weaken him militarily. The abbot to whom the gift was offered saw that the resistance of the soldiers and of the son would prevent the gift from coming to fruition. Consequently the abbot refused the gift and told the dying duke why. Duke Godfrey summoned his son and shamed him into agreeing to it. As soon as the father died, the son reneged on the gift and a long period of litigation began. The son argued "that he should not lose the friendship of his soldiers, in whose hand his power lay; his father was out of his mind in his last illness; he [the son] was going to look after his own affairs rather than to the ravings of his father."[38] This incident involved a large gift given by an important man, but it was mirrored in humbler dealings when the new monk's kin laid claims against the gift, seized it back, or simply never handed it over at all.

The Cistercians and some other new orders attempted to avoid these difficulties by forbidding entirely receptions *ad succurrendum*. They sought to prevent the reception of those who had no desire to be monks while healthy but came to conversion when it was clear that death was near. Cistercian charters contained a recurring proviso that a man would be received as a monk "if he shall come

according to the custom of the order."[39] That custom was specified in this text from a charter promising some benefactors the
right to enter: ". . . and they ought to be received in Berdoues if
they wish, if nevertheless they are able to come riding and unim-
paired in their members."[40] In effect this requirement meant
that to be eligible for reception a person must come to the monastery under his own power. Such a restriction would make it nearly
impossible for a man to take the Cistercian habit in his last,
debilitating illness. However, just as the Cistercians began to conform to the older orders in the kinds of property that they accepted, so too, by the later twelfth century, they were willing
to write into some charters provisions about taking a man no
matter what his condition. The need to round out domains, settle
claims, and honor benefactors gradually overcame the "custom of
the order." In 1186 Bernard of Logorsan gave to the Cistercians
of Gimont all his lands and abandoned his legal claims against the
property of the house. In return the monks agreed to receive him as
a *conversus* or a monk, as he wished. Not only did the monks waive
all requirements of health, but they conceded that "if by chance
he should fall ill, and not be able to come to Gimont on his own
feet or riding, then the monks ought to go for him up to seven
leagues, when they see his messenger."[41] The attempt to curb or
eliminate receptions *ad succurrendum* generally failed in the later
twelfth century because of social and economic pressures to offer it
to friends and patrons. However, procedures were worked out
that protected the interests of the laymen and of the religious.
The ideal situation for both parties was to negotiate the details of
the agreement before the final illness arrived, with its accompanying haste and emotion. The entrant would be assured of a
smooth reception when he wished it, presumably at the very last
moment, and the house would be assured of a gift that was more
stable because it was made in a calm atmosphere. Compacts and
prepayments with varying details were employed to arrange in advance such an orderly and mutually satisfactory reception *ad succurrendum*. One common way to work out such an agreement was
to make it a provision of some other transaction. Many charters

of gift, sale, confirmation, or settlement of dispute contained agreements about deathbed entry. The right to enter under known conditions was thus offered by the religious as a part payment for whatever was being purchased in the charter. The house had the security of knowing that if the giver or seller tried to renege on the agreement, he would be restrained by the threat of losing his guaranteed place. In 1183 a man made a deathbed gift to Conques of free passage through his portion of Le Port, a place where tolls were collected. Two knights who also possessed an interest in Le Port gave free passage and agreed to observe the dying man's gift. In return the knights were given the right to claim the habit *ad succurrendum* in return for a "good and acceptable portion of their goods."[42] Thus the gift and confirmation served as a kind of down payment that would be completed by a "good and acceptable portion of their goods" if they actually tried to exercise their option. Similarly a certain Bocherius gave a gift to the Breton monastery of Redon in return for reception *ad succurrendum*. The monks then sought the agreement of some relatives:

> Herveus, the son of Bocherius, and Judicalis the archdeacon, his nephew, conceded this gift; and Judicalis retained this, that if he should wish to be a monk, he would be received with all his money and with a large gift from his landed possessions.[43]

Thus Judicalis received the right to enter the house at some future time, and both he and the monks of Redon understood the conditions and financial arrangements that must precede the entry.

What emerges from this consideration of the practice of receiving the old, the injured, and the ill to religious life is that it was a social institution that always involved negotiations and conditioned agreements. It was a practice favorable to the religious because their habit was eagerly sought by the dying. Time and fear acted to the advantage of the monks. For the dying man and his family, it was an occasion for reconciliation and for righting wrongs.[44] For the religious it was a time for exhortation to penance, conversion, and almsgiving. It was only natural that among the wrongs to be righted were those of the entrant and his kin to the religious house that he wished to enter. A dispute of years' standing frequently ended on a deathbed attended by the religious. In addition to restitutions and recognitions of rights, there were new gifts accompanying the religious *ad succurrendum*, gifts that were at times suggested or demanded by the monks. Since the habit was highly valued, outsiders tried to arrange for its reception long before they would want it. The promise of reception under conditions was a privilege to obtain during dealings with religious houses. Thus in a variety of ways the reception of the aged and dying was a way for a religious house to tighten its hold on its patrimony and to increase it, a way to find leverage in dealing with its lay and clerical neighbors. But this meant that the religious habit became a nexus around which to negotiate, to form pacts, and to trade.

Child Oblation

It was only by way of exception that a religious received *ad succurrendum* recovered and became a permanent addition to the monastic community. Likewise, adult converts probably never constituted a majority of the religious in eleventh- or early twelfth-century communities. The major source of members for religious houses was children, the *oblati* or *nutriti* who had grown up in the community. Benedict's *Rule* had accepted as normal the practice by which children were given to a religious house by their parents and were raised there as full monks.[45] Benedict was not unique in this aspect of his legislation, for many of the extant monastic rules from late antiquity made provision for children in the community.[46] However, Benedict's contribution to this practice was that for him the oblate child was not a boarder or pupil, but was truly and permanently a monk who had no right to leave monastic life. His permanent vocation had been chosen for him by his parents.[47]

Premodern European society had little sense of children's rights, especially their right to choose a spouse or a career. For the middle and upper strata of society, marriage was a major economic event that was not to be complicated overmuch by the wishes of the children involved.[48] This same set of attitudes operated in the oblation of children to religious houses. Down to the twelfth century the dominant opinion was that expressed in canon forty-eight of the fourth Council of Toledo (633): "Either the devotion of the parents or the monk's own profession makes one a monk. Whichever one of these it is, the monk is bound."[49] On isolated occasions this view was challenged. The *cause célèbre* of Gottschalk of Orbais in the mid ninth century was partially due to his attempts to abandon the monastic life, even though he had been an oblate at Fulda. Due in large measure to the efforts of Hincmar of Reims and Hrabanus Maurus, Gottschalk had a very difficult time in his attempts to escape from the obligation placed on him as a child.[50] The exact disposition of his case is unknown, but a council at Worms in 868 reaffirmed the view that oblates were monks with no right to leave the cloister.[51]

In the eleventh century the practice of offering children to monasteries was deeply rooted and was sanctioned by religious sentiment, custom, and considerations of family pride and self-interest. As Richard Southern observed in *The Making of the Middle Ages*:

> . . . The number of those who came to monastic life as adults was never negligible; but it remains true that the proportion of the monastic population of the eleventh century, which had adopted the life by their own volition, was probably no greater than the proportion of volunteers in a modern army.
>
> The monasteries were filled with a conscript army. It was not an unwilling or ineffective army on that account: the ideal of monastic service was too widely shared for the conscription to be resented.[52]

To eleventh-century observers religious houses were inhabited by two distinct kinds of monks, the *nutriti* who had grown up in the monastery and the *conversi*, a term that then meant adults who entered the monastery as mature persons. There were frictions between the two groups, but contemporaries saw the division as quite normal and attributed to each group its own strengths and weaknesses.[53] However, in the twelfth century the institution of child oblation was attacked because of certain problems inherent in it that seemed to new sensibilities to outweigh its advantages.[54] In that century monasticism experienced a period of uncertainty. The total number of persons in religious life increased greatly, due in part to the rise of new orders. With that growth the numbers of unhappy, unfit, and apostate monks increased also, or so, at least, it seemed to contemporaries. A restless desire to move from house to house and from order to order posed a serious problem for the ecclesiastical authorities.[55] Contemporary opinion saw at least part of the reason for this unrest in infant and child oblation.

The reformed orders of the twelfth century reacted to the situation by refusing to accept new members below ages in the mid-teens, late teens, or even twenty. These monastic reformers forbade oblation largely because the presence of children in the cloister was disruptive and an impediment to the austerity and routine that they sought.[56]

In the older monastic tradition, whose origins predated the twelfth century, there was no such radical break with the reception of oblates. But even in that older tradition there was a recognition that the oblation of children often meant unfit, unhappy monks. Guibert of Nogent, a Benedictine abbot, wrote his autobiography about 1115–17, and he commented on the monks of his youth, most of whom had been oblates:

> Therefore in our day in the oldest monasteries, numbers had thinned, although they had an abundance of wealth given in ancient times and they were satisfied with small congregations, in which very few could be found who, through scorn of sin, had rejected the world, but the churches were rather in the hands of those who had been placed in them by the piety of their kinsmen early in life. And these, having little to fear on account of their own sins, as they imagined they had committed none, therefore lived within the walls of the convents a life of slackened zeal. They being allotted managements and outside duties in accordance with the needs or wishes of the abbots, were eager enough themselves to accept them but inexperienced in outside freedom from restraint and had easy opportunities for wasting church monies: these being accounted for as expended or as free gifts.[57]

The monks Guibert described were restless, tepid, without a sense of sin, and administratively inept. He traced this malaise to its origin in their entry into religious life as children, before they were experienced in the world or aware of their own sinfulness.

Likewise, Peter the Venerable, Abbot of Cluny, forbade the reception of anyone as a Cluniac monk before he was twenty years of age. Peter's explanation of the reasons for this ruling reveals the considerations that weighed with conscientious monastic leaders in attempting to check the practice of oblation:

> The reason for this ruling was the unconsidered and overly quick reception of youngsters, who put on the clothing of holy religion before they are able to possess any rational intelligence, and since they are enmeshed in boyish foolishness they disturb everyone; and that I may be silent about some things and lump together many other things for brevity's sake, they profit not at all to themselves, they impede the resolve of the other monks not merely a little, but sometimes a great deal.[58]

Abbot Peter's decision did not forbid the promise of the religious habit to children, but its actual reception was to be delayed until the twentieth year.[59]

Thus in the mid twelfth century child oblation was in decline, banished entirely in many of the new orders and regarded with ambivalence even within the older tradition.[60] However, the serious decline of child oblation should not obscure the fact that the practice was normal in the eleventh and early twelfth centuries and was criticized then only rarely. In a social system that gave parents wide powers of disposal over their children, many, perhaps most, of the youths offered to religious life saw this as a normal, accepted procedure. They came to choose or at least to accept what originally had been placed upon them. It is symptomatic of the acceptance of oblation that the monastic critics of the practice in the twelfth century did not deny the right of a parent to offer his child to God, but rather they attacked what they considered to be the unacceptable consequences of allowing children in the cloister.[61] Oblation retained its attractions even when criticized or banned. In spite of clear prohibitions against receiving children as monks, Cistercian abbots were regularly punished for it by the general chapter of their order. The guilty abbots apparently saw it as an advantageous practice from which it was frankly difficult to abstain, or else the abbots were under pressure from the surrounding lay world to preserve this time-honored and socially useful custom.[62]

When child oblation was common, religious and material interests were intertwined inextricably in the act of oblation, as they were in so many aspects of medieval religion. The parents who offered a child saw themselves performing a major work of piety and playing a role comparable to that of Old Testament figures who sacrificed or offered their children to God. Indeed, the canonist Gratian proposed as one of the possible defenses of payment for entry into religion an Old Testament model: ". . . Anna took Samuel with her when he was weaned, to the house of God in Silo, with three cows, and three measures of wheat and an amphora of wine."[63] The canonist Bishop Stephan of Tournai wrote in the later twelfth century on behalf of a parent to the abbot of Saint Bavo at Ghent:

> Warned by the example of the patriarch [Abraham], he wishes to offer one of his sons upon one of the mountains which the Lord has pointed out to him, i.e., your holy church, so that he may increase merit from the imitation of so great an example; and your convent may gather the profit of the holocaust in the daily service of himself and of his son.[64]

In the monastic theology of the time, the child was first and foremost a *hostia viva*, a living sacrifice, who would pray for his parents and the rest of his kin before God. He was an offering to expiate the sins of his parents:

> I, Bermond . . . of Dromon-Saint-Genies, am aware that I have been called to the rewards of heaven along with a multitude of innumerable peoples; yet, fearing that for the stain of my many sins and without the grace of God I may not be among the elect few, I hand over, give, and offer my son William with the will and advice of Richildis, his mother; . . . so that with him living henceforth under regular discipline, aided by his intercessions, . . . I may be worthy to be a coheir in the election of the servants of Jesus Christ.[65]

Because the child was a gift to God, his decision to leave the religious house could negate or frustrate his parent's good work.

Hence there was pressure on the child to remain, a pressure that operated even in the later twelfth century when the canon law guaranteed the child the right to leave at puberty.

The discussion of child oblation would be distorted unless this element of piety and of sacrifice to God is recognized as essential to the functioning of the institution. However, for a complete understanding of the social significance of oblation, the material interests of the family that offered a child must be examined. Between 1079 and 1087 Ulrich of Cluny described the *consuetudines*, or customs, of Cluny for Abbot William of Hirsau.[66] In his dedicatory letter to William, Ulrich congratulated the abbot for his decision to restrict, or perhaps to eliminate, the reception of oblates at Hirsau. In the course of the letter, Ulrich depicted in dark colors the unworthy motives that led some laymen to offer their children to religious houses:

> After they have their house, as I may say, full of sons and daughters, or if any of those children is lame or maimed or hard of hearing or blind or humpbacked or leprous or any other things of this sort which make him in some way less acceptable to the world, indeed they offer this one to God with a very eager vow, so that he may be a monk. Although clearly [they do it] not for the sake of God but on account of this only, that they may free themselves from bringing up and nourishing them, or that the situation may be more favorable to their other children.[67]

Ulrich charged that such oblates, whether well or ill, enervated the discipline of the monasteries that they entered. Indeed, in his view oblation of unwanted children was "that root from which alone almost all those monasteries were destroyed which have been destroyed in areas of German or of Roman tongue."[68] Ulrich's righteous anger at the motives for, and consequences of, child oblation is understandable. However, somewhat disingenuously he reserved all his criticism for the parents of the child and failed to mention that the oblate was normally not accepted *gratis* by the religious house. As was the case with virtually all kinds of monastic recruits, the child was accompanied by a gift of land, money, or some valuable concession. The monastic house as well as the

41

family had its material interests to be promoted by the entry of the child.

Ulrich mentioned two specific reasons why a lay family might be eager to offer a child: first, if it had too many children for whom to provide, and second, if a particular child was handicapped in some way. These two charges will be tested indirectly. The offering of a child to a religious house was often recorded in a formal document, many of which survive. In order to ensure the stability of the entry gift, the charters of oblation were often witnessed and approved by the other male children in a family. Consequently it is possible in many cases to know the number of male children in those families that offered oblates. The figures are of course *minima*, since female children were ordinarily not mentioned and a family might have absent male children or children born to it after the oblation. Out of sixty-one oblations (see table 1) in which the number of other sons is known, forty-two involved families with three or more sons and twenty-nine families had four or more sons.[69] Ulrich's assertion that the burdens of a large family were an important inducement to offer a child is also confirmed by literary evidence, although much of it comes from the thirteenth century.[70] William of Auvergne, bishop of Paris from 1228 to 1249, wrote:

> Others [monks] are cast into the cloister by parents and relatives just as if they were kittens or piglets whom their mother could not nourish; so that they may die to the world not spiritually but, as we say, civilly, that is so that they may be deprived of their hereditary portion and that it may devolve on those who remain in the world. . . .[71]

Although lay families provided the majority of oblates, there were others who sought positions for children. In order to combat clerical marriage, or nicolaism, as it was called by the eleventh-century reformers, the sons of priests had been forbidden to succeed their fathers directly in an ecclesiastical position.[72] As that legislation against clerical incontinence and hereditary benefices[73] grew more strict, there were some priests who found it convenient to provide a monastic career for their children, particularly

TABLE 1

NUMBER OF SONS IN FAMILIES OFFERING AN OBLATE

RELIGIOUS HOUSE AND YEARS	NUMBER OF SONS								Several
	1	2	3	4	5	6	7	8	
Saint Sernin									
1050-1100.....	...	...	...	...	...	...	...	...	2
1100-1150....	...	...	1	2	1	...	...	...	...
1150-1200.....	...	...	1	...	...	...	...	...	...
Saint Aubin									
1050-1100.....	2	...	...	1	...	...	...	...	4
1100-1150.....	...	...	1	...	...	...	...	...	...
1150-1200.....	1	1	...	1	...	...	...	...	3
Conques									
1050-1100.....	1	2	1	...	...	...	...	...	6
1100-1150.....	...	...	...	1	...	...	...	...	1
1150-1200.....	...	...	...	...	...	...	...	...	...
Saint Stephen of Beanie									
1050-1100.....	...	5	4	...	...	...	...	...	9
1100-1150.....	...	...	...	...	...	...	...	...	...
1150-1200.....	...	...	...	...	...	...	...	...	...
Aniane									
1050-1100.....	1	...	...	1	...	1	...	...	1
1100-1150.....	...	1	1	2	...	...	...	...	2
1150-1200.....	...	...	...	...	...	...	...	...	2
Saint Victor									
1050-1100.....	1	2	1	...	...	1	1	1	3
1100-1150.....	...	...	...	...	1	...	...	...	...
1150-1200.....	...	...	...	...	...	...	...	...	...
Gellone									
1050-1100.....	...	1	...	6	3	1	2	...	7
1100-1150.....	...	...	2	1	1	...	...	...	4
1150-1200.....	...	...	...	1	...	...	...	...	1
Redon									
1050-1100.....	...	...	1	...	...	...	...	...	2
1100-1150.....	1	...	...	...	...	...	...	...	1
1150-1200.....	...	...	...	...	...	...	...	...	...

since such children were freed from the legal stigma of being priests' bastards by entering religious life under a rule.[74]

Ulrich's companion charge against families offering children was that they placed in religious life handicapped children. The actual charters of oblation are not a useful source of information about the offering of such children. Naturally enough, a religious aura predominates in the charters; it would not have been seemly to mention that the oblate, the offering to God, was in some way blemished and was being dedicated to God's service for that reason. However, at rare intervals the charters are tantalizing even on this issue. For instance, it was normal that younger sons be offered as oblates, and older sons inherited the family property and pursued secular careers. Yet in a charter of the Holy Trinity at Vendôme, dated 1097, the situation was reversed: "Gaudinus of Malicorne [made a series of gifts] . . . , when he gave his firstborn son Warren to be a monk, to whom the whole *honor* of Gaudinus was to come if he had remained in the world. . . . "[75] There is no explicit proof in this charter that Warren was handicapped, but the very unusual circumstance that he was both the eldest son and also an oblate suggests that some factor of great weight to his family was at work in the oblation. The charter says nothing about Warren's special desire for religious life, nor does it say that the family offered him as a special gift to God for some particular favor. Hence there would seem to be a good possibility that the boy was deemed by his family to be unfit for secular life.

However, to obtain more conclusive evidence for Ulrich's assertion that religious houses were used as custodial institutions for handicapped children, it is necessary to turn to the writings of reformers, monastic and episcopal visitors, and literary figures. The following discussion is not an attempt to provide an exhaustive proof of Ulrich's contentions, but rather to suggest that he had indeed accurately identified one of the motives for child oblation.

Peter the Venerable issued statutes for the reform of the Cluniac Order between 1132 and 1146. In chapter 35 he discussed forthrightly the danger posed for the order by the reception of defectives of all kinds, including children.

> It is decided that no one is to be received as a Cluniac monk without the order and permission of the Abbot of Cluny, as is the custom, unless [the person is received] *ad succurrendum.* . . . The reason for this measure . . . was the very frequent and indiscrete reception of useless persons throughout almost every Cluniac house. As a result of this indiscrete reception of peasants, of children, of old men, of mental

defectives, and of others not useful for anything, the situation reached the state that such persons were almost a majority, and the frequent and detestable evils done by them . . . are heard frequently from all parts of the land.[76]

The chronicle of the abbey of Andrès in the diocese of Arras recorded the reaction of the new abbot who arrived at the house in 1161.

The honorable man was received with due deference and on his arrival, besides their [the monks'] practices, which he found misshapen, he was shocked and frightened at the deformity of the flock. For some were lame, some were crippled, some were one-eyed, some were cross-eyed, some blind, and even some missing a limb appeared among them; and almost all of these were of noble stock. Having seen this, the prudent shepherd was saddened and he contemplated what afterward the de-voted man fulfilled: for through thirty two years and more in which he ruled this place, he never permitted anyone to be a monk who had any defect in any part of his body.[77]

One must of course allow for rhetorical exaggeration in such liter-ary descriptions. However, it remains true that children with mild disabilities—the sources speak mostly of non-debilitating prob-lems[78]—were often candidates for oblation if their families could arrange it.

But, of course, superfluous and handicapped children were not the only ones whom a family might wish to place in religious life. Some youngsters entered for what were probably reasons of a pre-dominantly pious nature, to fulfill a vow or to atone for the sins of a parent. But special circumstances created smaller categories of youngsters for whom entry into religion constituted a solution to some problem. If a child was deprived of his parents or of his father in particular, other members of the kin group would provide for him. In most cases the child was taken into the household of a relative and was raised as one of the children of the family. How-ever, the sources indicate that not infrequently the kin discharged its duty by procuring for the child a place in a religious house. "[Her] relatives gave for Fania, daughter of Hugo and of Hermen-sendis, both of whom were dead, a part of the tithe of Ormeaux which the mother had held, and the land of La Greve and two shillings of rent. . . . "[79] It is important not to overestimate the force of kin ties. Entry into religion for an orphan was perhaps arranged as a way to get rid of a problem. Guibert of Nogent reported that when his widowed mother entered a pious seclusion, he was left with plenty of food and clothing but with no particular care or affection from his relatives, who were probably relieved when he decided to enter a religious house.[80]

It was especially the younger children in a family who could expect to be offered to a religious house in the event that their parents died. At times the dying parent had expressly provided that the child enter religion, as a source of prayers for his soul or as a convenient way to provide for the child.[81] The anonymous biographer of Edmund Rich noted the steps that Edmund's dying mother took to provide for her two young daughters:

> . . . And calling to herself Edmund, the brother of those virgins, . . . she placed them with a certain sum of money under his providence and protection: adding that as soon as an opportune moment offered itself, he should hand them over to a monastery to be wed to the Heavenly Spouse of virgins.[82]

If a dying parent did not or could not make such arrangements, the charters suggest that the child's surviving parent, siblings, or uncles often made the decisions necessary to place him in a religious house. Indeed, it is noticeable how frequently uncles and brothers figure in the charters as the oblators of the child and as the providers of his entrance gift.[83] At Gellone between 1077 and 1099 Rainelmus Guitardi and his two sons offered Hugo Guitardi, his nephew, whose father had died. The child's three other uncles and three brothers assented to the arrangement and to the gift, which was apparently taken from the deceased father's estate.[84] In many situations the brothers of the oblate took the leading role; for the death of the paterfamilias meant that there would be a division of the family assets among the heirs, and it was often perceived as more profitable to place the youngest child or children in religious life than it was to give them their full share. A charter of

Aniane, dated 1173, contained the provisions of such an arrangement:

> I, Raymond Bertrannus, who am son of the late Peter Bertrannus, with the advice . . . of my mother Alamanna, give . . . whatever my father Peter Bertrannus had from you . . . in the parish and in the district of Carcares . . . except for a vineyard which is between the vineyards of Raymond of Carcares and the vineyards of the Elemosinarius. . . . I concede to you everything else with my brother Peter, to whom these things suffice for [his] part of the paternal inheritance. . . . [85]

There were events besides death that could leave a child the equivalent of an orphan. For instance, when a man with children set off on a long trip, e.g., a pilgrimage, a crusade, or even a business trip, he had to make some provision for his minor children and unmarried daughters. Normally he must have entrusted them to his wife or relatives. But on occasion, for reasons that are generally not stated, those arrangements were not available. In that event he might turn to a religious house as the place in which to provide for his child. He had two options, either to make the child a religious or to board the child in a religious house until his return. The first option is recorded in a charter of Saint Peter of Chartres:

> I, R., vidâme of Chartres, . . . wish to make known that Philip of Tréon, wishing to go to Jerusalem, made his son Walter a monk in the monastery of Saint Peter of Chartres; and for the love of God and for his sake he gave . . . a meadow of the close, a vineyard, and land placed in the middle [and] also the tithe which Juhellus of Nonancourt held in his lifetime. [86]

On the other hand, some travelers were not so positive as Philip that they wished to make their child a religious. They exercised the second option and arranged for the religious house to keep the child in its custody until their return. However, even one of these might decide as a form of insurance that if he died abroad, the child should be made a religious:

> . . . Renaudus of Beré, before he set off on his trip, arranged his affairs thus. The forenamed Renaudus commended his possessions to

Lord Granus and to the Lady Abbess [of Ronceray] so that they might pay his debts from the houses. If it happened that he died in barbarous lands, he ordered that after his debts were paid, his daughter should be married to Christ and to the Virgin, His Mother, by means of the monastic habit, along with the remainder of his goods. If however divine grace should permit him to return, he would have his goods as free as he had possessed them before this arrangement.[87]

Finally, there were in the twelfth century deep yearnings among both the laity and the clergy for the *vita apostolica*, a life of poverty and preaching modeled on that of the apostles. In response to these aspirations there were laymen, laywomen, and clerics, some of them with dependents, who converted to the religious life in one of its formal or informal manifestations. In order to abandon the world, they had to find some haven for their children and spouses. When Guibert of Nogent's mother took up a life of pious seclusion near a monastery, she sent her little son to live in the monastery as a boarder, where he eventually took the habit.[88] In order to embrace the *vita apostolica* in the early twelfth century, Werimbald of Cambrai placed his wife, three sons, and one daughter in various religious houses.[89] Peter Abelard recommended the founding of double monasteries in which members of both sexes could be received, precisely because a man with dependents who wished to convert could thus be relieved of his responsibilities by taking them with him into the house.[90] The famous preacher Peter Waldo sent his two daughters into Fontevrault in order to free himself for a career of wandering preaching.[91] Individuals who wished simply to join a more conventional religious community, with no intention of adopting one of the extreme forms of the *vita apostolica*, also found it useful to place children in religion:

> The monks of Saint Aubin and Gerbert, a canon of Saint Magnobodus, had this agreement with one another: since by reflecting on his long experience, Gerbert discovered that clerical freedom in many ways closes the way of true salvation to clerics, he sought the more certain path of monastic discipline, . . . and at length to be received as a monk gratis as an act of kindness by the monks of Saint Aubin; and since he loved very much a certain little boy whom in some way he had fathered, for him also he asked persistently that when he was ac-

ceptable because of age for reception in the monastery (for he was then very small), he might be received by those same monks because of that same kindness. The monks both receive Gerbert gladly and for his sake they promise faithfully that they will receive the boy at the proper time. Gerbert recompensed the monks for that boy by thirty pounds of pennies and by two *arpents* of good vineyard, with vessels sufficient for collecting their yield, and one table at the gate of Angers paying twelve shillings of rent each year. . . . [92]

Thus oblation of children to religious life met a range of problems that might confront an upper-class family. The usefulness of oblation explains the willingness of those seeking it to negotiate and, indeed, to pay for it. It is probably true that the gift at entry was often freely conceded, in the sense that it was determined by negotiations between the house and the parents of the oblate, who felt no resentment about it. Perhaps some children were taken for free, but such oblates would leave little or no trace in the economic documents that constitute a cartulary.[93] However, even when these qualifications are granted, it remains true that custom and repetition had made a gift, whose exact provisions were worked out by the parties within the framework of their needs, an indispensable part of the act of oblation. Contemporaries presumed that any entrant would be accompanied by a gift, and the reception of a child in particular was a *beneficium*, a favor granted by the religious house,[94] which demanded some recompense. A charter of Saint Aubin implied clearly the contemporary view of oblation and gifts:

> A certain man, Berengar, wishing to make his little son a monk, sought with all supplication through his own efforts and through those of others that he might be received in the monastery of Saint Aubin. And since he knew that the boy was not going to be received gratis by the monks, he gave with his son to Saint Aubin a certain property which he had near the well.[95]

Finally, a charter of Saint Denys de Nogent-le-Rotrou, written about 1190, when child oblation was in decline, offered an insight into the emotions and values that surrounded an ordinary act of oblation. A knight offered his son and promised gifts, aid, and counsel if the child was received. The knight's brother seconded the request with a promise of other gifts if his nephew was received. The charter made clear that the father and uncle were doing an honorable thing, what any sensible persons should do to place a child in religion. The monastic prior who received the request was cast in the role of the good and faithful steward seizing an honest opportunity to increase the wealth of his church. The deal was a rather blunt *quid pro quo*, and was consummated to the satisfaction of all parties, with no hint that it might be illegal or dishonorable.[96]

Conclusion

From whatever perspective it is viewed, entry into monastic life in the eleventh and twelfth centuries was not simply a religious decision, though the religious element was generally present. Both the entrant and the religious house had needs to be satisfied and problems to be solved by entry. For the religious house and for the entrant, the gift at entry was simply part of the normal process for obtaining entry. Custom made that gift the focus of negotiations in the course of which problems were ameliorated and needs met.

1. B. Guillemain, "Chiffres et statistiques pour l'histoire ecclésiastique du moyen âge," *Le moyen âge* 59 (1953): 348, notes that at Clairvaux during Saint Bernard's abbacy, 888 men made profession as monks. That is an average of two per month, and *conversi* are not included. M.-A. Dimier, "Saint Bernard et le recrutement de Clairvaux," *Revue Mabillon* 42 (1952): 17-30, 56-68, 69-78, points out that there was a steady flow of monks from Clairvaux to its many foundations, and so the figure 888 gives no accurate picture of numbers at Clairvaux at any one time. Walter Daniel, *The Life of Ailred of Rievaulx*, trans. F. M. Powicke (London, 1950), p. 38, says that there were 140 monks and 500 *conversi* and hired laymen at Rievaulx during the abbacy of Ailred. However, there is some question whether the number 140 refers to monks alone or to both monks and *conversi*.

2. P. Schmitz, *Histoire de l'ordre de Saint Benoît* (Maredsous, 1948), 3:153. R. H. Snape, *English Monastic Finances in the Later Middle Ages* (Cambridge, 1926), p. 176, computes that English Cluniac priories for which figures survive had an average of 23 members in 1245-46, 26 members in 1262, and 18 members in 1279.

3. U. Berlière, "Le Nombre des moines dans les anciens monastères," *Revue bénédictine* 41 (1929): 231-61. A second article in *Revue bénédictine* 42 (1930): 19-42, gathers statistics on houses outside France.

4. Snape, *English Monastic Finances*, pp. 178-81.

5.   J. R. H. Moorman, *Church Life in England in the Thirteenth Century* (Cambridge, 1946), pp. 256–58; see also his appendix "Evidence of Numbers in English Religious Houses in the Thirteenth Century," ibid., pp. 402–12.

6.   J.-F. Lemarignier et al., *Histoire des institutions françaises au moyen âge*, vol. 3: *Institutions ecclésiastiques* (Paris, 1962), p. 227.

7.   *St. Victor*, vol. 1, no. 589, 1069; *St. Père*, vol. 1, no. 61, 1033–63; *St. Aubin*, vol. 1, no. 58, 1084; *Redon*, appendix, no. 71, 1128; *St. Trinité*, vol. 1, no. 260, 1077; *St. Victor*, vol. 2, no. 679, 1073; *Aniane*, no. 338, 1213.

8.   *Vigeois*, no. 281, ca. 1160: a self-confessed murderer entered; *St. Père*, vol. 2, no. 2, 1053; *St. Aubin*, vol. 2, no. 41, before 1095; *Conques*, no. 45, 1081.

9.   *Gellone*, no. 85, 1031–60; *Ste. Croix*, no. 6, 1191; *St. Père*, vol. 1, no. 7, 1081; no. 17, 1033–69; *Redon*, no. 384, 1095.

10.   *St. Victor*, vol. 1, no. 248, 11th cent.; no. 589, 1069; *Gellone*, no. 85, 1031–60; no. 223, 1077–99; *Conques*, no. 45, 1081.

11.   Peter Damian, *Rhetoricae declamationis invectio in episcopum monachos ad saeculum revocantem*, Migne, vol. 145, col. 369, divided converts to the monastic life into those inspired by divine grace and those worn down by punishment, i.e., disease or problems. Caesarius of Heisterbach added poverty as a motive for conversion (*Dialogus miraculorum*, ed. J. Strange [Cologne, 1851], 1:34).

12.   *Lettres d'Etienne de Tournai*, ed. J. Desilve (Paris and Valenciennes, 1893), p. 416.

13.   Letter to Warner, a monk of Canterbury (1104?), *S. Anselmi cantuariensis archiepiscopi opera omnia*, ed. F. S. Schmitt (Edinburgh, 1951), vol. 5, no. 335, pp. 271–72. See also J. Leclercq, "Nouvelle réponse de l'ancien monachisme aux critiques des cisterciens," *Revue bénédictine* 67 (1957): 92–93.

14.   "Fuit quidam magnus inter praevidentes; hic affirmabat dicens: Quia virtutem, quam vidi stare super baptisma, vidi etiam super vestimentum monachi, quando accipit habitum spiritualem" (Migne, vol. 73, col. 994). Compare *Vita beati Antonii Abbatis*, ibid., col. 155. Odo, a monk of Canterbury and later abbot of Battle, wrote a letter to his brother Adam in which he treated at length the monastic habit as a second baptism (*Vetera analecta*, ed. J. Mabillon, 2d ed. [Paris, 1723], pp. 477–78). Odo pursued the baptism-habit comparison in his sermons as well (J. Leclercq, "Profession monastique, baptême et pénitence d'après Odon de Cantorbery," *Studia Anselmiana* 31 [1953]: 124–32). In a charter describing the reception *ad succurrendum* of a badly injured man, parallels with baptism were evident in the language used to describe the act of putting on the habit (*Redon*, no. 389, 1144). For a systematic treatment of the theme of the religious habit as a second baptism, see J. Leclercq, *La Vie parfaite* (Paris, 1948), pp. 133–41.

15.   In popular belief demons could not hold a man responsible for sins committed before the taking of the habit (*Vita beati Antonii Abbatis*, Migne, vol. 73, col. 155; Peter the Deacon, *Chronicon casinense*, Migne, vol. 173, cols. 773–74). W. Brückner, "Sterben im Mönchsgewand. Zum Funktionswandel einer Totenkleidsitte," *Kontakte und Grenzen: Probleme der Volks-, Kultur- und Sozialforschung. Festschrift für Gerhard Heilfurth zum 60. Geburtstag* (Göttingen, 1969), pp. 259–77, describes twelfth- and thirteenth-century beliefs about the efficacy of the habit of a religious order to save its wearer.

16.   Even if the sick man had no intention of remaining a monk in the event that he recovered, the Anglo-Norman monk Ralph felt that there was hope in taking the habit: "Tamen numquam desperandum est de misericordia Dei. . . . Fortassis dicet ei Dominus: 'Licet aspiciam cor tuum obscurum et non parum tinctum tenebris infidelitatis, tamen signum clementiae meae, quo qui suscipiunt a damnatione solent liberari, suscepisti; nec propterea si te esse modicae fidei video, te damno, sed propter misericordiam meam libero,

qui etiam imperfectos in libro meo scribere soleo; et hoc ideo facio quia magis vitam peccatorum quam mortem diligo" (J. Leclercq, "La Vêture 'ad succurrendum' d'après le moine Raoul," *Studia Anselmiana* 37 [1955]: 162). In response to critics of lax receptions *ad succurrendum*, a twelfth-century Benedictine held that it was never too late to convert, because a man's eternal fate was decided on the last day of his life (Leclercq, "Nouvelle réponse," pp. 92–93).

17. "Accidit autem ut dictus abbas dives et pecuniosus, ut ditior adhuc existeret, ad matronam quandam in urbe graviter infirmantem, quam ipse noverat opimam, cum duobus monachis suis vel tribus importunus accederet, diraque carmina fundens, regnumque coelorum quasi sub certa sponsione promittens, et se sponsorem ad hoc ordinemque totum praestans . . . " (*Speculum Ecclesiae*, dist. 3, chap. 11, ed. J. S. Brewer. Rolls Series 21/4 [London, 1873], p. 179). Idungus of Prufening reported that the abbot who received him *ad succurrendum* promised that if he did as instructed by the abbot, the latter would answer for him to God (*Dialogus duorum monachorum* in R. B. C. Huygens, "Le Moine Idung et ses deux ouvrages: *Argumentum super quatuor questionibus* et *Dialogus duorum monachorum*," *Studi. medievali*, 3d ser., 13 [1972]:414). The monk Ralph contended that the reception of the monastic habit at death was the quickest way to find mercy with God and that the man who died in it was as the sun in heaven compared with an ordinary christian dying with the last rites of the church (Leclercq, "La Vêture," p. 164).

18. For another criticism of deathbed conversions, see *Liber de doctrina* of Stephen of Grandmont, in *Scriptores ordinis Grandimontensis*, ed. J. Becquet (Turnhout, 1968), p. 39.

19. "Hinc est quod ad eum omnes gentes, nationes, tribus et linguae benedictionum ejus accipiendarum gratia currunt: adeo ut ipsi derisores, qui huic Religioni in vita sua detrahunt, in morte tamen absque hujus Religionis habitu, scilicet cuculla, saltem ad succurrendum, securi esse non audeant" (*Vetera analecta*, p. 477).

20. Leclercq, "La Vêture," pp. 163–64.

21. Ibid., pp. 162, 163.

22. *Dialogus miraculorum*, 2:316–17. See also ibid., 2:298–99, for the tribulations of a monk who died without his habit.

23. *S. Wilhelmi constitutiones Hirsaugienses seu Gegenbacenses*, chap. 76, in *Vetus disciplina monastica*, ed. M. Herrgott (Paris, 1726), p. 444; A. Wilmart, "Les Ouvrages d'un moine de Bec: un débat sur la profession monastique au xiie siècle," *Revue bénédictine* 44 (1932): 37. Innocent III described the often hurried and confused conditions under which a sick man might receive the habit (Pott 252).

24. C. M. Figueras, "Acerca del rito de la profesión monástica medieval 'Ad Succurrendum'," *Liturgica* 2 (Montserrat, 1958): 380–93, describes the ritual of reception at death. See also *St. Trinité*, vol. 2, no. 391, ca. 1100, and no. 386, ca. 1100. The abbot of the Holy Trinity at the time, Geoffrey of Vendôme, asked the canonist bishop of Chartres, Ivo, whether reception by a simple monk had to be repeated by the abbot. Ivo replied that a reception by a simple monk could be repeated, but by no means had to be (*Correspondance*, ed. J. Leclercq (Paris, 1949), vol. 1, no. 41, pp. 164–69).

25. Figueras, "Acerca del rito," pp. 369–72; J. B. Valvekens, "Fratres et sorores 'ad succurrendum'," *Analecta praemonstratensia* 37 (1961): 323–28. Much legislation of religious houses and orders presumed the impending death of the new monk: Statutes of Peter the Venerable, no. 35; Statutes of Hugh V of Cluny, no. 8, in Charvin, *Statuts*, 1:30 and 43.

26. Benedict's *Rule* provided for a special official, the *infirmarius*, to care for sick monks (*Regula*, chap. 36). Many monastic houses of the twelfth century had an *infirmarius* and an infirmary for the care of sick monks and monks received *ad succurrendum*: see E. A. Hammond, "Physicians in Medieval English Religious Houses," *Bulletin of the History of Medicine* 32 (1958): 105–20. For information on the death of monks, see J. Leclercq,

"Documents sur la mort des moines," *Revue Mabillon* 45 (1955): 165-80; 46 (1956): 65-81.

27. Gratian, *Decretum, causa* XVII, *q.* I. In practice, from the mid-eleventh century the papacy demanded that the monk *ad succurrendum* be *compos mentis*, that is, in control of his mental faculties at the time of entry (JL 4520, 4560, 4625, 9707, 11036; Pott 36, 297). The failure of an entrant's spouse to give permission was also a reason to invalidate an entry *ad succurrendum*: Peter Damian, *Rhetoricae declamationis invectio*, Migne, vol. 145, col. 373; JL 4520; Marbod to Hildebert of Le Mans in *Veterum aliquot scriptorum spicilegium*, ed. L. d'Achery (Paris, 1677), 13:295; Figueras, "Acerca del rito," pp. 378-80.

28. *St. Trinité*, vol. 2, no. 528, ca. 1150: " . . . Quidam miles de Vindocino, Joscelinus nomine, de Rua Vassalorum, jam fere ad decrepitam etatem productus, mundumque et que mundi sunt deserere cupiens, vitam suam in monachi habitu finire disposuit. Hujus rei causa predictus Joscelinus per duos filios suos, . . . et per ceteros amicos suos, domnum Robertum abbatem Vindocinensem ad rationem mittens, quatinus eum pro Dei amore monachum faceret suppliciter exoravit. Domnus vero abbas, bone voluntatis Joscelini cognoscens effectum, ejus precibus et amicorum suorum peticionibus assensum prebuit, atque illum monachum fecit. Antequam vero Joscelinus monachus fieret, ut bona celestia lucraretur de temporalibus bonis . . . , ipsi Deo et sibi servientibus monachis . . . oblatus est."

29. G. Duby, "Dans la France du Nord-ouest au xiie siècle: les 'jeunes' dans la société aristocratique," *Annales. Economies, sociétés, civilisations* 19 (1964): 835-46, comments on the pressure from unmarried knights—the so-called *juvenes*—to have their fathers retire so that the sons could have their inheritance.

30. *St. Trinité*, vol. 2, no. 391, ca. 1100: " . . . Normannus, filius Drogonis de Monteaureo, captus a Gaufredo de Meduana et graviter vulneratus, se Deo vovit, et apud monachos . . . se fore monachum, si G. qui eum captum fecerat, hoc ei concederet, promisit. Quod ille, monachis rogantibus, concessit. Venerunt igitur monachi . . . et induerunt eum monachali habitu in roburdolio carceris, ubi captus tenebatur. Ille vero dedit . . . dimidium ecclesiae de Marthaiaco, cum omnibus redditibus suis." For other examples of men injured in feuds, wars, or otherwise, who sought the monastic habit, see *St. Père*, vol. 2, no. 24, 1101-12; *Redon*, no. 382, 1144; *St. Maur*, no. 59, 1141-45; *St. Aubin*, vol. 2, no. 872, ca. 1140. In an attempt to end tournaments, a council at Reims (1157) forbade those injured or killed in one to be accorded a Christian burial, even if they had become monks or *conversi* in a religious house (Mansi, vol. 21, col. 844). The abbey of Saint Bertin countered this attack on receptions *ad succurrendum* by seeking a papal privilege to receive even wounded men, *vulnerati* (JL 10134).

31. *St. Trinité*, vol. 2, no. 386, ca. 1100: "Denique isdem juvenis cadens in infirmitatem, mittens, fecit ad se venire monachos, videlicet mortem . . . metuens. Qui cum presentes adessent, donavit illis omnem suam partem, que sibi de Buisseello conveniebat. . . . Siquidem tunc rogavit ut eum fratres in suum consortium susciperent monachum; sed mater tunc contradixit, ne sola, . . . filii solatio destituta remaneret. . . . Tunc se omnimodis ut se monachum facerent deprecatus est. . . . Et sic eum tunc monachi monacum benedixerunt. Reliquit etiam tunc nobis quicquid ex jure paterno habebat apud Ulchas, post obitum matris. . . . Monachi itaque post hec afferebant ad monasterium, sed in via defunctus, ad monasterium usque prolatum est corpus." For other examples of youths or men apparently in their prime seeking the habit *ad succurrendum*, see *Azé*, pp. 56-57, ca. 1100; *St. Père*, vol. 2, no. 53, 1119-28; *St. Trinité*, vol. 1, no. 134, 1060; no. 487, ca. 1140; *Gellone*, no. 320, before 1140; *St. Aubin*, vol. 2, no. 841, 1157-89.

32. MGH, SS, 10:42-44. See *Azé*, pp. 56-57, ca. 1100, for a comparable relationship. S. Wood, *English Monasteries and Their Patrons in the Thirteenth Century* (Oxford, 1955), pp. 122-35, discusses the fact that lifelong association of house and patron might be capped by burial or by reception as a monk.

33. *St. Maur*, no. 26, 1040–45.

34. Figueras, "Acerca del rito," pp. 397–400.

35. *St. Aubin*, vol. 2, no. 872, ca. 1140: "Gauffridus de Uldone, in exercitu comitis Andegavensis apud Castrum Celsum graviter vulneratus et ad extrema perductus, in domum monachorum de Uldone se portari fecit, ibique habitum monachi devote petiit. Huic autem voluntati ipsius amici sui impedimento fuerunt, qui eum putantes posse vivere, ne monachus fieret dissuaserunt. Ipse vero tandem videns se morti proximum, . . . dedit . . . locum unius molendini in flumine Ligeris et bracam unam ad piscaturam, . . . et complanctum vinee Guihenoci Burelli, et omnia prata sua de Veteri Curte." For other instances of reluctance to receive the habit until death was assured, see *St. Trinité*, vol. 2, no. 386, ca. 1100; *St. Maur*, no. 28, before 1120; Caesarius of Heisterbach, *Dialogus miraculorum*, 2:316–17.

36. Innocent III to the Archbishop of Pisa, Pott 434. *St. Trinité*, vol. 1, no. 241, 1073, noted with some amazement that a man who had been a persecutor of the house entered *ad succurendum*, recovered, and remained for the rest of his life. The monastery of Saint Remy at Reims held in chains a man who recovered and sought to leave. He appealed to Pope Alexander III, who released him on the technical grounds that his wife had not consented to his entry (JL 11036).

37. *Rhetoricae declamationis invectio*, Migne, vol. 145, cols. 365–80.

38. *La Chronique de Saint-Hubert dite Cantatorium*, ed. K. Hanquet (Brussels, 1906), pp. 58–60. For other examples of gifts regretted, see *St. Père*, vol. 2, no. 103, ca. 1150; *Gellone*, no. 545, 1171. In *St. Trinité*, vol. 1, no. 168, 1064, the monastery had to return part of a gift when the dying man's wife and sons began weeping and claiming that they were being disinherited.

39. *Berdoues*, no. 197, 1181: ". . . Secundum consuetudinem ordinis ad religionem venire poterit." See also *Berdoues*, no. 645, 1181; *Gimont*, vol. 1, no. 8, 1147; vol. 3, no. 2, 1159.

40. *Berdoues*, no. 547, 1174: ". . . Et debent suscipi in Berdonis si voluerint, si tamen equitando et membris integris venire potuerint." The Carthusians issued a similar regulation between 1174 and 1222: "Supplementa ad Consuetudines Basilii," chap. 83, (*Analecta cartusiana*, vol. 1: *Die ältesten Consuetudines der Kartäuser*, ed. J. Hogg [Berlin, 1970], p. 232). The Grandmontine Rule, composed between 1139 and 1163, laid restrictions on the reception of the ill: Becquet, *Scriptores*, chap. 44, p. 88: ". . . Praecipimus ne quis infra viginti annos, aut homo infirmans, nisi equitando aut pedibus ambulando venire possit, in hac religione recipiatur." A bishop permitted the Order of Chalais to found a house in his diocese, but the order had to agree not to receive any diocesan subject for burial who was unable to come "on his own feet or riding, without the support of anyone" (*Chalais*, vol. 1, no. 79, 1199–1200). The Order of Artigas forbade its officials to receive anyone in sickness without permission of the prior (J. Becquet, "Les Chapitres généraux de l'ordre de l'Artige," *Revue Mabillon* 45 [1955]: 198, ca. 1200).

41. *Gimont*, vol. 2, no. 173, 1186: "Et si forte infirmaretur, et pedibus suis vel equitando Gemundum venire non posset, habitatores Gem. debent pro ipso ire, si nuntium ejus viderint, usque ad septem leucas." In return for a gift Gimont promised to receive a man "if nevertheless he is able to enter the monastery according to the custom of the order, and they ought to have him carried if that was necessary" (*Gimont*, vol. 6, no. 64, 1188). Ourscamp promised a donor that "they will receive me when I wish, no matter what sickness may hinder me" (*Ourscamp*, no. 306, 1190). See also *Berdoues*, no. 135, 1208.

42. *Conques*, no. 559, 1183.

43. *Redon*, no. 389, 1144: "Hoc concesserunt . . . Herveus filius jam dicti Boscherii,

et Judicalis, archidiaconus, nepos ejus, qui hoc retinuit quod si monachus esse vellet, cum tota pecunia et cum largo dono de terra sua reciperetur."

44. *St. Père*, vol. 2, no. 7, 1109.

45. *Sancti Benedicti regula*, chap. 59.

46. *Statuta sanctarum virginum*, chap. 7, in *Sancti Caesarii opera omnia*, ed. G. Morin (Maredsous, 1942), 2:104, sought to avoid receiving girls below age six or seven. See also *S. Aureliani regula ad monachos*, chap. 17, Migne, vol. 68, col. 390; *S. Donati regula ad virgines*, chap. 32, Migne, vol. 87, col. 284; *Regula ad virgines*, chap. 25, Migne, vol. 88, col. 1070; *S. Fructuosi Bracarensis Episcopi regula monastica communis*, chap. 6, Migne, vol. 97, cols. 1115-16; *Waldeberti regula ad virgines*, chap. 24, Migne, vol. 88, col. 1070.

47. G. de Valous, *Le monachisme clunisien des origines au xve siècle* (Paris, 1935), 1:40-41; J. R. Riepenhoff, *Zur Frage des Ursprungs der Verbindlichkeit des Oblateninstituts. Ein Beitrag zur Geschichte des mittelalterlichen Bildungswesen*, Münstersche Beiträge zur Geschichtsforschung, vol. 74/75 (Munster, 1939). A. Lentini, "Note sull'oblazione dei fanciulli nella Regola di S. Benedetto," *Studia Anselmiana* 18-19 (1947):220-25, challenges Riepenhoff's view that Benedict had not seen oblation as permanent. For the development of oblation in Western monasticism, see J. N. Seidl, *Die Gott-Verlobung von Kindern in Mönchs- und Nonnen-Klöstern oder de pueris oblatis* (Munich, 1872); M.-P. Deroux, "Les Origines de l'oblature bénédictine," *Revue Mabillon* 17 (1927):1-16, 81-113, 193-217, 305-51; and C. M. Figueras, *De impedimentis admissionis in religionem usque ad Decretum Gratiani*. Scripta et documenta, vol. 9 (Montserrat, 1957), pp. 45-88.

48. Lentini, "Note sull'oblazione," pp. 222-24. M. Sinopoli, "Influenza di Graziano nell'evoluzione del diritto monastico," *Studia Gratiana* 3 (1955): 336-37, discusses the parental rights over children that were acknowledged by Gratian. A. L. Smith, *Church and State in the Middle Ages* (Oxford, 1913), pp. 58-72, discusses twelfth- and thirteenth-century attempts to base the validity of marriage on the consent of the couple rather than on the wishes of their parents. A letter of Peter of Blois states clearly the power that an uncle felt that he held over an orphaned niece (*Petri Blesensis . . . opera omnia*, ed. J. A. Giles [Oxford, 1846], vol. 1, no. 54, pp. 162-63).

49. Mansi, vol. 10, col. 631: "Monachum aut paterna devotio, aut propria professio facit; quidquid horum fuerit, alligatus tenebit." This text was incorporated into many of the pre-Gratian canonical collections, including Burchard of Worms: *Libri viginti decretorum*, bk. 8, chap. 6, Migne, vol. 140, col. 793; Anselm of Lucca, *Collectio canonum*, bk. 7, chap. 179, Migne, vol. 149, col. 517; Ivo of Chartres, *Decretum*, pt. 7, chap. 30, Migne, vol. 161, col. 553. Peter Damian, *Rhetoricae declamationis invectio*, Migne, vol. 145, cols. 374-78, held that anyone who put on the monastic habit, willingly or unwillingly, was required to keep it.

50. K. Vielhaber, *Gottschalk der Sachse* (Bonn, 1956), pp. 15-17. For a contemporary defense of the legitimacy and permanence of oblation, see Hrabanus Maurus, *Liber de oblatione puerorum*, Migne, vol. 107, cols. 419-40.

51. Deroux, "Les Origines," pp. 1-16, 81-113, discusses Carolingian hesitations about the permanence of oblation. See also de Valous, *Le Monachisme clunisien*, 1:41-42. On canons 22 and 23 of the Council of Worms (868), see C. de Clercq, *La Législation religieuse franque de Louis le Pieux à la fin du ixe siècle* (Antwerp, 1958), p. 272.

52. R. W. Southern, *The Making of the Middle Ages* (New Haven, Conn., 1953), p. 162.

53. Ulrich of Cluny, in the dedicatory letter of his *Consuetudines*, contrasted those who entered religious life "aetate lasciva" and "imperio parentum," i.e., oblates, with those who entered "sponte sua, et majoris aetatis, solo Christo imperante," i.e., *conversi*. He clearly felt that the latter made better monks than the former (Migne, vol. 149, cols.

636-37). The *Liber Anselmi de humanis moribus per similitudines*, chap. 78, in *Memorials of St. Anselm*, ed. R. W. Southern and F. S. Schmitt (London, 1968), pp. 68-69, discusses the rivalry between *nutriti* and *conversi*. Guibert of Nogent, *De vita sua*, ed. G. Bourgin (Paris, 1907), bk. 1, chap. 8, pp. 23-24, notes the faults of oblates and contrasts them unfavorably with those who had entered religious life as adults.

54. For a brief account of the breakdown of the permanence of oblation in the twelfth and thirteenth centuries, see J. Orlandis, "Notas sobre la 'Oblatio puerorum' en los siglos xi y xii," *Anuario de historia del derecho español* 31 (1961):163-68; or Riepenhoff, *Zur Ursprung*, pp. 190-200.

55. The letters of Stephen of Tournai offer a varied perspective on the unrest among religious in the later twelfth century: *Lettres d'Etienne de Tournai*, ed. J. Desilve (Paris and Valenciennes, 1893). Letter one is a discussion of *transitus*, or transfer from one religious house to another, prompted by an inquiry from Grandmontine novices who wished to become Cistercians. Letters 15, 32, 58, 59, 101, 135, 264, and 288 are concerned with religious houses that refused to receive back members who had been expelled or had left. Letters 103, 134, 147, 150, and 169 concern *transitus*. On the legal question of *transitus* in the twelfth century, see M.-A. Dimier, "S. Bernard et le droit en matière de 'transitus'," *Revue Mabillon* 43 (1953): 48-82; and K. Fina, "*Ovem Suam Require*. Eine Studie zur Geschichte des Ordenswechsels im 12. Jahrhundert," *Augustiniana* 7 (1957): 33-56.

56. Guigo recorded the customs of the Grande Chartreuse between 1121 and 1127. Chapter 27 forbade the reception of anyone below the age of twenty (Migne, vol. 153, cols. 691-92). The Cistercian general chapter decreed in 1134 that no one was to be received as a novice before the completion of his fifteenth year (Canivez, *Statuta*, 1:31); in 1157 the chapter raised the minimum age to eighteen (ibid., p. 57). Cf. *Berdoues*, no. 614, 1186, in which a boy was promised reception when he reached eighteen. The Grandmontine Rule placed the age for reception at 20 (Becquet, *Scriptores*, chap. 44, p. 88).

57. Guibert de Nogent, *De vita sua*, bk. 1, chap. 8, pp. 23-24; translated by C. C. Swinton Bland as *The Autobiography of Guibert Abbot of Nogent sous Coucy* (London, 1925), pp. 28-29.

58. Charvin, *Statuts*, vol. 1, chap. 36, p. 30: "Causa instituti hujus fuit, immatura nimisque celer infantium susceptio, qui antequam aliquid rationabilis intelligentie habere possent, sacre religionis vestibus induebantur, et admixti aliis puerilibus ineptiis omnes perturbabant: et ut quedam taceam, et multa breviter colligam, et sibi nihil pene proderant, et aliorum religiosum propositum non parum, immo quandoque plurimum impediebant."

59. Ibid.: "Statutum est, ut nullus etiam ex concessione futurus monachus regularibus usque ad xx annos vestibus induatur." For examples of reception under the rubric *futurus monachus*, see *St. Aubin*, vol. 1, no. 661, 1106; no. 115, 1119-20. On the background to the statutes of Peter the Venerable, see D. Knowles, "The Reforming Decrees of Peter the Venerable, with a note by M. M. Postan," in *Petrus Venerabilis 1156-1956*, ed. J. Kritzeck and G. Constable, *Studia Anselmiana* 40 (Rome, 1956): 1-20.

60. Pope Alexander III freed Saint Augustine's at Canterbury from being forced to receive boys below the age of fifteen (JL 12709). Celestine III gave the same right to Saint John *in vineis* (JL 17475). In 1232 the papal visitor Matthew of Foigny set the minimum age for reception in Saint Vaast of Arras at fifteen, and he forbade the abbot even to promise entry to a boy below that age (M.-A. Dimier, "Les Statuts de l'abbé Matthieu de Foigny pour la réforme de l'abbaye de Saint Vaast [1232]," *Revue bénédictine* 65 [1955)]: 116).

61. See Bernard of Clairvaux's letter to his cousin Robert, who had left the Cistercians for the Cluniacs, claiming he had been an oblate at Cluny: *Sancti Bernardi opera*, vol. 7: *Epistolae*, ed. J. Leclercq and H. Rochais (Rome, 1974), especially pp. 5-7, where Bernard argues that oblation was good but entry to Cîteaux was better.

62. Cistercian general chapters in the twelfth century reiterated the ban on receiving underage recruits: Canivez, *Statuta*, vol. 1: chap. 16, p. 57, 1157; chap. 12, p. 72, 1160; chap. 26, p. 84, 1175; chap. 2, p. 95, 1184. The general chapter punished abbots for breaches of the regulations on age: ibid., chap. 47, p. 128, 1190; chap. 30, p. 139, 1191; chap. 55, p. 190, 1195; in 1201 the chapter increased the penalties for such admissions and complained that they were too frequent (ibid., chap. 4, p. 264). See also J. Lynch, "The Cistercians and Underage Novices," *Citeaux-Commentarii Cistercienses* 24 (1973): 283–97.

63. *Decretum, causa* I, q. II: " . . . Anna detulit secum Samuelum, postquam ablactatus fuerat, in tribus vitulis, et tribus modiis farinae, et amphora vini ad domum Dei in Sylo." Rudolph of Saint Trond, writing between 1123 and 1136, used the exemplum of Anna to defend the legitimacy of gifts offered along with oblates (MGH, *SS*, 10:422). *St. Victor*, vol. 1, no. 199, 1015, made a more general appeal to the example of Old and New Testament figures who offered children to God.

64. *Lettres*, no. 279, p. 351: "Exemplo monitus patriarche, filium quemdam suum super unum montium quem monstravit ei Dominus, ecclesiam scilicet vestram sanctam . . . desiderat immolari, ut eidem accrescat meritum ex imitatione tanti exempli, et universitas vestra in cotidiano servicio tam ipsius quam predicti filii fructum colligat holocausti."

65. *St. Victor*, vol. 2, no. 722, 1080–1103: " . . . Ego Bermundus, . . . de Dromone, sciens, . . . me vocatum esse ad premia regni celorum cum innumerabilium populorum multitudine, et, pro diversorum meorum peccaminum labe, nisi gratia Dei annuente, timens cum electione paucorum non esse, reddo, dono, offero quendam filium meum Guillelmum, cum domne Richildis matris ejus voluntate et consilio, . . . ut ab odierno die vivens sub disciplina regulari, adjutus intercessionibus ejus . . . , coheres esse merear in electione servorum Jhesu Christi." *Conques*, no. 477, ca. 1100: a boy was made a monk "for the salvation of the soul of our father and of all our kin"; *Redon*, no. 385, ca. 1050: a father offered his son *in hostiam vivam*; *St. Père*, vol. 1, no. 98, 1069–1100: a child was described as pouring out his prayers for his family and for mankind; *St. Aubin*, vol. 1, no. 83, 1082–1106; *St. Sernin*, appendix, no. 40, 1188: a child could serve as a substitute for his parent in religious life; *Redon*, no. 388, 1099–1128: the offering of a child was a meritorious act of penance for his parents. The concept of the monk as a living sacrifice was applied to adults as well: Guigo, *De vita solitaria*, in *Lettres des premiers chartreux*, ed. "Un chartreux" (Paris, 1962), 1:146.

66. Ulrich's *Consuetudines* are printed in Migne, vol. 149, cols. 635–778. On Ulrich of Cluny see E. Hauviller, *Ulrich von Cluny: ein biographischer Beitrag zur Geschichte der Cluniacenser im 11. Jahrhundert*, Kirchengeschichtliche Studien, vol. 3, pt. 3 (Munster, 1896).

67. Migne, vol. 149, cols. 635–36: " . . . Postquam domum habuerint, ut dicam, plenam filiorum et filiarum, aut si quis eorumdem claudus erit aut mancus, surdaster aut caecus, gibbosus aut leprosus, vel aliud quid hujusmodi quod eum aliquo modo saeculo facit minus acceptum, hunc quidem impensissimo voto ut monachus fiat offerunt Deo, quanquam plane non propter Deum sed propter hoc tantum ut seipsos expediant ab eis educandis et pascendis, vel aliis suis liberis possit esse magis consultum."

68. Ibid., col. 637: "Ego autem certus sum illam te radicem funditus exstirpasse, ex qua sola praecipue omnia sunt monasteria destructa quae destructa sunt vel in Teutonica vel in Romana lingua."

69. C. Blanc, "Les Pratiques de piété des laïcs dans les pays du Bas-Rhône aux xiᵉ et xiiᵉ siècles," *Annales du Midi* 72 (1960): 137–47.

70. Dimier, "Les Statuts," p. 116. Humbert of Romans, general of the Dominicans from 1254 to 1263, wrote in his *Speculum religiosorum*, in *Maxima bibliotheca veterum patrum* (Lyons, 1677), 25:721: "Et notandum quod multis de causis accidit quod in religione recipiuntur, qui ad religionem non sunt idonei. . . . Aliquando hoc accidit ex

parentum carnalium improbitate, qui filios suos in religione ponunt, ut ab se eos expediant, potius intendentes eorum corporalem provisionem, quam eorum salutem." Humbert also observed that the Cathar heretics in the south of France took girls as "oblates" from economically pressed noble families (cited in M. de Fontette, *Les Religieuses à l'âge classique du droit canonique* [Paris, 1967], p. 90, n. 8).

71. *Guilielmi Alverni opera omnia* (Paris, 1674), 1:234: "Alii vero a parentibus et propinquis, eo modo in claustro projiciuntur, quemadmodum catuli, et porculi, quos matres non sufficiunt enutrire, ut videlicet mundo non spiritualiter, sed (ut ita dicamus) civiliter moriantur, videlicet ut portione haereditaria priventur, et ad eos qui saeculo remanent devolvatur. . . . " A girl charged that her father and stepmother forced her to enter the Order of Sempringham in order to defraud her of her inheritance (Pott 2228). *Select Pleas of the Crown*, ed. F. W. Maitland, Selden Society I (London, 1888), no. 202, pp. 135–36, recounts a scheme to obtain a family's patrimony by marrying an heiress and placing her sister in a convent. See a canonist treatment of such tactics in G. Fransen, "Les 'Questiones' des canonistes: essai de dépouillement et de classement," *Traditio*, vol. 23 (1967), no. 62, p. 528. William Perault, a Dominican preacher active in the 1260s, criticized the practice of taking inheritances by forced religious profession, in sermon 71, incorrectly attributed to William of Auvergne in *Guilielmi Alverni opera omnia*, 2:248.

72. E. Vacandard, "Célibat ecclésiastique," *DTC*, vol. 2, cols. 2085–87.

73. C. N. L. Brooke, "Gregorian Reform in Action: Clerical Marriage in England 1050–1200," *Cambridge Historical Journal* 12 (1956): 1–21; C. N. L. Brooke, "The Composition of the Chapter of Saint Paul's, 1086–1163," *Cambridge Historical Journal* 10 (1950–52): 121–27; and B. R. Kemp, "Hereditary Benefices in the Medieval English Church: A Herefordshire Example," *Bulletin of the Institute of Historical Research* 43 (1970): 1–15.

74. R. Génestal, *Histoire de la légitimation des enfants naturels en droit canonique* (Paris, 1905), pp. 38–41, 80–90. For examples of priests placing children in monasteries, see *St. Aubin*, vol. 1, no. 41, before 1095; *Cîteaux*, no. 158, ca. 1160.

75. *St. Trinité*, vol. 2, no. 357, 1097: " . . . Gaudinus de Male-ibi-Cornaut, quando dedit filium suum Guarinum primogenitum, ad quem totus honor Gaudini reveniebat, si ipse in seculo remansisset. . . . "

76. Charvin, *Statuts*, vol. 1, chap. 35, p. 30: "Statutum est, ut nullus in monachum Cluniacensem recipiatur absque Cluniacensis Abbatis precepto et permissione, sicut mos est, nisi ad succurrendum. . . . Causa institui hujus fuit, . . . frequentissima inutilium personarum per cuncta pene Cluniacensia loca, et indiscreta susceptio. Qua indiscreta susceptione nunc rusticorum, nunc infantium, nunc senum, nunc stultorum, nec ad aliquod opus utilium, eo jam res pervenerat, ut talium personarum jam fere major numerus haberetur, et frequentia, ac nefanda mala ab eis commissa, . . . pene assidue a diversis partibus terrarum audiretur." In 1200 Abbot Hugh V issued a similar order (ibid., chaps. 4 and 5, p. 42).

77. *Chronica Willelmi Andrensis*, ed. J. Heller, MGH, SS (Hanover, 1879), 24:705: "Susceptus est cum honore debito vir honorabilis, et in suo adventu preter mores suorum, quos invenit degeneres, abhorruit et expavit deformitatem gregis. Quidam enim claudi, quidam contracti, quidam monoculi, quidam strabones, quidam ceci, quidam vero manci inter eos apparebant, et hii fere omnes genere nobiles existebant. Quo viso, prudens pastor indoluit et in se meditabatur quod postea devotus implevit; nam per annos triginta duos et amplius, quibus huic loco prefuit, nullum umquam monachari permisit, qui in aliqua parte corporis aliquem defectum habuit."

78. Ulrich of Cluny referred to a child who had been offered for a skin ailment and another for a foot problem (Migne, vol. 149, col. 636).

79. *Paraclet*, no. 83, before 1195: "Pro Fania, filia Hugonis et Hermensendis defunctorum, dederunt propinqui partem decime de Ulmellis quam mater tenuerat, et terram de Grevis, et duos solidos census. . . . "

80. *De vita sua*, bk. 1, chap. 14, p. 49.

81. *St. Aubin*, vol. 1, no. 71, 1060–81: a dying man left a son in the guardianship of the monastery; *St. Père*, vol. 2, no. 35, 1101–29: a woman who fell ill left an orphan for whom she was caring to the monastery; *Conques*, no. 477, ca. 1100: a family offered a child as a source of prayers for a deceased father. Parents even disposed of unborn children: *Gellone*, no. 320, before 1140; and J. Chevalier, "Formule d'oblation d'enfant tirée des archives de l'ordre de St-Ruf. XIIIe siècle," *Bulletin d'histoire ecclésiastique et d'archéologie religieuse des diocèses de Valence, Digne, Gap, Grenoble, et Viviers* 7 (1886–87): 87. Blanc, "Les Pratiques," p. 144, notes that oblation was often the fate of a child born after his father made a will.

82. *Vita beati Edmundi cantuariensis archiepiscopi*, in E. Martène and Ursin Durand, eds., *Thesaurus novus anecdotorum* (Paris, 1717), vol. 3, cols. 1779–80.

83. *Gellone*, no. 166, 1097; *Ronceray*, no. 346, ca. 1100; *Vigeois*, no. 269, 1092–1110; *Paraclet*, no. 50, 1145; Peter of Blois, *Opera*, vol. 1, letter 54, pp. 162–63; *St. Trinité*, vol. 2, no. 629, 1188–1200; *Paraclet*, no. 83, before 1194, contains notices of gifts by uncles for nieces and by brothers for sisters. For examples of brothers offering gifts for brothers, see *Gellone*, no. 206, 1082; *Vigeois*, no. 336, ca. 1164.

84. *Gellone*, no. 465, 1077–99.

85. *Aniane*, no. 246, 1173: " . . . Ego Raimundus Bertrannus qui fui filius quondam Petri Bertranni, cum consilio . . . matris mee Alamanne, dono . . . quicquid pater meus Petrus Bertrannus a vobis habuit . . . in parrochia et in terminio de Carchares . . . excepta vinea que est inter vineas Raimundi de Carcharesio et inter vineas elemosinarii . . . reliqua omnia . . . cum fratre meo, Petro, cui pro parte paterne hereditatis competunt, vobis concedo." *Gellone*, no. 206, 1082.

86. *St. Père*, vol. 2, part 3, no. 31, ca. 1147: "Ego, R., Carnotensis vicedominus, . . . notum fieri volo, quod Philippus de Treione, volens Jerosolimam proficisci, Galterium, filium suum, in cenobio sancti Petri Carnotensis monachum fecit; et, pro Dei amore et ejus gratia, pratum clausi, vineam atque terram sitam in medio, decimam quoque quam Juhellus de Nona Curia in vita sua manu tenuit, . . . contulit."

87. *Ronceray*, no. 358, ca. 1155: " . . . Renaudum de Bereio, antequam ad lucrandum peregre proficisceretur, res suas taliter disposuisse. Commendavit enim prefatus Renaudus res suas domno Grano et domine abbatisse, ut de domibus debita sua solverentur. Si vero in barbaris nationibus eum mori contingeret, precepit ut, post debita soluta, cum residuo rerum suarum filia ejus sponso Christo et Virgini matri sue monachali habitu conjugaretur; si autem divina gratia eum repatriare permitteret, res suas ita solutas sicut ipse ante hanc dispositionem possederat haberet." *Ronceray*, no. 354, 1120: a man who accompanied Count Fulk of Anjou to Jerusalem arranged for his daughter to be kept at Ronceray for three years, and then to be made a nun or married, as she chose.

88. Guibert of Nogent, *De vita sua*, bk. 1, chaps. 14–15, pp. 47–54.

89. *Gesta pontificum Cameracensium*, ed. C. de Smedt (Paris, 1880), pp. 130–31, ca. 1120.

90. T. P. McLaughlin, "Abelard's Rule for Religious Women," *Mediaeval Studies* 18 (1956): 259.

91. *Ex chronico universali anonymi Laudunensis*, ed. G. Waitz. MGH, SS, 26:447. Pontius de Lazario, a knight who converted to the Cistercians in the early twelfth century,

provided for his wife, daughter, and son by placing them in religious houses (Hugo Francigena, *Tractatus de conversione Pontii de Lazario, et exordio Salvaniensis monasterii*, in *Miscellaneorum liber tertius*, ed. S. Baluze [Paris, 1680], p. 208).

92. *St. Aubin*, vol. 1, no. 41, before 1095. *Conques*, no. 482, 1110: a husband and wife who intended to enter religious life offered "unicum filium suum"; *St. Père*, vol. 2, no. 82, 1130-50: a cleric who entered brought his young nephew with him "since he was unwilling to leave him outside." M.-A. Dimier, "Un Témoin tardif peu connu du conflit entre Cisterciens et Clunisiens," *Petrus Venerabilis*, pp. 81 ff., discusses the problems of a man who entered a Cistercian house and brought his little son to be educated as a boarder there. Hugh of Lincoln, youngest of three sons, was given to a house of regular canons by his father when the latter entered the canonry (*The Life of Hugh of Lincoln*, ed. D. L. Douie and H. Farmer [London, 1961-62], 1:5-6).

93. G. G. Coulton, *Five Centuries of Religion* (Cambridge, 1936), 3:34, says flatly that he knows of no case in which an oblate was received without a gift. The charters support this view. An adult might be received gratis, but a child was assumed to need a gift (*St. Aubin*, vol. 1, no. 41, before 1095). Rudolph of Saint Trond characterized an oblate as a liability, to be fed and clothed (de Borman, *Chronique*, 1:250).

94. *Les Ecouges*, no. 9, ca. 1150. Reception as a religious was called a *beneficium* in *Ronceray*, no. 405, 1111-20; no. 345, ca. 1137; and *St. Aubin*, vol. 2, no. 805, ca. 1170.

95. *St. Aubin*, vol. 1, no. 294, ca. 1070: "Quidam homo, nomine Beringerius, filium parvulum monachum facere volens, cum omni supplicatione per se et per alios petivit ut in monasterium Sancti Albini reciperetur. Et quia sciebat eum a monachis gratis non fore recipiendum, obtulit Sancto Albino cum filio suo quandam terram quam habebat ad Puteum."

96. *St. Denys*, no. 70, ca. 1190.

CHAPTER THREE

Gifts from Entrants
The Beginnings of Criticism

 In general, the social and economic transactions associated with the reception of the religious habit were accepted without comment before the twelfth century. However, there had been one relatively isolated period in which the open demand for money from new monks was criticized, although it was not explicitly condemned as simony. Charlemagne and his son Louis the Pious forbade, or placed limits on, the demand for money from entrants at least three times between 789 and 819. The texts were brief, as Carolingian legislation tended to be, and their exact interpretation is not entirely secure because their context is obscure.

The first text was in a series of instructions to royal inspectors, the *missi*. The instructions are designated as the *Duplex legationis edictum* and were probably issued on 23 March 789. The document reflected the general concern felt by Charlemagne and his advisors about greed on the part of abbots and other church officers. Chapter 3 warned such churchmen not to give more attention to earthly profit than they expended on the souls entrusted to them.[1] Chapter 15 ordered the *missi* to make sure "that no abbot should require a reward for the reception of a monk."[2]

In 794 Charlemagne held an empire-wide council at Frankfort to deal with the heresy of Adoptionism in Spain and the treatment of icons at Byzantium. Canon 16 of the council was probably a response to the findings of the *missi* of 789.

For we have heard [presumably from the *missi*] that some abbots, motivated by greed, demand gifts for those entering a monastery. Therefore it pleases us and the Holy Synod that money never be demanded for receiving brothers in the holy order [of monks], but rather they should be received according to the Rule of Saint Benedict.[3]

Benedict's *Rule*, chapter 58, allowed the entrant a choice in the disposition of his property. He could give his goods to the poor or to the monastery. In calling for a return to Benedict's practice, the Council of Frankfort was not criticizing gifts as such, but was attempting to reestablish their free-will character.

Louis the Pious supported the monastic reforms proposed by Benedict of Aniane. Between 816 and 819 the emperor translated into legislation the main features of the reform program at a series of imperial meetings.[4] The monastic legislation issued in August 816 and that of July 817 did not refer to payments for entry.[5] When the two sets of legislation were combined for an imperial assembly in 818–19, the anonymous compiler added this text: "That no one should be received for a gift, except him whom good will and merits commend."[6] This text apparently permitted gifts for an entrant, provided that he was acceptable on other grounds as well. In effect the criticism of forced gifts was narrowed to include only bribes for the acceptance of those who could not be accepted otherwise. I have found no similar direct criticisms of forced payments for entry in Carolingian capitularies or church councils either before 789 or after 819.

It is not entirely clear why Charlemagne and his son chose to attack these practices in the first place. Certainly the Carolingian rulers were deeply concerned about good order in the church, and such forced payments may have struck them as inimical to good order. However, there is evidence that one source for the legislation lay outside the Carolingian realm itself, in the Carolingian emulative rivalry with their Byzantine neighors to the east.[7] At Nicaea in 787 the Byzantines had convoked a great council, ecumenical in their view, to which Frankish representatives had not been invited. In canon 19 the council criticized in specific terms, for the first time in the history of the church, the requirement of a payment from an entrant to religious life.[8]

Scholars have long recognized that Charlemagne had a serious interest in the council, both because it was a calculated snub to him and because of its decrees on the veneration of icons or holy images. He and his advisers took great exception to the Byzantine promulgations on images and rejected them as heretical.[9] The Carolingian court had received a Latin translation of the acts of the second Nicaean council, and the nineteenth canon on monastic entry payments was no doubt included. This explicit Byzantine attack on entry payments was probably the stimulus to the Carolingian condemnations. Within seventeen months after Nicaea, Charlemagne issued his instructions to the *missi*, warning abbots not to require gifts. The borrowing entered the Carolingian legislation without acknowledgement of its source for two reasons. Carolingian relations with the Eastern Empire were strained; the Carolingians had vehemently attacked the council in which the prohibition first appeared, and consequently there was little incentive to make an open reference to the source for concern about payments.[10]

The Carolingian efforts against required entry payments spanned about thirty years. The issue failed to take root as a major or, indeed, a minor concern of the later Carolingian church. The prohibitions of payment were not repeated in subsequent royal capitularies or church councils, nor were they incorporated into important canonical collections,[11] probably because the Carolingian church reformers of the ninth century were reluctant to use recent texts as canonical authorities.[12] The legislation of 818–19, with its qualified prohibition of required payments, did serve as an addition to the False Capitularies of Benedict the Levite. However, that was not an exception to the reformers' reluctance to use recent texts, because the False Capitularies were by design a collection of recent secular texts favorable to reform.[13] Because of this neglect by ninth-century church councils and compilers of canonical collections, the issue of forced payments disappeared from active interest. When canonists began to concern themselves with entry payments in the second third of the twelfth century, the Carolingian texts played no significant role. Indeed, aside from some biblical and patristic citations, the oldest directly relevant text used by twelfth-century opponents of payments for entry was canon 7 of the

Council of Melfi (1089).[14] Thus in spite of Carolingian foreshadowings, the issue of the legitimacy of payment for entry into religion was a new one in the twelfth century.

Simony

The dissolution of the Carolingian Empire in the later ninth century had grave consequences for all aspects of society, including the church. The decay and eventual disappearance of the relatively firm Carolingian power, which had generally protected the church even while exploiting it, left it at the mercy of localistic, centrifugal powers. Especially in West Francia and in the Kingdom of Italy, effective social and political power generally fell into the grasp of the Carolingian bureaucracy and other regional strongmen who used the relative anarchy to consolidate their power.[15] The Scandinavian, Magyar, and Saracen invasions of the ninth and tenth centuries intensified the social disorganization left in the wake of the collapse of the Carolingian order.[16]

Among the consequences of that disorder were that preexisting problems of the church were aggravated and new problems arose. Much of the property accumulated by ecclesiastical institutions during the Carolingian era was alienated *de jure* or *de facto* into the grasp of the new regional rulers.[17] Along with the property, actual control over parishes and monasteries gravitated into lay hands. The dislocation and disruption of church life were severe. Indeed, a number of monasteries and dioceses ceased to exist in the most badly disorganized areas, such as Normandy and England.[18] Where ecclesiastical institutions continued to function, they were absorbed to a greater or lesser degree into the system of proprietary churches. The property and offices of the church often became, for practical purposes, part of a lay lord's patrimony. Ecclesiastical revenues, offices, and sacraments were treated by their lay and clerical holders as personal possessions that could be bought, sold, and used, like virtually any other form of property. In the vivid phrase of Emile Amann, the church was "au pouvoir des laïques."[19]

The net result of these developments in the life of the church was serious decline, especially when judged against the standard of the relatively orderly Carolingian church. Many of the economic, administrative, intellectual, and moral achievements of the ninth century were eroded during the times of troubles in the late ninth and tenth centuries.

However, the late tenth and first half of the eleventh centuries witnessed recovery and regeneration in many areas of Latin Christendom, coinciding with a general demographic and economic recovery. There were stirrings of reaction within the church against the disorganized state of affairs. Lorraine, Burgundy, Rome, and other areas were the sites of spontaneous and generally uncoordinated reform movements, which often worked for different ends and, indeed, sometimes at cross-purposes.[20]

In their attempts to attack the abuses in the feudalized and lay-dominated church, the reform movements created or revived intellectual tools. The abundant polemic literature produced by proponents and opponents of particular reforms was the forum within which such intellectual tools were employed and refined. These tools were intellectual techniques, attitudes, and value judgments that served to undermine and discredit conditions offensive to the reformers. They included a renewed interest in, and cultivation of, the canon law;[21] a stress on the hierarchical nature of the church that placed it beyond the legitimate control of laymen;[22] an emphasis on the papacy as the center and arbiter of ecclesiastical affairs;[23] and a concern for the moral reform of the clergy, including the enforcement of clerical celibacy.[24]

There was one further intellectual tool that is of central importance for this study. The full-blown concept of simony was a product of the struggle by the reformers to break lay control over the church.[25] The reformers saw in the buying and selling of sacred things, especially holy orders and church offices, a hateful crime, indeed, a heresy,[26] that was a root cause of the other problems facing the church. They sought to end the commerce in sacred things because they saw in it a source of profit and of encouragement to the lay and clerical exploiters of the church.

To be sure, the Carolingian church had also opposed the buying and selling of the sacraments and ecclesiastical offices. The term *simonia* and the constellation of ideas it connoted were relatively common in Carolingian documents.[27] However, when the reformers of the eleventh century sought to elaborate the concept of simony as a weapon with which to attack economic dealings in sacred things, they apparently could find little help or, more to the point, little prestige and authoritative weight in the writers of the Carolingian age. They turned instead to the texts of Christian antiquity, particularly to the writings of Pope Gregory I. His letter collection and sermons provided hints, comments, and key ideas that formed the elements for the fully developed concept of simony.[28] In addition to the texts of Pope Gregory, the eleventh-century polemicists drew on certain striking biblical texts for support. First and foremost, frequent use was made of the account of Simon Magus in the Acts of the Apostles, in which the Apostle Peter rebuffed his attempt to buy the power of the Spirit.[29] The punishment of Giezi with leprosy because he had demanded money for a cure wrought by his master, the prophet Elisha, was also cited often, and Giezi became the literary symbol of the simoniacal seller as Simon Magus was that of the buyer.[30] Christ's driving of the money-changers and dove-sellers from the temple also served the reformers well as a proof text.[31] Finally, Christ's admonition to the apostles to give freely what they had received freely completed the set of much-used biblical texts.[32] The reformers also cited the second canon of the Council of Chalcedon (451)[33] and the accounts of Simon Magus in the Apocrypha[34] to work out a concept of simony that was an effective ideological weapon in the struggle to loosen the grip of laymen on the church and to purify the relations of bishop to priest and of priest to people.[35]

The concept of simony has been treated often by scholars, especially from the viewpoint of its implications for the validity of sacraments performed or received simoniacally.[36] However, for the men of the eleventh century the term *simonia* had far richer connotations than those to be found in it by a primarily canonistic treatment. *Simonia* was a term that evoked a theological-historical myth of complexity and fascination for contemporaries. A charter of the monastery of Saint Victor at Marseilles, written about 1060, placed *simonia* in the broad context of the history of God's dealings with men. The charter recounted the story of the Creation of Man, the Fall of Man through sin, and his salvation by Jesus Christ. Then it continued:

> . . . And they [the apostles] were witnesses of the truth, and as long as they lived in the present life they strongly resisted the simoniacal heresy, obeying their Saviour who had commanded them, saying "Freely you have received, freely give." From among all of them there was one in the primitive church, the most blessed Peter, . . . who fought Simon Magus, from whom this unspeakable heresy took name and deed, by means of different arguments of word and act from Jerusalem all the way to great Rome. Peter acted in such a way that, having prayed to God, he cast down to earth his [Simon's] wicked body, which he saw flying in the air by magic arts; and not much later he subjected that body to a horrible death. That detestable heresy has spread so much that in modern times . . . there are scarcely any to be found in the ecclesiastical order who are not bound by the chain of this execrable evil.[37]

The view that was reflected in this charter depicted Simon Magus as a colorful anti-hero, the very first heretic, and his heresy the very worst of all.[38] Simon Peter, the first pope, was a rival and foil to Simon Magus, the first heretic.[39] The charter of Saint Victor also reaffirmed the note common to many reform-minded men of the eleventh century: that in their day simony had gained the upper hand and threatened to corrupt the church from top to bottom. Simony was visualized as a contagion, a filth that contaminated all it touched.[40] The frequency and seriousness of simony raised questions in some minds about the very survival of legitimate priesthood in the church.[41] Only when the deep disgust with which many reformers approached simony is understood can the reaction against it be comprehended and the often extreme forms which that reaction took.[42]

The *simonia* myth, with its biblical, canonical, and historical roots, was a potent and emotional force in the eleventh and twelfth centuries. There were disputes even within the camp of the reformers about the punishment appropriate for simoniacs and about the effects of simony on the sacraments. There were also attempts by some lay apologists to deny that certain practices were, in fact, simoniacal. But it is a clear index of the myth's acceptance that no one dared defend buying and selling of holy things in a theoretical way, as some did defend clerical marriage.[43]

By the middle of the eleventh century, the concept of simony had been defined and consequences had been drawn from it by the reformers that would have required a social revolution to realize in practice. To eliminate simony, as it was defined by the more extreme reformers, would have necessitated the severing of most of the customary ties by which laymen of high social station controlled and also supported the church.[44]

Concepts, once created and endowed with emotive force, persist. They are often transferred by intellectuals from one context to another with unexpected—sometimes unwanted—results. So it was when the concept of simony was applied to entry into religious life. The idea of simony had been elaborated to deal with gross and specific abuses, such as the outright sale of sacraments and ec- clesiastical offices. In the course of attacking such practices, a vigorous antisimoniacal propaganda program was pursued, and conscientious churchmen and laymen were sensitized to the prin- ciple that a *res spiritualis*, "a spiritual thing," ought not to be sold, with the term *sold* being understood in a broad sense to mean given for money, favor, or services rendered.[45] Thus, in a strictly logical sequence, anything included in the category of *res spiritualis* could be bought or sold only at the peril of simony. However, in human affairs it is often true that logical deductions from principles are not drawn immediately, if at all. It is one of the main conclusions of this study that it was a relatively long period of seventy-five years before the conclusion was firmly accepted that the religious habit and status were *res spirituales* and their sale simoniacal. The last major extension of the concept of simony was completed in the twelfth century, when economic dealings revolving about the entry into religion were perceived as potentially simoniacal.

It is clear that payment to become a monk was not one of those gross abuses against which the concept of simony was originally directed. To be sure, eleventh-century reformers were convinced that monks could and did commit simony. But there was nothing unique about their simony, which consisted in purchasing offices, e.g., an abbacy, and sacraments.[46] Their offenses were not different from those that any Christian could commit, so there was nothing "monastic" in their simony. The reformers apparently did not think that when a man gave a large gift or negotiated an agreement to become a monk he was thereby committing simony. I have found no eleventh-century list of simoniacal acts that included the purchase of the religious habit. At the very most, one may surmise that the vague terms that concluded such lists contained an implicit reference to entry into religion.[47] But such a surmise hardly seems justifiable. In the eleventh century simony was a common topic for conciliar legislation and for pamphleteering, and to find no explicit statement about the simoniacal nature of many entry agreements creates a strong presumption that contemporaries did not draw a connection between entry gifts and simony. Indeed, the first church council of the eleventh century that criticized the association of payment and monastic entry was that held at Melfi in 1089 by Pope Urban II, who was a former prior at Cluny. For the first time since the early ninth century, a church council forbade the requirement of a gift from those coming to be monks: "Let no abbot presume to demand a price from those who come to conversion, on any occasion of agreement."[48] The canon was repeated in a Roman council of 1099, held under the same pope.[49] This brief text did not use the term *simonia* to describe the practice that it criticized, and it is not absolutely certain that the canon was conceived within the framework of the *simonia* myth. It was only about thirty years later, in the 1120s, that clear, explicit criticism of required entry payments as simoniacal can be found in the sources. Before that time criticism was based on other grounds. The fact that gifts at entry were customary and normal did not shield them from unfavorable judgments in the eleventh and early twelfth centuries. Scrupulous churchmen perceived problems when the custom was abused, and two patterns of criticism of entry gifts appear in the sources. First, it was alleged that a gift obtained under dubious circumstances might be a form of "filthy gain"; second, it was argued that any gift might endanger the humility of the entrant.

"Seekers after Filthy Gain"

In his First Letter to Timothy, Saint Paul warned Christians against choosing men as bishops who were *sectantes turpe lucrum*, "seekers after filthy gain."[50] By the fifth century the phrase "filthy gain" was becoming an ecclesiastical commonplace that encompassed all modes of gaining income that were perceived as incompatible with the dignity of a cleric or a monk, such as usury or business.[51] The phrase took on a life of its own, and in the ninth century Carolingian capitularies and councils reiterated frequently the ban on clerics seeking *turpe lucrum* as businessmen (*negotiatores*),[52] agricultural agents or foremen (*vilici, conductores*),[53] usurers,[54] slick dealers,[55] and speculators in foodstuffs.[56] The prevailing canon law of the eleventh century perpetuated the view that particular forms of income were "filthy" for clerics, monks, and even all Christians. The *Decretum* of Ivo of Chartres, a canonical collection composed about 1094,[57] repeated the earlier tradition by forbidding to the clergy a whole series of practices on the grounds that they represented filthy gain. Ivo's work included under the ban usury,[58] buying crops cheaply at harvest and selling them dearly during famine,[59] and managing a business.[60] Monks in particular were warned to avoid all secular business in which profits were made.[61] In general, the category of *turpe lucrum* included any sort of greedy or 'shady dealing in which the clergy ought not to be involved. In a common literary antithesis, filthy or earthly gains were contrasted with the profit of souls, *lucrum animarum*.[62]

Since the category of *turpe lucrum* was firmly established in eleventh-century canon law, it was only natural that churchmen concerned about abuses of the custom of gifts at entry into religion should invoke it. Indeed, the Carolingian Council of Chalons in 813 set a precedent when it condemned bishops and abbots for inviting men to religious life on account of their money or property. The council specifically called the abuse a form of *turpe lucrum*.[63] Eleventh-century churchmen also found in the category of filthy gains a means to express disapproval of certain aspects of monastic entry gifts. When Abbot Warin of Saint Arnulf wrote to John of Fécamp about the case of a wealthy Jewish convert who had become a monk, he declared that if the convert left the monastery and took his considerable fortune with him, he should be allowed to do so because it was better for an abbot to save souls than to seek gold.[64] Peter Damian, citing directly the canon of Chalons (813), criticized monastic officials who enticed entrants to join their community in order to get their property. He declared that those officials

> do not love God, nor are they found to seek the profit of souls [*lucrum animarum*], [but] fired up by the pricks of filthy gain [*turpe lucrum*], they deceive some simple folk with their oily persuasions so that they may draw them by empty promises to the monastery.[65]

In a letter dated 1104–5, encouraging a hermit to send him recruits, Abbot Geoffrey of Vendôme expressed his uneasiness about venal receptions:

> Concerning the other one . . . whom you mentioned, if he seems to you to be of good life, take care to send him to us; and do not delay sending to us whatever clerics of upright life you find. We love in men honest poverty more than their proud riches. If they possess them, the riches ought not to be scorned; for they have their place. We seek nothing for making monks, but if something is offered we accept, since the Rule requires it to be accepted. Indeed, our order requires that we be such who give effort not for temporal gain [*lucris temporalibus*] but for gaining souls [*lucrandis animabus*].[66]

Geoffrey clearly hesitated about too close a connection between a man's wealth and his encouragement by monks to enter religion. He openly defended gifts, but he criticized the prelate who violated the norms of his order and whose excessive interest in wealthy recruits made him a "seeker after filthy gain."

Gifts as a Threat to Humility

Thus in the eleventh and early twelfth centuries, abuses of entry gifts were criticized as a base and unworthy means for a cleric to gain money, with no reference to simony. There was a second reason, rooted in an ancient tradition of monastic psychology, that prompted certain thinkers to have reservations about receiving *any* gift from an entrant. In a sermon delivered to monks about 1126–27, Peter Abelard criticized some religious houses for their venality in receiving new members:

> "If you wish to be perfect, sell all that you have, and give to the poor and come follow me." He did not say, "Come and bring what you have to us," but rather, "First offer your possessions to others and thus afterwards receive our possessions." But we, on the contrary, since we seek not so much the profit of the soul as of money, exhort anyone coming to conversion to bring what he has, and we do not so much give him our support as sell it.[67]

Abelard's sermon was a lengthy attack on monastic ambition and greed, which contradicted the ideal of withdrawal from the world. In the sentiments expressed and in its vocabulary, it stood in the long tradition of condemning forms of *turpe lucrum*. However, in his specific references to entry gifts, Abelard sounded another criticism as well:

> In which [procedure] we give him [the novice] a large occasion for temptation. Easily becoming proud about the things that he brought, he may grow angry and murmur when he lacks for anything; and he may complain that he is miserable and betrayed, since he sees himself equated with those who brought less or nothing at all. Cutting away all these excuses [for complaint], Christ therefore ordered [a man] to be taken naked rather than rich. He who ordered his disciples, "Freely you have received, freely give," wished to exhibit this first in himself, desiring not so much by his words as by his example to incite us to this. And it would have been much better and more upright for him [the convert] to have kept his goods so that he might have the fruit of charity from his own property, than by begging for others' goods to incur detriment of his reputation and to injure in a large way the dignity of the religious state.[68]

This opinion that a novice who brought a gift was particularly prone to the vices of pride and complaining was not original with Peter Abelard. Some of the monastic rules of late antiquity and of the early Middle Ages, especially in the Latin West, reveal a marked reluctance to accept gifts from new members. John Cassian, who was one of the earliest and most influential writers on monasticism in the West, spelled out the reasons for this reluctance in his *Institutes*, written at Marseilles about 420–24. Cassian said that the monks of Egypt refused to take a single coin from those who joined their group. The Egyptian monks had learned by bitter experience that the memory of a gift made the monk restless, insubordinate, and ready to abandon the monastic life when difficulties appeared.

> Therefore they refuse to receive from him money which is going to be put to the uses of the monastery; first, lest inflated by confidence in that gift he may not deign to equal himself to the poorer brethren; second, lest on account of this pride not descending to the humility of Christ, when he is unable to tolerate the discipline of the monastery, he may flee from it.[69]

When such monks left the monastery, they often sought the return of their gift, which led to litigation and distraction for the house. Thus Cassian expressed a tradition that saw in the gift at entry a direct danger to the humility of the monk and an indirect threat to the tranquility of the house. The *Regula monastica communis*, attributed to Fructuosus of Braga, a Visigothic abbot and bishop of the mid-seventh century, voiced a similar view. The *Regula* painted a gloomy verbal picture of the problems and scandals caused by men who left a monastery and sought the return of their entry gift. Its solution was a simple one: "When anyone requests to enter, let the monastery receive nothing from his resources, not even a single coin; but rather let him give all to the poor with his own hand. . . ."[70] The *Regula* thus interpreted literally the text of Matthew's Gospel that said, "If you would be perfect, go and sell all that you have, and give to the poor and come follow me." The prospective monk was obliged to give everything to the "poor of Christ," and he risked expulsion from the monastery if he gave anything to his immediate family, other relatives, the church, the ruler of the region, or his slaves,

> . . . since we see him not in the number of the apostles, but a fol-lower of Ananias and Saphira. May you know that such a person is unable in the monastery to come up to the standard of a monk, or to stoop to the poverty of Christ, or to acquire humility, or to be obedi-ent, or to persevere there forever; but when any reason for punish-ment or correction of the monastery by the abbot shall arise, immedi-ately he arises in pride and puffed up by the spirit of distaste, he leaves the monastery in flight.[71]

Such an absolute rejection of gifts from entrants was not feasi-ble economically for most religious houses. But even the more moderate monastic rules, such as that of Saint Benedict, which al-lowed the prospective monk to offer his goods either to the poor or to the monastery, were careful to insist that, whatever he did with them, the man was cut off from them.[72] The essential concern was the personal humbling of the new monk, the fostering in him of a psychological state befitting his new life. The *Regula mon-asterii tarnatensis* held that if a gift impeded the growth of the in-ner virtues of humility and poverty, then it would have been better for there to have been no gift at all:

> If they have offered a little part of their property to aid the expenses of the group, let them not be puffed up on account of this; from that action whence at first they desired to ascend they may afterward fall. What good is there in distributing wealth and in being made poor by giving to the poor, if the wretched soul is made more proud in scorning riches than it was in possessing them?[73]

Thus it was the consideration of pride on the part of the giver and of scandal or litigation if he reneged on his gift that made some monastic legislators reluctant to receive gifts from novices. Fear of simony was in no way an element of this thought pattern. The reluctance to receive gifts was embodied in authoritative texts, especially the *Institutes* of Cassian, whom Benedict recommended as reading matter for his disciples.[74] Therefore Abelard could crit-icize the gifts of entrants on the basis of this monastic psychology, with no reference to simony. Indeed, it would probably falsify its meaning to see a reference to simony in the sermon, which stated clearly that a gift at entry was dangerous because,

> easily becoming proud about the things which he brought, he may grow angry and murmur when he lacks for anything; and he may complain that he is miserable and betrayed, since he sees himself equated with those who brought less or nothing at all.[75]

Conclusion

In the late eleventh and early twelfth centuries, monastic thinkers accepted the basic legitimacy of gifts at entry into religious life. When the admission of a new member was motivated by mercenary considerations, the critics attacked it as the search for "filthy gains" and as an incitement to pride in the novice, who was supposed to be abandoning worldly pride. In spite of their willingness to criticize payments on those grounds, monastic thinkers before the mid-twelfth century seem to have been reluctant to admit that simony in the reception of new members was a danger, or even a significant possibility. The Paris theologian Peter the Chanter attributed an opinion to Bernard of Clairvaux, who was active from 1115 to 1153: "Abbot Bernard said that there could never be simony in the giving of a gift for making a monk, particularly when the monastery was poor."[76] The editor of Peter the Chanter's *Summa de sacramentis* was not able to find this opinion in the extant works of Bernard. However, whether or not Bernard himself said this, the opinion expressed was widely held among the religious. The entry gift, with all its implications of negotiations and pacts, was an all but unquestioned element of their tradition, open to criticism when abused, but not perceived as fundamentally wrong.

---

1. *Capitularia regum francorum*, ed. A. Boretius, MGH, *Legum sectio* 2 (Hanover, 1883), vol. 1, chap. 3, p. 63.

2. Ibid., chap. 15, p. 63: "Ut nullus abbas pro susceptione monachi praemium non quaerat."

SIMONIACAL ENTRY INTO RELIGIOUS LIFE

3. Ibid., canon 16, p. 76: "Audivimus enim, quod quidam abbates cupiditate ducti praemia pro introeuntibus in monasterio requirunt. Ideo placuit nobis et sancta synodo: pro suscipiendis in sancto ordine fratribus nequaquam pecunia requiratur, sed secundum regulam sancti Benedicti suscipiantur."

4. For an account of the cooperation between Louis and Benedict of Aniane, see S. Dulcy, *La Règle de saint Benoît d'Aniane et la réforme monastique à l'époque carolingienne* (Nimes, 1933), pp. 68-104.

5. J. Semmler, "Zur Überlieferung der monastischen Gesetzgebung Ludwigs des Frommen," *Deutsches Archiv für Erforschung des Mittelalters* 16 (1960): 309-88, traces the origins of the legislation of 816 and 817 and its relation to the legislation of 818-19.

6. *Initia consuetudinis benedictinae*, ed. J. Semmler in *Corpus consuetudinum monasticarum* 1 (Siegberg, 1963), Legislatio aquisgranensis, chap. 72, p. 533: "Ut nullus pro munere recipiatur in monasterio nisi quem bona voluntas et merita commendent."

7. W. Ullmann, *The Growth of Papal Government in the Middle Ages*, 3d ed. (London, 1970), pp. 104-5, describes the love-hate relationship that Charlemagne felt for the Eastern Empire. Ullmann's notes to those pages provide a bibliographical orientation to scholarly literature on the topic.

8. Canon 19, Migne, vol. 129, col. 487.

9. For an account of the Carolingian theological reasons for rejecting the image decrees of the Second Nicaean Council, see G. Haendler, *Epochen karolingischer Theologie. Eine Untersuchung über die karolingischer Gütachten zum byzantinischen Bilderstreit* (Berlin, 1958), pp. 27-43, 67-101. The main intellectual monument to the Carolingian rejection of the council was the elaborate theological treatise known as the *Libri Carolini*, ed. H. Bastgen, MGH, *Legum sectio 3, Concilia 2*, supplementum (Hanover, 1924).

10. Haendler, *Epochen*, pp. 27-30.

11. The following ninth-century canonical collections did not incorporate texts against forced payments for entry to religion: (1) *Decretales Pseudo-Isidorianae et Capitula Angilramni*, ed. P. Hinschius (Leipzig, 1863); (2) H. Mordek, "Die Rechtssammlungen der Handschrift von Bonneval—ein Werk der karolingischer Reform," *Deutsches Archiv für Erforschung des Mittelalters* 24 (1968): 339-434; (3) P. Fournier, "Le ms H 137 de l'école de médecine de Montpellier," *Annales de l'Université de Grenoble* 9 (1897): 357-89; (4) J. Rambaud-Buhot, "Un Corpus inédit de droit canonique de la réforme carolingienne à la réforme grégorienne," in *Humanisme actif. Mélanges d'art et de littérature offerts à Julien Cain* (Paris, 1968), 2:271-81.

12. P. Fournier and G. Le Bras, *Histoire des collections canoniques en Occident* (Paris, 1931-32), 1:93.

13. False Capitularies of Benedict the Levite are edited by F. Knust, MGH, *Leges*, vol. 2, pt. 2 (Hanover, 1837), pp. 17-158.

14. Mansi, vol. 20, col. 723.

15. For a useful survey of recent research on the nobility of the middle ages and its very diverse origins, see L. Genicot, "La Noblesse dans la société médiévale," *Le moyen âge* 71 (1965): 539-60. On the transformation of the international Frankish nobility into a constituent of the local seigneurs of the tenth century, see R. Poupardin, "Les grandes familles comtales à l'époque carolingienne," *Revue historique* 72 (1900): 72-95; and J. Boussard, *The Civilization of Charlemagne*, trans. F. Partridge (London, 1968), pp. 43-52.

16. M. Bloch, *Feudal Society*, trans. L. A. Manyon (London, 1961), pp. 3-38, describes the troubled period of the late ninth and tenth centuries. For further information and bibliography on various aspects of the invasions, see L. Musset, *Les Invasions: le second assaut contre l'Europe chrétienne, viie -xie siècles*, La nouvelle clio, vol. 12, 2d ed.

(Paris, 1965). A. d'Haenens, *Les Invasions normandes en Belgique au ix*ᵉ *siècle* (Louvain, 1967), pp. 151-62, argues that the actual damage wrought by the invasions has been exaggerated. The mental shock and anxiety persisted long after the physical aftermath had been repaired.

17. D. Herlihy, "Church Property on the European Continent, 701-1200," *Speculum* 36 (1961): 92-95, finds that between 876 and 976 the amount of ecclesiastical property dropped from 33 percent of all property to 26 percent. For alienations in Italy, especially in the diocese of Lucca, see C. Boyd, *Tithes and Parishes in Medieval Italy* (Ithaca, N.Y., 1952), pp. 87-102.

18. D. C. Douglas, *William the Conqueror: The Norman Impact upon England* (Berkeley and Los Angeles, 1964), pp. 105-6, notes that about 950 not a single monastery survived in Normandy. On England see D. Knowles, *The Monastic Order in England*, 2d ed. (Cambridge, 1963), pp. 31-36, and "The Evidence for the Disappearance of Monastic Life in England before 943," ibid., p. 695.

19. E. Amann and A. Dumas, *L'Eglise au pouvoir des laïques (888-1057)*, Histoire de l'église, vol. 7 (Paris, 1940). On proprietary churches see U. Stutz, *Geschichte des kirchlichen Benefizialwesens von seinen Anfängen bis auf die Zeit Alexanders III*, 2d ed., ed. H. E. Feine (Aalen, 1961), vol. 1. Stutz gives a précis of his views in "The Proprietary Church as an Element of Medieval Germanic Ecclesiastical Law," in *Medieval Germany, 911-1250*, trans. G. Barraclough (Oxford, 1939), 2:35ᵧ70.

20. For a brief survey of reform movements of the tenth and eleventh centuries, see Knowles, *Monastic Order*, pp. 25-57. For the Cluniac reform see G. de Valous, *Le Monachisme clunisien des origines au xv*ᵉ *siècle*, 2d ed. (Paris, 1970), vol. 1; or G. de Valous, "Cluny," *DHGE*, vol. 13, cols. 35-56. For an account of the reform emanating from Gorze, see K. Hallinger, *Gorze-Kluny. Studien zu den monastischen Lebensformen und Gegensätzen im Hochmittelalter*. Studia anselmiana, nos. 22/23 and 24/25 (Rome, 1950-51), 2 vols. On Gerard of Brogne and his short-lived reform, see F. Baix, "Brogne," *DHGE*, vol. 10, cols. 818-32. The *Revue bénédictine* 70 (1960) devoted the entire issue to Gerard of Brogne and his milieu.

21. Much of the polemic literature occasioned by the reform movements of the eleventh century was edited in the MGH, *Libelli de Lite* (Hanover, 1891-97), 3 vols. However, one of the most significant forms of that polemic, the reform-oriented canonical collection, was not represented there. For a survey of those collections and their significance, see Fournier and Le Bras, *Histoire des collections*, 2:4-7, and passim. See also A. Michel, *Die Sentenzen des Kardinals Humbert, das erste Rechtsbuch der päpstlichen Reform* (Leipzig, 1943), pp. 1-8; and J. J. Ryan, *Saint Peter Damiani and his Canonical Sources: A Preliminary Study in the Antecedents of the Gregorian Reform*, Pontifical Institute of Medieval Studies, Studies and Texts no. 2 (Toronto, 1956).

22. Ullmann, *Growth*, pp. 272-76, 413-46; G. Tellenbach, *Church, State, and Christian Society at the Time of the Investiture Contest*, trans. R. F. Bennett (Oxford, 1959), pp. 115-17, stresses the reformers' desire to force laymen to accept a subordinate place in the church.

23. G. Ladner, "Reformatio," *Ecumenical Dialogue at Harvard*, ed. S. H. Miller and G. E. Wright (Cambridge, Mass., 1964), pp. 172-90, treats Gregory VII's view that the pope had to be predominant in a "just" society. Similarly many of the canonical collections were papally-oriented: Fournier and Le Bras, *Histoire des collections*, 2:5-7. For other discussions of the papacy's role in reform, see Ullmann, *Growth*, pp. 275-76, and Tellenbach, *Church*, pp. 131-47.

24. For a brief treatment of measures against clerical marriage, see Amann and Dumas, *L'Eglise au pouvoir*, pp. 476-82. See also A. M. Stickler, "L'Evolution de la discipline du

célibat dans l'Eglise en Occident, de la fin de l'âge patristique au concile de Trente," in *Sacerdoce et célibat. Etudes historiques et théologiques* (Gembloux-Louvain, 1971), pp. 373–442.

25. For the meaning and application of the idea of simony before the Investiture Contest, see A. Leinz, *Die Simonie. Eine kanonistische Studie* (Freiburg im Breisgau, 1902); N. A. Weber, *A History of Simony in the Christian Church to 814* (Baltimore, 1909); R. A. Ryder, *Simony: An historical Synopsis and Commentary* (Washington, D.C., 1931); and H. Meier-Welcker, "Die Simonie im frühen Mittelalter," *Zeitschrift für Kirchengeschichte* 64 (1952-53): 61–93. None of these authors found a direct condemnation of forced entry fees as simoniacal before canon 19 of the Second Nicaean Council (787).

26. J. Leclercq, "Simoniaca heresis," *Studi Gregoriani* 1 (1947): 523–30. P. de Vooght, "La Simoniaca haeresis selon les auteurs scholastiques," *Ephemerides theologicae lovanienses* 30 (1954): 64–80, traces the rejection of the view that simony was in fact a heresy. The scholastic theologians saw it as a great crime, but not necessarily involving a doctrinal error, which would have made it a heresy.

27. Concilium vernense (755), canon 24, *Capitularia*, 1:37; Admonitio generalis (789), chap. 21, ibid., p. 55; Capitula ab episcopis Attiniaci data (822), chap. 6, ibid., p. 358; Capitula episcoporum Papiae edita (845-50) chap. 4, *Capitularia*, 2:81-82; Concilium Moguntinum (852), canon 25, ibid., p. 191.

28. Leclercq, "Simoniaca heresis," pp. 523–30, stresses the role of Gregory I in the formulation of the idea of simony, both because he wrote about it often and because of his prestige as an *auctoritas*. Gregory's letters were edited by P. Ewald and L. Hartmann, in MGH, *Epistolarum Tomi II* in two parts (Berlin, 1891–93); see the index under the word *heresis* for his comments on simony. Gregory also discussed the topic in his sermons, for example, Migne, vol. 76, cols. 1091-92, 1145-46, 1295.

29. Acts of the Apostles 8:18-25.

30. 4 Kings 5:16-27. See H.-J. Horn, "Giezie und Simonie," *Jahrbuch für Antike und Christentum* 8/9 (1965-66): 189-202.

31. Matthew 21:12-13; Mark 11:15-17; Luke 19:45-46.

32. Matthew 10:8.

33. *Conciliorum oecumenicorum decreta*, ed. J. Alberigo et al. (Freiburg im Breisgau, 1962), pp. 63-64; or Migne, vol. 129, col. 487.

34. E. Amann, "Simon le magicien," *DTC*, vol. 14, cols. 2130-40. See also the study and edition by L. Vouaux, *Les Actes de Pierre* (Paris, 1922), in which the rivalry of Peter and Simon forms a major theme.

35. E. Hirsch, "Die Simoniebegriff und eine angebliche Erweiterung desselben im elften Jahrhundert," *Archiv für katholisches Kirchenrecht* 86 (1906): 3-19, denies the view that lay investiture was perceived as a kind of simony in the eleventh century. Hirsch sees the idea of simony as defined in its essentials by the sixth century, and then adapted to new circumstances in the eleventh.

36. J. T. Gilchrist, "*Simoniaca haeresis* and the Problem of Orders from Leo IX to Gratian," in *Proceedings of the Second International Congress of Medieval Canon Law*, ed. S. Kuttner and J. J. Ryan (Vatican City, 1965), pp. 209-35, surveys the question from a canon law perspective, with bibliographical orientations to the abundant secondary literature on the topic. L. Saltet, *Les Réordinations: étude sur le sacrement de l'ordre* (Paris, 1907), chaps. 9-12, presents a solid general treatment of the problem of simony's effects on the administration of holy orders.

37. *St. Victor*, vol. 2, no. 832, 1 July 1060:" . . . Fueruntque veritatis testes, et, quandiu in presenti vixerint, fortiter obstiterunt symoniache heresi, obedientes suo salvatori qui eis

preceperat, dicens: 'Gratis accepistis, gratis date.' Ex quibus omnibus extitit unus in primitiva ecclesia, beatissimus scilicet Petrus, . . . qui Symonem magum, a quo hec nec dicenda heresis nomen et actum sumpsit, ab Jerusalem usque in maximam Romam, variis sermonum et actuum argumentis omnimodis obpugnavit, in tantum ut ab eo, oratione ad Deum fusa, scelestum corpus ejus, quod in aera magicis artibus volitari videbatur, id solo dejectum orribili non multo post morte plecteretur. Que detestanda heresis in tantum pullulavit, ut, modernis temporibus . . . vix repperiantur in ecclesiastico ordine constituti, qui non sint hujus nefandi sceleris vinculo colligati. . . . " Compare the account by Humbert of Silva Candida of the spread of simony from the ancient church to "modern times," *Libri III adversus simoniacos*, bk. 2, chaps. 35–36, ed. F. Thaner, MGH, *Libelli de Lite*, 1:183–85.

38. Leclercq, "Simoniaca heresis," pp. 524–25. Geoffrey of Vendôme, *Libellus IV*, ed. E. Sackur, MGH. *Libelli de Lite*, 2:690, wrote, "Igitur Simon magus non tantum hereticus, sed hereticorum primus et pessimus extitit." Humbert of Silva Candida, *Libri III*, bk. 2, chap. 34, *Libelli de Lite*, 1:182–84 discussed the proposition "How much worse than all heretics are the simoniacs!"

39. Humbert of Silva Candida, *Libri III*, p. 137, contrasts "piissimus Symon Petrus" with "impiissimus Symon Magus." Gerhoh of Reichersberg, *Liber de simoniacis*, ed. E. Sackur, MGH, *Libelli de Lite*, 3:269, charges that "Simon Magus sought to appear like Simon Peter."

40. Pope Alexander II called for the deposition of certain clerics at Cremona who "have been polluted with the simoniacal filth" (JL 4637). Simony was also called a plague (*pestis*) (Peter Damian, *Liber Gratissimus*, chaps. 18 and 29, ed. L. de Heinemann, MGH. *Libelli de Lite* 1: pp. 42, 59); and a wickedness (*pravitas*) (Geoffrey of Vendôme, *Libellus III*, MGH, *Libelli de Lite*, 2:688).

41. Damian, *Liber Gratissimus*, chap. 29, pp. 58–60.

42. For instance, much to his later regret, Leo IX took the extreme step of reordaining those clerics who had received simoniacal orders (Saltet, *Les Reordinations*, pp. 182–89; and J. Drehmann, *Papst Leo IX und die Simonie* [Leipzig, 1908], pp. 26–29). Individuals also experienced personal crises because of simony. According to a *Life* by Peter Damian, Domenicus Loricatus refused to exercise holy orders that he had received simoniacally (*AASS*, Oct., vol. 6, chap. 8, p. 622). This *Vita* was dated to 1061 by G. Lucchesi, "La 'Vita S. Rodulphi et S. Domenici Loricati' di S. Pier Damiano," *Rivista di storia della chiesa in Italia* 19 (1965): 173.

43. C. Mirbt, *Die Publizistik im Zeitalter Gregors VII* (Leipzig, 1894), p. 367, notes the lack of any defense of simony on the level of theory. Cf. Hirsch, "Die Simoniebegriff," p. 3. Clerical marriage had legal and historical support and was occasionally defended on a theoretical level, e.g., *Tractatus pro clericorum conubio*, ed. E. Dümmler, MGH, *Libelli de Lite*, 3: 588–96; and Sigebert of Gembloux, *Apologia contra eos qui calumniantur missas conjugatorum sacerdotum*, ed. E. Sackur, MGH, *Libelli de Lite*, 2: 436–48.

44. For some indication of the scope of social change implicit in anti-simoniacal propaganda, see the Council of Vienne (1060), canon 1, Mansi, vol. 19, cols. 925–26.

45. Gregory I was the source of this enumeration of ways to commit simony, by *munus a manu* (money), by *munus a lingua* (flattery), and by *munus ab obsequio* (undue service) (Migne, vol. 76, cols. 1091–92).

46. Council of Toulouse (1056), Mansi, vol. 19, col. 848; Council of Winchester (1076), canon 1, Mansi, vol. 20, col. 459; Council of Rouen (1074), Mansi, vol. 20, cols. 397–98.

47. Bernold of Constance, *Apologeticus*, chap. 7, ed. F. Thaner, MGH, *Libelli de Lite*, 2:66; Council of Rome (1059), Mansi, vol. 19, col. 898; Council of Rome (1078), canon 3, Mansi, vol. 20, col. 509.

48. Council of Melfi (1089), canon 7, Mansi, vol. 20, col. 723: "Nullus abbas pretium exigere ab eis qui ad conversionem veniunt aliqua placiti occasione praesumat."

49. Mansi, vol. 20, col. 964. In Gratian's *Decretum* this canon was added as a *palea* to *causa* I, *questio* II, canon 3, in the form, "Nullus abbas precium sumere vel exigere ab eis, qui ad conversionem veniunt, aliqua pacti occasione presumat."

50. 1 Timothy 3:8.

51. Canon 3 of Chalcedon(451) forbade all forms of *turpe lucrum* to the clergy (Mansi, vol. 7, col. 373).

52. Capitulare missorum generale (802), chap. 1, *Capitularia*, 1:92; "Le premier statut diocésain de Gerbald, évêque de Liège," canon 16, ed. C. de Clercq, *La Législation religieuse*, p. 356; Concilium parisiense (829), canon 28, *Concilia*, vol. 2, pt. 2, pp. 630–31.

53. Concilium parisiense (829), canon 28, *Concilia*, vol. 2, pt. 2, pp. 630–31; Episcoporum ad Hludowicum Imperatorem Relatio (829), chap. 10, *Capitularia*, 2:33; Concilium aquisgranensis (836), canon 8, *Concilia*, vol. 2, pt. 2, pp. 712–13.

54. Concilium cabillonense (813), canon 5, *Concilia*, vol. 2, pt. 1, p. 275; Concilium remense (813), canon 32, ibid., p. 256; Concilium parisiense (829), canon 53, ibid., pt. 2, pp. 645–48; Concilium aquisgranense (836), canon 8, ibid., pp. 712–13.

55. Capitulare missorum Niumagae datum (806), chap. 15, *Capitularia*, 1:132; Capitulare Septimanicum (844), chap. 7, ibid., 2:257; Edictum pistense (864), gloss on text, ibid., p. 319.

56. Capitulare missorum Niumagae datum (806), chap. 17, ibid., 1:132.

57. Ivo of Chartres, *Decretum*, Migne, vol. 161, cols. 47–1036.

58. Ibid., pt. 6, chaps. 65, 196, Migne, vol. 161, cols. 459, 489.

59. Ibid., pt. 6, chap. 201, Migne, vol. 161, col. 489.

60. Ibid., pt. 6, chap. 218; pt. 13, chap. 11, Migne, vol. 161, cols. 491–92, 805.

61. Ibid., pt. 7, chap. 108, Migne, vol. 161, cols. 568–69.

62. Capitula Qualiter (after 821), chap. 6, ed. H. Frank, in *Corpus consuetudinum monasticarum* (Siegberg, 1963), 1:353; Geoffrey of Vendôme, letter 49 of book 4, Migne, vol. 157, col. 186; Marbod to Vitalis of Savigny, letter 4, Migne, vol. 171, cols. 1474–75; Peter Abelard, sermon on John the Baptist, Migne, vol. 178, cols. 593–94.

63. Chap. 7, *Concilia*, vol. 2, pt. 1, p. 275.

64. *Vetera analecta*, ed. J. Mabillon, 2d ed. (Paris, 1723), col. 452.

65. Peter Damian, *Rhetoricae declamationis Invectio in Episcopum monachos ad saeculum revocantem*, Migne, vol. 145, col. 372: " . . . Qui nec Deum diligunt, nec lucrum animarum quaerere comprobantur, turpis lucri stimulis accensi, ita simplices quosque blanda persuasione decipiant, ut eos vanis promissionibus illectos, ad monasterium trahant."

66. Geoffrey of Vendôme, letter 49 of book 4, Migne, vol. 157, col. 186: "Alterum vero, . . . de quo iterum significastis, si vobis bonae vitae esse videtur, nobis mittere curetis; et quoscunque honestae vitae clericos inveneritis, nobis transmittere non differatis. Plus itaque in hominibus diligimus honestam paupertatem, quam superbas eorum divitias, quas si habuerint, respuendae non sunt; habent enim et illae locum suum, nihil tamen pro faciendis monachis quaerimus, sed si quid oblatum fuerit, quia illud Regula suscipi iubet, suscipimus. Ordo siquidem noster exigit ut tales simus, qui non lucris temporalibus sed lucrandis animabus operam demus." A. Wilmart, "La Collection chronologique des écrits de Geoffroi, abbé de Vendôme," *Revue bénédictine* 43 (1931): 241, dates this letter to 1104-5. See L. Compain, *Étude sur Geoffroi de Vendôme* (Paris, 1891), pp. 34–37, for the background to this letter.

67. Migne, vol. 178, sermon 33, col. 593: " 'Si vis perfectus esse, vade, vende omnia que habes, et da pauperibus et veni, et sequere me.' (Matth. 19:21) Non utique dicit: Veni, et affer quae habes ad nos, sed aliis prius eroga tua, et sic post modum, suscipe nostra. Nos vero e contrario quemlibet ad conversionem venientem, non tam lucrum animae quam pecuniae quaerentes, ut quae habet afferat exhortamur, nec tam ei nostra largimus quam

vendimus." D. van den Eynde, "Le Recueil des sermons de Pierre Abélard," *Antonianum* 37 (1962): 48-51, dates this sermon to 1126-27.

68. Migne, vol. 178, Sermon 33, cols. 593-94: "In quo ei profecto non mediocrem tentationis occasionem damus. Facile quippe de his quae attulit intumescens, quum quid ei defuerit indignatur et murmurat; et se miserum ac proditum clamat, quum se his coaequari viderit, qui minus, aut omnino nihil attulerit. Has igitur omnes occasiones Christus amputans, nudum magis quam suffarcinatum decrevit assumere. Qui enim discipulis praeceperat: 'Gratis accepistis, gratis date', hoc in se ipso primum voluit exhibere non tam verbo suo quam exemplo nos ad hoc cupiens incitare. . . . Ac longe melius vel honestius esset ei sua retinuisse, ut haberet de proprio fructum eleemosynae, quam ad aliena mendicantem famae suae detrimentum incurrere, et non mediocriter religionis propositae dignitatem laedere."

69. John Cassian, *Institutions cénobitiques*, ed. and trans. J.-C. Guy, Sources chrétiennes, no. 109 (Paris, 1965), bk. 4, chaps. 3-4, pp. 124-26.

70. Migne, vol. 87, col. 1125c: "Nihil enim de pristinis facultatibus suis in eumdem locum, ubi ingredi se petit monasterium, vel ad unum nummum recipiatur; sed et ipse manu sua cuncta pauperibus eroget. . . . " On the authorship of the *Regula monastica communis*, see C. J. Bishko, "Gallegan Pactual Monasticism in the Repopulation of Castile," in *Estudios dedicados a Menéndez Pidal* (Madrid, 1951), 2:514-15.

71. Migne, vol. 87, col. 1114b-c: ". . . Quia non eum in apostolorum numero, sed Ananiae et Saphirae sequacem videmus. Sciatis eum non posse in monasterio in mensuram venire monachi, neque ad paupertatem descendere Christi, neque humilitatem acquirere, neque obediens esse, neque ibidem perpetuo perdurare; sed cum aliqua occasio pro aliquo a suo abbate monasterii distringendi aut emendandi accesserit, continuo in superbiam surgit, et acediae spiritu inflatus, monasterium fugiens derelinquit."

72. *Sancti Benedicti regula*, chap. 58. In his provisions for receiving children, Benedict also sought to cut off the child from any hope that he possessed goods in the outside world (chap. 59). Other monastic rules that permitted gifts from entrants laid emphasis on the need to avoid giving the new monk a sense of pride in his offering: *La Règle du maître*, ed. A. de Vogüé, Sources chrétiennes, no. 106 (Paris, 1964), vol. 2, chaps. 87, 91. *Regula monasterii tarnatensis*, chap. 1, Migne, vol. 66, cols. 977-78; *Ferreoli Ucetiensis Episcopi Regula ad Monachos*, chap. 10, Migne, vol. 66, col. 963; *Aureliani regula ad monachos*, chaps. 3, 4, Migne, vol. 68, col. 389; *Regula Sancti Macarii*, chap. 24, Migne, vol. 103, col. 450. The same reluctance to accept gifts was expressed in the Carolingian commentary of Benedict's Rule, attributed to Paul Warnefrid: *Pauli Warnefridi commentarium in sanctam regulam* (Monte Cassino, 1880), chap. 58 pp. 442-43; chap. 59, p. 449. On the origin and authorship of this commentary, see W. Hafner, *Der Basiliuskommentar zur Regula s. Benedicti*, Beiträge zur Geschichte d. alten Mönchtums und d. Benediktinerordens, no. 23 (Münster, 1959).

73. *Regula monasterii tarnatensis*, Migne, vol. 66, col. 983c: "Nec ob hoc extollantur, si ad juvandas fraternitatis expensas quamcunque facultatum suarum particulam contulerint; et inde postmodum cadant, unde prius ascendere cupiebant. Quid prodest opes dispergere, et pauper fieri pauperibus erogando, si anima misera superbior efficiatur divitias contemnendo, quam fuerat possidendo."

74. *Sancti Benedicti regula*, chap. 73.

75. Migne, vol. 178, col. 593.

76. Peter the Chanter, *Summa de sacramentis et animae consiliis*, ed. J.-A. Dugauquier, Analecta mediaevalia namurcensia (Louvain and Lille, 1963), vol. 3, part 2a, pp. 213-14: "Abbas etiam Bernardus dixit quod nunquam in muneribus dandis ob monachandum aliquem potest esse Simonia precipue ut monasterio indigeat." Peter the Chanter also reported the opinion of "aliqui" to the effect that mere payment for reception in a monastery could not be simony so long as the payment did not involve the acquisition of a position in the house's hierarchy (ibid., pp. 60-61).

CHAPTER FOUR

Entry Payments as Simony

 This chapter will treat early twelfth-century attempts to apply the intellectual category of simony to the payments and transactions that customarily accompanied entrance to religious life. The major texts reflecting this attempt were those of Rudolph, abbot of Saint Trond; Gerhoh of Reichersberg; and Gratian, the Bolognese compiler of the *Decretum*.

Rudolph of Saint Trond

Sometime between 1123 and 1138, a controversy arose at Cologne concerning the gift demanded from a man who wished to place his son as an oblate in the monastery of Saint Panteleon. The dispute became heated and began to draw the interest of the city populace. The prior of Saint Panteleon, Sibertus, wrote for advice to Rudolph (ca. 1070–1138), a former abbot of Saint Panteleon and, at the time of the controversy, abbot of Saint Trond. Rudolph was experienced in the areas of canon law and the study of simony. He had compiled a canonical collection about 1100.[1] In addition, a notice of Mabillon indicated that Rudolph had written two works on simony, including one that was specifically concerned with the simony of monks.[2] Unfortunately, these three works seem to have perished. However, Rudolph's reply to the prior Sibertus does survive, in which he laid out his position on simony in entrance to religion. Sibertus' letter described the origins and issues of the controversy thus:

> A certain young boy was offered to us by his parents as an oblate, and because of their devotion they offered as much as they wished of their

wealth along with the boy. A certain man, richer in goods but poorer and greedier in will, saw this and was envious, and immediately he asked that his son be received. Much time was consumed in asking and denying, since his parents wished to introduce that boy by force, without a gift.[3]

It is important to remember that the monks had custom and precedent on their side in this quarrel.

At length, when his father was summoned in a friendly way, so that he might give to the church something from the goods which God had given him, he began to rage, saying that he was unwilling to commit simony. Seized by this fury, he struck us with much injury, he filled the markets and streets, he moved citizens and ecclesiastical persons, by declaring that we offer for a price that which we are ordered to give for free. He said "If indeed a rich commoner is easily admitted, [and] a nobler person coming simply [i.e., without a gift] is driven away by many excuses, then it appears obvious that not the person, but the money is sought. And when he, who at first was repudiated, has brought a sack of money and has merited the formerly denied entrance, who does not see how much simony is committed here?"

Since he was a well-known person of the city, this accusation disturbed us very much. At length, summoned again by clergy and laity, we answered as before that it was fitting and just, and not contrary to canonical rigor, that whoever wishes to join himself or one of his own to the church, while he has possessions whence he can offer, ought to offer [something] for the use of the same church. They said, however, "Monasteries are set up for this [purpose], so that whoever wishes to abandon the world ought rightfully to enter, and neither the occasion of poverty nor of any other thing should be an obstacle to him since those whom God unites and brings together, He fills with all good things."[4]

The father of the boy, and his lay and clerical supporters, made three charges against the monks of Saint Panteleon. First, they accused the monks of taking new recruits for money. Second, they asserted that monasteries should be open to all and that Saint Panteleon was not. Third, they declared that the monks should rely on God rather than on recruits for their needs. Rudolph of Saint Trond wrote a long reply to the letter of Sibertus, in which he attempted to meet these three criticisms. It is his reply to the first criticism that is significant for the problem of simony in entrance to religious houses.

Rudolph wrote to Sibertus that the charge was not serious, could not really be pursued in a court of law by the man, and therefore the monks should ignore their critics with "silent derision."[5] However, he agreed to write a reply because the charge was upsetting and scandalous for the monks. Rudolph took the offensive against the "rich but tight and greedy man,"[6] and he defended the premise that those who offer a child to a monastery are obliged to give with him that portion of their goods which the child would have received if he had remained in secular life.

> He wishes to cover himself and to purify himself with the name of piety, so that as if on account of simony . . . he may seem to retain what he retains on account of greed. If he wishes [both] to avoid simony and to shed avarice, let him do justice, for simony and avarice can not be done with justice. But what is the justice we ask him to do, so as to flee simony and avarice? Let him divide equally among his sons that which he is saving or retaining on account of his sons, or, as he lies, in order to avoid simony. But, he wishes to send one [son] from himself to give to God and to the holy church. This is very good; but nevertheless it is good and just that he send after him or with him his share. But I believe that he wishes to send [him] from the world for this purpose, that he may keep the boy's portion in his money-bag.[7]

The lines were clearly drawn, with Rudolph asserting that the money was owed to the boy and the father asserting that it was simony to demand the money. Rudolph accused the rich man of avarice, idolatry, and sacrilege because he was cheating his son, the monastery, and God out of their rightful due.[8] Rudolph questioned the sincerity of a man whose accusation of simony fitted in so well with his own self-interest.

However, the boy's father had certain religious and social attitudes on his side of the argument. Monastic theology held that the monk was dead to the world, and many of the relatives of monks, beginning especially in the twelfth century, interpreted that theological image literally and drew the conclusion that normal inheritance laws should prevail when a person "died" by entering religion.[9] Rudolph tried to counter that view by insisting that the image of the monk's death had another, contrary interpretation.

> May he give to him [the boy] what is his, may he hand over what he was keeping for him. But he says, "He is dead." Indeed, he is dead to the world, but he lives to God. His portion is owed to the poor of Christ and to the church. It is owed to them to whom he went; it is owed to Christ, for he has gone to him.[10]

Rudolph's opponent next declared that he would give the boy's goods to the poor, rather than to the wealthy monks. Rudolph insisted that the monks, because of their voluntary abnegation, were truer and worthier "pauperes Christi" than the worldly poor, who were still marked by greed and desire for goods. He concluded that it was to the monks that Christ was referring in the gospel when he told the rich young man to sell all he had and give to the poor.[11]

Furthermore, Rudolph returned to his major contention that the rich man could not legitimately choose whether or not to give the boy's portion to the monastery: "You say well, "The goods which I have I am going to give to the poor." The goods that you have, give to whatever poor you wish but allow the goods which are your son's to follow him to the monastery, where you offer him among the poor of Christ to follow the Lord."[12]

Rudolph's opponent apparently claimed that the *Rule* of Benedict was on his side as well, because Rudolph felt obliged to offer a rather forced exegesis of the text. Chapter 59 of the *Rule* said clearly that the parents ought to disinherit their child, and that only if they were unwilling to do so were they to give a gift with him to the house.[13] Rudolph omitted entirely the part of the text on disinheritance and concentrated his argument on the right of the parent to choose what to give, or, indeed, whether to give.

> Likewise in the text about the sons of nobles and of the poor. "If they should wish to offer anything for their reward as a gift to the monastery, let them make a donation to the monastery out of the possessions which they wish to give." He hears perhaps and is happy, because the blessed Benedict places this decision in his choice. But certainly the holy man would place this in the choice of no one, unless he knew

that the decision which ought to be made was going to be holy and just and pious. However, since what is holy and just and pious could not enter the will of this man, may he have his possessions in perdition. He wishes that his son be taken empty-handed, [then] let him bring it about that he is one of the number of those about whom the blessed Benedict writes. "But, who," he says, "have nothing at all, let them simply make the petition and may they offer their son with the oblation before witnesses."[14]

Thus Rudolph argued that this man could not choose, as the *Rule* allowed, because he was insincere and would choose incorrectly. Whereas it seems that Benedict's *Rule* foresaw the possibility of receiving the sons of rich men gratis, Rudolph restricted such receptions to the sons of the poor. The rich, in his view, must give a gift, or the child should be rejected.

Thus the burden of Rudolph of Saint Trond's positive argument was that the father was under a binding obligation to send the boy's portion to the monastery along with the boy. To support his claims, he referred to the *ius Dei et hominum*, and to the *lex optima ecclesiae* and the *leges imperiales*.[15] However, he did not cite these texts or specify them more exactly. Presumably, the terms *ius hominum* and the *leges imperiales* referred to the Code of Justinian, which provided that the undisposed goods and rights of a man entering monastic life should follow him.[16] The *lex optima ecclesiae* and the *ius Dei* are equally mysterious terms. It is recorded that Rudolph compiled a collection of canons and of scriptural excerpts, and was presumably familiar with earlier collections.[17] These terms may refer to adaptations of Justinian's law that had found their way into canonical collections,[18] or to certain biblical and patristic texts that he felt supported his view.[19] Indeed, there is a possibility that the terms were mere rhetorical embellishments to strengthen a weak case, a case without the support of prestigious *auctoritates*.

In addition to this positive task of proving that it was the father's duty to give his son's share to the monastery, Rudolph also set himself the negative task of rebutting the charges of simony made against the monks of Saint Panteleon. The main question at issue, raised by the rich man and his supporters, was the propriety of the monastery's refusal to receive an oblate without a gift. They had charged that the requirement of a gift with an entrant was simony. Rudolph attacked the sincerity of this charge, attributing it to the simple greed of the father.[20] However, he did make two attempts in his letter to deny that the reception of new monks with required gifts was, in fact, simony. He assumed that one of the characteristics of a simoniacal act was its clandestine nature. Using this assumption, he denied that an open, public gift made at an oblation could be simoniacal. "The holy Benedict orders that not a hidden, but a solemn gift be made to the monastery, which that wretch, seized by the furies, calls simony."[21] This argument was not developed at all, probably because a forced gift, even if public, was of questionable propriety and of dubious freedom from simony.

The second, more-sustained argument put forward to deny that a forced gift was simoniacal was that based on the father's obligation to give the boy's portion along with him. For if the father was obliged to give, then a forced gift was nothing more than the monastery seeking its due.

> For that portion, which ought to come to the son in the world, should by the law of God and of men follow him to the church to which he wishes to hand him over to God. However, to demand and to wish to have what is just is no simony, but much more is it rapine and avarice to keep what he ought justly to give.[22]

Rudolph pursued this argument and developed it, but finally he apparently could not find in it a convincing defense of forced gifts. For he admitted that the monks were wrong to demand a gift, and he advised them to proceed with caution in the matter.

> Therefore, brethren, pull back from a man of this type and don't touch his uncleanness, lest you seem both to join in idolatry through his greed and to incur the mark of simony because of it. Just as it is your duty to demand nothing from him or from anyone else for an affair of this type, so it was his duty, if he were a man of God and not of Mammon, to make a gift from the portion of his estate that would come to the son, along with him to the church that must hereafter feed and clothe him. But since he does not wish to do this, and you cannot and ought not to force him, but only to exhort piously, then he cannot and ought not to force you if you do not wish to receive his son.

Therefore, beloved brethren, flee every kind of simony, removing your hand from every gift. Very subtle simony is the art of the devil. It is threefold, . . . : for it is connected by three strands: undue service, gift, and flattery. Often, by these three at once, sometimes by one of them, he [the devil] trips up feet that seem to walk well, he binds up the eyes of some who think they have lynx-eyes. . . . If anyone offers to you himself or his son for reception in the monastery, with a sound eye of the mind and with full purity of heart, without any evil greed, may he hear through you the advice of Saint Augustine and the precept of Saint Benedict's Rule. . . . If he hears and obeys, it is well, you have saved his soul from death; if he does not obey, it is no iniquity or sin for you if you do not receive him. . . . Dear brothers, it is a major task in such affairs to retain great purity of mind, and no greed of avarice, since, just as every man who sees a woman and lusts after her has committed fornication in his heart, so every man who, through wicked greed, demands or desires anything, or even acts in hope of retribution, from ecclesiastical goods, is made a simóniac, and if not before the people, then certainly before the eye of God.[23]

In his treatment of this new problem, Rudolph of Saint Trond admitted that the charge made by the boy's father was, indeed, possible. He sought for the monks of Saint Panteleon to avoid both the appearance and the reality of such simony. At the same time he wished to preserve the custom of accompanying a new monk with an entrance gift. Indeed, his major line of defense for the monks was to argue that the gift was, according to the law of God and of men, obligatory on the part of the boy's father, because he owed to the boy and to the monastery what he would have given to the oblate if the child had remained in secular life.

Rudolph recommended specifically that the monks meet with the father and remind him in a pious, friendly way of his duty in the matter.[24] But they ought not to demand from him a gift. If he persisted in his refusal to give anything, then their course of action was to refuse entrance to the boy. Rudolph therefore left entrance contingent on money, and he never came successfully to grips with the father's accusation that had touched off the controversy:

If indeed a rich commoner is easily admitted, [and] a nobler person coming simply [i.e., without a gift] is driven away by many excuses, then it appears obvious that not the person, but the money is sought.

> And when he, who at first was repudiated, has brought a sack of money and has merited the formerly denied entrance, who does not see how much simony is committed here?[25]

Rudolph accepted as normal and just the custom according to which entrants, especially from the wealthy classes, were accompanied by a gift.

> Monasteries of monks have not been set up so that they may indiscriminately receive, clothe, and nourish at the expense of the church the sons of greedy rich men and [that] their fathers, eager for greed and avarice, may satisfy their money-bags from the due portion of their sons.[26]

In the case of such men, Rudolph felt that it was acceptable for the monks to bargain with the father and to refuse to receive his son if they didn't receive the gift that they thought appropriate. Thus, in spite of his opposition to simony, Rudolph went far to confirm the accusation that it was not the person but the money that was sought. To Rudolph's scale of values, simony was bad; but greed on the part of the new monk or his family was, in its way, worse.

Rudolph may indeed have been criticized by contemporaries for this reluctance to fault the monks vigorously enough for their admissions practices. The seventeenth-century scholar Mabillon recorded the following précis of the final books of Rudolph's lost *Seven Books against Simoniacs*: "In the fifth [book], he accuses himself that, in speaking of monks, he covers up their simonies. In the next two books, he cleanses himself of charges of this type."[27] The work in question seems to be, in chronology, the second of his two lost works on simony, and may indeed have been written in response to criticisms of the letter to Sibertus.[28] In any case, Mabillon's notice indicated that the problem of monastic simony was under discussion in the 1120s and 1130s in Rudolph of Saint Trond's cultural sphere.

Gerhoh of Reichersberg

Gerhoh of Reichersberg (1093–1169), the prolific polemicist for reform in the empire, left an interesting testimony to the new issue of simoniacal entry in his *Libellus de eo, Quod princeps mundi huius iam iudicatus sit*, or *Liber de simoniacis*.[29] The occasion for the composition of the work was a dispute about one of Gerhoh's theological views He upheld the position that the sacraments performed by heretics were *irrita*, without effect.[30] When he explained his position to Bernard of Clairvaux at Rome in 1133 and again at Bamberg in 1135, he was not able to convince the latter that his views were correct. Gerhoh therefore wrote this tract to Bernard, citing arguments and authorities to justify his position in the matter.[31] Ernst Sackur, who edited the tract in the *Monumenta Germaniae historica*, dated its composition to a period not long after the meeting of Gerhoh and Bernard at Bamberg in March 1135. Damian Van Den Eynde, who recently studied the entire corpus of Gerhoh's works, has shown that the work was revised three times by its author. The first revision, dated to the year from March 1135 to 1136 by Van Den Eynde, added a new conclusion,[32] in which Gerhoh wrote a brief disquisition on a new form of simony that had appeared in his own day.

> However, it is convenient now to say something about that most wicked plague, simony. Indeed, among all the little foxes which demolish vineyards, no little fox is worse or more clever than simony. For as a certain one says, "By what knot do I hold a face changing as Proteus?" Thus, we could say, by what knot may we hold simony, that very clever little fox, multifarious in aspect, a thousand-formed in dress, and almost always dissimilar not only to the other little foxes, but even to itself; so much so that when he destroys the vineyards of Christ, he sometimes appears in the costume of the vintner himself. For when he has begun to be recognized in any particular one of his pelts, he immediately puts on another, and sometimes he makes believe he is planting the vines which he is devastating. Sometimes and often this little fox is captured by the wise hunters of Christ and his pelt is taken. But now he finds such a pelt in which he can scarcely be recognized, when he uses craftiness in it, not in the way of a fox nor does he appear as a wild beast, but as if a tame sheep. For when the officials of monasteries demand gifts from those whom they receive in their congregation, they cover over that simoniacal avarice by the name of "offering"; quite improperly, for an offering is one thing, an exaction another. What is offered freely is one thing, another thing what is taken and forced even from unwilling persons. The blessed

Benedict in his Rule did not order [it] to be done thus: no rather, he forbade that to be done, teaching that poor people, who offer their sons, simply make a petition; however, he did not permit anything to be demanded from rich parents, but if they offered anything voluntarily, he agreed that it could be received, because a thing thus received could be called an offering, not an exaction. Indeed, when Christ was recommending to a certain rich young man a perfect conversion, he did not say, "Go, sell what you have, and bring it to me," but rather he said, "Give to the poor, and come follow me (Luc. 18, 22)." Also, when the apostle Peter was ruling the common life at Jerusalem, he demanded no one's goods, although he received as a voluntary offering those things placed at his feet. He did not demand that Ananias and Saphira hand over their possessions to Christ; but when the possessions were already offered, he demanded them for Christ and he exercised due punishment against the fraudulent holders of them.[33]

In this text Gerhoh treated briefly chapter 59 of the *Rule*, as Rudolph of Saint Trond had done, but he came to a diametrically opposed conclusion. Gerhoh used as his touchstone of judgment the voluntary nature of the entrance gift. He insisted that even the rich parent must be free to choose whether or not to make a gift with his child. Offerings were acceptable; exactions, under whatever name, were not. In addition to oblates, those adults who sought a *perfecta conversio* or who wished to join the *vita communis* could give of their goods if they wished, but they should not be forced to give.

It seems clear that Gerhoh regarded this practice of monastic leaders as a new form of that fox, simony, which can hide under all sorts of externally pious appearances.[34] The earlier chapters of this study have made clear that economic transactions accompanying entry were far older than 1135–36. Therefore, what this text testifies to is the relatively recent recognition, in Gerhoh's experience, of such transactions as simony.

There is an interesting methodological point to be made here in support of the recent date for the emergence of the issue of simoniacal entry. The *Liber de simoniacis*, in which this text appeared, was marked by a heavy use of authorities to prove its points.[35] The pages of the text are studded with quotations from papal letters, councils, and the fathers. Gerhoh of Reichersberg obviously commanded a wide arsenal of proof texts and liked to use them to buttress his views. Yet when criticizing this simony connected with entry into religion, he did a methodological *volte-face*. He could apparently find as authorities only Christ's advice to the rich young man;[36] the exemplum of Ananias and Saphira from the Acts of the Apostles;[37] and chapter 59 of Benedict's *Rule*, whose stress he had to change slightly in order to make it say what he wanted.[38] One may conclude that Gerhoh's sensitivity to simony was offended by forced "gifts" at entry into religion, but, as far as his citations show, he had almost no acceptable proof texts directly relevant to the issue. To use twelfth-century terms, he had *ratio* on his side, but only weak and sparse *auctoritates* and those mostly biblical.

Gratian

It remained for the canonist Gratian, who may have been a monk himself, to define this problem of simony and to point to a consistent approach to it. The critical factor in making payment for entry into religion a recognized form of simony was Gratian's decision to include a section to that effect in his systematic treatment of canon law, the *Decretum*. *Causa* I, *questio* II, was devoted to the problem "Whether money may be demanded for entrance to a monastery, and if demanded should it be paid?"[39] This was an important addition to the stock themes normally treated by canonists.[40]

Gratian composed his *Decretum* sometime between 1139 and 1150, and his difficulties in treating the problem reveal the state of the question before his own work.[41] Gratian's normal mode of procedure in the *causae*, or divisions, of his work was to state a case and then to answer certain questions about it. His answers were framed around *auctoritates*, or authoritative texts, drawn from councils, papal decretals, the fathers of the church, and other sources. By means of reasonings and comments, traditionally called *dicta Gratiani*, he sought to harmonize these often disparate and contradictory texts, and thereby to answer the questions that he had posed for himself. The original title of his compilation, *The*

Concordance of Discordant Canons, revealed the aim of the work and the procedure of harmonization that it followed.[42]

The problem of simony in entrance to religious houses was a difficult one for Gratian to treat according to his normal method, because he lacked one of the components for a solution. To state the matter clearly, Gratian, like Rudolph and Gerhoh, apparently did not have acceptable *auctoritates* to prove that payment to enter religious life was simony. The earlier canonical collections that he used as sources, such as those of Burchard of Worms and Ivo of Chartres, contained no texts directly relevant to the problem. The reason for this lack of help from earlier collections is not difficult to determine. The issue was a new one, almost unknown before Gratian's time. It was not one of the traditional questions of canon law, but it was in fact formulated by Gratian and his generation.

The case that Gratian set for himself to solve was stated in the prologue to *causa* I: "A certain man having a son offered him to a very rich monastery; he paid ten pounds demanded by the abbot and the brethren, so that his son might be received, but the latter was unaware of this by benefit of his age."[43] Gratian then proceded in the prologue to state one side and then the other of the argument about whether such a payment was licit. Here are his arguments in favor of gifts.

> Whether this is done licitly is proved by the course of both Testaments. For it is read in the first book of Kings that Anna took Samuel with her, after he was weaned, with three calves, three measures of wheat, and an amphora of wine to the house of the Lord in Silo. In the Acts of the Apostles it is read that "there was one heart and one spirit in the multitude of believers" nor did anyone call anything which they possessed to be his own; but all things were common to them. Each of them sold his fields, and placed their prices before the feet of the apostles. One of them, Ananias by name, fell dead before the feet of the apostle, having accepted a sentence of curse because he kept a part to himself, and so did his wife.
>
> Hence, it appears clearly, that those about to enter a monastery ought to offer their goods to the officials, and they ought not otherwise to be received unless they offer their possessions.[44]

This was a conclusion similar to that which Rudolph of Saint Trond defended, and which led the latter to justify the denial of entry to those who did not offer a gift. Gratian went on in the prologue to reject this view in part and to modify it in part.

> But, it is one thing to offer one's goods voluntarily, it is another to pay demands. Anna, the mother of Samuel, offered to the priests not things exacted or sought, but gifts [given] freely. The believers offered their goods freely to the apostles, so that they might serve the needs of those in want. It was not permitted to them to possess the goods while the persecution of the unbelievers continued. Also, Ananias was not damned because he was unwilling to offer his goods, but because he lied to the Holy Spirit [and] he defrauded partially the prices which he handed over to the apostles.
>
> Therefore, by these authorities, it is not permitted to demand anything from those about to enter, but [it is permitted] to receive things offered freely, since the former is damnable, but the latter is not.[45]

Thus Gratian criticized the Old and New Testament texts cited, among others, by Rudolph of Saint Trond to defend the insistence on gifts from entrants. Gratian argued, as Gerhoh of Reichersberg did, that the gift must be given freely, and could not be demanded, or even asked for, *petita*.

This prologue to *causa* I, *questio* II, was followed in Gratian's normal method of argumentation by ten chapters of *auctoritates* and four comments, or *dicta Gratiani*. The prologue and the four comments, that is, Gratian's own contribution, were the decisive places in which it was asserted that to demand payment, and to pay, for entry into religion were simoniacal. It is striking that the ten authoritative texts cited in the question are, with one exception, related to the problem obliquely, if at all.

The exception was chapter two, which was an apocryphal letter of Pope Boniface I, supposedly written in the early fifth century to the monks of Cagliari in Sardinia. In fact, the letter is a forgery that appears, as far as I can determine, nowhere else but in Gratian's *Decretum*.[46] It was entitled by Gratian, or his editors, "From those who come to conversion nothing should be demanded, nor should anyone be invited to conversion for a price." However, it dealt in fact solely with the second part of that title, that is, the invitation to conversion for a price.

The brethren of an abbey apparently sought a monk from another house to join theirs, perhaps as their abbot. The monks of the second abbey asked for a payment, because they were poor and were giving up a valuable asset. The monks of the first house consulted Pope Boniface, and he wrote the following reply.

> We have never read that the disciples of the Lord or those converted to their service brought anyone to the worship of God by means of a gift. . . . We also know that "every best offering and every perfect gift is from above," from whence he accepts the gift of good will who decides by a holy decision of deliberation to serve God freely. It stands, therefore, that he who accepts a price for any reception in a church sells a gift of God . . . ; the importunate man offering the price buys [a gift of God]. It is not necessary to draw the conclusion which follows about sellers and buyers of a divine gift. . . . Nevertheless, if he whom you seek is very useful to your need, let him come, let him begin to serve God freely, and let him bear piously the burden of his rule. Afterward, the Roman church permits you, as if by a kind of grant, to offer some gifts to his church as a comfort to the brethren, so long as every pact is absent, every agreement ceases, and there is no loss to your church.[47]

This letter forbade anyone to be paid to come to a religious house, because the desire to convert was a gift of God and ought not to be subject to venal treatment. However, the letter said nothing explicit about the man who paid for reception or the abbot who demanded payment to receive a new monk.

This text of the Pseudo-Boniface was, as noted above, an exception to the statement that the authorities cited in *causa* I, *questio* II, did not refer to simony in entrance to religious houses. The other chapters contained diverse material. Chapter one was a canon from the Council of Braga (572) that forbade bishops to demand anything for dedicating a church. Chapter two was the letter of the Pseudo-Boniface. Chapter three was a canon of a Roman council that forbade exactions by lesser officials on the occasion of the ordination of a priest. Chapter four was a quotation from Pope Gregory I that reinforced the prohibition to bishops and their officials about demanding gifts from those to be ordained. After these four *auctoritates*, Gratian inserted his own comment.

> By the authority of Boniface, it is shown openly that, just as no one is to be invited for a price to conversion, so likewise to no one should

entrance to a church be offered by the intervention of money. By the authority of Gregory, it is given to be understood that for entrance of a church it is not permissible to demand money, but that which is given freely may be accepted.[48]

Chapters five through ten of the *questio* dealt with the issue of whether a cleric of independent means ought to be supported at the expense of the church. The decision reached was:

> But, by these authorities, they are not prohibited from being received by a church, who were formerly rich and abandoned it all, as Peter, Matthew, and Paul; or those who distributed it to the poor, as Zacheus; or those who added it to the possessions of the church. . . . But, they [are prohibited] who, residing in the homes of their parents or being unwilling to leave their goods, wish to be supported by ecclesiastical wealth.[49]

These texts were relevant to one who entered the secular clergy and who had a choice as to the disposition of his property. However, they do not seem to be germane to the individual who became a monk or a regular canon, since his vows of poverty and of communal living effectively denied him any way to live at home or to retain his wealth personally. Therefore, such an individual would never be in the situation of being independently wealthy and also living from the monastic endowment as a monk.

Gratian concluded *causa* I, *questio* II, with an observation about the net result of his argument and his authorities: "It stands clearer than light by the authority of many that it is not permitted to demand money from those about to enter a monastery, lest he who demands and he who pays incur the crime of simony."[50]

However, the texts cited by Gratian had proved or demonstrated no such thing. Except for the letter of the Pseudo-Boniface, which referred to a man's being paid to come to a monastery, Gratian's *auctoritates* did not refer directly to simony in entrance to monasteries, as his initial case had been proposed. It is significant to note that one of Gratian's successors or copyists recognized this weakness and took steps to buttress the argument. Possibly sometime between 1140 and 1170, the third chapter of *causa* I, *questio* II, was added as a *palea*.[51] The new chapter began with a citation of the Council of Melfi, held under Urban II in 1089: "Let no abbot presume to take or demand a price from those coming to conversion, on the occasion of any pact."[52] The chapter was completed, perhaps at some later time, by a canon from a sixth-century Roman council forbidding anyone to seek profit out of priestly ordinations.[53]

In spite of any weakness that Gratian's argument may have had, his decision to include monastic simony in his *Decretum* was crucial for the issue. His opinions, expressed in the prologue and *dicta*, and his texts made simony in the entrance to religious houses a problem for canonists and, through them, for the whole church.

Thus one can date the concern about simoniacal entry to the period between 1123, the earliest date for Rudolph of Saint Trond's letter, and 1150, the latest date proposed for the composition of the *Decretum*. Other sources confirm that thirty-year period as formative for the issue of simoniacal entry. A council at London in 1127 issued a canon condemning "fixed exactions of money for receiving monks, canons and nuns."[54] In the late 1120s Urban II's canon of Melfi, directed against payments for entry, was incorporated into at least two canonical collections.[55]

There was nothing inevitable in the development that led to payments at entry being classified as simoniacal. The issue could have been ignored, as it had been for centuries, or could have continued to be classified as "filthy gain" or as a spiritual danger to the new monk. However, the twelfth century was acutely aware of the problem of simony, and it was natural for entry payments to be seen from the perspective of payments for a holy thing. When Gratian decided that such payments were indeed simoniacal, that view drove out all competing opinions, and a new intellectual and practical problem was posed for solution.

---

1. When Rudolph entered Saint Trond, Abbot Thierry commissioned him to make "quasdamque utilissimas compilationes, plenas plurimarum divinarum sententiarum scribendas et multorum decreta conciliorum" (*Chronique de l'abbaye de Saint-Trond*, bk. 8, chap. 3, ed. C. de Borman (Liège, 1877), 1: 122).

2. "Praeter istud Chronicon Rodolfus alia quaedam opuscula scripsit, quorum ipse in eo Chronico meminit, in primis, . . . volumen septem librorum quos contra simoniacos scripsit." Mabillon found a copy of the *Septem libri contra simoniacos* in the library of Gembloux, and he summarized it thus: "In primo libro, primam et maximam haeresim esse simoniam ostendit. In secundo deplorat, quod nihil maximum aut minimum tunc esset in domo Dei, quod qualicumque modo non esset venale. In tertio, ab agris incipiens, id est a presbyteris villarum, progreditur usque ad rectores et magistratus ecclesiarum, ostendens quomodo soleant clerici fieri, et ecclesias suscipere. In quarto ab agris transit ab [sic] urbes, agens de venditionibus praebendarum et omnium officiorum, quae sunt in Ecclesia. In quinto sibi objicit, quod de monachis loquens, simonias eorum dissimulet. In duobus posterioribus libris purgat se de ejusmodi objectis" (J. Mabillon, ed., *Vetera analecta*, 2d ed. [Paris, 1723], p. 471). W. Levison, "A Rhythmical Poem of about 1100 (by Rodulf of Saint-Trond?) against Abuses, in Particular Simony and Dancing in Churchyards," *Medievalia et humanistica* 4 (1946):12, n. 31, lists the four known, and presumably lost, manuscripts of the *Septem libri contra simoniacos*. The poem edited by Levison, if genuine, is further evidence of Rudolph's interest in the issue of simony.

3. "Oblatus est aliquando quidam puerulus nobis a parentibus suis, et devotione sua cum puero de facultate sua obtulerunt quantum voluerunt. Vidit hoc quidam ditior facultate, sed pauperior et avarior voluntate et invidit, statimque etiam suum filium suscipi rogavit. Multum temporis est in petendo et contradicendo consumptum, quoniam eundem puerum parentes vi intrudere voluerunt nudum" (de Borman, *Chronique*, 1:243–44). The letter of Rudolph to Sibertus is also available in MGH, *SS*, vol. 10, ed. R. Koepke (Hanover, 1852), pp. 319–24.

4. "Tandem pater eius familiariter conventus, ut de rebus quas sibi concesserat Deus aliquid conferret aeclesiae, coepit furere, dicens se nolle symoniam incurrere. Hac arreptus furia, multa nos pulsavit iniuria, replevit fora et plateas, cives et aecclesiasticas movit personas, contestans apud nos precio constare quae iubemur gratis dare. 'Si enim, inquit, plebeius nummatus facile admittitur, generosior simpliciter veniens multum excusationum repagulis repellitur; patet profecto, quia non persona sed pecunia requiritur. Dumque is qui primum repudiatus fuerat, sacculum pecuniae attulerit et denegatum introitum meruerit, quis non videat quantum hic symonia operetur et valeat?' Et quia nota et urbana fuit persona, satis nos inquietavit hac infamia. Tandem iterum conventi a clericis et laicis, respondimus id quod prius, quia esset competens et iustum, nec canonico rigori contrarium, ut qui se vel quempiam suorum aecclesiae vellet sociare, dum haberet unde posset, in usus eiusdem aecclesiae deberet conferre. Illi autem: 'Ad hoc, inquiunt, sunt instituta coenobia, ut quicunque seculo voluerit renuntiare, licenter debeat intrare, nec paupertatis aut alicuius rei occasio huic erit obstaculo, quia quos Deus coadunat et sociat, bonis omnibus replet et saciat" (de Borman, *Chronique*, 1:244).

5. "De re ergo, pro qua humilitas vestra parvitatem nostram dignata est consulere, prope a scribendo manum subtraxeramus, cum nemo sit qui inde vos provocet ad audientiam vel qui trahat ad iudicium, et vobis non minus quam nobis sint nota inde sacrae scripturae et apostolica precepta. . . . Tales silenti irrisione magis sunt pretereundi, quam amabili illis contentionis fune diutius trahendi" (ibid., p. 246).

6. ". . . Pecuniosus homo sed parcus et avarus . . ." (ibid.).

7. "Palliare se vult nomine pietatis et dealbare, ut quasi propter symoniam . . . videatur servare quod propter avariciam servat. Si vult vitare symoniam et exuere avariciam, faciat justiciam, nam symonia et avaricia non possunt fieri cum iusticia. Sed quam eum rogamus facere iusticiam, ut fugiat symoniam et avariciam? Inter filios aeque dividat quod propter filios sive propter vitandam symoniam, ut ipse mentitur, retinet et servat. Sed a se unum vult emittere et Deo dare et sanctae aecclesiae. Bonum hoc est utique; sed et nichilominus bonum et iustum est, ut mittat post illum sive cum illo partem suam.

SIMONIACAL ENTRY INTO RELIGIOUS LIFE

Sed credo ad hoc vult emittere e seculo, ut partem illius retineat in sacculo" (ibid., pp. 247–48).

8. "... Si post oblationem filii retinuerit quae illi debentur, idolatra erit et sacrilegus, idolatra propter avariciam, sacrilegus propter Dei et sanctae aecclesiae rapinam" (ibid., p. 248).

9. *Ourscamp*, no. 83, ca. 1140. C. Landry, *La Mort civile des religieux dans l'ancien droit français, étude historique et critique* (Paris, 1900); E. Durtelle de Saint-Sauveur, *Recherches sur l'histoire de la théorie de la mort civile des religieux* (Rennes, 1910).

10. "Reddat ergo illi quod suum est, reddat quod illi servabat. Sed: 'Mortuus est' inquit. Utique mortuus seculo, sed vivit Deo. Pauperibus Christi et aecclesiae pars ipsius detur. Illis debetur, ad quos perrexit, Christo debetur, ad eum enim perrexit" (de Borman, *Chronique*, 1:248).

11. Ibid., p. 257. Abelard, in a sermon on almsgiving, expressed a similar view about the greater merit of the voluntary poor over those who are poor by necessity: "Hi quidem, qui saeculo penitus abrenuntiantes apostolicam imitantur vitam, veriores sunt pauperes, et Deo propinquiores" (Migne, 178:568). The view that monks and others living under a rule were *veriores pauperes* was incorporated into canonical collections in two texts attributed to Gregory (*Quinque compilationes antiquae*, ed. E. Friedberg [Leipzig, 1882], pp. 36–37, Comp. I, bk. III, tit. 14; tit. 21).

12. "Bene dicis: 'Res quas habeo pauperibus confero.' Res igitur quas habes quibusvis pauperibus confer, sed res quae sunt filii tui dimitte eum ad monasterium sequi, ubi inter pauperes Christi ad sequendum Dominum eum tradis" (de Borman, *Chronique*, 1:257).

13. "De rebus autem suis aut in praesenti petitione promittant sub iureiurando, quia numquam per se, numquam per suffectam personam nec quolibet modo ei aliquando aliquid dant aut tribuunt occasionem habendi; vel certe si hoc facere noluerint et aliquid offerre volunt in eleemosynam monasterio pro mercede sua, faciant ex rebus quas dare volunt monasterio donationem. . . ." (Benedict's *Rule*, chap. 59).

14. "Item in sententiam de filiis nobilium vel pauperum: 'Si aliquid offerre voluerint in elemosina monasterio pro mercede sua, faciant ex rebus quas dare volunt monasterio donationem.' Audit forsitan et laetatur, quod in voluntate eius hoc ponat beatus Benedictus. Et certe vir sanctus in nullius voluntate hoc poneret, nisi sciret, quod debere hoc fieri sanctum et iustum et pium esset. Nunc, quia quod sanctum et iustum et pium est, non potest intrare istius voluntatem, habeat sibi res suas in perditionem. Vult ut vacuus suscipiatur eius filius, faciat ut de eorum sit numero, de quibus scribit beatus Benedictus. 'Qui vero, inquit, ex toto nil habent, simpliciter petitionem faciant, et cum oblatione offerant filium suum coram testibus' " (de Borman, *Chronique*, 1:249).

15. "Nam portio illa, quae debebat filio contingere in saeculo, iure Dei et hominum deberet eum sequi ad aecclesiam, ad quam eum vult tradere Deo" (ibid., p. 246).

16. *Corpus juris civilis*, vol. 3, *Novellae*, ed. R. Schoell and W. Kroll (Berlin, 1895), V, 5; CXXIII, 38. For a historical treatment of Justinian's measures concerning the property of religious, see R. Orestano, "Beni dei monachi e monasteri nella legislazione Giustinianea," in *Studi in onore di Pietro de Francisci* (Milan, 1956), 3:561–94.

17. De Borman, *Chronique*, 1:122.

18. C. G. Mor, "Le Droit romain dans les collections canoniques des Xe et XIe siècles," *Revue historique de droit français et étranger* 6 (1927): 512–24; and J. Imbert, "Le Droit romain dans les textes juridiques carolingiens," in *Studi in onore di Pietro de Francisci*, 3:61–67.

19. Rudolph relied heavily on a sermon of Augustine, whose theme was the criticism of men who say that they cannot give alms because they must provide for their sons.

Augustine argued that if a son died, his share should follow him as alms (Sermon 86, Migne, Vol. 38, cols. 526-29). In addition, Rudolph cited Benedict's *Rule*, chap. 59; Exodus 23: "Non apparebis in conspectu meo vacuus"; the exempla of Jesus being offered with gifts in the temple and of Anna offering Samuel with gifts to God; the exemplum of Ananias and Saphira, who were struck dead for holding back part of their gift; and the *vitae* of Saint Lucia and of Saint Lawrence, both of whom gave property and life to God.

20. The father was described as "miser et avaricia excaecatus" (de Borman, *Chronique*, 1:246); he was called a liar (p. 247); "what was holy and just and pious could not be part of his motivation" (p. 249); he was being led by "an evil spirit" (p. 250); he and his supporters were men who "spiritu avaritiae suae et parcitatis gravati, deorsum feruntur per vacua obloquii sui campestria" (p. 261).

21. "Non occultam sed solempnem rogat fieri beatus Benedictus ad monasterium donationem, quod iste miser arreptus a furiis appellat symoniam" (ibid., pp. 248-49).

22. "Nam portio illa, quae debebat filio contingere in saeculo, iure Dei et hominum deberet eum sequi ad aecclesiam, ad quam eum vult tradere Deo. Exigere autem et velle habere quod iustum est, symonia nulla est, magis vero rapina est et avaricia retinere quod iuste debeat dare" (ibid., p. 246).

23. "Recedite ergo, fratres, recedite ab huiusmodi homine et immundum eius nolite tangere, ne videamini et per eius avariciam idolatriae communicare, et per eandem notam symoniae incurrere. Sicut vestrum est nichil ab eo vel ab alio aliquo pro huiusmodi re exigere, ita et eius erat, si homo Dei esset et non mammonae, de portione hereditatis, quae filio deberet contingere, oblationem cum eo ad aecclesiam facere, quae eum amplius deberet et nutrire et vestire. Sed sicut ipse non vult hoc facere, et vos non potestis nec debetis eum compellere, sed pie tantum commonere, ita et, si filium eius non vultis suscipere, non potest nec debet ad hoc vos cogere" (ibid., p. 250).

"Ergo, dilectissimi fratres, fugite omne genus symoniae, excutientes manus vestras ab omni munere. Ars est diaboli subtilissima symonia. Triplex est . . . ; nam quibus connectitur tria sunt fila, obsequium, manus, lingua. His plerumque tribus simul, aliquando horum quovis uno quorundam innodat pedes, qui videbantur gradi simpliciter, quorundam prestringit oculos, qui se putabant linceos. , . . Si quis vel se vel filium suum obtulerit vobis in coenobio suscipiendum, simplici mentis oculo et tota cordis puritate, sine omni mala cupiditate, audiat per vos sancti Augustini consilium et regulae sancti Benedicti preceptum. . . . Si audierit et obaudierit, bene, salvastis animam eius a morte; si non obaudierit, neque iniquitas vestra neque peccatum si eum non receperitis. . . . Fratres karissimi, magnum opus est in tali re magnam habere mentis puritatem et nullam avariciae cupiditatem, quia, sicut omnis qui viderit mulierem ad concupiscendum eam, iam mechatus est eam in corde suo, ita omnis qui de aecclesiasticis donis mala cupiditate aliquid exigit vel concupiscit, plus dicam, vel in spe agit retributionis, symoniacus fit, et si non hic coram populo, certe coram divino oculo" (ibid., pp. 261-62).

24. ". . . Audiat per vos sancti Augustini consilium et regulae sancti Benedicti preceptum. . . ." (ibid., p. 262). In his initial letter Sibertus said that the monks had in fact summoned the father for a friendly discussion (p. 244). The father saw this as simoniacal pressure: "Quid calumpniaris servos Dei de symonia, pro eo quod familiariter te convenientes exuere voluerunt avaricia et post avariciam idolatria, nichil a te requirentes nisi quae dictat iusticia, exigit misericordia. . . ." (p. 251).

25. Ibid., p. 244.

26. "Monachorum coenobia non sunt ad hoc instituta, ut avarorum divitum filios inconsulte suscipiant, vestiant et nutriant aecclesiae stipendiis, et patres eorum de debita filiorum portione maiori studentes avariciae et questui satisfaciant suis marsupiis. . . ." (ibid., p. 259).

27. "In quinto sibi objicit, quod de monachis loquens, simonias eorum dissimulet. In duobus posterioribus libris purgat se de ejusmodi objectis" (*Vetera analecta*, p. 471).

28. In the prologue to the *Septem libri contra simoniacos*, as cited by Mabillon, Rudolph referred to a work of his called *Laberinthum primae simonis*, which must have predated the *Septem libri*. There is no way to prove that the *Septem libri* followed the letter to Sibertus, but it is suggestive that the *Septem libri*, from Mabillon's description, was directed partly against critics who said Rudolph was lenient to monastic simony.

29. The tract was edited by E. Sackur in MGH, *Libelli de Lite*, 3:239-72.

30. Sackur's historical introduction to the *Liber de simoniacis* discusses the events leading to its composition (ibid., 3:239-40). J. T. Gilchrist, "*Simoniaca haeresis* and the Problem of Orders from Leo IX to Gratian," in *Proceedings of the Second International Congress of Medieval Canon Law*, ed. S. Kuttner and J. J. Ryan (Vatican City, 1965), pp. 209-35, discusses at length the problem of the significance of the term *irrita* when it was used during the sacramental quarrels of the eleventh and early twelfth centuries.

31. MGH, *Libelli de Lite*, 3:240. On Gerhoh's attempts to convince Bernard of his views, see D. Van den Eynde, *L'Oeuvre littéraire de Géroch de Reichersberg* (Rome, 1957), pp. 34-42. P. Classen, *Gerhoch von Reichersberg: eine Biographie mit einem Anhange über die Quellen, ihre handschriftliche Überlieferung und ihre Chronologie* (Wiesbaden, 1960), pp. 78-86, discusses the origins of the work.

32. Van den Eynde, *L'Oeuvre*, p. 40. Classen, *Gerhoch*, pp. 408-9, agrees in essence with Van den Eynde's dating of the *Liber* and of the revision.

33. "Libet autem adhuc dicere aliqua de iniquissima peste, symonia. Inter omnes quippe vulpeculas, que demoliuntur vineas, nulla vulpecula nequior vel astutior symonia. Nam, ut quidam ait,
Quo teneo nodo mutantem Prothea vultus?
sic nos dicere possumus, quo teneamus nodo symoniam vulpeculam astutissimam, vultu multifariam, habitu milleformem, et pene semper non solum aliis vulpeculis, verum et sibimetipsi dissimilem, usque adeo, ut cum vineas Christi demoliatur, interdum in ipsius vinitoris habitu cernatur? Cum enim in una qualibet sua pelle dignosci ceperit, continuo aliam induit, et vineas, quas devastat, interdum se plantare simulat. Aliquando et multotiens haec vulpecula a sagacibus Christi venatoribus deprehensa est, et pelle sua spoliata, at nunc pellem talem invenit in qua vix dignosci possit, quando in ea non more vulpis utitur astutia, nec omnino apparet quasi bestia, sed quasi ovis domestica. Cum enim cenobiorum prelati ab his, quos in suum consortium recipiunt munera exigunt, ipsam symoniacam avaritiam nomine oblationis tegunt: nimirum satis improprie, cum aliud sit oblatio, aliud exactio; aliud quod sponte offertur, aliud quod etiam ab invitis aufertur et extorquetur. Non sic beatus Benedictus in regula sua precepit fieri: immo istud vetuit fieri, docens ut pauperes, qui pueros suos offerunt, simpliciter petitionem faciant, a divitibus autem parentibus non sinit quidem aliquid exigi; sed si quid sponte offerunt, acquiescit posse recipi, quod ita receptum potest appellari oblatio, non exactio, Christus etiam diviti cuidam perfectam conversionem suadens, non ait: Vade, vende que habes, et affer mihi; sed 'da,' inquit, 'pauperibus, et veni, sequere me.' Petrus quoque apostolus communem vitam Iherosolimis regens a nemine sua exigit: quamquam ea suis pedibus apposita, quasi voluntariam oblationem recepit. Ananiam et Saphiram sua Christo destinare non exegit; sed ea iam destinata Christo vendicavit, et in eorum fraudatores debitam vindictam exercuit" (MGH, *Libelli de Lite*, 3:268-69).

34. Gerhoh's insistence that simony has "a new skin," that of monastic entry payments, corroborates the view that such practices were only just beginning to be perceived as simoniacal about 1135-36.

35. One need only examine the text in the *MGH*, in which the editor used different type faces for the portions of the work citing authoritative texts. At its most extreme, Gerhoh's method of composition consisted in stringing together older texts, for example, pp. 249, 259. Van den Eynde, *L'Oeuvre*, p. 36, also notes Gerhoh's penchant for arguments well-buttressed by *auctoritates*.

36. Luke 18:18-25.

37. Acts 5:1-11.

38. The *Rule*, chap. 59, said simply, "But if they are unwilling to do this [i.e., disinherit the child] and they wish to offer something as a gift to the monastery for their own reward, may they make a donation to the monastery from gifts which they wish to give." In writing of forced gifts, Gerhoh strengthened Benedict's attitude by saying that "he forbade that to be done" and that "he did not permit anything to be demanded from rich parents." Gerhoh obviously read into the rule his own scruples about forced gifts and simony.

39. ". . . An pro ingressu monasterii pecunia sit exigenda, vel exacta persolvenda?" (*Corpus juris canonici*, vol. 1: *Decretum*, ed. E. Friedberg [Leipzig, 1879], p. 407).

40. The important pre-Gratian canonical collections, such as Burchard of Worms' *Decretorum libri viginti*, Migne, vol. 140, cols. 537-1058; and Ivo of Chartres' *Decretum*, ibid., vol. 161, cols. 59-1036, and his *Panormia*, ibid., vol. 161, cols. 1045-1344, had not given specific attention to simoniacal entry into religion.

41. The date of composition of the *Decretum* has been a much-discussed topic. P. Fournier, "Deux controverses sur les origines du Décret de Gratien," *Revue d'histoire et de littérature religieuse* 3 (1898): 235-80, reviews proposed dates of composition, offered from the twelfth to the fifteenth centuries, and discusses the critical reasons for and against each date. His conclusion is that the *Decretum* was composed about 1140 or shortly thereafter. This view is accepted by J. Rambaud-Buhot, *L'Age classique, 1140-1378* (Paris, 1965), p. 58. S. Kuttner, "Gratian," *Encyclopedia Britannica* (Chicago, 1968), 10: 707, suggests the period from 1139 to 1150 as that of composition. The most important recent dissent from this view has come from A. Vetulani, "Nouvelles vues sur le Décret de Gratien," in *La Pologne au Xe congrès international des sciences historiques à Rome* (Warsaw, 1955), pp. 83-105, who contends that the *Decretum* was composed circa 1105-20. This view has not been generally accepted. For a sympathetic criticism of Vetulani's position, see G. Fransen, "La Date du Décret de Gratien," *Revue d'histoire ecclésiastique* 51 (1956): 521-31, which defends the traditional date of about 1140 for the *Decretum*'s appearance.

42. S. Kuttner, *Harmony from Dissonance*: *An Interpretation of Medieval Canon Law* (Latrobe, Pa., 1960), offers a thoughtful essay on the procedures used by Gratian and other canonists to bring order out of their tangled sources and authorities. P. Torquebiau, "Corpus juris canonici," *DDC*, 4:616-20, has a useful illustration of Gratian's method of argument in the form of an analysis of his *distinctio* L.

43. "Quidam habens filium obtulit eum ditissimo cenobio; exactus ab abbate et a fratribus decem libras solvit, ut filius susciperetur, ipso tamen beneficio etatis hoc ignorante" (*causa* I, prologue).

44. "Hoc utrumque licite fieri, utriusque testamenti serie conprobatur. Legitur enim in primo libro Regum, quod Anna detulit secum Samuelum, postquam ablactatus fuerat, in tribus vitulis, et tribus modiis farinae, et amphora vini ad domum Dei in Sylo. I. In Actibus vero apostolorum legitur, quod 'multitudinis credentium erat cor unum et anima una,' nec aliquid eorum, que possidebant, quisquam proprium esse dicebat; sed erant illis omnia communia. Singuli vendebant predia sua, et ponebant precia eorum ante pedes apostolorum,

quorum unus, nomine Ananias, dum partem sibi reservaret, cum uxore sua Sapphira, sententia maledictionis accepta, ante pedes apostoli cecidit mortuus. 2. Hinc liquido aparet quod ingressuri monasterium sua debent offerre rectoribus, nec aliter sunt recipiendi, nisi sua obtulerint" (*causa* I, *q.* II, *pars.* 1).

45. "Sed aliud est sua sponte offerre, aliud exacta persolvere. Anna mater Samuelis non exacta neque petita, sed sponte munera sacerdotibus obtulit. Credentes sua sponte offerebant apostolis, ut indigentium necessitatibus deservirent, que instante persecutione infidelium eis possidere non licebat. Ananias quoque non ideo dampnatus est, quia sua nollet offerre, sed quia, Spiritui sancto mentitus, precia eorum, que apostolis obtulerat, ex parte fraudabat. Non ergo his auctoritatibus permittitur rectoribus ab ingressuris aliquid exigere, sed sponte oblata suscipere, quia illud dampnabile est, hoc vero minime" (ibid.).

46. C. S. Berardi, *Gratiani canones genuini ab apocryphis discreti.* . . . (Venice, 1777), part 2, pp. 241-43, notes that by reasons of style and of its complete absence outside the *Decretum*, the letter *Quam pio* of the Pseudo-Boniface must be apocryphal. A similar opinion was held by the *correctores romani* in their edition of 1584, and this was adopted by Friedberg, *Decretum*, col. 408. I have been able to find no evidence as to the age or purpose of the forgery; it is cited directly only in Gratian's work. There was in Rudolph of Saint Trond's letter to Sibertus an allusion that may be relevant to the problem: "Susceptiones igitur de aecclesiis et in aecclesiis maturarum et immaturarum personarum utique omnes debent gratis fieri. . . ." (de Borman, *Chronique*, 1: 249). Rudolph's letter in fact discussed only "susceptiones in aecclesiis," and the phrase "susceptiones de aecclesiis" received no comment. However, on the face of it, the phrase could refer to a practice similar to that criticized in *Quam pio*. If this interpretation is correct, then Rudolph's demand that "susceptiones de aecclesiis" be made without simony may indicate that the letter of the Pseudo-Boniface, or its views, were known outside Gratian's milieu.

47. "Numquam enim legimus Domini discipulos vel eorum ministerio conversos quempiam ad Dei cultum aliquo muneris interventu provocasse. . . . Scimus equidem, quod 'omne datum optimum, et omne donum perfectum desursum est,' a quo bonae voluntatis donum accipit qui sancto deliberationis arbitrio gratis Deo servire disponit. Restat ergo, ut qui pro aliqua ecclesiae susceptione munus accipit. Dei donum . . . vendat; munus autem largiens inportunus emat. Quid autem de divini doni venditoribus vel emptoribus consequatur, concludi necesse non est. . . . Verumtamen, si vestrae necessitati adeo est oportunus quem reperistis, dum tamen omnis absit pactio, omnis cesset conventio, nullaque vestrae ecclesiae fiat distractio, accedat, gratis Deo servire incipiat, suique regiminis devote gestet obsequium ac postmodum vos, quasi subsidii gratia, aliqua suae ecclesiae munera largiri fratrum solatio Romana permittit ecclesia" (*causa* I, *q.* II, canon 2 *Quam pio*).

48. "Auctoritate Bonifacii patenter ostenditur, quod, sicut nullus precio est invitandus ad conversionem, ita nulli pecuniae interventu ecclesiae largiri oportet ingressum. Auctoritate vero Gregorii datur intelligi, quod pro ingressu ecclesiae non licet pecuniam exigere, sed spontanee oblatam suscipere licet" (ibid., *dictum* after canon 4).

49. "Verum his auctoritatibus prohibentur ab ecclesia suscipi non illi, qui quondam fuerunt divites, et omnia reliquerunt, ut Petrus et Mattheus et Paulus, aut pauperibus distribuerunt, ut Zacheus, aut ecclesiae rebus adiunxerunt, . . . : sed illi, qui in domibus parentum residentes vel sua relinquere nolentes ecclesiasticis facultatibus pasci desiderant" (ibid., *dictum* after canon 7).

50. "Multorum auctoritatibus luce clarius constat, quod ab ingressuris monasterium non licet pecuniam exigere, ne et ille, qui exigit, et ille, qui solvit, symoniae crimen incurrat" (ibid., *dictum* after canon 10).

51. The problem of the *paleae*, i.e., additions to the *Decretum*, is disputed and complex. J. Rambaud-Buhot," Les *Paleae* dans le décret de Gratien," pp. 30–31, says that between 1140 and 1170 the *Decretum* received additions and corrections to fill gaps and to strengthen arguments. F. J. Gossmann, *Pope Urban II and Canon Law* (Washington, D.C., 1960), Catholic University of America Canon Law Studies, no. 403, studied the texts of Urban II as they appear in canonical collections. Out of twenty-four collections studied, the seventh canon of Melfi, Gratian's *palea*, appeared in only two, the Collection in Ten Parts, and the Collection of Saint Germain-des-Prés, both of which added the text as a supplement in the 1120s. On these collections see P. Fournier and G. Le Bras, *Histoire des collections canoniques en occident* (Paris, 1932), 2:285–306. The *palea* of Melfi was uncommon in canonical collections before the *Decretum*, and, indeed, the research of Madame Rambaud-Buhot, pp. 40–44, and of J. von Schulte, "Die *Paleae* im Dekret Gratians," *Sitzungsberichte der kaiserlichen Akademie der Wissenschaften*, Phil.-hist. Klasse no. 78 (1874): 287–312, indicate that in twelfth- and thirteenth-century manuscripts of the *Decretum*, this particular *palea* was not common.

52. "Nullus abbas precium sumere vel exigere ab eis, qui ad conversionem veniunt, aliqua pacti occasione presumat" (*causa* I, *q.* II, canon 3).

53. The text added to canon seven of Melfi was canon five of a council convoked at Rome by Gregory I about 595 (Mansi, 10: 435).

54. "Exactiones certas pecuniarum pro recipiendis canonicis, monachis, et sanctimonialibus, condempnamus" (*The Chronicle of John of Worcester, 1118–1140*, ed. J. R. H. Weaver [Oxford, 1908], Anecdota Oxoniensia, no. 13, p. 24).

55. The Collection in Ten Parts and the Collection of Saint-Germain-des-Prés, Gossmann, *Pope Urban II*, p. 94.

CHAPTER FIVE

The Canonists and
Simoniacal Reception

 Gratian's decision to dedicate a *questio* of his *Decretum* to simoniacal entry into religion was crucial for the evolution of the issue. Gratian's *Decretum* was one work in the long line of canonical collections. However, its use of certain technical innovations, such as illustrative cases and comments on the texts, and its avowed intention to harmonize and regularize the canon law, made it an outstanding example of its genre. Its appearance early in the intellectual revival of the twelfth century assured it of a place of importance in the schools. Although the *Decretum* never received official approbation from the church, it became the basic manual and source book for canonical studies in the second half of the twelfth century.[1] Training in canon law was a valuable asset for an ambitious man, and the *Decretum* was studied, glossed, and commented by many of those who attained high office in the church in the later twelfth century.[2]

It was the *Decretum*, with its format of authoritative texts and Gratian's own comments, that set the boundaries within which later canonists and moralists carried on the discussion of simony in the entrance to religious houses. As a legacy of a half-century of intense intellectual activity that centered on the *Decretum*, there survives an abundant, mostly unpublished, body of canonistic literature.[3] The comments on *causa* I, *questio* II, were the chief focus for a treatment of monastic simony that completed and expanded that of Gratian.

These commentaries were limited, more or less, to the issues raised by the *Decretum* and to the controversies in the schools about doubtful or disputed points in it. As a result of their common basis in the text of Gratian, the commentaries shared large amounts of traditional material and some stereotyped approaches. In addition, the canonists had the habit of quoting one another, often without acknowledgment, so that there was a considerable amount of overlapping comment. However, the canonists did differ in emphasis, in detail, and in particular opinions. Each succeeding commentator felt compelled to take account of, and to respond to, some of his predecessors on some issues. Thus later commentaries became more sophisticated as a result of the accumulation of opinions and of arguments. Certain issues were settled by a consensus of commentators, but many continued to be contested until the cessation of formal commentary on Gratian, in the early thirteenth century.[4]

The commentary as a literary form was, by its nature, discontinuous and disjointed, because of its obligation to follow the course of the authoritative text that was being commented. In the canonical commentaries on *causa* I, there was seldom a clear theoretical structure. Instead, the commentaries concentrated on interesting and disputed points. However, the decretists who wrote about simony in the entrance to religious life gave attention to six main issues, which they apparently thought required discussion and resolution.

I shall organize my discussion around the six issues. First, why was *ingressus monasterii*, entry to a monastery, a thing whose sale involved simony? Second, what difference was there between a payment for entry and an offering on the occasion of entry? Third, did the economic state of a religious house affect the problem of payment for entry? Fourth, could a man be induced to enter religious life for money? Fifth, what was to be done to the monk who was received simoniacally? Sixth, what was to be done with the money paid for entry?

1. Why Was the Entry of a Monastery a Thing Whose Sale or Purchase Involved Simony?

Gratian did not say in a direct way why the purchase of entry to a religious house was simoniacal. He noted in the prologue to *causa* I, *questio* III, that the *propositum religionis*, i.e., the religious state, was a spiritual thing.[5] This was no innovation, for it was a well-established view that the taking of the monastic habit was a second baptism. He noted in the same prologue that "not only those who receive spiritual things for a price, but also those who accept temporal things connected to spiritual things are judged simoniacs."[6] Thus he suggested that whether *ingressus monasterii* was itself a spiritual thing, or was merely connected to a spiritual thing, it was simoniacal to buy or sell it. Paucapalea, Gratian's earliest commentator, was content to allow the master's haziness by simply listing the position of monk among other ecclesiastical offices and orders, without further distinction.[7] Roland Bandinelli treated the issue succinctly: "But nothing ought to be demanded as a result of force or agreement for the acquisition of a holy thing, and therefore [it ought not to be demanded] for the entrance of a church."[8] However, as in the *Decretum* itself, Bandinelli's text left a certain ambiguity about whether the entry to a church was spiritual itself or an access to something spiritual.

The author of the *Summa Parisiensis*, writing about 1160, proposed an analysis that attempted to explain more clearly what made it simoniacal to purchase entry into religious life:

> Therefore, in order that we may establish some certainty over this matter, we say: Seeing that [holy] orders and ecclesiastical office and things connected to them, that is, things which cannot be had without them, such as prebends and the like; also fraternal society, i.e., that which lay converts dwelling in cloisters or in hospices have, I say, fraternal society and things connected to it, that is, which cannot be had without it, such as administration of the claustral offices —since all these things are such that it is simony to buy or sell them.[9]

This text, as it stands in Latin, is difficult to interpret, in part because the clauses that make it up are disorderly. T. P. McLaughlin, the editor of the *Summa Parisiensis*, noted several reasons for the confusion of the text. In the first place, it was a *reportatio*, notes on an oral lecture; in the second place, the scribe who copied the notes was not competent or careful.[10] In spite of these difficulties, the *Summa* seems to have divided things susceptible of simoniacal treatment into two categories. The first was the category of "[holy] orders and ecclesiastical office and things connected to them." This was a clear restatement of the traditional view that holy orders and positions in the church hierarchy, and their exercise, were subject to simoniacal manipulation.[11] The second category was that of "fraternal society, i.e., that which lay converts dwelling in cloisters and hospices have." This category was not a traditional one in the discussion of simony, and was apparently created to explain why payment for mere *ingressus monasterii* was simoniacal. The term *laicus conversus* probably designated that new category of members found in many twelfth-century religious houses. Such *conversi* joined the house permanently, took vows, and had their prescribed round of prayers and pious practices. However, they were separate from the monks. They were often illiterate and performed much of the hard physical work of the house.[12] Such "lay converts" were truly members of the religious community. One of their distinguishing features was that they did not receive any holy orders. Hence, to the author of the *Summa Parisiensis*, they stood as the very model of a kind of minimal member of a religious community, fully a part of it but receiving within it neither holy orders nor important administrative posts. When such a person paid to enter a religious house, what did he receive? By his status as a *laicus conversus*, he obtained neither orders nor offices. What he did obtain was "fraternal society," i.e., membership in a religious community. The author of the *Summa Parisiensis* defined more exactly the nature of that fraternal society: "May you distinguish thus, since in *prebenda* two things are understood, i.e., the external income of the prebend, and a certain spiritual adjunct, such as the communion of the brethren, participation in the choir, and in the chapter, etc."[13] Thus to participate as a full member in the ceremonies and way of life in a monastery was to enjoy its "fraternal society," even if the member held no office and exercised no holy orders in the house. The *Summa* explained the simoniacal nature of purchashing entry into religion by the fact that one thereby obtained a spiritual thing, *fraterna societas*, which was the sum total of rights and duties that a member of a religious community possessed. Even if the entrant remained a "lay convert," without holy orders or ecclesiastical office, the two traditional objects of simony, he did receive a spiritual thing subject to simoniacal treatment.

Thus, in contrast to the ambiguity of earlier decretists, the *Summa Parisiensis* held that the sale of the *ingressus monasterii* was simoniacal because it gave access to a spiritual thing, *fraterna societas*. The *summa* "De iure naturali," composed between 1171 and 1179, took a similar position when it classified *ingressus ecclesiarum* among things that were not themselves spiritual, but that were so closely linked to spiritual things that their sale was simoniacal.[14]

Peter the Chanter, a Paris theologian of the later twelfth century, had a pronounced interest in the problem of simoniacal entry, and was familiar with the canonical discussion of it. He wrote in his *Summa de sacramentis*:

> Some people say about congregations of monks, canons and nuns that it is not simoniacal to receive or to give [payments] in such places when no dignity [i.e., administrative position] is acquired there. Others distinguish, and say more correctly, that spiritual fraternity ought always to be given for free.[15]

The conciliar legislation and canonical commentators of the period after 1170 broadened Gratian's prohibition of payment for *ingressus monasterii* to include all forms of regular life. Nuns and canons were explicitly mentioned in the prohibition of simony at the Council of London in 1175.[16] Clement III, pope from 1187 to 1191, issued two decretal letters concerning canons, apparently regular and secular, who had entered their houses simoniacally.[17] In the late twelfth century, hospitals, which were generally structured as groups living under a religious rule, began to add to their statutes a prohibition of simony in entry.[18] The military order of the Templars was warned about simoniacal entry by Innocent III in 1213.[19] Indeed, the inclusion of all forms of religious life in community under the prohibition of simoniacal entry enabled Peter the Chanter to discuss entry into *aliqua congregatio*, without further qualification as to the nature of the group.[20]

In summary, most of the decretists who broached the question took the view that *ingressus monasterii* was not in itself a spiritual thing, but provided access to a spiritual thing, membership in a religious body. For that reason, its sale or purchase was simoniacal.

2. What Difference Was There between a Payment for Entry and a Gift Made on the Occasion of Entry?

Almost all those entering religious life were accompanied by a gift of some kind, a gift that was a normal, customary concomitant to entry. Indeed, there was a conviction among religious that it was only right for the gift to come with the new member. Rudolph of Saint Trond gave expression to that conviction when he wrote:

> For that portion which ought to come to the son in the world ought, by the law of God and of men, to follow him to the church in which he [the father] wishes to hand him over to God.[21]

Gratian and the decretists were not hostile to the view that a person entering religious life ought to make a gift, if he possessed the means to do so. Gratian took note of that view, though without embracing it, when he wrote:

> Hence it appears clear that those about to enter a monastery ought to offer their goods to the officials [of it], and unless they offer their goods, they should not otherwise be received.[22]

Stephan of Tournai, whose *summa* on the *Decretum* was composed about 1159, supported the entrance gift as a moral necessity.

> Certain people say that they do not hold him perfect, who leaves all his goods to his parents, and gives nothing to the needy church which he enters. . . . For there are many who leave all their goods to their parents and take the habit of poverty, not from a love of poverty, but so that they may enrich their parents, or so that they may be made bishops. . . .[23]

The commentator Sicardus of Cremona, writing about 1179–81, likewise took a favorable view of entry gifts when he wrote:

Money demanded conditionally from those who have entered is a permitted procedure. No, indeed, it ought to be done as a counsel of perfection, if the weakness of our era would sustain it, so that none of those rich persons who could be supported on their family's wealth should be received in a church unless he left his goods to his parents . . . or distributed them to the poor . . . or added them to the possessions of the church. . . .[24]

The decretists evidently had no quarrel with the entrance gift as such. However, the rising concern in the twelfth century about simony in entrance to religious houses called into question the customary connection of entry and gift.

As the controversy at Saint Panteleon revealed, there were individuals who drew the conclusion that there need be, indeed should be, no entrance gift at all.[25] There was support for such a negative view of entrance gifts in some of the monastic rules of late antiquity and in twelfth-century criticism of monastic venality.[26] Some canonists entertained, at least as a debating topic, the idea that individuals rich enough to give a gift were not eligible for reception in religious houses at all. Gratian had taken care to point out in his *dictum* after chapter 7 of *causa* I, *questio* II, that those who had been rich were not prohibited from entry into religion, provided that they disposed of their wealth to their relatives, to the poor, or to the church.[27] The *Summa coloniensis* composed about 1169, proposed the following opinion as a debating point to be rejected: "Therefore, if those with possessions are not to be gathered in monasteries, then neither are those who give [entrance gifts], since he who gives has [possessions]."[28]

If such opinions had become widespread in the twelfth century, major adjustments would have been necessary in the economic life of religious houses, since entrants were important both for bringing new possessions and for assuring the security of properties already held. In fact, however, in spite of the views of a few theorists, the decretists had no intention of anything so revolutionary as an end to gifts on the occasion of entry into religion. They concentrated instead on the nature of those gifts.

113

The key words, recurring in the conciliar decrees and canonists' comments of the twelfth century, were *exactio* and *pactio*, which denoted concern about compulsion and negotiation connected with entry into religion. Gratian formulated one of the significant distinctions when he wrote, "But it is one thing to offer one's goods voluntarily, it is another to pay exactions."[29] Roland Bandinelli echoed this comment, with significant modifications:

> On this point it must be noted that some of those things which are offered are put forward voluntarily, others under pressure; likewise, some by agreement, others by pure generosity. . . . Therefore, we say nothing at all should be demanded nor if demanded paid; nor should anything be given by pact for entrance of a church.[30]

These texts of Gratian and Roland Bandinelli make clear that the nexus of gift and entrance was not to be broken. However, the nexus had to result from the free-will offering of a gift by the new entrant. The consensus of decretist opinion was that if a gift was demanded of a new entrant, and consequently was not a result of a free-will offering, it was simoniacal. Any gift offered voluntarily by the entrant was acceptable, indeed, praiseworthy.[31] The notion of exaction, which stood in opposition to that of free-will offering, served as a means of distinguishing simoniacal fees from legitimate gifts, and thus justified the entry gift, within given limits.[32]

There was a second, more complex issue with which the canonists had to deal. That was the situation in which entry was preceded, not by an exaction, but by a pact or agreement. For instance, Rudolph of Saint Trond had recommended to the monks of Saint Panteleon that the father who was reluctant to give a gift with his son "hear from you the advice of saint Augustine[33] and the command of saint Benedict's Rule." Rudolph advised the monks to meet with the father and to reason with him about a gift. He insisted that such a discussion be handled carefully, without giving in to greedy or simoniacal intentions.[34]

This sort of negotiatory meeting constituted a major problem for those concerned about the integrity of monastic entry. It was often unnecessary to fix an amount or to demand overtly anything from the prospective monk or his family. The latter were frequently quite willing to offer a reasonable gift in order to obtain a place for a child or an adult. The burning question in the normal situation must have been the size and nature of the gift, rather than whether there would be a gift. A discussion about entry and gift, as recommended by Rudolph of Saint Trond, must often have turned into a bargaining session, as happened at Saint Denys de Nogent-le-Rotrou about 1190.

> When Dom Nicholas presided over the church of St. Denys, a certain knight, William of Villula, approached him and asked humbly that he consent to make his son William a monk, for the love of God and of him. He promised that he was going to place many goods there and that he would, as best he could, give his aid and counsel in all things [to the monastery], if his request received the effect he desired. Orricus, the brother of the forenamed William, promised that he would do similar things, if what they sought was fulfilled. The prior, bearing diligently the care of the church committed to him and desiring to improve it during his tenure of office, decided that he would satisfy their will, if they worked to give something . . . from their revenues along with the boy.[35]

The brothers consented to the prior's suggestion, and they offered two tithes and the confirmation of earlier gifts along with the boy. In this charter there was no fixed sum sought, and there was no clear demand for a gift. Indeed, the two brothers took the initiative in offering to give something for the reception of the boy. Yet there was an air of commerce about such agreements, and the decretists felt that such a bargain before reception was trading in holy things and that such a child was received in religious life because his relatives paid, voluntarily to be sure, a considerable sum for his entry.

To support their view, the canonists could cite the general prohibition in the law against simoniacal pacts for acquiring any holy object.[36] But they also relied heavily on the letter of the Pseudo-Boniface to justify their objection to the particular form of bargaining that accompanied entry into religion. In that letter the pope had given permission to a group of monks to receive a new member from another monastery. "But nevertheless, if he whom you seek is so useful to your need, let him come, provided however that every pact is absent and every agreement ceases. . . . "[37] On the basis of this very explicit text, the decretists banned pacts and agreements, either on the part of the entrant or the house, to give anything in return for entry into religious life.

A problem subsidiary to that of pacts and agreements was the timing of a gift. Apparently there was a view current that a pact to give a gift before or at entry was forbidden, but that a pact about a gift to be transferred after the actual entrance was acceptable.[38] As will be demonstrated in section three of this chapter, gifts agreed on after entry were allowed for the special case of entrants to impoverished houses. But, as a general proposition, the canonists were not willing to admit that a pact about an entry gift could be legitimized by any temporal subterfuge. The author of the *Summa Parisiensis* attacked such manipulations that were intended to conceal either a pact or a demand: "Money ought not to be demanded [nor] if demanded given, either along with the entrant, or before or after [entry], since that is simoniacal. But, if it is offered freely, then before or after it is laudably received or given."[39] A commentator on the early thirteenth-century *Compilatio* III summarized this view of the effect of timing on pacts and agreements: "But is one able to offer something at the time when he is received? Lawrence said no . . . John and Vincent said—and I believe well— that it is permitted to give at that time so long as a pact does not precede, since if a pact precedes, then neither before nor after [reception] is it licit to give. . . . "[40] Thus the canonists agreed that no simoniacal pact or demand could be legitimized merely by delaying the payment until after the actual entrance into the religious house.

Finally, the decretists were interested in whether the ultimate use of money received by pact or by exaction made any difference in evaluating the act itself. Rufinus wrote, " . . . Although some say that then without sin money can be demanded for entrance, when something is demanded with the intention that the sum exacted should afterward be spent in the need of the church or the aid of the poor."[41] In the course of his argument, Rufinus rejected such an opinion, as did several of the later canonists.[42] The *Summa coloniensis* noted:

> I say nothing should be demanded from those who are to be received, for the sake of any pious act, as Alexander says in the chapter "Ex multis", toward the end: "We establish that no cleric of whatever grade should dare to offer anything for a benefice in a church either to the fabric of the churches or to the coffers of the churches or even what is to be offered to the poor, since, with scripture as witness, he who receives [something] illicitly, so that he may give well, is burdened rather than aided.[43]

The decretists held that the ends, even pious ones, for which an entry gift was exacted could not justify the exaction itself.

In summary, Gratian's commentators and successors branded as simoniacal all exactions, all pacts, and all temporal subterfuges in receiving new religious. The canonical norm for judging gifts was their free-will character; otherwise, they were simoniacal.

3. Did the Economic State of a Religious House Affect the Problem of Payment for Entry?

There was one significant modification that many decretists brought to their opposition to pacts and demands for payment on the occasion of entry into religion. One of the practical realities of the later twelfth century was that religious houses varied significantly in size and income. For a house with a substantial endowment, the gifts brought by entrants probably did not constitute a crucial percentage of its annual income. However, for houses on the poorer end of the spectrum, the reception of a member without an increase in income could conceivably work a hardship.[44] The twelfth-century decretists were normally administrators at some time in their careers, and, in any case, they were concerned with the workings of a complex institution, the church. They were aware that the income accompanying a new entrant was, in practice, a necessity for a poor house. Their treatment of Gratian's text gradually adapted it to the problems of poor religious houses.

The Bolognese decretist Rufinus upheld as a matter of course

Gratian's opposition to forced payments and to pacts on the occasion of entry. However, he introduced a new element, not found in Gratian's treatment of simoniacal entry, when he took account of the economic condition of the house.

> If anyone who possesses his own income in abundance is received by a church that is not particularly rich, it is demanded of him either that he add his income to the goods of the church, or that he live off his own possessions and not seek support from the church.[45]

In the *Decretum* itself Gratian's focus had been upon the wealth of the entrant rather than upon the poverty of the church being entered.[46] Rufinus shifted the stress to the financial state of the religious house. If it was poor, it could lay down certain conditions for the reception of a wealthy entrant. Since the entrant could choose whether or not to live off—and therefore to retain—his own property, Rufinus felt obliged to point out that this procedure was not intended for persons entering a house under a rule of poverty,

> . . . even though certain defenders of evil custom drunkenly think these texts apply to regular canons. But how, from these authorities, is it granted to regular canons to live from their own or their parents' goods, since they ought to possess nothing personal, but ought to have all things in common.[47]

Gratian had posed this difficulty of exegesis for his interpreters because he had not distinguished carefully in *causa* I, *questio* II, between clerics entering houses living under a rule of poverty and those entering communities whose members retained personal property. His original question had been formulated around *ingressus monasterii*, but it became at times *ingressus ecclesiae*, i.e., entrance to any ecclesiastical body that received members.[48] Gratian's concern was to prevent wealthy persons from living at the expense of the church, but his choice of authoritative texts centered on secular rather than regular clergy.[49] He had cited three texts about clerics who had the option to retain their personal wealth, and he concluded:

> But by these authorities, they are not prohibited from being received by a church, who were formerly rich and left it all . . . or gave it to

the poor, . . . or added it to the possession of the church . . . : but they are prohibited who reside in the homes of their parents or who, unwilling to leave their goods, desire to be supported by ecclesiastical income.[50]

It is evident that Gratian framed his opinion about rich men entering a church on the model of secular clerics, who had the option to retain and live from their personal wealth. When his commentators attempted to apply this opinion to regular clergy, they found themselves in the untenable situation of seeming to recommend that clergy bound to personal poverty nonetheless be given the choice of retaining their personal property, a view that Rufinus denied. The author of the *Summa coloniensis*, writing about 1169, recognized this anomaly and tried to correct it by distinguishing between two types of reception:

> Therefore, let this be the opinion in this question, that one may never demand from those to be received, but sometimes from those already received, that they give their goods to the church or that they not demand support from it. I say "received" to support [i.e., perhaps novitiate], but not to profession, since the rule does not allow personal property to professed religious.[51]

Stephan of Tournai, writing about 1159, adapted the exception for poor churches directly to the needs of religious houses living under a rule of poverty: "Note however that if any monastery is so poor that it cannot provide for those who convert, in that case an abbot may well demand from one offering himself to the monastery, and having some possessions, that from which he who is converted may derive necessities."[52]

Huguccio, whose work was a summation of much that preceded him, reiterated the opinion that a man of means entering a poor church should choose whether to give his goods away or to live from them at no cost to the church.[53] But, he also proposed the alternate solution, used by Stephan, which fit well the needs of a religious house living under a rule of poverty:

> If nevertheless the church is so poor that it cannot provide for more than are there, then the prelate can legitimately say to a person wishing to enter that church, "This church is so poor that it cannot provide

for those in it and therefore we cannot receive [you]. But if you have [resources] whence you can live, we are prepared to receive you and you may offer to the church [something] from which it may provide for you." There is not noted here the vice of greed and of simony, but the necessity of the church is simply made known.[54]

Thus Huguccio offered the potential entrant the choice whether to make a gift so that a poor house could receive him or to forgo entry because of the church's poverty. This was a choice adapted to the needs and circumstances of a regular house.

This exception for the poor religious house met an obvious need, and it became, in one form or another, a permanent part of the discussion of simony in entrance to religious life.[55] However, the exception threatened to reopen the way for simoniacal pacts and demands. The canonists tried therefore to hedge it with qualifications that would prevent abuse.

Some decretists feared that the ability or willingness to make a gift would become the determining factor in receiving new members.[56] A conciliar canon of the early thirteenth century does indicate that some French houses rejected those candidates who stood on their right not to make a gift.[57] Some canonists proposed that a man be formally received first, and only after reception should the house's poverty be discussed with him. Rufinus was a proponent of this measure:

> It should be recognized that sometimes money is demanded from those to be received and sometimes from those who have already been received. Likewise, sometimes [it is demanded] absolutely, and sometimes conditionally. . . . Thus, money is never to be demanded absolutely or conditionally from those who are to be received. . . . However, from those who have been received, it is not to be demanded absolutely at all, nor conditionally except in this single situation.[58]

The "single situation" was, of course, that in which a wealthy man entered a poor church. In Rufinus' view it was not enough that a poor church demand only from those already received. The demand had to be made "conditionally" rather than "absolutely." I interpret these terms to mean that not every religious house could request a gift from every person received, but that only poor houses could ask a gift of well-to-do entrants, and even then without compulsion.

But to receive a person and only then to ask for a gift for his support could be inconvenient and embarrassing if he would not or could not make a gift. The *Summa coloniensis*, and later Huguccio, upheld the opinion that poverty justified mentioning the house's finances even before an individual was received: "But nevertheless if the poverty of the monastery is so severe that an increase in the number of persons would require an increase in the endowment, in such a case we do not disapprove of indicating the situation of the place to those seeking entry."[59] The *Summa coloniensis* went so far as to suggest, without explicit disapproval, the idea of fixing fees for entrance of such poor places: "Certain persons go so far as to say that even fixed entry fees are permitted in this case, using as a justification for their opinion the custom of monks."[60]

Peter the Chanter, who discussed the exception for poor houses on a number of occasions, gave it a careful minimalist interpretation, along the lines followed by Huguccio:

> Likewise, if any congregation is so much in need that it can not receive more brethren, if anyone seeks its membership, they can licitly demand from him enough from which he can be supported there for so long as he lives. But when he has died, they ought to give those things back, unless he voluntarily wishes to hand them over. But, if they demand from him a perpetual revenue, it is simony, since they could exist without it.[61]

Peter prescribed a different procedure in his *Verbum abbreviatum* when he recommended that a poor house receive an applicant on his merits to a form of spiritual, nonresident membership, and then agree to receive him as a resident member of the congregation if he was able to provide it with a life revenue for his support.[62] Thus Peter the Chanter recommended, at different times, both the demand from those already received and the demand from those to be received. Apparently, if a house was truly poor and if its motives were pure, then either procedure was acceptable.

The successors of Gratian, in fifty years of discussion, had attempted to balance the legitimate needs of a poor house against the crime of simoniacal reception of new members. They held to a ban on all forced gifts and pacts, but with the important proviso that a poor religious house could make known its plight to a potential recruit, and could ask the recruit to provide his own support either before or after the house received him.

4. Could a Man Be Induced to Enter Religious Life for Money?

Gratian had introduced into the learned discussion of monastic simony an issue that derived from the letter of the Pseudo-Boniface, cited in *causa* I, *questio* II, canon 2. The letter dealt with the case of monks who asked the pope whether it was licit for them to pay another monastery for a monk whom they wished to join their congregation, perhaps as their abbot. The pope replied that the purchase of a religious vocation would be simony, because it was a divine gift that inspired a person to choose to enter a religious house.[63] Gratian's authority and the fact that the Pseudo-Boniface was almost the only *auctoritas* in the *Decretum* that pertained directly to monastic simony were such that the propriety of paying a man to come to religious life became a standard item in discussions about monastic simony. Gratian's commentators decided that it was illicit to induce anyone to enter religious life by means of a gift.[64]

Peter the Chanter lectured on the problem at Paris in the last two decades of the twelfth century, and his views are an adequate summary of earlier canonist opinion:

> It is asked if it is permitted to anyone to sell himself for taking the religious habit. . . . For example, [suppose] someone is invited to the monastic habit by an abbot who sees that his church needs such a person. The man says that he has a poor little mother whom he neither wishes nor is able to leave all alone, or [he has] an unmarried sister or [he is] in debt. It is asked whether it is permitted to him to offer himself without a pact, so that, i.e., with the intention that, he would enter their monastery if they would free him from debt? In such a case, a pact is ruled out by *causa* I, *questio* II, *Quam pio* [i.e., Pseudo-Boniface].[65]

But there were apparently people who could see little harm in paying a man's debts so that he might enter religious life. Indeed,

Peter's treatment is followed by several sentences, perhaps by a student taking notes on the lecture, that expressed doubt about the whole basis for calling this simony. "But does not intention result in simony? But such a simony, if it is simony, does not seem to have much impiety about it. But, is it not simony when reception of the religious habit is arranged for a price? And likewise, if it is simony, is it not a mortal sin?"[66]

Caesarius of Heisterbach told with satisfaction of a man of learning who entered the Premonstratensians under the condition that they pay his debts: "When the provost of the aforementioned monastery learned of that [condition], he very gladly paid the money, and the scholastic immediately took the habit."[67] Thus even in the first third of the thirteenth century, when Caesarius wrote, the simony in paying a good man to come to religious life was not always evident. However, the letter of the Pseudo-Boniface and the force of the canonical tradition deriving from it convinced most canonists that to pay a man to come to religious life was the purchase of a gift of God; and so, in a strictly technical sense, it was simony.

Although this form of simony was certainly not so common as payment offered by the entrant, it was not merely an academic fantasy. Charters reveal that monasteries were, at times, willing to pay debts on the property of an entrant in order to obtain the endebted property. The entrant, for his part, was freed from the debts and could give the endebted property as part or all of his entrance gift. At Vigeois in the Limousin about 1165-71, just such a series of bargains was concluded with an impoverished family.[68] The charter reveals that over a period of years, the monks of Vigeois received three brothers and the son of one of them. The monks paid their considerable debts, provided the men with monastic garb and bedclothes, and gave a corody for life to the wife of one brother. In return the monastery brought back into its direct possession this family's estate, which was apparently in origin a fief from the monastery. By paying off the debts of the sons of Peter Fulcherius, the monks were able to take over the property and exploit it as they wished. Thus the practice of paying a man to take the habit could redound to the benefit of the house, if the man brought with him endebted properties and rights that the monastery could redeem and retain.

However, the consensus of canonist opinion was that it was wrong to be paid to enter religious life, just as it was wrong to pay for entry. The only acceptable form of gift at entry was a free-will offering by the entrant or the monastery, in which neither pact nor compulsion had a place.

5. What Was to Be Done to a Monk Whose Entry Was Simoniacal?

One of the conditions of the case envisioned by Gratian in *causa* I was that it concerned a boy who was too young to understand his father's payment to the monks for his reception.[69] Gratian introduced this element so that he would have the opportunity to discuss the effect of ignorance on the boy's guilt. His conclusion was: "In this instance, however, there was not ignorance of the law, but of a fact, and of a fact about which he was not obliged to know. Therefore, the ignorance about his father's crime excused him from the guilt of the crime. Even if he had known it, he could not grasp it because of the weakness of his age."[70] As a consequence of the manner in which Gratian set up his hypothetical case, the child was not personally guilty of simony, and his punishment for simoniacal entry did not enter into discussion. Furthermore, Gratian never said specifically what was to be done about an adult who was simoniacally received nor about the prelate who received him simoniacally.

The appropriate punishment for simoniacs was a complicated problem, and that complexity was reflected in Gratian's *causa* I, *questio* I, which contained 130 authoritative texts. Gratian attempted to harmonize the disparate opinions about simony and simoniacs that the canonical and theological traditions contained. It was a monumental task. Indeed, the decretist Everard of Ypres noted simply that the punishment of simoniacs was not fixed but arbitrary.[71]

However, in spite of the complexity of the issue, the punishment of the pure type, i.e, of the conscious, adult simoniac, was still governed by norms laid down in canon two of the Council of Chalcedon (451):

> If any bishop shall have performed an ordination for money and shall have given for a price that grace which cannot be sold, and if he shall have ordained for money a bishop or a priest or a deacon or any one of those who are included in the clergy; or if he shall have appointed by money for the sake of his most wicked gain a *dispensator* or a *defensor* or anyone who is placed under the rule; he, who was proved to be attempting this, will lose his own rank, and he who was ordained will profit in no way from this ordination or promotion which was performed by means of business. But may he be kept from that dignity or job which he received through money. But if anyone is a go-between for such wicked and unspeakable givings and takings, if indeed he is a cleric, may he fall from his rank; but if he is a layman or a monk, may he be anathema.[72]

Thus, in the classic case, the simoniac purchaser was to lose that which he had gained illicitly, and the other party to the transaction, the seller, was to be removed from his position as well.

Twelfth-century commentators on the *Decretum* did not normally broach the question of punishment for an abbot who received members simoniacally. Perhaps this was so because, at least on the level of theory, there was little incertitude: the offender was subject to the sanctions against any simoniacal seller, i.e., deposition. Innocent III confirmed that view at the Fourth Lateran Council.[73]

On the other hand, the punishment of the monk who was received simoniacally did interest the commentators. If a simoniacal monk was treated strictly according to canon two of Chalcedon, he would lose the illicitly gained object, presumably the monastic habit. However, one of the persistent problems of religious houses in the twelfth century was that of members seeking to leave, either legally or by apostasy.[74] The canonists, as they were no doubt aware, would have contributed to this problem if they had insisted that monks guilty of simony be forced to abandon the monastic habit. One can conjecture that individuals who wished to escape from the religious life would "confess" to simoniacal entry, and thereby win expulsion from the habit. The canonist

Rufinus, who had aided religious houses by promoting the exception for poverty, also came to their assistance in this matter.

> It is usual to ask at this point (since such promotions, as the council of Chalcedon says, profit in no way) . . . , whether anyone made a monk by means of money given or received or by any promise ought to be stripped of the monk's habit. To which we say that just as if any monk should be made a bishop by means of money, he would not lose the sacrament of order—which is what it is whether received well or badly—but he would lose the dignity of the sacrament, [for] to obtain that alone he gave money. For he would not care about the sacrament, if the dignity could exist apart from the sacrament. Just so, when anyone is made a monk in a particular place by means of money received or given, he ought to be deprived of that on account of which he gave or received money, i.e., he should not be a monk in that place: for it was on account of the place that the money was given. He ought not simply to be stripped of the monastic habit; for money was not given so that he could be a monk, but so that he could be a monk there.[75]

By asserting that the monk who entered simoniacally gained, not the religious habit, but the habit-in-a-particular-place, Rufinus was able to respect the letter of canon two of Chalcedon and also to avoid encouraging apostasy from the religious life. He recommended penal exile to another monastery, a procedure that punished the simoniac while respecting his life-long commitment to God's service.[76]

The *Summa coloniensis* advised the same punishment for the guilty monk, but it was more explicit than Rufinus about the motives for such a recommendation.

> Therefore, with the exception of this case [i.e., the case of a payment to enter a poor monastery], if anyone is made a monk by means of money, it is asked whether he ought to be stripped of the habit. He did not give money so that he might be made a monk, but so that he might be a monk in that place. As a result, he ought to be removed from that place [but] not separated from the austerity of religious life, lest if we say this, we would open the way for fugitives.[77]

The author of the *Summa coloniensis* wanted to avoid making simoniacal entry an excuse to flee the "austerity of religious life," since the life of a monk was, in itself, a punishment.[78]

This opinion of the canonists about the fate of a simoniacal monk met a need, and it was apparently adopted in theory[79] and in practice. Pope Alexander III, himself a decretist and commentator on Gratian, adopted such a view in a decretal letter dealing with a case of simoniacal entry that was referred to him.[80] Pope Clement III issued a decretal letter between 1187 and 1191 that espoused the decretist opinion, but with the important qualification that the monastery into which the simoniacal monk was exiled should be stricter than the one that he had illicitly entered.[81] The decretal letters of Alexander and Clement were incorporated in the *Compilatio* II, a canonical collection of papal letters that was put together between 1210 and 1212.[82] Finally, the sixty-fourth canon of the Fourth Lateran Council prescribed as the preferred punishment of simoniacal entrants a penal exile to a house of stricter life (*arctior regula*).[83]

By the late twelfth century the canonists generally agreed that simony could not be an excuse for escape from monastic vows. The guilty religious was to be sent to a house of stricter rule for penance. If no house of exile could be found, the religious could remain in his own monastery, but stripped of seniority and of the right to promotion.[84] In this way guilt could be punished without any concession to the attempts to escape from religious life.

6. What Was to Be Done with the Money Paid for Entry?

Apparently, the decretists never responded to this problem diectly, but they laid down principles that were used by early thirteenth-century glossators to solve it. In *causa* I, *questio* III, canon 2, Gratian cited a letter addressed to the bishop of Rouen and to all Gauls. The letter, which concerned simoniacal reception of office, was signaled in the *Decretum* as sent by a Gregory, and Friedberg attributed to it the era of Gregory VII. In part the letter said: "For whoever has wished to serve God by taking up religion both loses the merit and is stripped of the benefice he received, if he accepted anything. Therefore, by the force of reason, he is compelled to give back what he received unjustly, and not to retain whatever he received for the sake of filthy gain."[85]

This text became the focus for a discussion of what to do with money illicitly given or received in a simoniacal transaction. The decretists did not treat the particular case of money paid for entry into religion. They concentrated on the more inclusive situation of money paid for any spiritual thing, including such entry.

Some of the early decretists took the text at more or less face value and held that the money should be returned to the giver. Paucapalea cited a *lex Justiniani* which had ordered that "it [the money] should be claimed for the church whose priesthood he wished to buy. If however he is a layman, who accepted anything for this reason, or was an intermediary in the affair, those things which were given should be demanded in double from him and claimed for the church."[86] Paucapalea dissented from this view. He explained that Justinian's law was the rigorous position, but that Gratian's chapter recommending the return of the price to the giver was a result of ecclesiastical mercy.[87] Rufinus likewise upheld a simple interpretation of the text:

> There were some who said that the money should not be returned to him who gave it, but should be given to the church or to the poor. However, this is not "to give back," but to despoil; for "to give back" is to hand over to him who had it before. Therefore, it will be more sound to judge that it ought to be returned to the perverse giver. . . .[88]

Like Paucapalea, Rufinus did not admit that the giver had a strict right to the return of the money: ". . . . Not that the giver himself is able to claim back what he gave for an immoral end. But, the money is returned to him in his eternal opprobrium, so that he may have it in damnation, since he thought that he could possess a gift of God for money."[89] Rufinus argued further that such money was unclean and should not be put in the coffers of the church or given to the poor.[90] Therefore, a simoniacal giver should have his money returned when his transaction was thwarted.

In the situation in which the guilty giver was not an individual but a church, Rufinus came to the same conclusion, but for a different reason. He based his contention on the canonical opinion that "the crime of an individual ought not to result in the damage of a church."[91] This was a view designed to protect the interests of an ecclesiastical corporation against the incompetence and misdeeds of a person who held a responsible position in it. Rufinus argued that a church should not lose its money because an official committed a crime. Thus Rufinus held that a simoniacal giver, whether an individual or a church, should have his money returned.

The view that a simoniacal religious corporation should have its money back was generally accepted by the decretists, with the understanding that the individual officials responsible for the crime be punished.[92] In contrast, the problem of what to do if the giver was an individual had a more complicated evolution. Apparently, many of the decretists could see no reason why a simoniac should be so fortunate as to have his money back when his illicit negotiation failed. Stephan of Tournai noted:

> It [*causa* I, *questio* III, canon 2] seems to indicate that he who received anything from the sale of spiritual things ought to return [it] to him from whom he received [it]. But, since both are on a par because of immorality, he who gave cannot demand return, since in an immoral affair the situation of the possessor is better.[93]

This uneasiness about rewarding either the giver or the receiver of a simoniacal payment was allayed by adopting the view of Justinian, cited by Paucapalea, that the money should go to the church whose office the simoniac tried to buy.[94]

Basing themselves on the practice current in punishing the crime of calumny, Sicardus of Cremona and the author of the *summa* "Tractaturus magister," both writing in the late 1170s, expressed the view that neither the giver nor the receiver of a simoniacal payment should receive the money. Instead, it should be awarded to the party injured in the transaction, i.e., to the church that was involved.[95] The *summa* "De iure naturali" expressed the same view:

> Likewise, it is said that money simoniacally received ought to be returned. . . . But to whom, since neither the giver has a right to get it back nor does the receiver have a right to keep it? Therefore, the situation of the possessor will not be the better [of the two]. They say it ought to be returned to the church in whose injury it happens to have been given, by the example of money offered on account of

129

calumny, which is not returned to the giver, nor is it permitted to the receiver to keep it, but is conceded to him in whose calumny it was given. . . .[96]

The decretists proposed other alternatives that would also have avoided giving benefit to the simoniacs; for instance, that the money be returned to the giver's heir,[97] if he had one, or to a stricter monastery in which such lapsed simoniacal clerics were to be placed.[98] However, the solution that awarded the money to the church that had been injured was apparently the most successful. The *Summa Lipsiensis* described the situation about 1186 as one in which the "injured church" solution prevailed without dissent.[99]

However, the decretists apparently did not directly broach the specific question of the payment made by a man for entry into religious life. In such a case there were problems inherent in the award of the money to the monastery. The decretists agreed that the simoniacal entrant was not to be stripped of the religious habit, but was to be sent to another house for penance. Some measure had to be taken to free the house of exile from the economic burden of its prisoner. The decretists might have found a solution to this problem in a text of the *Decretum* itself. In *causa* XVI, *questio* VI, canon 4, a letter of Pope Gregory the Great had prescribed for lapsed clerics a penal entry into a monastery. His letter ordered that support be provided for the lapsed clergymen out of their own personal resources, "lest if they are stripped [of their possessions], they might be a burden to the place into which they were thrust."[100] The decretists had cited this text for other purposes, but so far as I have been able to determine, they did not explicitly connect it to the fate of simoniac monks. That connection was drawn in the early thirteenth century by the decretalists, commenting on a letter of Pope Alexander III.

Alexander touched briefly on the issue of money in his letter about the simoniacal entry of the priest "F." The pope had written:

. . . If you [his investigator] find the situation as reported, may you admonish immediately and, in all strictness, compel the abbot and

the monks to return the money so unworthily received to the fore-
named F., . . . may you order the said F. that he seek to serve the
Lord in another monastery in the monastic habit.[101]

This letter ordered the return of the money to F. and his entry into
another house, but it did not draw an explicit connection between
these two commands. The letter posed a problem in the case of
the money because it seemed to contradict the general trend of
decretist thinking, which favored the award of the money to the
injured church. It remained for the glossators, commenting on this
decretal in the early thirteenth century, to account for the fact
that, in the case of simoniacal entry, the illicitly paid money
should be returned to the giver.

Alan, writing about 1210, explained the discrepancy thus: "Note
that money simoniacally received ought to be restored to that
institution in whose injury it was given. . . . Nevertheless, it is
found returned to him who gave it as an act of mercy. . . .[102]
Thus, for Alan, the variance from normal was due simply to an act
of kindness on the part of Alexander III. A second glossator, writing about the same decretal, offered a more subtle explanation:

> But why is it owed to him rather than to the monastery in whose prej-
> udice it was given? . . . Solution, the money cannot remain with
> the monastery, lest the monks receive some profit from it, for which
> they have made themselves unworthy. To the second [objection],
> we say that the monastery is given no injury here, since it loses noth-
> ing if the possessions of others are returned. . . . Likewise, this is
> done in favor of the second monastery, as in causa XVI, questio VI,
> De lapsis; otherwise as a rule it is owed to the [first] monastery.[103]

In this text the glossator linked the return of the money explicitly
to the entry of the priest F. into a second house; the money had been
returned to him for the sake of the second house, and the reference to Gregory the Great's letter makes it clear that the priest F.
was to use his money for his support at the second house. By re-
interpretation, Alexander's letter has been reconciled with the desire not to return the money to the simoniacal giver. If the monk
arranged in some way not to enter another house, then the commentator recommended that he not receive the money, which was

to remain with the first monastery. The canonist Albert, writing about 1215, summarized the reasonings of his predecessors:

> . . . Money given for simony ought to be given to that church in whose shame it was paid. . . . Solution, Alan said the procedure [i.e., award to injured church] was the common law, but this [Alexander's return of the money] is to be understood as done by way of dispensation and mercy. Others say it is done because of the crime of the abbot and of the monks, which is described here, since if the money remained with the monastery, the monks would feel a benefit of which they had made themselves unworthy. It seems to me that the money ought not to be returned to a cleric returning to the world, but it should remain with the church. . . . If, however, he must go to [another form of] religious life, that which is said here obtains, lest he may be a burden to the secondary monastery.[104]

On the basis of Alexander's letter, the early thirteenth-century decretalists decided the fate of the money paid for entry. The money was returned to the simoniacal monk in the case that he was to be placed in another house for penance. But if the simoniacal entrant did not remain in religious life, then the normal procedure should prevail in which the money remained with the church in whose injury it was paid.

It is vain to seek complete agreement among the canonists who treated the issue of simoniacal entry into religion. They wrote over a period of seventy-five years and with different emphases and focuses of concern. However, the canonists went far toward developing the theoretical implications of Gratian's decision to include in his *Decretum* a case involving simoniacal entry into religion. They defined a series of thorny issues and proposed various solutions to deal with them. On account of their work the broad intellectual principles governing the discussion of simoniacal entry had been formulated and disseminated widely by the year 1200, although many of the specific issues and, more significantly, the practical measures to be adopted were still open to disagreement.

THE CANONISTS AND SIMONIACAL RECEPTION

1. For a treatment of the *Decretum* as a canonical collection, and as an intellectual phenomenon in its own right, see G. LeBras, J. Rambaud-Buhot, and C. Lefebvre, *L'Age classique 1140-1378, sources et théorie du droit* (Paris, 1965), Histoire du droit et des institutions de l'Eglise en Occident, no. 7.

2. LeBras et al., *L'Age classique*, pp. 10-11. C. E. Lewis, "Ricardus Anglicus: A *familiaris* of Archbishop Hubert Walter," *Traditio* 22 (1966): 469-71, notes that Hubert Walter, archbishop of Canterbury from 1183 to 1205, had several canonists in his household and among his advisers. S. Kuttner and E. Rathbone, "Anglo-Norman Canonists of the Twelfth Century," *Traditio* 7 (1949-51): 279-358, trace the interrelations of academic and administrative careers among several late twelfth-century English canonists. L. Genicot, "Aristocratie et dignités ecclésiastiques en Picardie aux XIIᵉ et XIIIᵉ siècles," *Revue d'histoire ecclésiastique* 67 (1972): 436-42, finds that at Beauvais a high percentage of non-nobles holding important positions in the church were university masters; i.e., university training could compensate for lack of noble blood. W. Holtzmann, "Die Benutzung Gratians in der päpstlichen Kanzlei im 12. Jahrhundert," *Studia Gratiana* 1 (1953): 323-49, stresses that from the pontificate of Alexander III (1159-81), the papacy was in the possession of canonists, and that many members of the curia were canonists as well.

3. The most useful guide to the canonical literature of the twelfth and thirteenth centuries remains S. Kuttner, *Repertorium der Kanonistik 1140-1234* (Vatican City, 1937). This indispensable work may be updated by reference to the journal *Traditio*, which published from 1955 to 1970 an annual report and bibliography on developments in the study of medieval canon law. Since 1971, the annual report and bibliography appear in the *Bulletin of Medieval Canon Law*, New Series.

4. Kuttner, *Repertorium*, pp. 123-207, lists no *summa* on the *Decretum* written later than the second decade of the thirteenth century. The formation of separate collections of papal decretals, which were studied and glossed by canonists, led to a gradual shift in canonical studies from the *Decretum* to the decretals (LeBras et al., *L'Age classique*, pp. 290-305). J. Rambaud-Buhot, "Les *Paleae* dans le décret de Gratien," *Proceedings of the Second International Congress of Medieval Canon Law,* ed. S. Kuttner and J. J. Ryan (Vatican City, 1965), pp. 23-44, describes attempts to bring the *Decretum* up to date in the later twelfth century by adding appendixes of useful texts and of papal letters. Such attempts proved unsatisfactory, and gave way to decretal collections.

5. "Sed adhuc obicitur, qui ingressuri monasterium pecunias tribuunt, non propositum religionis, sed participationem stipendiorum ecclesiae emunt. Temporalia ergo, non spiritualia ementes, nequaquam simoniaci habendi sunt. 1. His ita respondetur: Non solum qui spiritualia, sed etiam qui temporalia eis annexa precio accipiunt symoniaci iudicantur" (*Decretum, causa* I, *q*. III, prologue; cf. *distinctio 47*, canon 9).

6. Ibid.

7. Archpriest, archdeacon, canon, monk, and any cleric were positions or orders not to be sold because they were subject to a *regula* (J. F. von Schulte, ed., *Die Summa des Paucapalea über das Decretum Gratiani* [Giessen, 1890], p. 52).

8. "Nichil vero pro adeptione sacrae rei ex coactione vel pactione est exigendum, nec ergo pro introitu ecclesiae" (F. Thaner, ed., *Die Summa Magistri Rolandi, nachmals Papstes Alexander III, nebst einem Anhange incerti auctoris Questiones* [Innsbruck, 1874], p. 13).

9. "Ut igitur aliquam certitudinem super hujusmodi constituamus, dicimus: quia ordo et officium ecclesiasticum et his annexa, quae scilicet sine his haberi non possunt, ut praebendae et similia, fraterna etiam societas, scilicet quae est conversorum laicorum in claustris vel in ptochiis manentium, fraterna inquam societas, et annexa his, scilicet quae

sine his haberi non possunt, sicut administrationes officiorum claustrum—cum haec omnia talia sunt quod ea emere vel vendere simonia est" (T. P. McLaughlin, ed., *The Summa Parisiensis on the Decretum Gratiani* [Toronto, 1952], p. 79).

10. "The scribe was very careless at times and frequently it seems that he could not make out what he was copying. . . . Often he has written in a clear hand words which do not exist and phrases which have no possible meaning" (McLaughlin, *Summa Parisiensis*, p. ix).

11. The basic distinction between offices and holy orders as objects of simony derived from the second canon of Chalcedon, cited by Gratian in *causa* I, *questio* I, canon 8, which is quoted below in note 72. However, it was the work of twelfth- and thirteenth-century canonists that clarified the distinction between an ecclesiastical order and an ecclesiastical position: see D. E. Heintschel, *The Medieval Concept of an Ecclesiastical Office* (Washington, D.C., 1956) Catholic University of America Canon Law Studies, no. 363.

12. U. Berlière, "La *familia* dans les monastères bénédictins du moyen age," *Mémoires de l'Académie royale de Belgique*, 2d ser., vol. 29, fasc. 2 (Brussels, 1931), documents the complex structure of inhabitants that a religious house could have. C. DuCange, *Glossarium Mediae et Infimae Latinitatis*, ed. G. A. L. Henschel (Paris, 1842), 2:583, cites three texts of the twelfth and early thirteenth centuries that indicate that *laici conversi* were individuals who lived in a monastery, but were not monks. E. P. Sauvage, "Vitae B. Petri Abrincensis et B. Hamonis Monachorum Coenobii Saviniacensis," *Analecta Bollandiana* 2 (1883): 511, contains a text that states that a *laicus conversus* at Savigny was a layman who took the religious habit, but remained a layman.

13. "Distingues itaque quoniam in praebenda duo intelliguntur, scilicet fructus exterior praebendae et quoddam spirituale annexum, ut est communio fratrum, participatio chori, capituli, et huiusmodi" (McLaughlin, *Summa Parisiensis*, p. 93). In at least two other places, the *Summa* added details to this view of membership in a religious body as a spiritual thing: "Similiter dicimus de praebenda, circa quam tria considerantur: consortium spirituale fratrum, jus recipiendi stipendia et ipsa stipendia. Consortium spirituale emere simonia est. Jus etiam recipiendi stipendia nomine praebendae vendere simonia est" (pp. 79–80). "Quaeritur de eis qui emunt victualia a monachis, et dicimus: si ita emunt ut etiam habeant fraternitatem eorum, simoniacum est, alias non" (p. 93).

14. "De simoniacis qui spiritualia emunt, vendunt, vel adnexa spiritualibus. Spiritualia, ut sunt gratie virtutum, dignitates ordinationum, consecrationes ecclesiarum etc. Adnexa spiritualibus, ut ingressus ecclesiarum, ius decimationum, prebendarum, administrationum et similium, que vendere simoniacum est" (summa "De iure naturali," Durham University, Cosin V III 3, fol. 41^r, cited by K. W. Nörr, "Die Summen 'De iure naturali' und 'De multiplici iuris divisione'," *Zeitschrift der Savigny-Stiftung für Rechtsgeschichte*, Kanonistische Abteilung, no. 48 (1962): 142). At least one decretist, the author of the *Summa coloniensis*, writing about 1169, held that the *ingressus monasterii* was itself a spiritual thing: "Cum enim ingressus monasterii res spiritualis sit, gratis, non ob munerum largitionem concedendus est" (BN lat. 14997, fol. 51^r).

15. "De collegiis cenobiorum, canonicorum, monialium, dicunt aliqui non esse symoniacum accipere vel dare in talibus, quando ibi nulla dignitas adquiritur. Alii distingunt et melius dicunt quod spiritualis fraternitas gratis semper concedenda est" (*Summa de sacramentis*, ed. J.-A. Dugauquier (Louvain and Lille, 1963), vol. 3, pt. 2a, p. 60).

16. Mansi, 22:149e.

17. "De regularibus canonicis," JL 16562; "Venerunt," JL 16620: these letters were incorporated in the *Compilatio* II, bk. 5, tit. 2, chaps. 7 and 8, and were commented by canonists.

THE CANONISTS AND SIMONIACAL RECEPTION

18. *Statuts d'hôtels-Dieu et de léproseries*, ed. L. LeGrand (Paris, 1901), pp. 26, 36, 44, 194–95. J. Imbert, *Les Hôpitaux en droit canonique* (Paris, 1947), pp. 249–50, especially note 7, discusses simony in the entrance to hospitals in the work of thirteenth-century canonists.

19. Pott 4783. See also *La Règle du Temple*, ed. H. de Curzon (Paris, 1880), pp. 153, 228, 234, 287–88, 311, 343; and *Die Statuten des Deutschen Ordens nach den ältesten Handschriften*, ed. M. Perlbach (Halle, 1890), pp. 86–87, 164.

20. Dugauquier, *Summa de sacramentis*, vol. 3, pt. 2a, pp. 14–15.

21. De Borman, *Chronique*, 1:246. Peter the Chanter attributed a similar view to Bernard of Clairvaux (Dugauquier, *Summa de sacramentis*, vol. 3, pt. 2a, pp. 213–14). A text of regular canons likewise criticized those who held back their property when they entered religious life (J. Leclercq, "Documents pour l'histoire des chanoines réguliers," *Revue d'histoire ecclésiastique* 44 [1949]: 566–67; the text cited by Leclercq was also incorporated into Robert of Bridlington, *The Bridlington Dialoque*, ed. and trans. a religious of C.S.M.V. [London, 1960], p. 56).

22. "Hinc liquido aparet, quod ingressuri monasterium sua debent offerre rectoribus, nec aliter sunt recipiendi, nisi sua obtulerint" (*Decretum, causa* I, *q.* II, prologue). Gratian modified this view substantially by insisting that the entrant must have a free choice as to whether or not to give his property.

23. "Dicunt quidam, quod non habent eum perfectum, qui omnia bona sua relinquit parentibus et nil dat ecclesiae indigenti, quam intrat. . . . Nam multi sunt, qui omnia bona sua parentibus relinquunt et assumunt pauperatatis (*sic*) habitum, non paupertatis amore, sed ut ditentur parentes, vel ut possint episcopari" (J. F. von Schulte, ed., *Die Summa des Stephanus Tornacensis über das Decretum Gratiani* [Giessen, 1891], p. 146). John of Faenza, relying on Stephan of Tournai's text, repeated the opinion almost verbatim (BN lat. 14606, fol. 51ᵛ). The author of the *Summa coloniensis* also criticized those who gave no gift, or who gave a small gift when they could have given more: "De his intelligende sunt [i.e., the text of the *Decretum* critical of wealthy entrants] qui se propriis facultatibus de toto exuere nolentes, pro modica et particulari largicione ecclesias sartina sue persone et sumptibus ob hanc causam quaesitis gravare non metuunt. Unde prosper: non est meum dicere quale peccatum cibos pauperum presumendo commitunt, qui ecclesiàm quam de propriis facultatibus iuuvare debuerant insuper suis expensis gravant" (BN lat. 14997, fol. 51ʳ).

24. "Peccunia exigi ab ingressis conditionaliter. Hoc licitum est, immo de perfectionis consilio faciendus esset, si defectus nostri temporis sustineret, ut nullus divitum qui possunt paternis opibus sustentari in ecclesia susciperetur nisi sua parentibus relinqueret . . . vel pauperibus distribueret . . . vel ecclesie rebus adiungeret . . . " (BN lat. 14996, fol. 40ʳ).

25. De Borman, *Chronique*, 1:243–44. At least one canonist held that there should be no gift at entry: "Set nunquid eo tempore, quo quis recipitur, potest aliquid offerre? Lau . . . dixit, quod non, ut I. Q. I Emendari (c. 104) et Q. II Quam pio (c.2)" (F. Gillmann, *Des Laurentius Hispanus Apparat zur Compilatio III auf der staatlichen Bibliothek zu Bamberg* [Mainz, 1935], p. 72).

26. See above, chapter 4, pp. 72–75.

27. *Decretum, causa* I, *q.* II, *dictum* after canon 7.

28. "Si ergo non sunt in cenobiis colligendi habentes tunc nec dantes quoniam habet qui dat" (BN lat. 14997, fol. 51ʳ). The author went on to refute this position: "Econtra Samuelum ablactatum anna in tribus vitulis et tribus farine modiis et anphora vini optulit in domum domini in silo. Et in primitiva ecclesia qui se numero fidelium adnunabant vendebant omnia, ponentes precia eorum ante pedes apostolorum. Quorum unus ananias quia de precio fraudavit et spiritui sancto mentiri praesumpsit accepta maledictionis sen-

tentia expiravit. . . . Similiter ex premissis exemplis habes quod liceat offerentem suscipere . . . " (ibid.).

29. "Sed aliud est sua sponte offerre, aliud exacta persolvere" (*Decretum, causa* I, *q.* II, prologue).

30. "Ad hoc notandum est, quod eorum, quae offeruntur, alia sponte, alia coacte praestantur; item alia pactione, alia mera liberalitate. . . . Dicimus ergo nichil omnino exigendum nec exactum solvendum nec pactione aliquid pro ingressu ecclesiae erogandum" (Thaner, *Die Summa*, p. 13).

31. "Non ergo his auctoritatibus permittitur rectoribus ab ingressuris aliquid exigere, sed sponte oblata suscipere, quia illud dampnabile est, hoc vero minime" (*Decretum, causa* I, *q.* II, prologue). The *Summa Parisiensis* noted that, in the proper circumstances, an entrance gift was a praiseworthy thing: "Non debet exigi pecunia [nec] exacta dari vel cum intrante vel ante vel post quia simoniacum est. Sed si gratis offeratur, tunc ante vel post laudabiliter recipitur et laudabiliter datur" (McLaughlin, *Summa Parisiensis*, p. 92). The *summa* "Tractaturus magister" noted, "Huius questionis negativa simpliciter est vera. Sponte tamen oblata post factum non sunt respuenda non precedente duntaxat conditione vel intentione" (BN lat. 15994, fol. 32^r).

32. "Eorum que dantur alia sponte, alia dantur coacte. Item alia pactione, alia mera liberalitate. Nichil vero pro ingressu ecclesie vel pro alicuius sacrae rei datione vel acceptione per pactionem vel exactionem ab aliquo est requirendum vel pactum vel exactum persolvendum" (summa "Cum in tres partes," BN lat. 16540, fol. 2^r). For other expressions of the distinction between a free-will, legitimate offering and an exaction, see the Council of Melfi (1089), Mansi, 20:col. 723; the Council of London, canon 3 (1127), in *The Chronicle of John of Worcester*, ed. J. R. H. Weaver (Oxford, 1908), p. 24. Gerhoh of Reichersperg's *Liber de simoniacis* criticized forced gifts as simoniacal exactions, no matter what euphemism hid them: "Cum enim cenobiorum praelati ab his, quos in suum consortium recipiunt, munera exigunt, ipsam symoniacam avaritiam nomine oblationis tegunt: nimirum satis improprie, cum aliud sit oblatio, aliud exactio; aliud quod sponte offertur, aliud quod etiam ab invitis aufertur et extorquetur" (MGH, *Libelli de Lite*, 3:269).

33. Augustine's sermon 86, Migne, vol. 38, cols. 526–29, dealt with excuses used by the rich to justify their failure to give alms to the poor.

34. De Borman, *Chronique*, 1:261–62.

35. "Tempore quo domnus Nicolaus ecclesie Beati-Dionisii preerat, miles quidam Guillermus videlicet de Villula ipsum adiit, atque ut filium suum, Guillermum nomine, pro Dei suoque amore, monachum facere dignaretur humiliter postulans, promittebat etiam se bona plurima inibi collocaturum, suumque auxilium et consilium in omnibus pro posse adfuturum, si peticio ejus effectum, ut desiderabat, consequeretur. Orricus vero frater prefati Guillermi similia se facturum si impleretur quod petebant fideliter spopondit; prior denique ecclesie sibi commisse sollicite curam gerens, eamque, suo tempore, ampliare desiderans, voluntati eorum satisfacturum ita decrevit si de reditibus suis, cum ipso puero, . . . aliqua conferre satagerent" (*St. Denys*, no. 70, ca. 1190).

36. *Decretum, causa* I, *q.* II, prologue. Cf. Pott 3235.

37. "Verumtamen, si vestrae necessitati adeo est oportunus quem reperistis, dum tamen omnis absit pactio, omnis cesset conventio . . . accedat . . . " (*Decretum, causa* I, *q.* II, canon 2). The decretists laid stress on opposition to pacts in their treatment of the letter of the Pseudo-Boniface: "Respondit papa quod haec quaestio difficilis sibi videtur quia inaudita. Tandem dicit quia ex pacto nihil dare debent, sed accedat ille gratis quem sibi credunt necessarium, et postea si voluerint gratis monasterio in subsidium aliquid dare, poterunt licite" (McLaughlin, *Summa Parisiensis*, p. 92). "Respondet apostolicus, non licere ex pactione, tamen postquam factum fuerit, permittit aliquid dari fratribus illius coenobii, cui prius praeerat" (Schulte, *Die Summa des Stephanus*, p. 145).

38. In his comments on *causa* I, *questio* II, canon 2, *Quam Pio*, Huguccio expressed the view that the timing of a gift could make a difference in assessing its legitimacy: *"Post-modum*, quod non ante ne presumatur symonia, quum enim aliquid licet post quod non licet ante. . . . Quum aliquid licet ante quod non post. . . . Quum quod non licet ante nec post . . . " (BN lat. 3892, fol. 120ᵛ). The Pseudo-Boniface had recommended that the richer monastery give a gift to the poorer house after the monk had come gratis. The *summa* *"Tractaturus magister"* had approved gifts made after the actual entrance: "Sponte tamen oblata post factum non sunt respuenda, non precedente duntaxat conditione vel intentione . . . " (BN lat. 15994, fol. 32ʳ). A gloss to *Compilatio* III, book 5, title 2, canon 6, *Tua*, likewise approved of gifts after reception: "Non tamen receptionis tempore, set postmodum, I. Q.I Emendari et Q. II Quam pio" (Gillmann, *Des Laurentius Hispanus*, p. 72).

39. "Non debet exigi pecunia [nec] exacta dari vel cum intrante vel ante vel post quia simoniacum est. Sed si gratis offeratur, tunc ante vel post laudabiliter recipitur et laudabiliter datur" (McLaughlin, *Summa Parisiensis*, p. 92). The *summa* "De iure naturali" likewise held that timing was irrelevant in judging the simoniacal nature of a gift: "Contraitur autem simonia a pecunia, ab obsequio et lingua, pactione apud homines, intentione apud deum, licet non precesserit pactio. Unde simoniacum intentio facit per obsequium et linguam, pactio per pecuniam, quocumque tempore detur vel accipiatur. Neque enim tantum est simonia dandi et accipiendi, set etiam dati et accepti, quandoque nulla precedente pactione, si intentione, quia promotus es, post dederis . . . " (Nörr, "Die Summen," p. 142). Huguccio also argued that in the case of entry into religious life, the timing of a gift was irrelevant, if the gift was required: "Hic intitulatur ii quaestio scilicet an in progressu [sic] ecclesie peccunia sit exigenda vel exacta persolvenda. Haec quaestio nullam habet dubitationem quia certum est quod in progressu [sic] monasterii, id est cuiuslibet ecclesie, peccunia non est exigenda vel si fuerit exacta persolvenda non est, quia uterque symoniacum est, scilicet exigere vel exactam persolvere sive ante susceptionem sive post susceptionem. Utrumque enim prohibetur scilicet ante et post . . . " (BN lat. 3892, fol. 120ʳ).

40. "Set nunquid eo tempore, quo quis recipitur, potest aliquid offere? Lau. [O:Laur] dixit quod non, . . . Jo. et vi. dixerunt et credo bene, quod licet illo tempore dare, dummodo . . . talis . . . paccio non precesserit, quia si pactum precedit, nec ante nec post dari licet . . . " (Gillmann, *Des Laurentius Hispanus*, p. 72).

41. " . . . Licet quidam autument tunc sine peccato pecuniam pro ingressu exigi, cum aliquid ea intentione exigitur, ut exactum postmodum in necessitatem ecclesie vel pauperum alimoniam erogetur" (Singer, *Die Summa*, p. 224). John of Faenza reported a similar view: "Quidam male putant exigendam si exacta postmodum in necessitatem ecclesie vel alimoniam pauperum erogetur" (BN lat. 14606, fol. 51ʳ).

42. " . . . Que sententia penitus exsufflanda videbitur, si illud cap. Gregorii ad memoriam reducatur, 'Non est putanda' (27), supra q.I et infra II cap" (Singer, *Die Summa*, p. 224). John of Faenza also contradicted the opinion that he had reported, "Sed infringitur hoc ex decreto gregorii, 'Non est putandum' . . . " (BN lat. 14606, fol. 51ʳ).

43. "Nichil inquam a suscipiendis cuiuscumque pietatis obtentu exigendum, ut ait alexander capitulo 'ex multis' circa finem: Constituimus ut nullus cuiuscumque gradus clericus pro ecclesie beneficio audeat aliquid conferre aut in ecclesiarum fabrica vel in donariis ecclesiarum seu etiam quod pauperibus erogetur quia teste scriptura qui ma/le accipit ut bene dispenset gravatur potius quam iuvetur" (BN lat. 14997, fol. 51ʳ-51ᵛ). The reference is to a letter of Alexander II, JL 4722.

44. Bonaventura, *Opera omnia* (Quaracchi, 1898), 8:369–70. Odo Rigaud, *Registrum*, p. 361.

45. "Si aliquis, qui census proprios exuberanter possidet, susceptus est ab ecclesia, que non admodum dives est, exigetur ab eo, ut vel censum suum ecclesie rebus annumeret vel suis rebus incumbat et sumptum de ecclesia non requirat . . . " (Singer, *Die Summa*,

p. 224). John of Faenza repeated Rufinus' view and added to it a reason why a rich person should not be allowed to keep his wealth after entry: "Si aliquis qui census proprios exuberatur [sic] possidet, susceptus est ab ecclesia quae non admodum dives est, exigetur ab eo vel ut censum suum ecclesie rebus annumeret vel de ecclesia sumptum non requiret, maxime cum occasione rerum suarum occupatus servitio desit ecclesie" (BN lat. 14606, fol. 51ʳ).

46. *Decretum, causa* I, *q.* II, canons 6, 7, 8, 9. 10.

47. " . . . Licet quidam prave consuetudinis defensores illa decreta ebriose sentiant data pro canonicis regularibus. Sed quomodo ex auctoritatibus illis indulgetur canonicis regularibus vivere de propriis aut de bonis parentum, cum nullum proprium possidere, sed omnia in · commune habere debeant?" (Singer, *Die Summa,* pp. 224–25). Stephan of Tournai made a similar comment about the applicability of Gratian's texts to regular clergy (Schulte, *Die Summa des Stephanus,* pp. 145–46). John of Faenza followed Rufinus on the issue: "Quidam dicant hoc dici de canonicis regularibus, sed quomodo ex autoritatibus illis indulgeretur canonicis regularibus vivere de bonis parentum aut de propriis cum nullum proprium possidendum, sed omnia in communi habere debeant" (BN lat. 14605, fol. 51ʳ).

48. "Secundo, an pro ingressu ecclesiae sit exigenda pecunia, vel si exacta fuerit, an sit persolvenda?" (*Decretum, causa* I, prologue). "Sequitur secunda questio, qua queritur, an pro ingressu monasterii pecunia sit exigenda, vel exacta persolvenda?" (ibid., *q.* II, prologue). "Auctoritate Bonifacii patenter ostenditur, quod, . . . ita nulli pecuniae interventu ecclesiae largiri oportet ingressum" (ibid., *dictum* after canon 4). "Multorum auctoritatibus luce clarius constat, quod ab ingressuris monasterium non licet pecuniam exigere . . . " (ibid., *dictum* after canon 10).

49. Ibid., canons 6, 7, 8, 9.

50. "Verum his auctoritatibus prohibentur ab ecclesia suscipi non illi, qui quondam fuerunt divites et omnia reliquerunt, . . . aut pauperibus distribuerunt, . . . aut ecclesiae rebus adiunxerunt . . . : sed illi, qui in domibus parentum residentes vel sua relinquere nolentes ecclesiasticis facultatibus pasci desiderant" (ibid., *dictum* after canon 7.

51. "Hec ergo sit in hac questione sententia ut nunquam a suscipiendis sed a susceptis quandoque exigi debeat ut res suas ecclesie adnuerent vel sumptus ab ea non postulent. Susceptis dico ad sustentationem, non ad professionem, quia professis regulam propria habere non licet" (BN lat. 14997, fol. 51ʳ). Stephan of Tournai also commented that Gratian's opinions and texts were not always appropriate for regular clergy: "De secularibus dicit, nam regularibus aequaliter distribuendum, vel generaliter de omnibus . . . " (Schulte, *Die Summa des Stephanus,* p. 146).

52. "Nota tamen, quia, si aliquod coenobium ita pauperrimum est, quod non possit sufficere his qui convertuntur, in hoc casu abbas ab offerente se coenobio et habente aliqua, bene potest exigere id, unde habeat necessaria qui convertitur" (Schulte, *Die Summa des Stephanus,* p. 145). John of Faenza proposed a similar · view in his *summa*: "Nota si aliquod cenobium its pauper est quod nec possit suficere his qui convertuntur, in hoc casu abbas ab offerente se monasterio vel cenobio et habente aliqua bene potest potest [sic] exigere unde habeat necessaria qui convertuntur" (BN lat. 14606, fol. 51ᵛ).

53. "*Autoritate bonifacii. c. quam pio.* Ad versionem [sic], id est, ad fidem et cultum dei, *gregorii c. Sicut episc.* Item opponitur ad id quod dixerat, scilicet quod pro ingressu ecclesie nichil est exigendum a suscipiendis vel susceptis, sed omnes quot recipiuntur debeirent [sic] gratis suscipi et suscepti pasci de rebus ecclesie, exceptis talibus de qualibus locuntur sequentia capitula. A talibus enim et videtur posse exigi ut sua temporalia conferant ecclesie vel abstineatur a sumptibus ecclesie vel locantur" (BN lat. 3892, fol. 120ᵛ).

138

54. "Si tamen ecclesia est adeo pauper quod non possit pluribus quam ibi sunt sufficere, licite potest dicere prelatus volenti illam ecclesiam intrare: ecclesia ista adeo pauper est quod non potest presentibus sufficere et ideo non possumus suscipere. Sed si tu habes undɔ possis vivre parati sumus te recipere et tu offeras ecclesie unde ipsa possis [sic] etiam tibi sufficere. Non notatur hic vicium cupiditatis et symonie, sed simpliciter declaratur necessitas ecclesie" (BN lat. 3892, fol. 120ʳ).

55. "Nota si aliquod cenobium ita pauper est quod nec possit suficere his qui convertuntur in hoc casu abbas ab offerente se monasterio vel cenobio et habente aliqua bene potest exigere unde habeat necessaria qui convertuntur" (BN lat. 14606, fol. 51ᵛ). "Conditionaliter potest ab eo exigi qui ingressus est ecclesiam quae divitiis non habundat, et habet de patrimonio vel de alio unde vivere potest" (*Summa monacensis*, Munich, Clm 16084, fol. 16ʳ). "Suppone quod monasterium adeo extenuatum quod non potest pluribus sufficere. Numquid possunt aliquid exigere? Credo sic in hunc modum, 'Frater, scias quia res huius monasterii pluribus sufficere non possunt; si volueris intrare ducas unde vivere possis" (Tancred on *Compilatio* I, bk. 5, tit. 2, canon 7, BN lat. 15399, fol. 51ᵛ). "Sed quid si monasterium ad quod volo transire non sufficit in possessionibus ad sustinendum plures quam habeat. Respondetur: licite potest a me aliquid petere pro mea sustintacione" (Guilelmus on *Compilatio* I, bk. 5, tit. 2, canon 7, BN lat. 3932, fol. 56ʳ).

56. "Non inde habemus quod ab eo qui, cum nichil promittit, monasterium petit, propter ingressum liceat exigere. Similiter ex premissis exemplis habes quod liceat offerentem suscipere; non tamen quod a suscipiendo fas sit quicquid exigere vel propter oblata susipere" (*Summa coloniensis*, BN lat. 14997, fol. 51ʳ). Peter the Chanter held that, in cases of extreme need, the ability to make a gift could be taken into account: "Aliquis accedit ad pauperem locum ubi sunt quatuor heremite vel monachi quorum singuli habent suum panem tantum. Petit recipi ad conversationem inter illos. Illi, ostendentes paupertatem suam, petunt ut faciat assignari locum unde habeat victum et vestitum tempore vite sue. Accedit dives aliquis et paciscitur cum illis de procurando eo in victu et vestitu suo tempore vite sue. Est ne hec pactio symoniaca? Non credit et distinguit inter causam propter quam et causam sine qua non fieret cum fieri non possit. Causa enim sine qua non fieret, cum fieri possit, est causa propter quam, principalis scilicet non secundaria, et ista inducit symonia in huiusmodi, reliqua non" (Dugauquier, *Summa de Sacramentis*, vol. 3, pars. 2a, 16).

57. "Praecipimus etiam sub poena suspensionis [ne] ab ingressuris claustrum, vel pastus vel vestimentum exigantur, neque denarii, neque aliud in fraudem praedictorum, ita quod propter hoc non repellantur" (canon 27, Council of Paris [1213], Mansi, 22:833b; also in Council of Rouen [1214], canon 30, Mansi, 22:911d).

58. " . . . Sciendum est quod pecunia aliquando exigitur a suscipiendis, aliquando a susceptis; item aliquando absolute, interdum conditionaliter. . . . Itaque a suscipiendis nec absolute nec ullo modo conditionaliter pecunia est exigenda. . . . A susceptis autem nullo genere absolute exigenda est nec conditionaliter, nisi in hoc solummodo casu" (Singer, *Die Summa*, p. 224). The *Summa Monacensis*, written about 1175⁻78, made the same point: "Aliquando peccunia exigitur ab ingressis, aliquando ab ingressuris; quando ab gressuris simonia committitur. Quando ab ingressis refert utrum absolute vel conditionaliter exigatur. Si absolute quidem exigit, simoniam incurrit; si autem conditionaliter nequaquam" (Munich Clm 16084, fol. 16ʳ). The *summa* "Tractaturus magister" reported the same opinion, but not necessarily as its own: "Quidam tamen volunt distinguere inter recipiendos et receptos, dicentes a recipiendis nil omnino esse exigendum nec a receptis absolute, sed conditionaliter si volunt percipere stipendia ecclesie, quoniam ipsi habundant et ecclesia indiget . . . " (BN lat. 15994, fol. 32ʳ). Sicardus of Cremona set up the question of receiving money from those received and from those about to be received in the form of a chart:

139

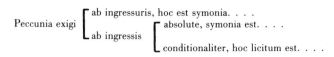

Peccunia exigi [ab ingressuris, hoc est symonia. . . .
ab ingressis [absolute, symonia est. . . .
conditionaliter, hoc licitum est. . . .

(BN lat. 14996, fol. 40ʳ). J. Weitzel, *Begriff und Erscheinungsformen der Simonie bei Gratian und den Dekretisten*, Münchener Theologische Studien, Kanonistische Abteilung, vol. 25 (Munich, 1967), p. 134, note 52, cites this text of Sicardus from Munich Clm 4555, fol. 20ʳ. However, in his printed citation the meaning was reversed:

Peccunia exigitur [ab ingressuris, hoc est simoniacum. . . .
ab ingressis [conditionaliter, haec est simonia. . . .
absolute, hoc licitum est.

It would require an examination of the manuscript used by Weitzel to determine whether this difference was due to a real divergence in the text, or to an error of transcription or printing.

59. "Verumtamen si cenobii nimia paupertas sit intantum ut adaucto numero personarum necesse sit augeri patrimonium, ibi statum loci significare introitum petentibus non improbamus" (BN lat. 14997, fol. 51ᵛ). For Huguccio's comment see above, note 54. Stephan of Tournai also defended the mention of the house's economic state before reception of a new member (Schulte, *Die Summa des Stephanus*, p. 145).

60. "Quidam plus dicunt etiam taxationes hoc casu licere, habentes quo tueantur hanc suam opinionem cenobitarum consuetudinem" (BN lat. 14997, fol. 51ᵛ).

61. "Similiter, si aliqua congregatio egeat in tantum quod non possit plures recipere fratres, si quis petit fraternitatem ipsius, possunt ab eo licite exigere tantum unde possit ibi sustentari, quamdiu vixerit; sed eo mortuo debent illa reddere, nisi velit ea sibi gratis conferre. Si vero exigant ab eo perpetuum, symonia est, cum sine illo esse possent" (Dugauquier, *Summa de sacramentis*, vol. 3, pars. 2a, 14).

62. "Si autem monasterium eguerit, ita quod offerentem se illi, sine pecunia recipere non possit vel sustentare, spiritualem fraternitatem ei concedat, non corporalem; vel in exceptionem pauṛertatis suae, et sustentationem vitae illius exigere potest ab eo, ut eum recipiat, et temporales redditus, quibus tantum sustenetur dum vixerit. Quod si perpetuos exegerit, jam manifesta cupiditas vitiosum facit ingressum" (*Verbum abbreviatum*, chap. 38, Migne, 205:130‑31). Radulphus Ardens, apparently a disciple of Peter the Chanter, included this text, with minor modifications, in his *Speculum universale*, bk. 12, chap. 73, BN lat. 3240, fol. 128ʳ. Concerning Radulphus see M.-T. d'Alverny, "L'Obit de Raoul Ardent," *Archives d'histoire doctrinale et littéraire du moyen âge* 15/17 (1940‑42): 403‑5; and J. Gründel, *Das "Speculum Universale" des Radulphus Ardens*, Mitteilungen des Grabmann-Instituts der Universität München, vol. 5 (Munich, 1961), p. 3.

63. *Decretum, causa* I, *q.* II, canon 2, *Quam pio.*

64. It is striking how often the commentators summed up the letter in a single sentence, and then went on to treat merely verbal difficulties: see McLaughlin, *Summa Parisiensis*, p. 92; Singer, *Die Summa*, p. 225; Huguccio, BN lat. 3892, fol. 120ᵛ; *summa* "Omnis qui iuste iudicat," Rouen ms. 743, fol. 50ᵛ-51ʳ.

65. "Queritur si alicui liceat vendere seipsum ad religionis habitum . . . suscipiendum. Verbi gratia. Aliquis invitatur ad monasticum habitum suscipiendum ab abbate vidente ecclesiam suam indigere tali persona. Dicit ille se pauperculam matrem habere quam nec vult, nec potest derelinquere desolatam vel sororem innuptam, vel se obligatum ere alieno.

THE CANONISTS AND SIMONIACAL RECEPTION

Queritur an liceat ei sine pactione ita vendicare se ipsum ut, scilicet ea intentione, ingrediatur monasterium illorum si liberaverint eum ab ere alieno. Pactio enim in tali casu excluditur, Ca. I, Q.II, Quampio" (Dugauquier, *Summa de sacramentis*, vol. 3, pars. 2a, 45-46). The *summa* "Tractaturus magister" made a similar point: " . . . Non debet aliquid promitti alicui ut convertatur . . . sed forte posset ei fieri spes aliqua, non certa pactio" (BN lat. 15994, fol.32ʳ). A twelfth-century charter of the Cistercian house of Berdoues offers a confirmation of Peter the Chanter's hypothetical cases. The abbot provided a dowry for the daughter of a monk, in order that the monk would confirm a gift he and his sons had made at the time of his entry (*Berdoues*, nos. 481 and 482).

66. "Nonne intentio symoniam inducit? At symonia talis, si symonia est, non multum videtur habere impietatis. Sed nunquid non est symonia cum religiosi habitus susceptio redigatur sub pretium? Nunquid item si symonia est mortale peccatum?" (Dugauquier, *Summa de sacramentis*, vol. 3, pt. 2a, p. 46).

67. "Quod cum intellexisset praepositus praedicti monasterii, pecuniam libentissime solvit, et Scholasticus statim habitum suscepit" (*Dialogus Miraculorum*, ed. J. Strange [Cologne, 1851], 1: 228).

68. *Vigeois*, no. 338, 1165-71.

69. *Decretum, causa* I, prologue.

70. "In hoc autem non fuit ignorantia iuris, sed facti, et illius, quod non oportuit eum scire. A reatu ergo criminis excusat eum ignorantia paterni delicti, quod etsi oportuisset eum scire, infirmitate tamen etatis deprehendere non poterat" (ibid., *q*. IV, *dictum* after canon 13).

71. "Queritur quae penitentia sit simoniacis iniungenda. Respenditur, non est auctoritate taxata sed arbitraria" (*Summula decretalium quaestionum*, Reims ms. 689, fol. 23ʳ).

72. "Si quis episcopus ob pecuniam fecerit ordinationem et sub pretio redegerit gratiam, quae non potest venundari, ordinaveritque per pecunias episcopum aut presbyterum seu diaconum vel quemlibet ex his, qui connumerantur in clero, aut promoverit per pecunias dispensatorem aut defensorem vel quemquam, qui subiectus est regulae, pro suo turpissimo lucri commodo: is, cui hoc adtemptanti probatum fuerit, proprii gradus periculo subiacebit, et qui ordinatus est, nihil ex hac ordinatione vel promotione, quae est per negotiationem facta, proficiat. Sed sit alienus ea dignitate vel sollicitudine, quam per pecunias adquisivit. Si quis vero mediator tam turpibus et nefandis datis vel acceptis exstiterit, si quidem clericus fuerit, proprio gradu decidat, si vero laicus aut monachus anathematizetur" (J. Alberigo et al., eds., *Conciliorum oecumenicorum decreta* [Freiburg im Breisgau 1962], pp. 63-64). Gratian included this canon in the *Decretum, causa* I, *questio* I, canon 8.

73. Alberigo, *Conciliorum*, canon 64, pp. 240-41.

74. The letters of Stephan of Tournai, who was himself a decretist, contain much information about the restlessness among religious in the second half of the twelfth century. He interceded for repentant apostates, and for religious seeking legal permission to transfer from one order to another (*Les lettres d'Etienne de Tournai*, ed. J. Desilve [Paris-Valenciennes, 1893], nos. 1, 15, 32, 57, 101, 103, 135, 264, 288). In *causa* XX, *questio* IV, *dictum* after canon 3, Gratian had forbidden a monk to take a pilgrimage vow without his abbot's permission, precisely because such a vow might be used to escape from regular life and discipline. See also K. Fina, "*Ovem Suam Require*. Eine Studie zur Geschichte des Ordenswechsels im 12. Jahrhundert," *Augustiniana* 7 (1957): 33-56.

75. "Queri solet hic, cum tales promotiones, sicut ait Calcedonense concilium, in nullo proficiant . . . , utrum aliquis per pecuniam datam vel acceptam vel per aliquam pro-

missionem factus monachus monachico habitu debeat expoliari? Ad quod dicimus quoniam sicut, si aliquis monachus ordinaretur in episcopum per pecuniam, non amitteret sacramentum ordinis—quod sive bene sive male susceptum est id, quod est—amitteret tamen sacramenti dignitatem, propter quam solam optinendam et non propter sacramentum dedit pecuniam,—non enim de sacramento curaret, si a sacramento dignitas absisteret—: ita et quando per pecuniam acceptam vel datam aliquis in aliquo loco fit monachus, debet eo privari, propter quod dedit vel accepit pecuniam—scil. ne ibi sit monachus; propter hoc enim pecunia data est. Non autem simpliciter expoliandus est habitu monachali; non enim pecunia oblata est, ut monachus fieret, sed ut monachus esset ibi" (Singer, *Die Summa*, pp. 229-30).

76. Penal exile as a form of punishment was in use in the twelfth and thirteenth centuries within religious orders: see Canivez, *Statuta*, vol. 1, chap. 5, 1202; vol. 2, chap. 68, 1233; chap. 7, 1247; vol. 3, chap. 3, 1262.

77. "Hoc ergo casu excepto, si quis per pecuniam monachus efficitur utrum habitu expoliandus sit queritur. Ad hoc non dedit pecuniam ut monachus fieret, sed ut ibi monachus esset. Unde et ab eo loco removendus, non ab austeritate religionis seperandus ne si hoc dixerimus, profugis viam pandamus" (BN lat. 14997, fol.51ᵛ). Sicardus of Cremona held the same view: "Queritur itaque si aliquis interventu peccunie effectus monachus sit monachico habitu expoliandus. Videtur, quia nullus ex promotione quae est per negotionem facta proficiat. . . . Respondeo, privetur eo cenobio sed non illo habitu. Non enim data est pecunia propter habitum" (BN lat. 14996, fol. 43ʳ-43ᵛ).

78. John of Faenza commented that the habit itself was a *pena*, a punishment: "Queritur cum tales promotiones in nullo proficiant, . . . utrum aliquis per pretium monachus Sancti Proculi factus monachico habitu debeat expoliari. Dicimus quod non habitum, cum pena sit, sed monasterio privabitur. Non enim propter habitum sed propter monasterium pretium dedit" (BN lat, 14606, fol. 52ᵛ).

79. In addition to Rufinus, John of Faenza, Sicardus of Cremona, and the author of the *Summa coloniensis*, Everard of Ypres, also recommended penal exile for a simoniacally received religious: "Queritur utrum aliquis interventu pecunie monachus factus monachico sit habitu expoliandus. Responditur: Videtur privandus illo cenobio non habitu" (*Summula decretalium quaestionum*, Reims ms. 689, fol. 22ᵛ); and so did the author of the *Summa Lipsiensis*: "Quid fiet de eo qui monachus factus est per pecuniam? Nunquid debet monachico habitu expoliari sicut iste qui ecclesiam emit? Et dicimus quod non habitu spoliabitur cum hoc pena sit. Sed monasterio privabitur, non enim propter habitum sed propter monasterium pecuniam dedit" (Rouen ms. 743, fol. 51ᵛ).

80. *Veniens*, JL 14149.

81. *De regularibus*, JL 16562.

82. E. Friedberg, *Quinque compilationes antiquae nec non Collectio Canonum Lipsiensis* (Leipzig, 1882). For the origin and dating of the *compilationes*, see Kuttner, *Repertorium*, pp. 322-85; R. Naz, "Compilationes (Quinque Antiquae)," *DDC*, 3:1239-41; and Le Bras et al., *L'Age classique*, pp. 227-32.

83. " . . . tam recipiens quam recepta, sive sit subdita sive praelata, sine spe restitutionis de suo monasterio expellatur, in locum arctioris regulae, ad agendum perpetuam poenitentiam retrudenda" (Alberigo, *Conciliorum*, p. 240).

84. Master Honorius recommended an unpleasant readmission if a house of exile were not available, "Solutio: dici potest in eodem posse retrudi qui nihominus [*sic*] locum emptum amittitur nec enim ibi erit ut frater sed potius ut in ergastulum detrusus et ita amitit quod ibi habebat honoris, eis qui sunt honeris remanentibus" (BN lat. 14591, fol. 61ʳ). Canon 64 of the Fourth Lateran Council provided that if no house of exile was available,

"ne forte damnabiliter in saeculo evagentur, recipiantur in eodem monasterio dispensative de novo mutatis prioribus locis et inferioribus assignatis" (Alberigo, *Conciliorum*, pp. 240-41).

85. "Nam qui sub religionis obtentu Deo famulari voluerit, si quid acceperit, et meritum perdit, et beneficio accepto frustratur. Rationis ergo vigore cogitur quod iniuste recepit restituere, et quicquid turpis lucri gratia receperat non tenere" (*Decretum, causa* I, *q.* III, canon 2). Loewenfeld attributed the letter to Gregory VII (JL 5276).

86. " . . . Ecclesiae vendicetur, cuius voluit sacerdotium emere. Si autem laicus est, qui pro hac causa aliquid accepit, vel mediator rei factus est, ea quae data sunt, in duplum ab eo exigantur, ecclesiae vendicanda" (Schulte, *Die Summa des Paucapalea*, p. 55). The *lex Justiniani* is *Novella* VI, c. i, 9, in *Corpus juris civilis*, vol. 3, ed. R. Schoell and R. Kroll (Berlin, 1895), p. 38.

87. "Sed illud decretum de ecclesiastica mansuetudine, istud vero Iustiniani de rigore iuris intelligitur dictum" (Schulte, *Die Summa des Paucapalea*, p. 55).

88. "Fuerunt hic qui dicerent pecuniam restituendam non ei, qui dedit, sed ecclesiae vel pauperibus dandam. Sed hoc non restituere esset, sed potius destituere; restituere enim est prius habenti reddere. Erit ergo magis intergrum estimare perverso datori pecuniam reddendam esse . . ." (Singer, *Die Summa*, pp. 226-27).

89. ". . . Non quod ipse dator repetere possit quod ob turpem causam dedit; sed in sempiternum ejus obprobrium reddetur sibi pecunia, ut secum sit in perditionem, quia existimavit donum Dei pecunia possideri" (Singer, *Die Summa*, p. 227). Everard of Ypres, in his *Summula decretalium quaestionum*, agreed: "Queritur cui pecunia sit reddenda an fisco vel ecclesie vel pauperibus vel datori. Respondeo datori reddenda cui dicendum est quod petrus symoni, 'Pecunia tua tecum sit in perditione.' " (Reims ms. 689, fol. 22ᵛ).

90. "Non igitur ecclesiae huiusmodi pecunia est offerenda nec pauperibus danda—pro eo quod precepit Dominus filiis Israel, ut afferrent oleum de olivis purissimum ad concinnandas lucernas in tabernaculo Domini [et] quia non de alienis, sed de nostris bonis elemosinam facere debemus . . ." (Singer, *Die Summa*, p. 227).

91. "Cum ergo clericus alicuius ecclesiae dat alicui pecuniam de ecclesia, ut ad ecclesiam serviturus adveniat, tunc et dator et acceptor graviter puniendus est, pecunia autem ecclesiae restituenda est, quia delictum persone in dampnum ecclesiae non est convertendum, ut j. C. 16, q.6 Si episcopum" (ibid.). See *Decretum, causa* XVI, *questio* VI, canon 2, for the legal basis for this view.

92. " . . . In eo casu loquitur, quando aliquis bono zelo ad praelaturam emitur a fratribus, reddi debet ecclesiae, quoniam et in hoc casu turpiter facit, non qui dat, sed qui recipit" (Schulte, *Die Summa des Stephanus*, p. 147). "Queritur cui restituet. Si dixerimus hoc decretum de eo tamen loqui qui a clerico alicuius ecclesiae pecuniam accipit ut ad illam ecclesiam veniat serviturus, . . . licet qui sic peccuniam ecclesiae dat vel accipit tamquam symoniacus graviter sit puniendus, tamen peccunia est ecclesie restituenda quia delictum persone non est convertendum in damnum ecclesie . . ." (John of Faenza, BN lat. 14606, fol. 52ʳ). See also the *summa* "Tractaturus magister," BN lat. 15994, fol. 32 ʳ, Huguccio, BN lat. 3892, fol. 121ᵛ. Nörr, "Die Summen," pp. 161-63, has a collection of texts from decretists on the issue of the fate of money simoniacally received.

93. "Videtur innuere, quod, qui aliquid acceperit ex venditione spiritualium, ei, a quo accepit, debeat restituere. Sed cum uterque sit in pari causa turpitudinis, qui dedit non poterit repetere; quoniam in turpi causa melior est conditio possidentis. Sed restituere cogitur non danti, sed ecclesiae vel pauperibus" (Schulte, *Die Summa des Stephanus*, p. 147).

94. *Novella* VI, c. i, 9.

95. "Videtur quod non fisco sed potius ecclesie, quia data est in iniuriam ecclesie ut XVII, q.IIII Si quis in atrio" (Sicardus of Cremona, BN lat. 14996, fol. 43ᵛ). The *summa* "Tractaturus magister" mentioned giving the money to the church as one possibility among several: "Queritur cui cum potior sit conditio possidentis . . . nec ecclesia debet lucra querere ex iniquitate . . . nec de talibus debet fieri elemosinas. . . . Potest dici quod ecclesie in conpensationem iniurie, ar. XVII, q. IIII Si quis in atrio, XV, q. ult. Cum multe; vel ipsi qui dedit in detestationem persone, sicut legitur dixisse petrus simoni . . ." (BN lat. 15994, fol. 32ʳ). Nörr, "Die Summen," p. 162, says that the injury concept, used as a way to claim the illicit payment for the church, was cited for the first time by Sicardus and the "Tractaturus magister."

96. "Item pecunia simoniace accepta dicitur restituenda. . . . Set cui, cum nec dans habet repetitionem nec accipiens retentionem? Non ergo melior erit causa possidentis. Dicunt eam esse reddendam ecclesie, in cuius iniuriam constat esse datam, exemplo pecunie ob calumpniam prestite, que nec danti redditur nec accipienti retinere permittitur, set ei conceditur, in cuius calumpniam data est . . ." (Durham University, Cosin V III 3, fol. 42ʳ, cited in Nörr, "Die Summen," p. 161).

97. "Nota quod pecunia symoniaca debet restitui non ei qui dedit, set eius heredi . . ." (*summa* "Permissio quedam," cited in Nörr, "Die Summen," p. 162; see also Schulte, *Die Summa des Stephanus*, p. 147).

98. ". . . Vel si heredes non habeat districtiori monasterio, in quod retraditur . . ." (*summa* "Permissio quedam," cited in Nörr, "Die Summen," p. 162). The *Summa Lipsiensis* reported the opinion, though without embracing it: "Dicunt quidam quod debet restitui non ei qui dedit, sed eius heredi ut infra XVI, Q. ult Constituit vel si heredes non habeat districtiori monasterio in quo retrudetur ut infra XVI. Q VI De lapsis" (Rouen ms. 743, fol. 51ʳ).

99. "Queritur cui debet restitui pecunia. . . . Secundum alios debet restitui ecclesie ad cuius iniuriam et ad cuius precium data est pecunia. . . . Horum sententiam applicamus, approbamus quia haec hodie optinet sine quaestione" (Rouen ms. 743, fol. 51ʳ).

100. ". . . Ne, si nudentur, locis, in quibus dati fuerint, sint onerosi" (*Decretum*, *causa* XVI, *q*. VI, canon 4). This text, JL 1112, was an excerpt from Pope Gregory's register, bk. 1, no. 42; cf. MGH, *Epist. Gregorii I Papae Registrum Epistolarum*, ed. P. Ewald and L. Hartmann (Berlin, 1891), 1:67, lines 7 ff.

101. ". . . Si ita esse inveneris, abbatem et monachos ad restituendam pecuniam praefato F. tam indigne acceptam, instanter admoneas et cum omni districtione compellas . . . , praecipias dicto F., ut in alio monasterio in habitu monastico Domino studeat deservire" (JL 14149).

102. "Nota pecuniam simoniace receptam ei restituendam, in cuius iniuriam data est. . . . Ei tamen, qui dedit, invenitur ex misericordia restituata . . ." (gloss to *Compilatio* I, bk. 5, tit. 2, *Tua*, cited in F. Gillmann, "*Magister Albertus Glossator der Compilatio II*," *Archiv für katholisches Kirchenrecht* 105 [1925]: 149).

103. "Set cur ei, cum potius monasterio, in cuius preiuditium pecunia data est debeatur . . . ? Solutio: penes monasterium pecunia remanere non potuit, quin monachi inde lucrum sentirent, quo penitus se fecerunt indignos. Ad secundum dicimus, quod nullo dampno hic afficitur monasterium, cui nil deperit, si que sunt aliena, reddantur. . . . Item in favorem secundi monasterii hoc fit, ut s. XVI, q. VI De lapsis, alias regulariter monasterio deberetur . . ." (Gillmann, "Magister Albertus," p. 149).

104. ". . . Quod pecunia propter symoniam data ei ecclesie dari debet, in cuius ignominiam fuit soluta. . . . Solutio: dixit Al . . . , quod illud est ius commune, hoc ex dispensatione et misericordia intelligitur. Alii dicunt, quod propter delictum abbatis et

144

monachorum fit, quod hic dicitur, quia monachi, si remaneret peccunia apud monasterium, sentirent lucrum, quo se fecerunt indignos. Mihi videtur, quod clerico in seculo remanenti non debet reddi peccunia, set remanet apud ecclesiam. . . . Si autem debet ad religionem transire, optinet, quod hic dicitur, ne sit honerosus secundo monasterio . . ." (ibid. pp. 148-49). The Premonstratensians made just such a distinction between novices leaving their order to enter another order and novices returning to the world: "Sin autem aliquis remanere voluerit [correct to noluerit], quia promisit se ad aliam communem vitam, consilio abbatis cum his que attulit se transferat. Si vero ad seculum redire voluerit, nihil ei reddetur, sed lazaris vel aliis pauperibus quicquid attulit sub testimonio distribuatur" (R. van Waefelghem, "Les premiers statuts de l'ordre de Prémontré: le clm 17. 174 [XIIe siècle]," *Analectes de l'ordre de Prémontré* 9 [1913]: 38).

CHAPTER SIX

Measures against
Simoniacal Entry, 1163–1198

 The work of the canonists was primarily an intellectual achievement—the definition of a problem and the elaboration of measures to deal with it. Theirs was an activity of the lecture hall and the study, but not necessarily of the real world. It remains now to trace the consequences of the canonists' concern with simoniacal entry, as those consequences appeared in the church at large. The accession of Innocent III to the papal throne in 1198 heralded a major shift in the intensity of the campaign against simoniacal entry, and therefore this chapter will concentrate on measures taken against monastic simony before Innocent, and the next chapter on Innocent's role, which culminated in the sixty-fourth canon of the Fourth Lateran Council.

Papacy and Episcopate, 1163–1198

Alexander III, the first of the popes trained as a canonist, was also the first to attempt to translate into practice the views of the canonists on simoniacal entry. Roland Bandinelli had been one of the earliest students of the *Decretum*, and he completed a succinct commentary on it between 1143 and 1145.[1] In that work he broached the question of simoniacal entry and treated it briefly:

> In the second question, "Whether money may be demanded for entry of a church, etc." At this point it should be noted that of those things which are offered, some are put forward willingly, others as a result of force; likewise, some by pact, others by simple generosity. But nothing

ought to be demanded by force or pact for entrance to a church. Therefore, we say nothing at all should be demanded or [if] demanded paid,
nor should anything be asked by pact for the entrance to a church.[2]

Bandinelli's commentary was one of the earliest of the genre,
and consequently it did not have as its background the complicated
academic discussions of several generations of decretists. However,
in brief compass it stated adequately the central canonist theme of
entry into religious life free from force or pact. From the modest
scope of his comments, it would be unwarranted to conclude that
Bandinelli the canonist was exceptionally interested in the question of simoniacal entry. He gave the issue the same brief treatment that he accorded to most topics in his commentary. But the
passage stands as proof that Bandinelli was aware of the problem
of simoniacal entry from at least the mid-1140s.

Bandinelli's subsequent career was deeply marked by his studies
of canon law. When, in 1159, he was elected pope under the name
Alexander III, he began a twenty-two year pontificate of major
significance for the future development of the papacy and the
church.[3] He approached the problem of ruling the church with an
armory of intellectual models, value judgements, and ideas that
derived in great part from his study of canon law.[4]

In view of his canonist training, it is probably no accident that
Alexander III was the first twelfth-century pope to take an active
interest in the crime of simoniacal entry into religious houses.
At Tours in 1163 he gathered a council to pursue the goals of reform and church unity. At that council, apparently for the first
time since 1099, a papally presided assembly legislated against
simoniacal reception of monks:

> Avarice is not satisfactorily refuted among the people if it is not
> avoided in every way by those who are seen to be members of the
> clergy, and particularly those who, having spurned the world, profess
> the name and rule of religious. Therefore, we prohibit that any money
> be required from those who wish to go to religion. . . .[5]

As its preamble indicates, this canon was directed against forms
of simony practiced by religious, and it forbade several other varieties of monastic malpractice. Apparently, the framers of the

canon thought that the demand for a payment from those wishing to enter religious life was an actual or potential source of scandal to the people. The canon contained no specific punishment for the various monastic simoniacs who were criticized. It was content to threaten them with the fate of Simon Magus, i.e., damnation.[6]

This lack of a particular sanction was not uncommon in twelfth-century conciliar canons, which were frequently intended simply to alert public opinion to an abuse, create guilt feelings among offenders, and arouse the concern of the important ecclesiastics and laymen attending the council.[7]

However, the failure of the Council of Tours to specify a sanction for simoniacal entry may indicate that the pope and bishops present intended that the well-known general sanction against simony be applied, i.e., the loss of the position simoniacally gained and the deposition of the simoniacal seller. The course of decretist discussion in the 1160s and 1170s, that is, after the Council of Tours, called into question the application of the normal sanctions against simoniacal religious, primarily because of a reluctance to encourage apostasy from the religious habit.[8] The Council of Tours and its canon "Non satis" reflected the rather rudimentary state of the issue in the early 1160s, when the focus of attention was on the simoniacal prelate but not on the simoniacally received monk.

When Alexander III again took up the issue of simoniacal entry at the Third Lateran Council in 1179, the new conciliar canon "Monachi non pretio" reflected the decretist arguments of the preceding sixteen years, and it incorporated sanctions designed to meet the reluctance of canonists to expel monks from the religious habit, even if that habit were obtained simoniacally:

> Let monks not be received for a price in a monastery. . . . However, if anyone were pressed and gave anything for his reception, may he not ascend to holy orders. May he however who took the payment suffer the loss of his office. . . . May an abbot who does not take care diligently in these matters know that he will suffer the loss of his office.[9]

The guilty entrant was to be punished by declaring him ineligible, or *irregularis* as the canonists designated the condition, to receive further holy orders.[10] Such an ineligibility served the dual role of punishing the simoniac monk while not allowing him any opportunity to escape from his commitment to the religious life. In these two functions it responded to the similar concerns of the decretists, although I have found no recommendation of this particular punishment among the decretists whom I have studied. The decretists who addressed themselves to the appropriate punishment for a simoniac entrant generally recommended penal exile to another religious house.[11] The punishment of simoniac religious by declaring them ineligible to receive holy orders may be an innovation of the Third Lateran Council, or of Alexander himself. On the other hand, the council's decision to depose an abbot who had received a monk simoniacally was the normal punishment for all forms of simony, and could be applied readily because the deposed abbot would remain a monk.

In addition to these two important conciliar texts, Alexander issued a decretal letter, "Veniens," that had several points in common with the academic discussion of the issue of simoniacal entry. Unfortunately, the recipient of the letter and its exact date are not known:

> F., a priest, who came before us, told us on his own authority that the abbot and brethren of Saint R. were unwilling to receive him as a monk until he agreed to give them for reception as a monk thirty shillings; when the agreement had been concluded, on the following day they put on him the monastic habit, and those same monks demanded thirty shillings, the abbot ten, and the *familia* twelve for a meal, asserting that this was on account of the custom of the monastery.[12]

The priest F. had complained before Alexander III that he had been compelled to pay fifty-two shillings for entry into the monastery of Saint R. Since F. had initially agreed to pay thirty shillings, it is clear that he objected to the new sum required rather than to the payment as such. For Alexander, it was the procedure itself that was objectionable.[13] The entry of F. for a fee in cash would probably have proceeded smoothly, if the payment to the abbot and that to the *familia* had been settled as amicably as that due to the monastic community. From the letter it is probable that F. saw the dispute as breach of contract, rather than simony.

Alexander remarked in his letter that the sole proof for the priest's accusations was his personal assertion. Therefore, the pope instructed the local bishop to investigate the situation:

> . . . If you find the situation as described, may you immediately urge and with all pressure compel the abbot and monks to return to the forementioned F. the money so unworthily received; and suspending the abbot and the senior persons of the monastery from the execution of office because of an excess of such a great wickedness, may you order the said F. that he strive to serve the Lord in another monastery in the monastic habit.[14]

Because they had participated in this simoniacal reception, the abbot and the important members of the community were to be suspended from office, that is, they lost the right to exercise any of the functions given to them by their positions within the house. This punishment was similar to the *privatio officii* prescribed by the Third Lateran Council, but was less severe in that the guilty parties did not actually lose the positions that they had abused. Presumably, some ecclesiastical judge, perhaps Alexander himself, would have to decide the duration of the suspension and its final outcome, either reintegration into office or deposition.[15] The illicitly received money was to be returned to F., and he was to be ordered to enter another house. Alexander's letter said pointedly that F. had been received as a monk, and the bishop investigating the case was to ensure that F. remained a monk in some other monastery.

The return of the illicitly used money and the exile of the simoniac monk were measures frequently proposed in the decretists' discussion and, indeed, sometimes in conjunction with one another. It is difficult to know for certain whether the pope's letter suggested the solution to the decretists or the decretists themselves were the source used by Alexander. As a matter of policy, Alexander III did not cite the sources for his decisions.[16] In this case Alexander was probably depending on the decretists, perhaps on the decretist Rufinus. The latter composed his *summa* on the

151

Decretum between 1157 and 1159, i.e., before Alexander became pope. In that work Rufinus proposed both that the payment be returned to the illicit giver and that the simoniacal monk be sent to another house.[17] Alexander's adoption of this view reenforced its use by later decretists, who could cite his authority for it.[18]

The canons "Non satis" of Tours (1163) and "Monachi non pretio" of the Third Lateran Council (1179) and the decretal letter "Veniens" represented different stages in the development of Alexander's views on the subject of simoniacal entry and of the measures required to cope with it. The apparent chronological sequence of the texts was the canon of Tours, the decretal letter, and then the canon of the Third Lateran council.[19] The three texts reflected Alexander's growing awareness of the complexity of the problem and of the academic discussion about it. Over a period of about fifteen years, Alexander's views became more complex. From a position of silence on the fate of the guilty monk, he moved in his decretal to the provision that the monk F. receive his money and enter another monastery. By 1179 he apparently had adopted the general proposition that simoniac entrants should be ineligible for holy orders. His treatment of the simoniac abbot developed from silence to suspension, and finally to deposition from office. The three texts also testify to a certain independence from the academic canonists, since, at the Third Lateran Council, Alexander chose a solution that was, so far as I know, not commonly proposed by the decretists for simoniac monks, that of making the simoniacs *irregulares*.

The texts of Alexander III were significant in at least three ways for the development of the issue of simoniacal entry into religious life. First, they took an abuse that was, so to speak, invented by Gratian and his commentators and gave it full legal standing as a crime with punishments tailored to it. Second, Alexander's decisions to condemn simoniacal entry at Tours and at the Lateran gave the issue a major dose of publicity in two of the largest ecclesiastical gatherings of the second half of the twelfth century.[20] Finally, and most significantly, these three texts of Alexander became, in their turn, a stimulus to further canonical discussion and elaboration. The texts were incorporated into the new canonical collections of the later twelfth century, which were intended to supplement Gratian and to embody the new papally created canon law.

In the twelfth century the significance of a conciliar canon or of a papal decretal for future development was, to a large degree, determined by its inclusion or lack of inclusion in the larger canonical tradition. No matter what its intrinsic interest, if a text remained hidden in a papal register or in a monastic cartulary, its role in future legal development was likely to be nil. The importance of Alexander's three texts lies in the fact that they were incorporated into new canonical collections, were explicated and commented by canonists, and their solutions were woven back into the fabric of the canonistic discussion of the problem of simoniacal entry.[21]

In addition to the two conciliar canons and the decretal letter in which the activity of Alexander III is clearly visible, there was one council (or perhaps two) held in England during his pontificate that may reflect his influence. After a vacancy of more than two years following the murder of Thomas Becket, the see of Canterbury was filled in 1173 by the election of Richard, the Benedictine prior of Saint Martin's at Dover.[22] The election was disputed, and Richard was forced to go to the papal curia to vindicate his claim to be the rightful archbishop of Canterbury. Alexander III ruled in his favor, and the pope consecrated Richard at Anagni on 7 April 1174.[23]

Archbishop Richard's relations with the pope during the remaining seven years of Alexander's reign were, from an official point of view, close. Richard served often as judge-delegate of the pope, and was a frequent recipient of papal letters. Charles Duggan, in his study of English decretal collections, stressed Richard's role as the recipient of many of the letters that were ultimately incorporated into the English decretal collections. Indeed, Richard was perhaps responsible for the creation of decretal collections composed in part of the letters that he had received from Alexander III.[24]

Archbishop Richard has been credited with two church councils in which simoniacal entry was condemned. The first is the

Council of Westminster (1173), in the course of which Richard was elected archbishop. Thirty-seven canons were attributed to this council by the eighteenth-century editor of councils, David Wilkins.[25] The twenty-fourth canon said, "Let nothing be demanded for receiving monks, canons, [or] nuns in a monastery."[26] In fact, the unique manuscript in which these canons survive does not attribute them to the Council of Westminister (1173), but notes simply that they were canons of a council of Archbishop Richard, without specifying a place or date.[27] The canons attributed to Westminster (1173) may represent a schema drawn up for the Council of Westminster in 1175. However, the differences between the canons of Westminster (1173) and those of Westminster (1175) are such as to give support to the view that the canons of Westminster (1173) are in fact a record of some undated council held during Richard's pontificate, i.e., 1173–84.[28]

In any case, from 11 May to 18 May 1175, Archbishop Richard presided at a council at Westminster in which he personally promulgated a set of canons that were, in general, a reworking of certain elements of Gratian's *Decretum* for local needs. This council was one of the earliest examples of the explicit use of the *Decretum* as a model for the canons of a local synod.[29] The eighth canon of Westminster (1175) was an amalgamation of the seventh canon of Melfi (1089), as it appeared in the *Decretum*, and the third canon of the Council of London (1127): "From the decree of Pope Urban. May no prelate presume, in receiving a monk or a canon or a nun, to take or to demand a price from those who come to conversion, by reason of any pact. However, if anyone shall have done this, may he be anathema."[30]

There is to my knowledge no conclusive evidence that Richard of Dover derived his concern with the problem of simoniacal entry from Alexander III. It is quite possible that Archbishop Richard, with his experience as a monastic prior, papal judge-delegate, and patron of canonical collections, was aware of the problem from other sources. His interest may simply reflect the growing concern on the part of the hierarchy of the church about simoniacal entry. However, leaving aside the probably authentic but undated first "Council of Westminster," it is striking that at Westminster in 1175, less than a year after he left the court of a pope clearly interested in the issue, Richard chose to legislate against the practice. His was the only non-papal council of Alexander's pontificate that I have found to have done so. Whether Richard acted as a disciple of Alexander or as a prelate independently interested in the abuse of simoniacal entry, his council or councils are a further example of the manner in which the concerns of the canonistic schools were transformed into ecclesiastical practice.

There was at least one other prominent figure at the court of Alexander III who expressed an interest in preventing simoniacal entry to religious houses. Albert de Mora had taught at Bologna and may have written a commentary on Gratian's *Decretum*. He was a cardinal-deacon at the papal curia by 1155–56, and for thirty years thereafter he served the papacy in various capacities. In 1178 he was chosen by Alexander III to be papal chancellor, and in 1187 Albert was elected pope as Gregory VIII. He died after a reign of only 57 days.[31]

In 1167–70 Albert de Mora founded a regular canonry dedicated to Saint Andrew at Benevento, his natal city. To govern his foundation, he issued a series of *observantiae* or *institutiones* to serve as a supplement to the Rule of Saint Augustine, under which the canons lived. In 1187 Pope Urban III issued a papal bull recounting and confirming those *institutiones*.[32] The second provision of the regulations dealt with the new entrant and his property. In essence it declared that the entrant was permitted, but not required, to make a modest free-will offering for his clothing during the period of probation. If he gave or promised more than was proper, both the entrant and the official who received it were to be suspended from their religious duties until the papacy had judged them. After the entrant had taken his final vows, he or his friends could give a gift, if they wished.[33] Albert's provisions for his foundation provide another insight into the critical role that canonists played at the papal court in spreading the new concern about illicit entry.

The only other papal text on monastic simony that I have been able to find before the pontificate of Innocent III is a response of Clement III (1187–91) to the bishop of Saragossa in Spain:

> You wished to consult us about regular canons or monks who had entrance by simony, which they knew about and arranged. Since many authorities are found to have given an opinion on this subject, for that reason we respond nothing but what has been laid down, that they completely give up the place which they attained in that way, and that they go to solitudes or to other stricter monasteries, in which they may lament ceaselessly so wicked an offense.[34]

This decretal letter dealt with the classic case of an adult who entered a monastery by simoniacal means, of which he was aware and with which he cooperated. Writing about forty years after the compilation of the *Decretum*, the pope noted that there was a tradition on the subject; "many authorities" had treated it. In a commonplace of ecclesiastical legislation, Clement insisted that he was not innovating, but was repeating "what has been laid down." The authorities who had spoken presumably included his predecessor Alexander III, but Clement may also have been drawing on the work of the decretists. The command that the guilty religious give up his position in the monastery, and go to "solitudes," i.e., perhaps a hermitage or to another monastery for perpetual penance, derives from the canonists' solutions. Clement himself may be responsible for the detail, not found in Alexander's texts, that the monastery of exile be stricter than the one that had been entered simoniacally.[35] The latter provision became normal in the canonical commentaries of the later twelfth century, and was adopted by Innocent III on a number of occasions.[36] Clement's letter to the bishop of Saragossa suggested the possibility that some of the simoniacs were not personally guilty because the money involved had been given without their knowledge. Clement ordered that religious who were simoniacs in a technical sense but who were not personally guilty should be put through a legal charade, in which they were expelled from their illicitly gained positions and then reintegrated into them. If their continued presence in the community was scandalous to the other religious or to the populace, the simoniacs could be placed in another house of the same order, i.e., of the same strictness of rule.[37] Clement's indulgence toward those religious who were guilty of simony in a merely technical sense was clearly derived from the similar stance taken by Gratian and his commentators toward any simoniac in similar circumstances.[38] This distinction between actually and technically guilty monks and canons points to the fact that the problem had moved from the classroom to the world. Nuances and modifications of this sort were required when the officials of the church actually enforced a regulation and had to adapt it to circumstances.

Clement's letter foreshadowed in a number of ways the solutions to the problem of simoniacal entry that were adopted later by Innocent III. This was no accident, because Clement's letter entered the larger canonical tradition by being included in the *Compilatio* III, a collection of letters of Clement III and Celestine III put together by John of Wales in 1210-15.[39]

Aside from its clarification and reenforcement of the law, Clement's decretal letter "De regularibus" has significance for the comprehension of the process whereby the issue of simoniacal entry became a matter of concern to the church at large. Prior to the accession of Alexander III, there is almost no evidence that anyone besides the canonists in their lecture halls and studies took an interest in the crime of simoniacal entry into religion. Alexander's legislation at Tours and at the Third Lateran Council attested to his personal interest in the problem. However, it is significant that his decretal "Veniens" had been written because a man who was willing to pay thirty shillings for entry felt himself wronged when compelled to pay fifty-two shillings instead. To judge from the decretal, the priest F. acted more from anger at the price increase than he did from the realization that he and the monks of St. R. had committed simony by their initial agreement. In contrast, Clement III's decretal "De regularibus" arose in the initiative taken by a local bishop who had to deal with a scandalous situation in his own diocese. The bishop of Saragossa was concerned about a problem of simony that had come to his attention, but was apparently not secure enough to move on his own authority to correct it. Although conciliar texts represent the collective, if perhaps passive, action of bishops against the practice, this text of Clement III is one of the earliest examples of an individual bishop taking initiatives against simoniacal entry. There is, of course, no assurance that this was in fact the first instance of such action. It does indicate that by 1187–91, the approximate date of Clement's decretal, the crime of simoniacal entry had begun to attract the interest of bishops, who then sought to take measures against it. It had moved from the lecture hall to the world.

The action of the bishop of Saragossa was not an isolated event, but had at least one counterpart in England. When the Carthusian Bishop Hugh of Lincoln (1186–1200) visited the convent of Nun-Coton at some time during his pontificate, he found that the nunnery was burdened by an excessive number of members relative to its resources. Hugh attempted to set the house's financial affairs in order. With the agreement of all parties, he fixed the maximum numbers in the house for the future at thirty nuns, ten lay sisters, and twelve male *conversi*. No one was to be admitted until the congregation had been reduced to those numbers.[40]

Apparently, the strained financial situation caused by the excess numbers had led the nuns to admit members for money, i.e., simoniacally, because Hugh also decreed: "Since the simoniacal wickedness has led many into error and ruin, we, who wish to provide for the salvation of souls, strictly prohibit that a man or woman ever be received there by pact for money or for any temporal thing."[41] The text recording the results of the visitation made no reference to any sanctions imposed by Hugh of Lincoln against the religious who had been received simoniacally or against their receptors. Hugh simply forbade for the future any form of simony in receptions. His brief provisions about simony do not seem to derive in any specific way from the jurisprudence of the era, either papal or decretist. Hugh had been a Carthusian before his election to the see of Lincoln, and perhaps he was not well versed in the most recent developments in canon law. What is noteworthy is that Hugh was aware of the evils of simoniacal entry and took measures to prevent it in the future by a formal prohibition and by a reduction in the number of religious. His procedure during the visitation was pastorally oriented, i.e., he sought improvement of the situation without punishments. However, his prohibition of simoniacal reception of new members is a further indication that in the last fifteen years of the twelfth century some local bishops were aware of the problem and were moving to solve it.

Religious Orders, 1160–1198

By 1198 the papacy and at least some members of the episcopate had begun to translate into practice the strictures and theorizings of the canonists about simoniacal entry. They were not alone in this, for many of the religious orders that were founded between 1160 and 1198, or that drew up a code of legislation during that period, included provisions against simoniacal reception.

Such legislation by religious orders against simony was an innovation, motivated by the contemporary concern with the issue. None of the monastic rules from antiquity had given attention to the problem.[42] Between 789 and 819 the Carolingian rulers forbade forced payment for entry into monasteries, but their interest in the issue lapsed in the mid-ninth century and had no perceptible effect on subsequent developments.[43] In the twelfth century there was a discernible division between orders drawing up codes of legislation before and after the 1150s. The legislation of religious orders promulgated before the 1150s contained no provisions against simoniacal entry. The issue of simony apparently did not exist among the religious orders in the first half of the twelfth century. The fact that the rule or legislation of an order did not include a provision against simoniacal entry is, of course, merely negative evidence, which supports an argument *ex silentio* about the nonexistence of concern with simoniacal entry within that group. This is admittedly not a strong form of argument when used by itself. However, the failure of legislation issued before the 1150s to mention such simony becomes more significant when linked to the fact that much of the legislation composed or revised after the 1150s did contain anti-simoniacal provisions.

Such a contrast supports the view that a change of attitude toward entrance practices occurred in the middle of the twelfth century.

No extant Premonstratensian rulings forbid simony in entry. The order codified its legislation in about 1131-34,[44] in about 1174,[45] and in 1236-38,[46] and none of those law codes mentions simoniacal entry. The sparse records of the order's general chapters, collected by Valvekens, are also silent on the issue.[47] Either the Premonstratensian measures against such simony have been lost, a real possibility in view of the meager survivals of chapter rulings, or the order never legislated against simoniacal entry. In any case, this order, which took its form in the early twelfth century, did not emend its successive legislative codes to provide a place for the subsequent concern with simoniacal entry.

The Carthusian legislation of the twelfth century exhibited a pattern of development from silence to explicit condemnation of simony in entry. Guigo, the fifth prior of the Grande Chartreuse, recorded the customs of the house between 1121 and 1127.[48] His work contained no direct reference to simoniacal entry, although it advised the prior to proceed with circumspection in dealing with the property of novices.[49] About 1139 the Carthusian priors began to meet in general chapters to legislate for the order. Some chapter decisions and liturgical regulations survive from the period 1139 to 1170, but they contain no reference to simoniacal reception of new members.[50] About 1170 Prior Basil organized earlier chapter decisions into a code, his *Consuetudines*. Chapter 43, paragraph 5, of Basil's code forbade the Carthusians to demand anything from the property of a novice or to encourage a novice to make an offering of any kind.[51] Between 1174 and 1222, during the priorates of Guigo II and Jancelinus, the Carthusian general chapters continued to meet, and their decisions survive as undated additions to Basil's *Consuetudines*.[52] Chapter 8 of the additional decisions stated simply that nothing whatsoever should be demanded from novices.[53] Chapter 60 ordered the punishment of those priors who demanded clothing or anything else from a novice, and it prescribed deposition for a prior whose illicit demand was actually met.[54] Thus the first evidence of Carthusian concern about simoniacal reception of novices appeared about 1170. In the next generation the general chapter reiterated the prohibition more explicitly and provided serious punishments for breaches of the law.

The Cistercians took their first timid steps against simoniacal entry in 1198 and 1212. Perhaps the considerable prestige of the order, rooted in its austere and zealous past, protected it from criticism on the score of entry practices. Indeed, it may be that the reception practices of the Cistercians were free, in contemporary eyes, of simoniacal associations. However, examination of the Cistercian cartularies of Gimont, Berdoues, Cîteaux, and Ourscamp has revealed that, by the second half of the twelfth century, entry to those houses was frequently hedged with conditions and financial arrangements similar to those practiced at other Benedictine houses.[55]

According to Peter the Chanter, Bernard of Clairvaux believed that it was very difficult to commit simony in entering a poor house.[56] This opinion may indicate a certain reluctance on the part of Cistercians to admit the simoniacal nature of many entry agreements, a reluctance mirrored in the paucity of Cistercian chapter rulings on the problem. In an interesting article Ulrich Stutz demonstrated that the Cistercians were hostile to certain views that they regarded as innovations introduced into the canon law by Gratian.[57] In 1188 the Cistercian general chapter had ordered: "May those who possess the book called the Collection of Canons and the *Decreta* of Gratian keep them more hidden away, so that they may be brought out when necessary; may they not be kept in the common book chest, because of the various errors which can arise from them."[58] Stutz held that this ruling of the Cistercian general chapter was not an expression of opposition to canon law as such, but was a measure of prudence designed to shield Cistercian monks from knowledge of certain contradictions between Cistercian practices and the work of Gratian, which was, by 1188, the major canon law text. The outstanding areas of opposition identified by Stutz were the issues of the propriety of pastoral work

161

by monks, and of the reception of tithes by monks. Although Stutz said nothing about simoniacal entry in his article, his basic point can be extended by recognizing that the Cistercian abbots may have objected to Gratian's undoubted innovation in the matter of simoniacal entry.

In any case, for an order that legislated annually on all sorts of topics, it is remarkable how little was said about the property of new monks at entry. In a laconic text of 1198, the general chapter ordered, "Concerning the goods of novices, may it be observed as it is contained in the Rule."[59] The annual legislation of the general chapter was normally prompted by circumstances, and this text was presumably an admission that the goods of novices were, in some cases and in some way, not being treated as the *Rule* of Benedict required. The essential feature of the *Rule* on this point was that the novice had free disposition of his goods, provided that whatever course he chose had the effect of stripping him completely of all temporal goods.[60] Thus the ruling of 1198, ordering a return to the *Rule*, may constitute an oblique admission that the freedom of novices to dispose of their goods was in some manner being narrowed. However, it is best not to press this brief text too much, since it is frankly not clear exactly what it was intended to accomplish.

In 1212 the general chapter approached the problem again: "It is forbidden by the general chapter that membership in our order be promised to anyone if any sort of price intervenes."[61] This text, forbidding the promise of membership in return for a payment, was directed against agreements that, in effect, purchased the right to enter a monastery at some future date.[62] The phrase "interveniente quocumque pretio" was common in anti-simoniacal texts, and is a clear indication that the abuse forbidden was perceived as simony.

Except for these two rather narrow texts, there is in the records of the Cistercian general chapters and in the codifications of the twelfth and early thirteenth centuries no general prohibition of simoniacal entry. The Cistercian general chapter, with its Europe-wide membership and contacts, could not have been unaware of the opposition to such entry, especially during the reign of Innocent III, who took wide, well-publicized initiatives against it. I believe that the Cistercians did, in fact, become more aware of the problem, but chose not to issue a general decree about it. The decisions of 1198 and 1212 indicate that they moved in a tentative, piecemeal way, punishing individual crimes without issuing an over-all decree. The vigorous anti-simoniacal campaign of Innocent III made it clear where church law stood on the issue, and the Cistercians adopted that law without incorporating it into their own statutes.[63] This observation is confirmed by the fact that in the period after the Fourth Lateran Council, which had condemned simoniacal entry in canon 64, the Cistercian general chapter acted as if simony of that sort were forbidden, even though no specifically Cistercian text was cited. In 1220 the abbots of the order were forbidden to dispense in the case of simony, but were commanded instead to bring such cases to the general chapter for settlement.[64] In 1222 "the abbot of Bloomkamp, who confessed publicly in the general chapter that he received many monks and *conversi* to conversion under a condition, which is a form of simony, is deposed on the spot."[65] In 1225 John Godard, the abbot of Fontmorigny, was illegally deposed as a result of a conspiracy in which one monk claimed to have had a simoniacal entry in order to defame the abbot of the same crime. Godard was ultimately reinstated.[66] Rulings of the general chapter for the remainder of the thirteenth century presupposed an opposition to simony that must have been grounded in the general canon law of the church, rather than in the specific rulings of the Cistercian chapter.[67] Thus it was during the pontificate of Innocent III that the Cistercians began to acknowledge the seriousness of simoniacal entry and to move against it. Such views had not been part of their ethos during the early or middle twelfth century, as that ethos is reflected in surviving legislative texts.

The Cluniacs also took their first recorded steps against simoniacal entry during the pontificate of Innocent III, and those steps were both clearer and more specific than the Cistercian measures had been. In 1196 Celestine III had empowered Hugh IV, abbot of

Cluny, to enforce older statutes and to make new statutes for the order.[68] Hugh IV died in 1198 and was succeeded by his nephew, Hugh V, who had been abbot of Reading in England. Hugh V undertook a complete revision of the statutes of the order, and the newly created general chapter of the order also issued a revised set of statutes during his term of office.[69] Hugh's own statutes were issued on 29 October 1200, and they included a provision clearly inspired by the canonists' opposition to simoniacal entry.

> May no one be received by a pact in a monastery. Since often and in many places it happens that entrance of a monastery is offered with money or a pact intervening (although this is forbidden by the sacred canons and causes a danger to the souls of both, that is, of the receivers and of the received), we decree that no one henceforth may be received in a monastery by pact or price, and that nothing be demanded from an entrant. But if anyone has brought something voluntarily, may his devotion not be rejected.[70]

The very next provision of Hugh's statutes provided a significant commentary on the prohibition of such receptions.

> And since that plague [simony] has crept in especially from the reception of feeble and useless persons, we order that only those are to be received as monks who are fit for the service of God, and not a burden to the brethren, and are useful to the monastery.[71]

Thus Hugh V linked simony specifically to the reception of unfit persons in Cluniac houses, persons who paid in order to obtain an entry that they probably could not have otherwise received. Hugh had before him when he worked the statutes issued by Peter the Venerable in 1132–46.[72] Peter too had complained of the reception of useless, unfit persons, but he had not linked such receptions to simony.[73] In the sixty years since Peter's statutes, the problem of "useless" recruits had come to be seen in the perspective of simony, a sign of the intellectual change that had occurred in that period. Hugh's rewriting and updating of Peter's statute on useless recruits forced him to take account of an issue that had scarcely existed in Peter's day.

In 1205–6 the Cluniac general chapter issued a set of statutes, and its second provision was a rewriting of Hugh V's legislation of

1200. Both texts began and ended on the same note,[74] but the general chapter's text broadened the focus to include all forms of simony, whereas Hugh's text had singled out monastic receptions.[75]

Thus in the early thirteenth century, perhaps under papal pressure or else simply in response to the new sensitivity to simoniacal entry, the Cluniac Order placed itself firmly in opposition to the pacts and payments at entry that violated the canon law.

The Cluniacs, the Carthusians, and the Cistercians, groupings that had taken form long before the 1150s, reacted to the problem of simoniacal entry rather reluctantly late in the twelfth or early thirteenth centuries, when the pressure against the illicit practices exerted by the canonists and by Innocent III was at its greatest. By way of contrast, a number of the religious orders that were founded or that legislated for the first time in the second half of the twelfth century made opposition to simoniacal entry an integral part of their statutes.

The Grandmontines arose in the diocese of Limoges early in the twelfth century under the leadership of Stephen of Muret (d. 1124). They were marked by a desire for extreme simplicity and for utter separation from the world.[76] The tiny group of ascetics apparently needed no written regulations in its early years, and it was only under the fourth prior of Grandmont, Stephen of Liciac (1139–63) that the Grandmontines received a formal rule. Although the dating of the rule is not certain, Dom Jean Becquet, a researcher and editor of Grandmontine texts, has suggested the decade 1150–60 as that of its composition.[77] If the dating is correct, then chapter 45 of the rule is one of the earliest prohibitions of simoniacal entry by a functioning religious order.

> But indeed, may the pastor of this congregation, in receiving brethren, consider with greatest care only the will of God and the salvation of souls, [thus] guarding himself and all his disciples entirely from every kind of simony, and faithfully fulfilling that precept of the Lord: "Freely you have received, freely give" (Matt. X).[78]

To judge from the documents of early Grandmontine history, the founders of the group mistrusted the role of temporal goods as motives for any spiritual actions. In several places in his rule, Stephen of Liciac warned his brethren against acting in spiritual affairs for temporal ends.[79] On occasion he used the term *simony* to describe such actions.[80] In the *Life* of Saint Stephen of Grandmont, a work composed in 1188–89 but based on a text of the 1150s, anti-simoniacal opinions were attributed to the group's founder.[81] Thus the prohibition of simoniacal reception of new members was a manifestation of a more general Grandmontine reluctance to trade spiritual things for temporal ones.

The customary of Grandmont, composed about 1170–71, reinforced this concern with simoniacal entry. Chapter 64 of the customary was a detailed attempt to define what was and was not licit at entry.

> Since we propose to follow the steps of our Saviour for the grace which He gives us, by His example the simoniacal heresy is to be rooted out entirely from our religious group. Therefore, all [of us] in everything, and especially in receiving brethren, avoiding every form of simony, damn entirely what the Redeemer Himself damned when He ejected all buyers and sellers from the Temple. Also, faithfully observing that precept of the Lord, "Freely you have received, freely give," we make no mention through ourselves or through another person to any man wishing to enter our congregation about buying clothes, about bringing the equipment for a horse, about bringing money, or about any other thing in which simony could be noted.[82]

Thus the customary went so far as to forbid even the mention of the normal entrance gifts of the period, so as to avoid any hint of simony. If the novice took the initiative in bringing up the subject, it could be discussed with due caution. Three situations were envisioned in the text. First, an entrant might wish to know what a new monk needs; in that case, he should be informed, though without any inducement to bring the things himself.[83] Second, an entrant might seek the advice of the Grandmontines about the disposition of his property; in that event it was permitted to advise him.[84] Finally, if the entrant decided to give some of his goods to the Grandmontines, they could be accepted, provided that no solicitation had been employed.[85] The gift had to be utterly free and spontaneous. If any Grandmontine violated these conditions in receiving a new member or in seeking entrance gifts, he was to be punished "with such strictness that the discipline of one might be the correction of many."[86]

These Grandmontine texts reflected a heightened sense of concern about simony, but they did not use the vocabulary or turns of expression common to the canonists. The imagery and references in the Grandmontine texts were biblical rather than legal. The Grandmontine texts seem to be relatively independent formulations of the concern about simoniacal entry; they were rooted as much in the peculiarly Grandmontine concerns as they were in the discussions of the canonists.

The situation was different with the rule of the Order of Sempringham, in which the verbal influence of the canonists seems indisputably present. Gilbert of Sempringham gradually elaborated the constitution of his order of nuns and canons during the second and third quarters of the twelfth century.[87] The rule of his order, as it survives, apparently dates from about 1180,[88] when Gilbert was still alive, though almost ninety years old. Chapter nine of the rule declared:

> Obeying the provisions of the holy canons, we damn the hateful heresy of simony, prohibiting under anathema that anything be demanded for entrance of the monastery from any man or woman to be received among us; but if anything were offered freely, it will be permitted to receive it, provided that every illicit pact or exaction is excluded. Also in other spiritual things and affairs, we prohibit the same vice of simony, and we denounce him, whosoever shall have offended, as one destined to the lot of the first Simon, the author of this wickedness, [to go] with his money to damnation.[89]

As this chapter of the rule of Sempringham announced in its first phrase, it was inspired by the "holy canons," and probably by those canons as embodied in Gratian or in his commentators, since the crime of simoniacal entry was not condemned specifically in earlier canonical collections. Unlike the Grandmontine texts, the vocabulary of the Gilbertine text is rather close to that found in the *Decretum* and in the works of the decretists. Since the decretists' vocabulary was highly stereotyped, it is not possible to link this text to a specific decretist or school of decretists. But the language and ideas were derived from contemporary canonistic science.[90] This example is the earliest that I have located of clear links between the activities of the canonists and the governance of an actual religious order, with relation to simoniacal entry.

The Order of the Holy Trinity, devoted to the redemption of captives, was founded in the 1190s, and received approval for its rule from Innocent III in December 1198. The order was marked by its Parisian origins. The founder, John of Matha (ca. 1150–1213), was a Paris master in theology,[91] and the rule itself had been reviewed by Odo of Sully, bishop of Paris, and Robert, abbot of Saint Victor, before Innocent III approved it.[92] Chapter seven of the rule dealt with those who wished to enter the order.[93] The economic arrangements were spelled out, and it was specifically forbidden to demand anything for reception. The rule provided that if the decision was taken after the year of probation not to admit the novice, he should be allowed to leave with everything that he brought.[94]

Some late twelfth- and thirteenth-century rules for hospitals, which were generally organized as religious congregations, also included provisions against simoniacal entry:

> May no brother or sister be received by condition of purchase or of other promise. . . . [95]

> May no one be received in our society unless he is of good reputation, nor should we have regard to money rather than to uprightness; and if any upright person ought to be received, may he request membership for love of God and may he receive it for love of God. May nothing be sought from him, but if he should bring something, that may be received for the service of the poor.[96]

In the thirteenth century entrants to hospitals were sometimes required to swear that they had not, directly or indirectly, committed simony in order to obtain a place.[97]

In conclusion, the period between 1163 and 1198 was marked by attempts in councils, papal decretals, episcopal visitations, and the legislation of religious congregations and orders to translate into practice the canonistic concern about simoniacal reception of religious. Before mid-century this had not been true, and religious orders that took form earlier were reluctant to condemn practices that were customary among them. These admittedly fragmentary records indicate that in the later twelfth century wide circles of those involved, i.e., religious, abbots, and members of the hierarchy, became aware of the issue. The work of the canonists began to erode the customary practices surrounding entry into religion and led to the growing rejection of hitherto accepted pacts and payments. The pontificate of Innocent III heightened the legal and also the propagandistic campaign against monastic simony and saw its condemnation at the Fourth Lateran Council in 1215.

1. M. Pacaut, "Roland Bandinelli," *DDC*, 7:704. Bandinelli taught canon law at Bologna from about 1139 to 1142, and he was therefore a contemporary, and perhaps a collaborator, of Gratian (ibid., cols. 703-4).

2. "Secundo, an pro ingressu ecclesiae pecunia sit exigenda, etc. Ad hoc notandum est, quod eorum, quae offeruntur, alia sponte, alia coacte praestantur; item, alia pactione, alia mera liberalitate. Nichil vero pro adeptione sacrae rei ex coactione vel pactione est exigendum, nec ergo pro introitu ecclesiae. Dicimus ergo nichil omnino exigendum nec exactum solvendum nec pactione aliquid pro ingressu ecclesiae erogandum" (*Die Summa Magistri Rolandi nachmals Papstes Alexander III, nebst einem Anhange Incerti Auctoris Quaestiones* ed. F. Thaner [Innsbruck, 1874], p. 13).

3. For some significant examples of Alexander's role in crystallizing church practice, see E. W. Kemp, "Pope Alexander III and the Canonization of Saints," *Transactions of the Royal Historical Society*, 4th ser., 27(1945): 13-28; E. W. Kemp, *Canonization and Authority in the Western Church* (Oxford, 1948), pp. 82-94; C. Duggan, *Twelfth-Century Decretal Collections and Their Importance in English History* (London, 1963), pp. 19-22, 32-34; M. Baldwin, *Alexander III and the Twelfth Century* (Glen Rock, N.J., 1968), pp. 177-217.

4. M. Pacaut, *Alexandre III, étude sur la conception du pouvoir pontifical dans sa pensée et dans son oeuvre* (Paris, 1956), pp. 59-77. W. Holtzmann, "Die Benutzung Gratians in der päpstlichen Kanzlei im 12. Jahrhundert," *Studia Gratiana* 1:345, notes that it was during Alexander's pontificate that the *Decretum* began to be used regularly at the papal curia as a legal guide and source book.

5. "Non satis utiliter avaritia redarguitur in populo, si ab iis, qui in clero constituti videntur, et precipue qui contempto seculo religiosorum nomen profitentur et regulam, modis omnibus non cavetur. Prohibemus igitur ne ab iis qui ad religionem transire voluerint, aliqua pecunia requiratur . . ." (William of Newburgh, *Historia rerum Anglicarum*, ed. R. Howlett [London, 1884], Rolls Series 82/1, bk. 2, chap. 15, p. 136). The canon is also printed in Mansi, 21:1178c-d.

6. "Hoc autem Simoniacum esse, sanctorum patrum auctoritas manifeste declarat. Unde quisquis hoc de cetero praesumpserit attentare, partem se cum Simone non dubitet habiturum" (William of Newburgh, *Historia*, bk. 2, chap. 15, p. 136).

7. C. R. Cheney, "Legislation of the Medieval English Church," *English Historical Review* 50 (1935): 202-3.

8. See above, pp. 124-27. Alexander subscribed to the view that no occasion should be given to a religious to abandon his vow (JL 11316).

9. "Monachi non pretio recipiantur in monasterio. . . . Si quis autem exactus pro sua receptione aliquid dederit, ad sacros ordines non ascendat; is autem qui acceperit, officii sui privatione mulctetur. . . . Abbas etiam qui ista diligenter non curaverit, officii sui iacturam se noverit incursurum" (*Conciliorum Oecumenicorum Decreta*, ed. J. Alberigo et al. [Freiburg im Breisgau, 1962], p. 193).

10. See the fundamental article by F. Gillmann, "Zur Geschichte des Gebrauchs des Ausdrücke 'irregularis' und 'irregularitas'," *Archiv für katholisches Kirchenrecht* 91 (1911): 49-86. See also G. Oesterlé, "Irregularités," *DDC*, 6:42-66, and G. Oesterlé, "De potestate abbatum dispensandi ab irregularitatibus," *Liturgica* 2(Montserrat, 1958): 465-81. According to Gillmann, the fact of *irregularitas* was very old, but the expression was used for the first time as a technical term by the decretist Rufinus about 1157-59 to describe the absence of qualifications required for admission to holy orders.

11. See above, pp. 126-27.

12. "Veniens ad nos F. presbyter simplici nobis relatione proposuit, quod abbas et fratres sancti R. noluerunt eum in monachum recipere, quousque illis pro monachatu triginta solidos dare convenit; conventione autem facta statim sequenti die eum monasticum habitum induerunt, et iidem monachi triginta solidos, abbas vero decem, et familia duodecim pro pastu, asserentes, hoc esse de consuetudine monasterii, postularunt" (JL 14149). Loewenfeld dates the letter to 1159-81, and designates the recipient as "Gregorio(?) Episc. Tridentino." However, there was no Gregory on the episcopal throne of Trent during Alexander III's pontificate. A Brackmann, *Germania Pontificia*, ed. P. Kehr (Berlin, 1910), 1/1, p. 403, no. 10, suggests that the see intended was Tudertinum-Todi, which was governed by Bishop Gratian from ca. 1144 to 1179.

13. In agreement with canonist opinion, Alexander objected to force or pact, but not to entrance gifts as such (JL 11036, 11316).

14. ". . . Si ita esse inveneris, abbatem et monachos ad restituendam pecuniam praefato F. tam indigne acceptam, instanter admoneas, et cum omni districtione compellas, et, abbatem et maiores personas monasterii pro tantae pravitatis excessu ab officii exsecutione suspendens, praecipias dicto F., ut in alio monasterio in habitu monastico Domino studeat deservire" (JL 14149).

15. The decretalist Albert noted that the suspension of the abbot and officials was the consequence of an investigation, and deposition likewise would come only after investigation: "Nota inquisitione inducere/suspentionem, non aliter autem depositionem ab ordine" (BN lat. 3932, fol. 97ʳ, *ad verbum* "suspendas").

16. Holtzmann, "Die Benutzung," pp. 328-30. Urban III (1185-87) was one of the first popes to cite an authority, in JL 15820, ibid., pp. 333-34.

17. *Summa decretorum*, pp. 229-30, recommended penal exile for simoniac monks; pp. 226-27 recommended that the illicit payment be returned to any simoniac. However, Rufinus did not link explicitly the return of the money with entry to another house. Perhaps it was Alexander's decretal "Veniens" that linked the two. See also JL 11316, in which Alexander ordered the return of an entrance gift in order that a monk could enter another house.

18. The early thirteenth-century "Ius naturale," an *apparatus* on the *Decretum*, cited "Veniens" to support the prohibition against forced gifts (BN lat. 15393, level a, fol. 84ʳ, *ad verbum* "pro ingressu"). Tancred's commentary on *Compilatio* I, book 5, canon 7, also cited "Veniens" against pacts at entry (BN lat. 15399, fol. 51ᵛ). Alan, in his commentary on Compilatio I, book 5, canon 2, *ad verbum* "restituant," cited "Veniens" in support of the view that a simoniacal payment should be returned to the giver: "Ei tamen, qui

dedit, invenitur ex misericordia restituta, ut extra tt (=titulos) 'Veniens' " (cited in F. Gill-mann, "Magister Albertus Glossator der Compilatio II," *Archiv für katholisches Kirchen-recht* 105[1925]: 149).

19. If the bishop to whom "Veniens" was addressed was Gratian of Todi (ca.1144-79), then the letter was probably composed before the Third Lateran Council.

20. R. Foreville, *Latran I, II, III et Latran IV* (Paris, 1962), pp. 118-19, notes that Tours was attended by 17 cardinals, 124 bishops and archbishops, and 400 abbots and lesser prelates; and, pp. 387-90, that the Third Lateran Council was attended by at least 287 bishops and archbishops and 21 cardinals.

21. The decretal "Veniens" was included in the *Compilatio II*, composed between 1210 and 1215 by John of Wales, and edited in E. Friedberg, *Quinque compilationes antiquae nec non collectio canonum Lipsiensis* (Leipzig, 1882), V. 2. 1. The decretal was also included in the collection of Gilbert, made about 1208: R. von Heckel, "Die Dekretalen-sammlungen des Gilbertus und Alanus nach den Weingartener Handschriften," *Zeitschrift der Savigny-Stiftung für Rechtsgeschichte*, Kanonistische Abteilung 29(1940): V. 2. 1. The sixth canon of Tours(1163), "Non satis," was included in the *Compilatio I*, 5. 2. 7. In addi-tion, Duggan, *Twelfth-Century Decretal Collections*, p. 72, found the canon of Tours in the *collectio belverensis*, composed soon after 1175. E. Friedberg, *Die Canonessammlungen zwischen Gratian und Bernhard von Pavia* (Leipzig, 1897), p. 185, recorded the canon "Non satis" in seven canonical collections composed between 1163 and 1191. The tenth canon of the Third Lateran Council (1179), "Monachi non pretio," was included in the *collectio cantuariensis* (ca. 1182) and the *collectio roffensis* (ca. 1181-85) (Duggan, *Twelfth-century Decretal Collections*, pp. 73, 77); Friedberg, *Die Canonessammlungen*, p. 52, no. 16, notes six collections composed between 1179 and 1191 that included "Monachi non pretio." A systematic survey of canonical collections of the last quarter of the twelfth century would uncover more instances of use of these texts of Alexander III.

22. W(illiam) H(unt), "Richard," *Dictionary of National Biography* (London, 1896), 48:191-94; M. Chibnall, "Richard of Canterbury," *New Catholic Encyclopedia*, 12(1967): 477-78.

23. JL 12365.

24. Duggan, *Twelfth-Century Decretal Collections*, p. 75: ". . . The most remarkable feature in the whole range of English primitive collections: namely the high proportion of their total contents of Canterbury, Exeter and Worcester provenance; or, to stress the personal aspect, the large proportion of decretals received by Richard, Bartholomew and Roger, their respective bishops." See also ibid., pp. 122-23, 149, for Richard's frequent service as a judge-delegate and his probable promotion of the compilation of decretals that he and others had received.

25. *Concilia Magnae Britanniae et Hiberniae* (London, 1737), 1:474-75.

26. "Pro monachis, canonicis, monialibus in monasterio recipiendis nihil exigatur" (ibid.; also in Mansi, 22:143).

27. Duggan, *Twelfth-Century Decretal Collections*, p. 92, n. 7, reports that the canons attributed to Westminster(1173) survive in Cotton ms. Claudius A IV, fol. 191vb-192va, under the heading "Concilium Ricardi Cantuariensis."

28. Cheney, "Legislation," p. 208, suggests that the canons attributed to Westminster (1173) may represent a preliminary draft of the council of 1175, or they may record an-other council held by Richard. Duggan, *Twelfth-Century Decretal Collections*, pp. 92-93, stresses that the decrees of Westminster(1173) are quite different from those of West-minster(1175).

29. E. Seckel, "Canonistische Quellenstudien I. Die Westminster Synode 1175, eine Quelle falscher oder verfälschter Canonen in den nachgratianischen Sammlungen,"

SIMONIACAL ENTRY INTO RELIGIOUS LIFE

Deutsche Zeitschrift für Kirchenrecht, 3d ser., 9 (1899): 176–77, notes that, with two exceptions, the canons of Richard's council were an adaptation of the *Decretum* to local needs. See also Holtzmann, "Die Benutzung," pp. 345–46. The prologue to the canons, as reported in *Gesta Regis Henrici Secundi Benedicti Abbatis*, ed. W. Stubbs(London, 1867), Rolls Series 49/1, pp. 84–85, stresses Richard's personal initiative and authority in promulgating the canons.

30. "Ex decreto Urbani Papae. Nullus praelatus, in recipiendo monacho, vel canonico, vel sanctimoniali, pretium sumere vel exigere ab his, qui ad conversationem veniunt, aliqua pacti occasione praesumat. Si quis autem hoc fecerit, anathema sit" (*Gesta Regis Henrici*, p. 87; also in Mansi, 22:149e).

31. On Albert de Mora, see Paul Kehr, "Papst Gregor VIII. als Ordensgründer," *Miscellanea Francesco Ehrle* II. *Studi e Testi* 38 (Rome, 1924): 248–58.

32. Urban III's Bull, "Cum ex iniuncto nobis," issued 26 March 1187, was published in Kehr, "Papst Gregor VIII," pp. 267–75, and in Paul Kehr, *Papsturkunden in Benevent und in der Capitanata, Nachrichten der Göttinger Gesellschaft der Wissenschaften*, Phil.-hist. Klasse(1898), vol. 1, no. 16, p. 82.

33. "Nichil tamen pro receptione sua promittat, nisi tantum si habuerit quod ad simplicem habitum su[um secun] dum institutionem domus uisum fuerit expedire. Tempore quoque probationis, si facultatem habuerit, de proprio induatur, ne domum, cui utilis ex accessu forte non extitit, ex recessu afficiat detrimento. Si quis autem ultra hoc ante plenam receptionem suam quicquam dederit aut promiserit, tam dantem quam accipientem ab omni sacri altaris officio tamdiu statuimus remouendum, donec per Romanam ecclesiam misericordiam consequatur et ad eius arbitrium culpam suam expurget. Post professionem autem, si uel is qui recipitur vel amici ejus gratis aliquid ecclesiae dare uoluerint, licite recipi poterit et teneri, dum tamen tale sit, quod de usuris, rapina vel furto non constet dantibus prouenisse et de quo litigium non uideatur ecclesie imminere; quod utique in cunctis, que uobis ab aliquibus offerentur, statuimus observandum" (Kehr, "Papst Gregor VIII," p. 268).

34. "De regularibus canonicis seu monachis nos consulere voluisti qui per simoniam ingressum ipsis scientibus et machinantibus, habuerunt. Unde, quum super hoc auctoritates multae reperiantur expressae, non aliud, quam statutum est, respondemus, ut locum, quam taliter adepti sunt, omnino dimittant, et solitudines seu alia monasteria districtiora adeant, in quibus tam exsecrabilem excessum sine intermissione deplorent" (JL 16562). This decretal letter was included in *Compilatio* II, bk. 5, tit. 2, canon 7.

35. Alexander's "Veniens" recommended that the simoniac monk go to another monastery. Later commentators added that the new monastery should be stricter, in order to make "Veniens" conform to Clement's "De regularibus." Damasus' commentary on *Compilatio* II, bk. 5, tit. 2, canon 1, "Veniens," *ad verbum* "in alio monasterio" added: "districtiori ar. infra e. de regularibus" (BN lat. 3930, fol. 91ʳ). Albert, in his commentary on the same text, made the same comment (BN lat. 3932 fol. 97ʳ). The *apparatus* to the *Decretum*, "Ecce vicit leo," specified that a simoniac monk "tenetur renunciare et in alio monasterio magis districto debet animam suam salvare" (BN nouv. acq. lat. 1576, fol. 142ʳ). Master Honorius assumed that it was normal for a simoniac monk to be placed in a stricter house, and he dealt with the question of what to do if no stricter house were available (BN lat. 14591, fol. 61ʳ).

36. Pott 1403, 4783; canon 64 of the Fourth Lateran Council.

37. "Si autem ignorantibus ipsis pecunia data fuerit, cogas eos ad renunciandum loco eidem, et postmodum in ipsum reducere, si ibi absque scandalo potuerint remanere, vel in alio, qui sit de ordine ipso, ad serviendum Deo poteris collocare" (JL 16562).

38. *Decretum, causa* I, *questio* V, embodied Gratian's view that a child who was una-

ware of his father's simoniacal machinations could be treated leniently. The *summa* "Cum in tres partes," composed between 1160 and 1171, summarized Gratian's position well: "Quinto loco queritur si liceat isti esse in ecclesia vel fungi ordinatione quam paterna pecunia est assequutus. Ad quod dicimus, si eo ignorante pater pecuniam dedit et ipse postquam id scivit ecclesie seu dignitati paterna pecunia adepte abrenuntiavit, tam in ecclesia quam in ordinibus non de rigore iuris sed de indulgentia manere permittitur" (BN lat. 16540, fol. 3ᵛ).

39. R. Foreville, "Clément III," *DHGE*, 12:1107-8, notes that Clement's pontificate foreshadowed that of Innocent III in a number of ways, to which can be added the treatment of simoniac monks. The *Compilatio* II was published in Friedberg, *Quinque compilationes antiquae*, pp. 66-104.

40. "Cum ad congregationem ancillarum Christi de Cotun, causa visitationis ex officii nostri debito faciendae accederemus, ad ea quae didicimus ibidem corrigenda, remedium studuimus adhibere. Advertentes igitur multitudinem monialium ampliorem quam sustinere valeant domus illius facultates, habitare, statuimus, cum consensu magistri, priorissae, et conventus, quod congregatio monialium, de caetero, trigintarium numerum non excedat, sororum numerus sub denario concludatur, duodecim fratres conversi ad officia ruralia sint ibidem exercenda. . . ." (Migne, vol. 153, cols. 1113-14). "Nulli vero religionis habitus in eadem domo tribuatur, donec minutus fuerit praesens conventus ad numerum praetaxatum, nisi propter manifestam domus utilitatem, et hoc ex speciali licentia dioecesani" (ibid., cols. 1114-15).

41. "Quia Simoniaca pravitas plures in errores et interitum adduxit, animarum saluti providere volentes, districte prohibuimus, ne vir vel mulier, pro pecunia vel re qualibet temporali recipiatur unquam ibidem ex pacto" (ibid., col. 1116b). However, Hugh himself was willing to provide a reception feast for the monks of Saint Neot's when they received his wardrobe-keeper into their community (*The Life of Saint Hugh of Lincoln*, ed. D. Douie and H. Farmer [London, 1961-62], 2:3-4).

42. I have examined the monastic rules listed in *Clavis Patrum Latinorum*, ed. E. Dekkers, 2d ed. (Steenbrugen, 1961), *Sacris Erudiri* 3 (1961): 407-17.

43. *Duplex Legationis Edictum* (23 March 789), in MGH, *Capitularia*, vol. 1, chap. 15, p. 63; Synod of Frankfort (794), in ibid., chap. 16, p. 76; Monastic Capitulary of Louis the Pious (818-19), in ibid., chap. 75, p. 348.

44. R. van Waefelghem, "Les premiers statuts de l'ordre de Prémontré: le clm 17.174 (xiiᵉ siècle)," *Analectes de l'ordre de Prémontré* 9 (1913): 1-74.

45. E. Martène, *De antiquis ecclesiae ritibus*(Antwerp, 1737), 3:890-926.

46. Pl. Lefèvre, *Les Statuts de Prémontré réformés sur les ordres de Grégoire IX et d'Innocent IV au xiiiᵉ siècle* (Louvain, 1946).

47. J. B. Valvekens, "Acta et decreta capitulorum generalium ordinis Praemonstratensis," *Analecta Praemonstratensia* 42 (1966): i-ix, 1-22; 43 (1967): 23-42.

48. Guigo's *Consuetudines* are printed in Migne, vol. 153, cols. 631-760.

49. Ibid., cols. 683-86.

50. *Die ältesten Consuetudines der Kartäuser*, ed. James Hogg, in *Analecta Cartusiana*, 1 (Berlin, 1970): 92-141.

51. *Consuetudines Basilii*, ibid., pp. 142-218, chap. 43: "Nullus autem ex nostris de rebus Nouitij aliquid postulet, nec ad procurationem faciendam ab aliquo nostrum Nouitius instruatur" (p. 207).

52. *Supplementa ad Consuetudines Basilii*, ibid., pp. 219-40.

53. "A Nouitiis cum venerint, nichil penitus exigatur" (ibid., chap. 8, p. 221).

54. "Qui vestes vel aliud exegerit a Nouitio, sit extra sedem quadraginta diebus, et totidem abstinentias faciat sine misericordia. Si jam exactio ad effectum venerit, Prior amittat obedientiam" (ibid., chap. 60, p. 229).

55. A promise of future reception in return for a gift: *Gimont*, pt. 6, no. 74, 1180; pt. 4, no. 67, 1187; pt. 6, no. 100, 1187; *Berdoues*, no. 378, 1180; no. 524, 1182; no. 159, 1185; *Ourscamp*, no. 306, 1190; no. 723, 1192. A person received in return for a gift or concession to the monastery: *Gimont*, pt. 1, no. 100, 1183; pt. 3, no. 63, 1183; *Berdoues*, no. 378, 1180; no. 204, 1182; no. 524, 1182; no. 411, 1186. Gifts offered in return for services and receptions connected with death: *Gimont*, pt. 3, no. 53, 1183; pt. 2, no. 173, 1186; *Berdoues*, no. 35, 1185; *Ourscamp*, no. 354, 1179; no. 402, 1189.

56. *Summa de sacramentis*, ed. J.-A. Dugauquier (Louvain and Lille, 1963), vol. 3, part 2a, pp. 213-14.

57. U. Stutz, "Die Cistercienser wider Gratians Dekret, "*Zeitschrift der Savigny-Stiftung für Rechtsgeschichte*, Kanonistische Abteilung, no. 9 (1919), pp. 63-98. Pages 84-94 discuss the contradictions between the *Decretum* and the Cistercians on the issues of monks exercising *cura animarum*, receiving certain types of revenues, and possessing tithes of other men.

58. "Liber qui dicitur Corpus Canonum, et Decreta Gratiani apud eos qui habuerint secretius custodiantur, ut cum opus fuerit proferantur; in communi armario non resideant, propter varios qui inde possunt provenire errores" (Canivez, *Statuta*, vol. 1, no. 7, p. 108).

59. "De rebus novitiorum sicut continetur in Regula, sic observetur" (ibid., no. 8, p. 225).

60. "Res si quas habet, aut eroget prius pauperibus aut facta solemniter donatione conferat monasterio, nihil sibi reservans ex omnibus; quippe qui ex illo die nec proprii corporis potestatem se habiturum scit" (*Sancti Benedicti regula monachorum*, ed. P. Schmitz, 2d ed. [Maredsous, 1955], chap. 58, p. 122).

61. "Inhibetur a Capitulo generali ne cui, interveniente quocumque pretio, consortium Ordinis nostri promittatur" (Canivez, *Statuta*, vol. 1, no. 2, p. 389).

62. In 1262 the general chapter forbade the practice of promising membership for some future date (ibid., vol. 3, no. 4, pp. 1-2). For examples of such promises see *Gimont*, pt. 5, no. 56, 1168; pt. 3, no. 1, 1169; pt. 1, no. 31, 1173; pt. 6, nv. 61, 1173; *Berdoues*, no. 19, 1205; no. 16, 1191. In 1236-38 the Premonstratensians also forbade the practice (Lefèvre, *Les Statuts*, p. 27).

63. V. Hermans. "De novitiatu in ordine Benedictino-Cisterciensi et in iure communi usque ad annum 1335," *Analecta sacri ordinis Cisterciensis* 3 (1947): 24, also concludes that Cistercian opposition to simoniacal reception was based on the common law rather than on specific legislation of the order.

64. Canivez, *Statuta*, vol. 1, no. 29, p. 523.

65. "Abbas de Florido Campo qui in Capitulo generali publice confessus est quod multos monachos et conversos sub conditione ad conversionem recepit, quod est species simoniae, deponitur in instanti" (ibid., vol. 2, no. 40, p. 21). The monks of Bloomkamp apparently did not see the crime as serious because in 1223 the general chapter noted: "Abbas de Florido Campo qui depositus fuit propter symoniam quam confessus est in Capitulo generali, et iterum in eadem domo est promotus, tanquam ex ore proprio iudicatus, deponitur in instanti" (ibid., no. 36, pp. 29-30).

66. The abbot of Clairvaux was punished for deposing the abbot of Fontmorigny. The chief conspirator at Fontmorigny was treated harshly: "De sene illo miserrimo, qui huius inordinatae depositionis fuit malitiosissimus procurator, dicendo se ipsum simoniacum, ut abbatem suum respergeret infamia simoniae, de quo solo verbum huius infamiae emanavit, mittatur in Claramvallem et sit ibi omni sexta feria in pane et aqua per annum, et in capitulo eisdem diebus accipiat disciplinam" (ibid., no. 55, p. 46). On the career of John

Godard, abbot of Fontmorigny, see C. H. Talbot, "Two Opuscula of John Godard, First Abbot of Newenham," *Analecta sacri ordinis cisterciensis* 10 (1954): 208–67.

67. See, for example, Canivez, *Statuta*, vol. 2, no. 7, p. 316; no. 3, p. 335; vol. 3, no. 3, p. 300.

68. JL 17420.

69. G.de Valous, "Cluny," *DHGE*, vol. 13, cols. 77–78, on Hugh V.

70. "Ne quis in monasterio pactionaliter recipiatur. Quoniam plerumque, et in plerisque locis accidit, quod ingressus monasterii pecunia vel pactione interveniente conceditur, cum hoc sit sacris canonibus inhibitum et periculum utrobique vertatur animarum, tam recipientium, quam recipiendorum. Statuimus ne ullus de cetero in monasterio pactione seu precio recipiatur, nec ab ingrediente quicquam exigatur. Sed si quis sponte quicquam abtulerit, non respuatur ejus devotio" (Charvin, *Statuts*, vol. 1, no. 3, p. 42).

71. "Et quoniam ex susceptione debilium et inutilium personarum, ista precipue pestis irrepsit, precipimus, ut nonnisi tales recipiantur in monachos qui apti sint servitio Dei et non onerosi fratribus, et utiles monasterio" (ibid., no. 4. p. 42).

72. Hugh cited Peter the Venerable by name and renewed a provision of the latter's legislation in ibid., no. 6, pp. 42–43.

73. Ibid., no. 35, p. 30.

74. *Incipit* of Hugh's text: "Quoniam plerumque, et in plerisque locis accidit, quod ingressus monasterii. . . . " *Incipit* of the general chapter's text: "Quoniam plerumque et in plerisque locis accidit, quod beneficia spiritualia. . . . " *Explicit* of Hugh's text: "Sed si quis sponte quicquam abtulerit, non respuatur ejus devotio." *Explicit* of general chapter text: " . . . excepto quod de monacho dicit beatus Benedictus, quod ejus devotio sponte oblata non respuatur."

75. "Quoniam plerumque et in plerisque locis accidit, quod beneficia spiritualia pactione conferantur interveniente; cum hoc sit sacris canonibus inhibitum, et legi divine contrarium, prohibemus statuendo ne prioratibus dandis vel recipiendis, pro obedientiis, pro ecclesiis et capellanis, pro monachis recipiendis, sepultura, seu aliis rebus vel officiis spiritualibus, pactione mediante aliquid offeratur vel promittatur, excepto quod de monacho dicit beatus Benedictus, quod ejus devotio sponte oblata non respuatur" (Charvin, *Statuts*, vol. 1, no. 2, p. 55).

76. There is an invaluable collection of Grandmontine documents in *Scriptores ordinis Grandimontensis*, ed. J. Becquet (Turnhout, 1968), Corpus Christianorum, Continuatio Medievalis, no. 8. The rule of Grandmont is also accessible in Migne, vol. 204; cols. 1135–62. J. Becquet, "La Règle de Grandmont," *Bulletin de la Société archéologique et historique du Limousin* 87 (1958): 9–36, analyzes the rule and stresses its high valuation of extreme simplicity and its provisions intended to avoid all secular concerns and contacts.

77. J. Becquet, "Bibliothèque des écrivains de l'ordre de Grandmont," *Revue Mabillon* 53 (1963): 62–63; and J. Becquet, "Grandmont," *Catholicisme* 5: 192–93.

78. "Quinetiam pastor huius congregationis, seipsum et omnes discipulos suos, ab omni genere simoniae prorsus custodiens, et illud Domini praeceptum: 'Gratis accepistis, gratis date,' fideliter adimplens, in suscipiendis fratribus solam Dei voluntatem et animarum salutem summa discretione consideret" (Becquet, *Scriptores*, no. 45, p. 88).

79. The rule viewed any service to laymen or to patrons of the order as "simoniacal" (Becquet, *Scriptores*, no. 29, p. 83). The *Liber de doctrina* of Stephen of Muret, composed before 1157, criticized monks who took pride in the fact that their presence attracted gifts from their families (Becquet, *Scriptores*, p. 10; see also ibid., no. 5, p. 73; no. 19, p. 80; no. 24, p. 82).

80. "Talibus verbis vir bonus experiebatur si ille [a novice] firmum relinquendi saeculum cor haberet. Simoniacum enim eum aestimaret, si cuiuslibet terrenae rei promissione in religionem veniret" (ibid., chap. 4, p. 6). "Cum soli Deo, cuius servitus libertas est, serviendum sit vobis ex debito, si datores locorum in quibus habitatis, pro eisdem locis, vos sibi deservire postulaverint, potius ipsa loca vos iubemus deserere, quam hac intentione quodlibet etiam minimum eis petentibus tribuere. Aliter enim non huius mundi veri peregrini, sed velut ceteri cultores agrorum, tributa debentes essetis. Iniustum quoque et simoniacum esset pro eo quod quislibet erogando pauperibus, Deo obtulit, eidem datori temporaliter deservire, et non soli Deo, cuius amore totum illud reliquit" (ibid., no. 29, p. 83). *

81. On the origin and dating of the *Vita*, see J. Becquet, "Les premiers écrivains de l'ordre de Grandmont," *Revue Mabillon* 43 (1953): 125-30, and Becquet, "Bibliothèque," pp. 66-67. In the *Vita* Stephen of Muret, the founder of the group, warned his followers in a secret talk that to pray in return for money was simony (Becquet, *Scriptores*, pp. 324-25).

82. "Quoniam Salvatoris nostri vestigia pro gratia quam ipse nobis largitur sequi proposuimus, ipsius exemplo a religione nostra simoniaca heresis est radicitus evellenda. Omnes igitur in omnibus et precipue in suscipiendis fratribus omne genus simonie vitantes, omnino damnamus quod ipse Redemptor damnavit, cum omnes vendentes et ementes de templo eiecit. Illud ita [que prece] ptum Domini 'Gratis accepistis, gra [tis et date,' fide] liter observantes, de veste emend [a, de equita] tura adducenda, de pecunia afferen[da aut de] qualibet alia re ubi simonia notari p[ossit], cuilibet viro nostram congregationem [ingredi] cupienti, nullam sive per nos, sive [per alium] mentionem faciamus" (J. Becquet, "L'Institution: premier coutumier de l'ordre de Grandmont," *Revue Mabillon* 46 (1956): chap. 64, p. 26; Becquet, *Scriptores*, chap. 64, p. 525). The brackets in the text indicate damaged portions of the manuscript used for Becquet's edition.

83. "Si vero nos interroget quibus utimur vestibus et que sunt necessaria ad nostram religionem venientibus, rei veritas ei simpliciter manifestetur" (ibid.).

84. "Si autem de dispositione et distributione rerum suarum postulat a nobis consilium, legitime super hoc ei consulatur" (ibid.).

85. "Quod si [libera] voluntate et sine [nostra inquisitione] et absque pacto sua nobis presentet beneficia, more et auctoritate apostolorum huiusmodi possumus recipere" (ibid.).

86. "Si quis frater huiusmodi preceptum transgredi presumpserit et simonie reus extiterit manifeste, per solum pastorem tanta districtione super hoc iudicetur, ut disciplina unius sit correctio multorum" (ibid.).

87. For a study of Gilbert and his order, see R. Graham, *St. Gilbert of Sempringham and the Gilbertines* (London, 1901); see also R. Foreville, *Un Procès de canonisation à l'aube du XIIIe siècle. Le livre de saint Gilbert de Sempringham* (Paris, 1943).

88. The Rule of Sempringham was edited in W. Dugdale, *Monasticon Anglicanum*, ed. J. Caley, H. Ellis, and B. Bandinel (London, 1830), vol. 6, part 2, pp. I-XCIX, intercalated between pages 946 and 947. The original Dugdale edition was also printed in L. Holste, *Codex regularum* 2d ed. (Augsburg, 1759), 2:466-536. D. Knowles, *The Monastic Order in England* 2d ed. (Cambridge, 1963), p. 205, n. 1, warns that the *Monasticon Anglicanum* edition omitted portions of the text without signaling the fact.

89. "Sacrarum canonum statutis obtemperantes, detestabilem execramus Symoniae haeresim, sub anathemate prohibentes, ne ab aliquo viro, seu muliere inter nos suscipiendo, pro ingressu monasterii aliquid exigatur; set si quid fuerit sponte oblatum, suscipere licebit, omni illicita pactione, sive exactione exclusa. In aliis quoque rebus et negotiis spiritualibus, idem symoniae vitium inhibemus, et eum, quicumque fuerit aggressus, parti Symonis primi, hujus sceleris auctoris, cum sua pecunia in perditione deputatum denuntiamus" (*Monasticon Anglicanum*, vol. 6, part 2, p. xxxiii).

90. A comparison of the Rule of Sempringham (RS), chapter 9, with the *Decretum* (D), *causa* I, *questio* II, prologue reveals two verbal similarities that almost prove direct borrowing. RS: "ne . . . pro ingressu monasterii aliquid exigatur"; D: "an pro ingressu monasterii pecunia sit exigenda." RS: "set si quid fuerit sponte oblatum, suscipere licebit"; D: "sed sponte oblata suscipere."

91. A. de l'Assomption, *Les Origines de l'ordre de la Très-Sainte-Trinité d'après les documents* (Rome, 1925), pp. 33 ff. See also P. Deslandres, *L'Ordre des Trinitaires pour le rachat des captifs* (Rome and Toulouse, 1903), 1:20-30. John of Matha's masters at Paris are, unfortunately, not identified (de l'Assomption, *Les Origines*, pp. 33-34).

92. De l'Assomption, *Les Origines*, p. 38. For an account of the genesis of the rule and the part played by the bishop of Paris and the abbot of Saint Victor, see Pott 483.

93. "Si quis huius ordinis frater esse voluerit, primo per annum cum expensis suis praeter victum, habito suo et omnibus suis retentis, in ordine pro Deo serviat; et post annum, si bonum et conveniens videatur ministro domus et fratribus et illi, et locus vacaverit, recipiatur. Nihil tamen pro receptione sua exigatur. Si quid tamen gratis dederit, recipiatur . . . " (Pott 483, printed in Migne, vol. 214, col. 448).

94. "Tribuatur ei modeste licentia cum omnibus quae attulit recedendi" (ibid.).

95. "Que nus frères ne sereurs ne soit recheus par condition d'acat ou d'autre proumesse . . . " (statutes of the leper house of Noyon [late twelfth century, revised in mid-thirteenth], in L. LeGrand, *Statuts d'hôtels-Dieu et de léproseries* [Paris, 1901], chap. 1, pp. 194-95).

96. "Nullus autem recipiatur in nostram societatem nisi bone opinionis exstiterit, nec habeamus ad pecuniam sed pocius ad honestatem respectum; et si aliqua honesta persona recipienda fuerit, pro amore Dei petat fraternitatem et pro amore Dei recipiatur. Nichil autem petatur ab ea, sed, si aliquid secum attulit, illud ad utilitatem pauperum suscipiatur" (statutes of the hospital of Angers [ca. 1200], ibid., chap. 18, p. 26).

97. "Si quis ingredi in domum voluerit, per annum probabitur in-habitu seculari. Anno peracto, si domus ei placuerit, vel si talis fuerit ejus conversatio quod non debeat reprobari, in congregatione fratrum recipiatur. Antequam induatur habitu religionis istius, jurabit quod, nec per se nec per alium, dederit aut promiserit, aut indebitum servitium fecerit per quod istius domus ingressum speraverit optinere" (statutes of the hospital of Montdidier [1207-33], in ibid., chap. 3, p. 36). See also statutes of the hospital of Paris (ca. 1220), ibid., chap. 3, p. 44; statutes of the Hospital-Comtesse at Lille (ca. 1250), ibid., chap. 2, p. 81; statutes of the leper house at Brives (1250), ibid., chap. 5, p. 207, chaps. 33, 34, p. 213; statutes of the Hotel-Dieu-le-comte at Troyes (1263), ibid., chap. 1, p. 105; statutes of the Hospital of Pontoise (ca. 1265), ibid., chap. 13, p. 141.

CHAPTER SEVEN

Innocent III
And Simoniacal Entry

 The five popes who succeeded Alexander III in the years 1181–98 were interested, in varying degrees, in the reform of the church and its institutions. They initiated or promoted some of the reforms that were subsequently adopted by Innocent. However, their relatively brief reigns, their personalities, and the troubled political situation prevented them from carrying their reforms to fruition. Innocent III had the good fortune of a long reign and a favorable conjuncture of political events that enabled him to espouse a number of older reforms and to initiate new departures. One of the chief characteristics of Innocent's reign was a commitment to reform in almost all areas of church life and practice.[1]

The reform of the regular clergy, in its organization and practices, was an area in which Innocent expended much effort. He sought to eliminate abuses and to revitalize structures, partly in the hope of winning useful allies for his larger reform ideals.[2] Certain aspects of his reform program for the regular clergy have been well studied, for instance, his efforts to organize independent religious houses into provinces for chapter meetings and mutual visitation on the Cistercian model.[3] Other aspects of his program, however, have been left in relative obscurity. Innocent's attack on simoniacal entry into religious life is one such neglected subject. Opposition to such entry and measures against it formed a significant minor theme in Innocent's relations with the various forms of the regular clergy.

In at least two points Innocent's career as a student intersected the rising concern about simoniacal entry into religion. At Paris, in the 1180s, he had been a fellow student of men who later in their careers were interested in the problem, for example, Robert de Courson.[4] Certainly he was in the milieu out of which much of the intellectual concern with this simony arose. Indeed, because of the congruence of Innocent's reformist views with those of the Paris masters who were in the circle of Peter the Chanter, John W. Baldwin has suggested that it is legitimate to consider Innocent a member of that circle.[5] After 1187 Innocent studied canon law at Bologna with the great lawyer Huguccio, whom the pope later made bishop of Ferrara.[6] When Lothario dei Segni was elected pope in 1198, he was well prepared by his theological and canonical training to deal with the problem of simoniacal entry into religion.

Innocent's surviving registers contain a considerable number of letters to religious orders and to individual houses that criticized them for rumored or proven abuses of unspecified character and exhorted them to correct the objectionable situation.[7] In view of Innocent's explicit activities against simoniacal entry, it is quite probable that some of these critical and hortatory letters had illicit entry practices as one of their targets. However, the clear and specific measures taken by him against such simony are sufficient to demonstrate his interest in eliminating what was by 1198 certainly perceived as a crime.

In 1200 the archbishop of Canterbury and apostolic legate, Hubert Walter,[8] held a council at London in which he promulgated canons based on those of the Third Lateran Council of 1179, but modified for English conditions. One portion of the fourteenth canon was an almost unchanged reissue of canon ten, "Monachi non pretio," of the Lateran Council: "Let not monks be received for a price in a monastery. . . . However, if anyone was pressed and gave anything for his reception, may he not ascend to holy orders. May he, however, who took the payment suffer the loss of his office."[9]

This canon was not a dead letter, as events quickly revealed. In

1201 Hubert Walter sent a messenger, perhaps a canonist since his title was "master," to Innocent III, informing him that, in the course of a canonical visitation of religious houses in his diocese, he had discovered conditions contrary to the canons against simoniacal entry. Hubert Walter's letter is lost, but Innocent's response, sent in May or June 1201, advised the archbishop on several points of procedure.

> Your messenger, the beloved son Master A., on your behalf, proposed that when you were visiting the Canterbury diocese according to the custom of your predecessors, in order to correct what required correction and to institute that which, according to God, you saw should be instituted, you discovered that the simoniacal wickedness was flourishing in monasteries, among regular canons, and in religious places, so that in those places many were received for a price, who should instead be received freely, nay rather even invited to the observance of religion.[10]

Thus, in common with his contemporary Hugh of Lincoln,[11] Hubert Walter had apparently included in his visitation questionnaire some sort of inquiry about the reception practices prevalent in the houses visited. Innocent's response to the archbishop supplied more details about the discovery: "Therefore, since a large number is involved in the case, you are not certain whether severity should be lessened to some degree, or whether you should exercise against such [persons] the rigor of canonical discipline."[12] Hubert Walter's hesitations about what to do in the face of so large a number of guilty religious are understandable. Judged rigorously against the standard of the canon law, the entry of many otherwise respectable religious[13] must have been tainted. The archbishop was apparently unwilling to punish large numbers of simoniacs without some consultation with the pope. The problem of numbers in cases of simoniacal entry was a persistent one, and Innocent proposed several solutions to it over the course of his pontificate. In this particular case his response was centered not on the numbers involved but on the manner in which their guilt was discovered.

Therefore, we respond thus to your inquiry, that if an accusation had been canonically presented before you against those who were marked by the stain of this kind, then after the crime has been proved in a legal way, you may exercise the revenge of canonical severity against both those giving and those receiving [illicit payments]. But, if you found out about this only in the course of your inquiry during visitation, you may direct those who were received in such places by simoniacal wickedness to be removed from them [and] you may send them to stricter monasteries for penance.[14]

The visitation of a religious house was, in theory, a procedure conducted in secret and whose results were generally not revealed to outsiders for fear of scandal.[15] Thus if Hubert Walter learned of the simony only in the course of visitation, it was presumably hidden from the public. Innocent's demand that the guilty religious be sent to a stricter house for penance was borrowed from the decretal "De regularibus" of Clement III.[16] The matter would thus be kept within bounds, avoiding public scandal, and yet the guilty religious would be punished.

On the other hand, if the archbishop had discovered the simony by way of a public accusation formally laid before him, then the matter was, or soon would be, notorious, and a full judicial process with normal punishments was necessary to discourage other simoniacs and to assure the public of the church's intention to deal seriously with offenders. In the event of public notoriety, Innocent held that no lessening of severity on account of numbers was to be allowed. Thus, from his first public treatment of simoniacal entry, Innocent pursued a policy of calibrating the punishment to fit the circumstances of the crime.

Innocent also specified a punishment for the abbots and other monastic leaders who had participated in simoniacal receptions:

May you impose a fitting penance on the abbots, abbesses, priors, other prelates and their officials, and until they perform it, may you suspend them from the execution of holy orders, and [may] you order your [suffragan] bishops to strive to observe this procedure in their dioceses. Nevertheless, that can be received gratefully which was offered freely, without being prescribed.[17]

The canonists had generally avoided the issue of what to do to a prelate who had received new members simoniacally. Perhaps they could see no reason why such a prelate should not be treated like any other simoniac prelate, i.e., deposed. In any case, Innocent III filled that apparent gap in legal theory by ordering that if the crime was made known by accusation,[18] the offending prelate should be struck with the full severity of the canons, i.e., deposed. But, if the offense was discovered during a secret visitation, the guilty prelate was to be suspended from his sacred and administrative functions until he or she performed a suitable penance.[19]

Innocent terminated his response to Hubert Walter by a restatement of the principle that gifts, provided that they were freely offered, were in no way discouraged by his letter. This decretal, "Dilectus filius," was incorporated into the first official collection of Innocent's decretals, composed at the pope's order by Peter Collevacino in 1210. The collection was directed to the law schools at Bologna for use in the courts and in the classrooms.[20]

In October 1201 Innocent sent a letter to the prior and brethren of the Lateran monastery, ordering them to observe the constitutions of Alexander III, i.e., the canon "Monachi non pretio" of the Third Lateran Council, which forbade simoniacal receptions, as well as the monastic abuses of religious keeping personal money and traveling alone among lay people.[21]

Innocent's registers of letters for the years 1200–1202 do not survive intact, and, as a consequence, for those years few traces can be found of Innocent's activities against simoniacal entry of religious. However, in 1207 Robert de Courson, a canon of Noyon and master in theology, accompanied the archbishop of Sens in visitation of the monastery of Vezelay. Innocent commissioned them to investigate rumors of irregularity in the house. The visitors reported to him that the rumors of incontinence, fiscal irregularities, and simoniacal reception of new members were true. On the basis of this report, Innocent took the extreme step of deposing and ejecting from the house the abbot, the prior, the *decanus*, the

almoner, the cellarer, the third prior, three priors of outlying possessions, and the chaplains of both the abbot and the prior. They
were distributed among houses of stricter rule, and could never
again hold positions of authority without papal permission. In
the case of Vezelay, simony in receptions was merely one of a constellation of abuses, but it is significant that it was singled out
for condemnation in the report of the visitors and in Innocent's
measures for restoring order.[22]

In an undated letter, which Potthast attributed to the year 1210,
the abbot of Bec was advised by Innocent how to deal with monks
who had incurred canonical irregularity, either because they had
struck other religious or had entered simoniacally. The abbot
may have initiated this correspondance with the pope to avoid
visitation by the diocesan bishop.[23] Innocent first recounted the
details of the abbot's question:

> From your report we have learned that some of the monks of your
> monastery—certain of them fell under the canon of the promulgated
> sentence because of violent striking with hands [and] others had a
> simoniacal entry there—have received holy orders without having ob-
> tained the benefit of absolution or the grace of a dispensation, and
> in due course they have not feared to minister in those holy orders.[24]

The monks who had struck other religious were required to go to
the pope for absolution because, since canon 15 of the Second
Lateran Council of 1139, all dealings with that crime had been reserved to the pope.[25] The monks who had entered Bec simoniacally were ineligible to receive or to exercise holy orders because
the Third Lateran Council of 1179, in its tenth canon, had declared
that such religious were *irregulares.*[26] The simoniac monks at Bec
had taken holy orders and had exercised them, and therefore had
incurred automatic excommunication for violation of the canon.
Innocent advised the abbot:

> Since it is necessary for them to come to the Apostolic See, and you
> say that it is to be feared lest they may wander in coming to our pres-
> ence, and may incur damage to that very salvation for which they
> come, you are concerned about their salvation and have asked that
> we act mercifully in this matter.[27]

Note that the monks were required to go to Rome, not because they had entered religious life simoniacally, but because they had incurred excommunication as a result of their taking holy orders while *irregulares*. Innocent expressed full confidence in the abbot's discretion and continued his decision:

> . . . Also considering that we tolerate for the sake of religious life many things among the regular clergy which we would not allow in others, we order through Apostolic letters that . . . , saving the general constitution of the council [of 1179] which dealt with those who are known to have had simoniacal entry, you may deal with them by our authority as you see is expedient for the salvation of their souls in the matter that they received orders in that way and subsequently ministered in them.[28]

Thus Innocent empowered the abbot to deal with the monks, without the necessity that they go to Rome for absolution from their excommunication. He was careful to add that the Third Lateran Council should be observed; i.e., after the excommunication was lifted, the simoniac monks were not henceforth to exercise the orders that they had taken. The monks were absolved for receiving and exercising orders while ineligible, but they were not free from the irregularity contracted when they entered religious life simoniacally.

Innocent's pronouncements on the problem of simoniacal entry up to 1210 were prompted by consultations from concerned prelates. In 1210 he took a wide personal initiative when he attacked the problem on a large scale, apparently without reference to any particular case. In a letter of 17 April, directed to the bishops and archbishops of France, he declared:

> We have heard very often and from many people that in certain monasteries of monks, nuns, and of other religious located in your dioceses, a damnable custom—no, rather a damned and rightfully damned abuse—has persisted up to this point that almost no person is received in them without the stain of simoniacal wickedness. Therefore, lest we may seem by ignoring a cry so often repeated to favor [the practice], . . . we order . . . that once a year each of you, in the course of visiting monasteries of this type in your dioceses, forbid under threat of anathema that henceforth any person be re-

ceived in them by a wickedness of this type, [and] always denouncing this same [crime] in your synods, may you do with Apostolic authority to those whom you find so received what you see is expedient to salvation and to honesty, with the obstacle of appeal removed.[29]

Innocent's order for annual visitation of suspect houses and for denunciation of the crime in episcopal synods was symptomatic of his desire to encourage regular episcopal supervision as a primary tool of reform, in this instance among regular houses subject to diocesan correction.[30] His order for frequent denunciation of the crime, both during visitation and in diocesan synods, was a characteristic attempt to publicize the campaign against simoniacal entry. Just as in 1201 he had ordered the bishops of the province of Canterbury to follow the procedure outlined for Hubert Walter, so in 1210 he commanded the episcopate of France to act in a regular fashion against the practice.

Innocent left to the bishops' discretion the treatment of simoniac religious, without any reference to the Third Lateran Council. This was in contrast to the order given to the abbot of Bec, perhaps in the same year, to act in such a way as to observe the provisions of the council. This explicit permission to the bishops not to invoke the full rigor of the law was based on considerations implicit in the first sentence of the letter. If, in certain monasteries, almost no one had entered without simony, then a strict enforcement of the canon law would have stripped such places of most of their clergy, dispersing them to stricter houses for punishment and, in effect, annihilating the guilty houses. This was the same problem of numbers that Hubert Walter had put to the pope a decade before, and that Innocent had sidestepped then by his decision that the punishment would be determined by the manner in which the offense had become known. In the decade since Hubert Walter's letter, Innocent must have become aware that large numbers of otherwise respectable religious were involved in the crime of simoniacal entry, and that a more lenient procedure for them was necessary.

In any case, from 1210 to 1215 Innocent gave more attention to the fate of those numerous religious who were simoniacs out of ignorance and simplicity, rather than out of malice. Ultimately,

Innocent developed two procedures, founded on a distinction between those who were only technically simoniacs and those who were
personally guilty of simony.

Preparation for the Fourth Lateran Council

On 19 April 1213 Innocent issued letters to the prelates and
princes of Christendom, summoning them to a general council
that was to convene at Rome on 1 November 1215.[31] On that
same 19 April Cardinal Robert de Courson was made apostolic
legate "in partibus Gallicanis" to preach a crusade and to prepare
for the council.[32] Between June 1213 and May 1215, the legate
held regional councils at Paris, Rouen, Reims, Bordeaux, Clermont-Dessous, and Montpellier, and attempted unsuccessfully to
convoke a council at Bourges. The canons of Paris, Rouen, and
Montpellier survive more or less *in toto*, and the canons of Bordeaux survive apparently in part, in a letter to King John of England listing the canons that concerned his crown and realm.[33]
By analogy to Paris and Rouen, there were probably canons issued
at Reims and Bordeaux, but they do not survive.

At Paris in June 1213 and at Rouen in February-March 1214,
Robert de Courson issued elaborate sets of very similar reform
canons that reflected the concerns of Innocent III, and that foreshadowed in many particulars the canons of the Fourth Lateran
Council.[34] Sections two and three of Courson's canons, contain-
ing approximately fifty canons in all, were directed respectively
to male religious and to nuns.

In canon one of section two, the council at Paris referred explicitly to Innocent III's letter of 1210 to the French bishops and
indicated that the letter was sufficient guidance for the council.[35]
In canons 27 of Paris and 30 of Rouen, the councils defined
more explicitly their opposition to simoniacal entry: "We order
under pain of suspension that neither food nor clothing be demanded from those about to enter a monastery, nor money, nor
anything in circumvention of the foresaid [prohibitions]; likewise
that they not be rejected on account of this."[36]

This canon reiterated the view expressed by Innocent to Hubert

Walter that a guilty prelate be suspended from office. It also forbade a monastery to reject an entrant because he refused, quite legitimately, to give anything for his reception. This last point was a new element in the discussion of simony, and may represent one of the ways religious houses adapted to the new scruples about gifts, i.e., they rejected those who offered no "voluntary" gift.

A council was held at Montpellier by the legate Peter of Benevento on 8 January 1215, with the apparent cooperation of Robert de Courson. Its twentieth canon decreed: "Likewise we order that no one be made a canon or a monk under any condition or pact through which anything should be given for his reception."[37]

In view of Innocent's interest in simoniacal entry, it is reasonable to assume that he included that topic in the list of subjects to be treated by his legates in councils. The verbal agreement of the canons issued at Paris and at Rouen indicates that Robert de Courson had a sort of program that, with local variants for local needs, he promulgated at each council that he convoked.[38] Thus Innocent used at least two legates, Robert de Courson and Peter of Benevento, to publicize the crime of simoniacal entry and to prepare the prelates of the church for his own measures against it at the Fourth Lateran Council.

However, it is important to see that Innocent was probably not the sole source for these canons. Robert de Courson himself may also have been a contributor to the formulation of the canons against simoniacal entry. At the very least, he was representative of the university-trained masters who provided much of the impetus of the intellectual attack on the problem.[39] Robert had been a student at Paris, roughly contemporary with Innocent, of the theologian and moralist Peter the Chanter. In their fundamental article Marcel and Christiane Dickson date his studies with Peter to the years 1196–97, the very period in which Peter was probably composing his *Summa de sacramentis*, with its attention to the complexities surrounding simoniacal entry into religion.[40] From approximately 1204 to 1210 Robert de Courson was a master in theology at Paris, and between 1204 and 1208 he composed his own *summa*, a copy of which exists in the Bibliothèque Nationale ms. latin 14524. In 1207, as visitor of Vezelay for Innocent III, he acquired experience investigating actual cases of simoniacal entry.[41]

In at least two sections of his *summa*, Master Robert discussed the problem of simoniacal entry and its consequences. He assumed, with little discussion, that payment to enter a religious house was simoniacal, and he addressed himself to the practical question of what an individual religious should do if his entry into religious life was simoniacal.

> Likewise, since scarcely any monastery can be found in the cisalpine church whose entrance is given free, it is asked what should be advised to monks and nuns who, through the intervention of money, were introduced into a congregation of monks or nuns. For it is a fact that, since they do not enter through the door, but climb in by some other way, either through threats, or only by reason of blood relationship or of a gift or of some sort of greed, they incur the stain of simony.[42]

Master Robert responded to the problem of these religious as a moralist and spiritual director, rather than as a canonist. He left it to the conscience of the individual religious to decide on the course to follow. He laid down as a criterion of choice the relative strictness of life in the religious house. If the house was lax, then the member was advised to seek *transitus* to a stricter house; if the monastery was itself a house of strict rule—he used Cistercians and Carthusians as examples—then in accord with the general principles governing *transitus*,[43] the religious had to remain there and to expunge his sin with special penances from the abbot.[44]

In his treatment of penance, Master Robert again broached the question of simoniacal entry: "However, what should be advised to a whole convent where all their goods are derived from simony or from rapine; or some goods from licit sources and some from rapine . . . ?"[45]

As was conventional in a theological *quaestio* of this sort, Master Robert discussed the merits of various alternatives: for example, advising a troubled monk to remain in his monastery; advising him to leave it for another; or advising him to confide in his abbot. Depending on other circumstances, Robert approved or disapproved of each of the alternatives. His relatively long treatment of the question reveals clearly that he saw that any solution to the troubled religious' problem involved grave inconveniences and moral dangers. Finally, as a last resort in a hopeless case, he opted for the extreme solution of dispersion of the house.

> Likewise there is another sad and almost insoluble situation which everywhere creates a huge slaughter of souls. Imagine a certain monastery which has not received for free all the monks whom it has, but rather [took them] through the intervention of money. Now at last the abbot with the whole chapter recognizes himself along with all the rest to have contracted the stain of simony. And now all are about to die, or the feast of Easter is near, and they wish to atone worthily for all their crimes, according to your judgment, you who are their bishop. What will you advise? You know that everyone entered unworthily, and that they have nothing except what they got through simony. You know also that the foresaid demon cannot be driven out unless a full restitution is made, if possible. Therefore, you ought to tell them that they should all go away destitute rather than perish there.[46]

These texts reveal that Robert de Courson had more than a passing acquaintance with the moral problems caused by simoniacal entry into religion. It seems clear that he, and other Paris-trained masters at the curia, advised and cooperated with Innocent III in his formulation of measures against this form of simony. The existence and influence of university-trained theologians and lawyers points to one of the chief sources of Innocent's opposition to the practice and of the diffusion of that opposition to the rest of the church.

On 25 July 1213, that is, during the mission of Robert de Courson to France and the Low Countries, Innocent sent a letter to another of his legates, Albert of Vercelli,[47] the patriarch of Jerusalem, then resident at Saint John of Acre because of the Saracen conquest of his see. The legate was informed of the pope's reaction to a situation that had come to light in the Order of the Templars.[48] In this letter Innocent expressed more formally than he had done elsewhere two of the central reasons for his opposition to simoniacal entry. The practice was simultaneously a danger to the soul of the individual religious and a scandal to others, presumably to other religious and to outsiders who might learn of it. Innocent saw his predecessors in the papacy as the chief opponents of such simony, and, in his view, their various measures against it had not been effective.[49] He felt obliged to renew the attack with measures of his own. "We have learned that some people have entered simoniacally that house of the Templars, to which the eyes of many look, although, as we accept from the letters of your Fraternity, [they did this] from simplicity rather than from malice, simplicity offering the opportunity for the offense."[50]

Thus, in the pattern established by Hubert Walter and by the abbot of Bec, the legate had laid before the pope instances of simoniacal entry that he had uncovered among the Templars. The reference of the legate to the *simplicitas* of the offenders is significant, for it pointed to the major obstacle to any full attack on monastic simony in the early thirteenth century. The objectionable nature of many entry arrangements was not well known among ordinary religious and aspirants to religious life. Simoniacal entry into religion had first been perceived and elaborated as a crime in the schools of canon law and theology in the last forty years of the twelfth century. Those who had had contact with the schools, and by 1213 that included many leaders of the church, were often sensitized to the issue. But individuals entering the order of the Templars, accompanied by the customary negotiations and payments, probably did so in good faith, even though many church leaders and intellectuals rejected that customary procedure as simoniacal. This hard factual situation was, no doubt, the chief reason why Innocent attempted to publicize the crime by means of episcopal visitations, diocesan synods, and regional councils. His instructions to the legate Albert contained a demand for publicity for the crime within the order of the Templars:

Therefore, in order to exclude the danger of such *simplicitas*, We order your fraternity through apostolic letters that you strictly prohibit on Our behalf the master and brethren of the Templars that

191

nothing be demanded for the reception of anyone; and that you cause it to be prohibited firmly by them in all the houses of their order. Not even under the pretext of an "aid" should there be an exaction, since the camouflage of a name does not change the guilt of a crime.[51]

As in the cases at Canterbury in 1201 and in the French church in 1210, Innocent used the occasion of a scandal to inform a large segment of the church—in this case, and I believe for the first time, an entire religious order—about the evils of simoniacal receptions. For the future the full rigor of the law was to apply to the Templars:

> However, if hereafter anyone shall have admitted someone in that way to the forementioned order, may both the admitter and the admitee be punished in that in which he sinned: let him be expelled forever from the order without hope of restitution, [and] he should be transferred to another order of stricter rule, in which he may lament the guilt of so damnable a fault.[52]

The full rigor of the law for the guilty parties in simoniacal entry was to be penal exile to a stricter order, without hope of returning to the Templars. This was, of course, the solution based on Clement III's decretal letter "De regularibus."[53] But Innocent accepted a more lenient procedure for those who had committed the crime before his letter had removed all doubt on the subject. That is to say, he recommended mercy for those who had acted with *simplicitas*: "However, if urgent necessity or clear utility demand it, you may act more gently with those who up to now have sinned by *simplicitas*, just as the prudence of your discretion sees fit."[54]

Thus, from at least 1201 to 1213, there was a continuing current of concern on the part of Innocent III about the practice of simoniacal entry into religion. His responses to the concrete cases that came before him were complex and varied. Evidently he attempted to take into account such mitigating factors as the numbers of guilty and their degree of personal, conscious guilt. He promoted public attacks on the practice as a way to educate those potentially or actually involved in such simony. This concern found its final expression in the sixty-fourth canon of the Fourth Lateran Council.

Fourth Lateran Council (1215)

Innocent's great council, which held its first session on 11 November 1215, was a major effort to promote and to publicize a largely preexisting reform program, and to win cooperation for it from the church's hierarchy and from secular rulers. Groundwork for the council had been laid by legates and by consultations with church leaders, but its canons probably represent the concerns and decisions of Innocent and his immediate advisers. The assembly itself, attended by 412 bishops, 800 abbots and priors, and hundreds of delegates representing secular rulers, cathedral chapters, and Italian cities, was large and unwieldy. The relative brevity of the council's sessions would seem to prove that Innocent and the curia had the major role in the formulation of the seventy canons that were promulgated.[55]

There were four canons that dealt with the crime of simony in various of its forms. Canon 63 forbade payments for installing or consecrating prelates. Canon 65 forbade bishops to extort money for filling positions. Canon 66 ordered that the sacraments be provided for free, provided that the "laudable customs" of giving gifts by the laity were observed.[56] Canon 64 was devoted to simony in the entrance to religious houses: "Since the simoniacal stain has infected so many nuns to such a degree that they receive scarcely any as sisters without a price, and they wish by pretext of poverty to palliate a crime of this sort, we prohibit entirely that this be done henceforth. . . ."[57]

From the study of earlier texts dealing with simoniacal entry into religion, one is totally unprepared for the fact that this canon is directed primarily against women religious. In the treatment accorded to the issue by canonists and theologians in the later twelfth and early thirteenth centuries, nuns were mentioned, but there were few indications that they were in some way particularly guilty of simoniacal receptions. Not one of the instances reported by the letters of Alexander III, Clement III, or Innocent III involved female religious. The only case I have found before 1215 is that of Nun-Coton, visited by Hugh of Lincoln between 1186 and 1200.[58]

In the thirteenth century critics of simoniacal entry shifted their stress from religious in general to female religious in particular. Of course, male religious continued to be mentioned for simoniacal reception practices, but the relative increase in the frequency of complaints against nuns, especially Benedictine nuns, was striking.[59] That shift in emphasis quite probably reflects a shift in reality. In the three decades straddling the year 1200, many of the religious orders of men, including the Cistercians and the Cluniacs, took measures to forbid simoniacal entry.[60] For these houses of men, with their generally larger economic base, it was easier to abandon or, at least, to camouflage some of the more objectionable elements of the customary entry arrangements. On the other hand, the poorer women's houses were more constrained to retain the practice of demanding an income with their new members.[61] Also, monks could help support themselves by managing the properties of their houses, but the relatively strict claustration of female religious prevented them from contributing much to their own expenses. In any case, it seems that the required entry fee, or dowry, which was an institutionalization of the earlier simony, was more characteristic of women's than of men's houses in the thirteenth century and later.[62]

Canon 64 of the Fourth Lateran Council continued by prescribing for those who committed simony after its promulgation the same penalty that had been inflicted on those Templars who were denounced by the legate Albert: "[We] institute that whoever henceforth shall have commited such a wickedness, both receiver and received, whether she be subject or prelate, shall be expelled from her monastery without hope of return, [and] shall be forced into a place of stricter rule to do perpetual penance."[63]

As a concession to the numbers involved and to the *simplicitas* of those who might have acted in good faith in paying for their entry, the canon provided a gentler punishment for those who had entered before 1215. They were to be removed from their present houses, but allowed to reenter other houses of the same order.[64] Then, expressly as a further concession to numbers, the canon authorized a second procedure for those who had entered simoniacally before 1215: "But if by chance they cannot be conveniently placed elsewhere on account of large numbers, lest by chance they should wander damnably in the world, they may be received again by way of dispensation in the same monastery, having changed their earlier positions and having received lower ones."[65] Thus, in effect, a guilty religious could be expelled and received again in the same monastery, but with the loss of all the privileges that she had gained by seniority. This provision was a guarantee that the guilty religious would remain in religious life, no matter what other punishment was inflicted. The Lateran canon was directed specifically to nuns, but its provisions were intended for all regular religious: "We want this observed even about monks and other regular clergy."[66]

After the canon had defined the procedures to be followed in dealing with the religious who were simoniacs before and after 1215, it demanded publicity, which had characteristically accompanied almost all of Innocent III's moves against simoniacal entry: "But, lest they may be able to excuse themselves through *simplicitas* or ignorance, we order that diocesan bishops cause this canon to be published throughout their dioceses each year."[67]

Thus the Fourth Lateran Council provided a treatment for simoniac religious, calibrated according to degree of guilt and the numbers involved. It also ordered the implementation of a regular mechanism, the annual condemnation by the diocesan bishop, with which to attack the problem. No element of the canon was entirely new, since Innocent had experiemented with the problem for fifteen years. But canon 64 was a complete formulation that reflected the results of those years of trial and error in the face of a serious practical problem.

1. For a characterization of Innocent III as an ecclesiastical reformer, see A. Fliche, "Innocent III et la réforme de l'église," *Revue d'histoire ecclésiastique* 44 (1949): 89–152. See also the valuable comments of H. Tillmann, *Papst Innocenz III* (Bonn, 1954), pp. 152–85. M. Maccarone, "Riforma e sviluppo della vita religiosa con Innocenzo III," *Rivista di storia della chiesa in Italia* 16 (1962): 29–72, treats of Innocent's reform measures for religious life.

2. Tillmann, *Innocenz III*, pp. 180-85, discusses Innocent's attempts to use Cistercians as legates, visitors, preachers, and reformers of other religious orders. These efforts were only moderately successful, and the pope turned to other groups, such as the Franciscans and the *Humiliati*, which were more amenable to his active purposes of preaching and evangelizing (H. Grundmann, *Religiöse Bewegungen im Mittelalter* [Berlin, 1935], pp. 70-169). But, in the first decade of his pontificate, Innocent tried to harness the Cistercians and other regulars to his purposes. In 1198 he empowered the famous Parisian preacher Fulk of Neuilly to promote a crusade and to join to his work any Black monk, Cistercian, or regular canon whom he felt necessary (Pott 408). In 1206 Innocent committed the evangelization of the pagan Livonians on the Baltic to any religious, especially Cistercian, who wished to volunteer (Pott 2901).

3. U. Berlière, "Innocent III et la réorganisation des monastères bénédictins," *Revue bénédictine* 32 (1920): 156-58. Canon 12 of the Fourth Lateran Council ordered the establishment of triennial chapters and regular mutual visitation by all independent religious houses. W. A. Pantin, ed., *Documents Illustrating the Activities of the General and Provincial Chapters of the English Black Monks, 1215-1540* (London, 1931-37) Camden Third Series, nos. 45, 47, 54, provides a rich selection of texts concerned with the chapter mechanism as it operated among English Benedictines. In the immediate aftermath of the Lateran Council, the chapter system was instituted in many areas; but outside England, it seldom attained the regulariy needed for it to take root. U. Berlière, "Les Chapitres généraux de l'ordre de Saint Benoit," *Mélanges d'histoire bénédictine* 4 (Maredsous, 1902): 52-171, lists all the known chapter meetings of independent Benedictine houses. Canon 12 of the Fourth Lateran Council ordered meetings for regular canons as well as for monks. H. E. Salter, ed., *Chapters of the Augustinian Canons* (London, 1922) Canterbury and York Series, no. 29, prints documents about English chapter meetings; and G. G. Meersseman, "Die Reform der Salzburger Augustinerstifte (1218) eine Folge des IV. Laterankonzils," *Zeitschrift fur schweizerische Kirchengeschichte* 48 (1954): 81-95, edits the records of three chapter meetings at Salzburg in 1218, 1221, and 1224.

4. On Innocent's student career, see M. Maccarrone, "Innocenzo III primo del suo pontificato," *Archivio della R. Deputazione romana di Storia patria* 66 (1943): 59-134; and Tillmann, *Innocenz III*, pp. 4-9.

5. J. W. Baldwin, *Masters, Princes, and Merchants: The Social Views of Peter the Chanter and His Circle* (Princeton, N.J., 1970), 1: 342-43.

6. Tillmann, *Innocenz III*, p. 8.

7. Pott 4680 to the Cluniac General Chapter complained about the state of La Charité; Pott 1695 concerned Thorney Abbey; Pott 3142 criticized Vezelay; Pott 4262 concerned Saint Victor at Marseilles. Berlière, "Innocent III," pp. 35-39, cites many other examples of Innocent's letters complaining about conditions in Benedictine houses. Many of these letters do not specify clearly the nature of the problems criticized.

8. On Hubert Walter in his dual role as churchman and king's man, see C. R. Cheney, *Hubert Walter* (London, 1967), pp. 49-134. Cheney (pp. 159-71) stresses the importance of the canonists who served in Hubert Walter's entourage. See also C. R. Young, *Hubert Walter, Lord of Canterbury and Lord of England* (Durham, N.C., 1968).

9. Mansi, 22:720-21.

10. "Dilectus filius magister A. nuncius tuus pro parte tua proposuit, quod, quum Cantuariensem dioecesim secundum praedecessorum tuorum consuetudinem visitans, ut quae corrigenda sunt corrigas, et statuas quae secundum Deum videris statuenda, in monasteriis et canonicis regularibus, et religiosis locis pullulasse repereris simoniacam pravitatem, ita, quod in eis multi pretio sunt recepti, qui potius gratis recipi debuissent, immo etiam ad religionis observantiam invitari" (Pott 1403). The full text is printed in Migne, vol. 216, col. 1231.

11. In the course of a canonical visitation between 1186 and 1200, Hugh found simoniacal receptions at the nunnery of Nun-Cotton (Migne, vol. 153, cols. 1113-16).

12. "Dubitas igitur, an, quia multitudo reperitur in causa, severitati sit aliquid detrahendum, an in tales exercere debeas rigorem canonicae disciplinae" (Pott 1403).

13. In his letter to Innocent, Hubert Walter had apparently noted that many of those involved were otherwise respectable, because Innocent commented that many were people who deserved to be invited to religious life, rather than being forced to pay for entry: "in eis [monasteries] multi pretio sunt recepti, qui potius gratis recipi debuissent, immo etiam ad religionis observationem invitari" (Pott 1403).

14. "Nos igitur inquisitioni tuae taliter respondemus, quod, si adversus eos, qui labe fuerint huiusmodi maculati, accusatio coram te fuerit canonice instituta, postquam crimen ordine fuerit iudiciario comprobatum, tam in dantes quam in recipientes canonicae severitatis exerceas ultionem. Quodsi de hoc tibi per solam inquisitionem constiterit, eos, qui per simoniacam pravitatem in locis talibus sunt recepti, ab illis amotos ad agendam poenitentiam ad monasteria dirigas arctiora" (Pott 1403).

15. C. R. Cheney, *Episcopal Visitation of Monasteries in the Thirteenth Century* (Manchester, 1931), pp. 64-71. Cheney points out that religious communities resented the presence of secular clerics during visitation, and they exerted themselves to keep the visitation an affair between the bishop and themselves. The religious orders that maintained discipline by means of mutual visitation of their own houses also tried to keep secret the irregularities discovered during visitation. The Cistercians attempted to prevent members from divulging information damaging to the order (Canivez, *Statuta*, vol. 1, no. 42, 1195; no. 2, 1208). In their revised statutes of 1236-38, the Premonstratensians formally condemned anyone who divulged the secrets of the order, because such persons were "destroyers of the Order" (Pl. Lefèvre, *Les Statuts de Prémontré reformés sur les ordres de Grégoire IX et d'Innocent IV au XIIIe siècle* [Louvain, 1946], Bibliothèque de la Revue d'histoire ecclésiastique, fasc. 23, p. 126, no. 24).

16. JL 16562.

17. "Abbatibus autem et abbatissis, prioribus, praelatis quibuslibet et officialibus eorundem iniungas poenitentiam competentem, et, donec illam peregerint, eos a sacrorum ordinum exsecutione suspendas, iniungens episcopis tuis, ut hanc formam per suas dioeceses studeant observare. Illud tamen gratanter recipi poterit, quod fuerit sine taxatione gratis oblatum" (Pott 1403).

18. The letter specified that if a formal accusation was made, then both the giver and receiver of the simoniacal payment were to receive the "revenge of canonical severity."

19. Among the Cistercians, abbots whose offense did not merit deposition were frequently punished by removal from their functions for a specified period of time or by a specified penance, or both (Canivez, *Statuta*, vol. 1, no. 30, 1191; no. 4, 1201; no. 26, 1205).

20. The decretal collection, the *Compilatio* III, was sent by Innocent to the law schools at Bologna (Pott 4157). The *Compilatio* III is edited by E. Friedberg, *Quinque compilationes antiquae* (Leipzig, 1882), pp. 105-34. On the compiler of the collection and its genesis, see S. Kuttner, *Repertorium der Kanonistik 1140-1234* (Vatican City, 1937), pp. 355-68. Innocent's letter "Dilectus filius" was also included in two canonical collections formed about 1208, that of Bernardus Compostellanus (H. Singer, "Die Dekretalensammlung des Bernardus Compostellanus antiquus," *Sitzungsberichte der kaiserlichen Akademie der Wissenschaften in Wien*, Phil.-hist. Klasse, no. 171 (1914), V. 3. 2); and that of Alanus (R. von Heckel, "Die Dekretalensammlungen des Gilbertus und Alanus nach den Weingartener Handschriften," *Zeitschrift der Savigny-Stiftung für Rechtsgeschichte*, Kanonistische Abteilung, no. 29 (1940), V. 1. 4).

21. "Priori et fratribus Lateranensibus mandata dat super observatione constitutionum

SIMONIACAL ENTRY INTO RELIGIOUS LIFE

Alexandri papae, qui inhibuit monachum pro pretio recipi in monasterio ac habere peculium ac solum inter seculares ambulare" (Pott 1494). The actual letter belonged to a now-lost volume of Innocent's register. The tenor of the letter is known through an index of letters published by A. Theiner, *Vetera Monumenta Slavorum Meridionalium historiam illustrantia* (Rome and Zagreb, 1863), 1: 60, no. 170. The "Constitutions of Pope Alexander" mentioned in the summary are in fact the elements of canon 10, "Monachi non pretio," of the Third Lateran Council, as a comparison of the order of the two texts reveals (J. Alberigo et al., eds., *Conciliorum oecumenicorum decreta* [Freiburg im Breisgau, 1962], p. 193).

22.   Pott 3142. The full text is printed in Migne, vol. 215, cols. 1185-87, no. 89. One charge against the abbot was "quod Simoniacum habuisset ingressum, et quosdam in fratres receperit et aliquibus prioratus concesserit per Simoniacam pravitatem" (col. 1185c-d). Certain monks gave testimony against the abbot: "Quidam vero quod in ingressu ejus pro ea et cum eo commiserunt Simoniam, proprio juramento monstrabant, licet singuli fuerint in suo testimonio singulares" (col. 1186a).

23.   Pott 4158, 4159, 4160 are undated letters from Innocent III to the abbot of Bec. The first prohibited visitation of Bec by the diocesan bishop, unless the house were gravely defamed by upstanding persons. The second letter empowered the abbot to recall to Bec certain monks whose conduct in the priories was scandalous. The third letter empowered the abbot to deal with cases of violence and of simoniacal entry discovered in the house. The letters derive from ms. 149 of the Bibliothèque d'Avranches, fol. 78ᵛ, on which see *Catalogue générale des manuscrits des bibliothèques publiques des départements* (Paris, 1872), 4:503. The letters may refer to an interrelated group of events revolving around the diocesan bishop's attempt to visit Bec canonically. In any case, the letters underline the fact that simoniacal entry was only one of Bec's problems.

24.   "Ex tua insinuatione didicimus, quod nonnulli monasterii tui monachi quorum quidam per violentam manuum injectionem inciderunt in canonem sententiae promulgatae: alii vero Simoniacum ibi habuerunt ingressum, absolutionis beneficio seu dispensationis gratia non obtentis, sacros susceperunt ordines, et in eis non sunt veriti postmodum ministrare" (Pott 4160). The full text is in Migne, vol. 217, cols. 275-76.

25.   "Item placuit, ut si quis suadente diabolo hujus sacrilegii reatum incurrit, quod in clericum vel monachum violentas manus injecerit, anthematis [*sic*] vinculo subjaceat: et nullus episcoporum illum praesumat absolvere, nisi mortis urgente periculo; donec apostolico conspectui praesentetur, et ejus mandatum suscipiat" (canon 15, Mansi, 21:530c). This canon had been enacted previously at Clermont-Ferrand (1130) (canon 10, Mansi, 21:439d); and at Reims (1131) (canon 13, Mansi, 21:461b). Sometime after 1139, Gratian included it in his *Decretum, Causa* XVII, *questio* iv, canon 29. On the subject of irregularity contracted from striking clerics, see JL 14025, 14119.

26.   On *irregularitas* see F. Gillmann, "Zur Geschichte des Gebrauches des Ausdrücke 'irregularis' und 'irregularitas'," *Archiv für katholisches Kirchenrecht* 91 (1911): 49-86; and G. Oesterlé, "De potestate abbatum dispensandi ab irregularitatibus," *Liturgica* 2 (Montserrat, 1958): 465-81. P. Huizing, "The Earliest Development of Excommunication *Latae Sententiae* by Gratian and the Earliest Decretists," *Studia Gratiana* 3 (1955): 277-320, traces the development of automatic punishments for certain crimes, such as simony and striking a cleric.

27.   " . . . De quorum salute sollicitus postulasti, ut cum eos venire ad Sedem Apostolicam oporteret, et verendum asseras ne ad nostram veniendo praesentiam vagarentur, et salutis cuius causa veniret incurrent detrimentum, misericorditer super hoc agere dignaremur" (Pott 4160).

28.   " . . . Considerantes quoque quod religionis favore multa in regularibus, quae non pateremur in aliis, sustinemus: per apostolica scripta mandamus, . . . servata generali

constitutione concilii circa eos qui noscuntur ingressum Simoniacum habuisse, super eo quod taliter receperint ordines, et in eis postmodum ministraverint, auctoritate nostra facias cum eisdem prout animarum suarum saluti videris expedire" (Pott 4160). Innocent's letter did not settle the problem of simoniacal entry at Bec, for on 20 December 1220 Honorius III had to respond to another inquiry from Bec. In that case he ordered the simoniacs to be placed in priories of the house, and to be forbidden reentry to Bec itself (Pressutti 2901).

29. "Multoties audivimus et a multis quod in quibusdam monachorum, monialium et aliorum religiosorum monasteriis per vestras dioeceses constitutis consuetudo damnabilis, imo damnatus et damnandus abusus usque adeo inolevit, ut pene penitus nulla persona recipitur in ipsis absque labe Simoniacae pravitatis. Ne igitur clamorem toties iteratum videamus, . . . simulando fovere, universitati vestrae . . . mandamus . . . , quatenus semel in anno hujusmodi monasteria singuli per vestras dioeceses visitantes, sub ana-thematis interminatione vetetis, ne qua persona de caetero recipiatur in eis per hujusmodi pravitatem, semper in vestris synodis denuntiantes hoc ipsum, et circa eas quas sic receptas invenietis, auctoritate apostolica, sublato appellationis obstaculo, statuatis quod saluti et honestati videretis expedire" (Pott 3976; the full text is printed in Migne, vol. 217, col. 198, no. 144).

30. Berlière, "Innocent III," pp. 145-47. Cheney, *Episcopal Visitation*, pp. 17-53, dis-cusses attempts to maintain the discipline of the regular clergy by means of episcopal visitation.

31. The papal letter convoking the council was "Vineam Domini Sabaoth" (Pott 4706). For an account of the recipents of the letter, see A. Luchaire, "Innocent III et le quatrième concile de Latran," *Revue historique* 97 (1908): 225-35.

32. Pott 4711. For a study of Cardinal Robert de Courson and his legation, see the excellent article by M. and C. Dickson, "Le Cardinal Robert de Courson: sa vie," *Archives d'histoire doctrinale et littéraire du moyen âge* 9 (1934): 53-142. For an account of Robert de Courson's activities in northern France and Flanders during the winter of 1213-14, see S. Hanssens, "De legatiereis van Robert van Courson in Vlaanderen en Henegouwen," in *Miscellanea historica in honorem Alberti de Meyer* (Louvain and Brussels, 1946), 1: 528-38.

33. The canons issued at Paris in June 1213 are printed in Mansi, 22:817-54, where they are dated incorrectly to 1212. The canons of Rouen, February-March 1214, are printed in Mansi, 22:897-924. The canons that survive from the council at Bordeaux, 26 June 1214, are printed in a letter from Robert de Courson to King John of England (T. Rymer, *Foedera, conventiones, etc.* [London, 1836], vol. 1, pt. 1, p. 122). The canons of Montpellier, 8 January 1215, are printed in Mansi 22:935-54. No canons are extant from the Council of Reims (winter 1213-14) or of Clermont-Dessous (July 1214).

34. Dickson, "Le Cardinal Robert de Courson," pp. 124-26.

35. "De ingressu itaque monachorum simoniaco licet habeamus speciale mandatum domini papae ad archiepiscopos et episcopos per totum regnum Franciae, quod in hoc articulo bene sufficere potest . . . " (Mansi, 22: 826a-c). This provision was repeated in Rouen, canon 1 (Mansi, 22:905e-906a).

36. "Praecipimus etiam sub poena suspensionis [ne] ab ingressuris claustrum, vel pastus vel vestimentum exigantur, neque denarii, neque aliud in fraude praedictorum, ita quod propter hoc non repellantur" (Canon 27 of Paris, Mansi, 22:833b; canon 30 of Rouen, Mansi, 22:911d).

37. "Ut nullus admittatur cum pacto aliquid dandi pro receptione. Item praecipimus, ut nullus in canonicum vel monachum admittatur, cum aliqua conditione, vel pacto, per quod aliquid debeat pro receptione ejus dari" (Mansi, 22:944c). The wording of this canon differs from those issued by Cardinal Robert at Paris and Rouen on the same subject. This

fact indicates that the legate Peter of Benevento had also been instructed to legislate against simony, but was apparently free to express the prohibition in his own way.

38. Dickson, "Le Cardinal Robert de Courson," pp. 124-26, comments on the striking continuity of program between the councils of Paris and Rouen, and that of the Fourth Lateran Council. C. R. Cheney, "Legislation of the Medieval English Church," *English Historical Review* 50 (1935): 197-98, notes that a papal legate issued his own canons, as authorized by his papal mandate, and that those canons were binding decrees, not to be altered by bishops and enduring after the termination of his legateship.

39. Baldwin, *Masters*, vol. 1: 315-43, examines the influence of university masters, particularly those affiliated with Peter the Chanter at Paris, on the decisions of the Fourth Lateran Council. He traces their views on capital punishment, ordeals, clerical celibacy, and marriage. The council adopted the masters' views on ordeals and marriage. It is apparent that the council also adopted the views of canonists on the issue of simoniacal entry into religion.

40. Dickson, "Le Cardinal Robert de Courson," pp. 64-65. The editor of Peter the Chanter's *Summa de sacramentis*, J.-A. Dugauquier, dated that work to 1191-97 (*Summa de sacramentis et animae consiliis* (Louvain and Lille, 1961), 3:1, *prolegomena*, 185). Baldwin, *Masters*, vol. 2, appendix 2, pp. 241-65, questions the firmness of Dugauquier's dating of the *Summa*. Baldwin agrees that it was compiled about 1191-97, but that the material in it was the product of a school career that extended over many years.

41. Pott 3142. The account of his investigations at Vezelay is printed in Migne, 215:1185-87.

42. "Item cum vix inveniatur in ecclesia cisalpina aliquod monasterium cuius in/troitus gratis concedatur. Queritur quid consulendum sit monachis et sanctimonialibus qui ad interventum pecunie intromissi sunt in collegium monachorum et monialium. Constat enim quod cum non intrent per hostium sed ascendunt aliunde vel per violentas preces vel intuitu sanguinis tantum vel muneris aut cuiuscumque cupiditatis labem incurrunt simonie" (BN lat. 14524, fol. 38ʳ-38ᵛ).

43. On the legal principles governing *transitus* in the middle and later twelfth century, see M. A. Dimier, "Saint Bernard et le droit en matière de *transitus*," *Revue Mabillon* 43 (1953): 48-82; and K. Fina, "*Ovem suam require*. Eine Studie zur Geschichte des Ordenswechsels in XII. Jahrhundert," *Augustiniana* 7 (1957): 33-56.

44. "Solutio: claustrum quod sic emitur aut locus est voluptatis aut est locus carceris. Si voluptatis consulendum est eis ut exeant velud usualiter contingit in domibus monachorum regalium in quibus adeo splendide epulantur tamquam dives ille qui induebatur purpura et bissa epulabatur cotidie splendide. Istis consulendum est ut exeant et ad artiorem locum penitentie se transferant ut dignam pro comissa simonia et aliis peccatis penitentiam agant. Si vero locus est carceris qui emitur velut claustrum cisterciense vel cartusiense non oportet ut arciorem locum petant quia vix arciorem invenirent; ibi ergo lugeant commissa et preter traditionem regule aliquam specialem ab abbate recipiant penitentiam intuitu commisse simonie" (BN lat. 14524, fol. 38ᵛ).

45. "Quid autem sit consulendum toti conventui ubi omnia bona eorum sunt de simonia vel de rapina aut quedam de licite acquisitis, quedam de rapinis . . . " (BN lat. 14524, fol. 38ᵛ).

46. "Item alius lugubris casus et quasi insolubilis qui late dat infinitam stragem animarum. Ecce monasterium quoddam quod omnes monachos quos habet non gratis sed ad interventum pecunie suscepit. Nunc tandem cognoscit abbas cum toto capitulo se cum omnibus labem simoniae contraxisse, et modo omnes sunt in articulo mortis vel instat solemnitas pascalis et volunt condigne satisfacere de omnibus ad arbitrium tuum qui es prelatus eorum. Quid consules eis? Tu scis quod indigne omnes introierunt et quod

nichil habent nisi per simoniam acquisitum, et scis quod non expellitur predictum demonium nisi plena fiat restitutio si potest fieri. Ergo debes eis dicere ut omnes abscedant nudi pocius quam ibi pereant" (BN lat. 14524, fol. 14ᵛ). Another version of this text, with slight variations, is edited in J. Petit, *Theodori . . . poenitentiale* (Paris, 1677), pp. 371-72. See also V. L. Kennedy, "Robert Courson on Penance," *Mediaeval Studies* 7 (1945): 316-17, where these and similar texts are edited and discussed for the light they shed on Robert de Courson's views on penance. See Baldwin, *Masters*, vol. 2, p. 82, note 36, for another text of Robert de Courson on simoniacal entry.

47. P. Marie-Joseph, "Albert de Verceil," *DHGE*, 1:1564-67. Albert of Vercelli composed a brief rule for the Carmelites, between 1205 and 1214, but it contained no mention of simony. The rule is printed in a confirmation by Honorius III, Pott 7524. M.-H. Laurent, "La Lettre 'Quae honorem conditoris' (1 octobre 1247): note de diplomatique pontificale," *Ephemerides Carmeliticae* 2 (1948): 10-16, provides a critical edition of the rule, as modified by papal order in 1247.

48. "Vitium pravitatis in Giezi leprae morbo et in Simone Mago perditione damnatum in regularibus transire non debet inultum; quoniam eo damnabilius ab illis committitur quo periculosius tales cadunt sibi meritum et aliis per exemplum" (Pott 4783; printed in Migne, vol. 216, cols. 890-91, no. 90).

49. "Licet autem contra pestem istam mortiferam diversis temporibus a praedecessoribus nostris diversa prodierint instituta, nondum tamen usque adeo mortificari potuit quin etiam in terra quae funiculus est haereditatis Dominicae multos infecerit et effecerit sic habitus religiosi participes quod sanctae religionis expertes" (Pott 4783).

50. "Ipsam quoque domum militiae Templi, ad quam oculi respiciunt plurimorum, quosdam intelleximus Simoniace introisse, simplicitate tamen potius quam malitia, prout ex litteris tuae fraternitatis accepimus, simplicitate occasionem praestante delicto" (Pott 4783).

51. "Ad excludendum igitur talis simplicitatis periculum, fraternitati tuae per apostolica scripta mandamus quatenus magistro et fratribus militiae Templi ex parte nostra districte prohibeas et ab eis facias per omnes domos sui ordinis firmiter inhiberi ne pro alicujus receptione aliquid exigatur, nec etiam sub praetextu subventionis ad exactionem procedatur hujusmodi, cum superficies nominis reatum criminis non immutet" (Pott 4783).

52. "Si quis autem de caetero quemquam taliter admiserit ad ordinem supradictum, utque tam admittens videlicet quam admissus puniatur in quo deliquit, ab eo sine spe restitutionis perpetuo expellatur, ad alium districtioris regulae ordinem transferendus, in quo tam exsecrabilis culpae reatum poenitentia condigna deploret" (Pott 4783).

53. JL 16562.

54. "Cum his autem qui hactenus simplicitate peccarunt, si urgens necessitas aut evidens utilitas postularit, mitius agere poteris, prout tuae discretionis prudentia viderit expedire" (Pott 4783). The Templars were apparently not willing or able to solve their problems of simoniacal entry, because in the term of the Grand Master Herman of Perigord (1233-44), a veritable crisis over the issue arose. For the details of the crisis, see H. de Curzon, ed., *La Règle du Temple* (Paris, 1886), pp. 285-88.

55. R. Foreville, *Latran I, II, III et Latran IV* (Paris, 1965), Histoire des conciles oecumeniques, no. 6, pp. 391-95, on the numbers present at the council; see also pp. 251-52.

56. The canons of the Fourth Lateran Council are printed in Alberigo, *Conciliorum*, pp. 206-47; see also Mansi, 22:953-1086.

57. "Quoniam simoniaca labes adeo plerasque moniales infecit, ut vix aliquas sine pretio recipiant in sorores, paupertatis praetextu volentes huiusmodi vitium palliare, ne id de caetero fiat, penitus prohibemus . . . " (*Conciliorum*, p. 240).

58. Migne, vol. 153, cols. 1113-16.

59. Gerald of Wales declared that almost no nuns were received in Cluniac nunneries without a price (*Gemma Ecclesiastica, dist.* II, chap. 126, pp. 289-90). Jacques de Vitry, writing about 1223, commented that though Cistercian nuns were still rather strict on the issue, most other nunneries were guilty of simoniacal reception (*The Historia Occidentalis of Jacques de Vitry*, ed. John F. Hinnebusch, Spicilegium Friburgense, no. 17 (Fribourg, 1972): 116-17). Raymond of Pennaforte was probably the author of a visitation manual for archdeacons, written about 1230, that singled out Benedictine nuns for special criticism about simoniacal receptions, which happened in their houses "quasi communiter et fere semper" (*Summa pastoralis,* in *Catalogue générale des manuscrits des bibliothèques publiques des départements* [Paris, 1849], 1:630-31). For other explicit criticisms of the reception practices of nuns, see Bonaventura, *Opera omnia* (Quaracchi, 1898), 8:369-70; Gilbert of Tournai's *Collectio de scandalis ecclesiae* (1274), edited by A. Stroick in *Archivum Franciscanum historicum* 24 (1931): esp. 57. Thirteenth-century papal registers also provide evidence for simoniacal entry to nunneries, e.g., Pressutti 592, 2522, 3154, 3737, 6100.

60. See above, pp. 159-68.

61. Bonaventure explicitly pointed to poverty in his defense of reception practices among the Poor Clares: "Ubi vero pecunia recipitur propter personam, quam alias libenter reciperent, si haberent unde eam pascerent; non videtur esse simonia, dummodo forma cum intentione concordet. Et hoc modo sustinemus, quod Sorores sanctae Clarae recipiunt 'pecuniam cum personis,' si quando oportet, eas plures personas recipere quam de facultatibus monasterii congrue valeant sustentari" (*Opera omnia,* 8:370).

62. Indeed, it was only after the Council of Trent that dowries were generally acknowledged as licit: see T. M. Kealy, *Dowry of Women Religious* (Washington, D.C., 1941), Catholic University of America Canon Law Studies, no. 134, pp. 4-38; A. Leinz, *Die Simonie. Eine kanonistische Studie* (Freiburg im Breisgau, 1902), pp. 15-30; and R. E. Kowalski, *The Sustenance of Religious Houses of Regulars* (Washington, D.C., 1944), Catholic University of America Canon Law Studies, no. 199.

63. " . . . Statuentes ut quaecumque de caetero talem pravitatem commiserit, tam recipiens quam recepta, sive sit subdita sive praelata, sine spe restitutionis de suo monasterio expellatur, in locum arctioris regulae, ad agendam perpetuam poenitentiam retrudenda" (*Conciliorum,* p. 240).

64. "De his autem quae ante hoc synodale statutum taliter sunt receptae, ita duximus providendum ut remotae de monasteriis, quae perperam sunt ingressae, in aliis locis eiusdem ordinis collocentur" (ibid.).

65. "Quod si propter nimiam multitudinem alibi forte nequiverint commode collocari, ne forte damnabiliter in saeculo evagentur, recipiantur in eodem monasterio dispensative de novo mutatis prioribus locis et inferioribus assignatis" (ibid., pp. 240-41).

66. "Hoc etiam circa monachos et alios regulares decernimus observandum" (ibid., p. 241).

67. "Verum ne per simplicitatem vel ignorantiam se valeant excusare, praecipimus ut dioecesani episcopi singulis annis hoc faciant per suas dioeceses publicari" (ibid.).

CHAPTER EIGHT

The Aftermath of the
Fourth Lateran Council

 Innocent III died less than a year after the close of the Fourth Lateran Council, too soon to see its consequences in the life of the church. The influence of the council on subsequent developments is complicated because each of seventy canons had its own history of implementation or neglect.[1] There are many indications that the sixty-fourth canon, directed against simoniacal entry into religion, was taken seriously and was enforced in varying degrees during the second and third quarters of the thirteenth century, although the final result was less than the reformers wanted.

In both ecclesiastical and lay affairs, the thirteenth century was an age of law and lawyers. In that society the permanent survival of the new attitudes toward entry payments was virtually assured when the developments that had taken place since Gratian were incorporated into the official legal codes of the church. By the later twelfth century the papacy had become in theory and in fact the major source of legislation in the church, primarily through its judicial decisions, which were accepted as precedents for the future. As the papal decisions grew in number and in importance, Gratian's *Decretum* became outdated and had to be supplemented and completed by collections of papal decretal letters, which were studied and glossed by the canonists alongside the *Decretum* itself.[2] The practice of making collections of papal decretals sped up the dissemination of new decisions. For example, Innocent's decretals on simoniacal entry had been incorporated during his own lifetime into several such collections, thus making the decisions readily available to law students and judges.[3] However, the existence of many unofficial decretal collections was inefficient and disorderly. Pope Gregory IX wished to unify and organize the canon law, and in 1234 he issued an authoritative collection, the *Decretales*.[4] The major decisions of his predecessors on simoniacal entry issued during the previous seventy years were included, and the effect was like the layers of an archeological site. Book five, title three of the *Decretales* was devoted to simony. Chapter eight consisted of Alexander III's canon of Tours (1163), chapter 19 was Alexander's decretal letter "Veniens," chapter 25 was Clement III's decretal letter "De regularibus canonicis," chapter 30 was Innocent III's decretal letter "Dilectus filius," and chapter 40 was the sixty-fourth canon of the Fourth Lateran Council.[5] Thus, in a formal and solemn way, the prohibitions against simoniacal entry were encased in the major canonical authority of the era and were studied and glossed by teachers of canon law for centuries.

Formal prohibitions, however, are by no means equivalent to effective implementation. One of the main themes of papal action in this area had been the tension between the demands of the law and the demands of fair, orderly administration; or to put the dilemma another way, there had been a tension between legal theory and practical constraints. In spite of his convictions Innocent III had been compelled to take into account mitigating factors, in particular, the numbers of religious involved and the *simplicitas* or ignorance of the offenders. His two successors in the papacy, Honorius III and Gregory IX, upheld the legal principles at stake while also bending to meet realities. The maximum punishment prescribed for simoniacal entry was deposition of the guilty official and penal exile to a stricter house for the guilty entrant. It is striking how rarely those penalties were invoked in the generation after Innocent's death. If an abbot was guilty of multiple crimes, among which was the reception of new members simoniacally, he might be deposed.[6] But in those cases in which only simoniacal receptions were at issue, the abbot was rarely accused or reprimanded.[7] The reason for this leniency lay in the dearth of competent administrators among religious communities. The letters of Innocent III, Honorius III, and Gregory IX reveal that capable, honest, firm officials were not common enough among the religious houses of the early thirteenth century. One could not afford to depose otherwise acceptable prelates for any but the most serious crimes. The canonist Hostiensis remarked that, in cases of simoniacal entry, "perhaps it was not useful to monasteries to remove their experienced administrators."[8] In one instance in which a prelate was singled out for accusation, the motive was primarily political. In 1237 King Henry III of England wished to prevent papal confirmation of the election of Simon of Elham, prior of Norwich, to the see of Norwich. As was common in England, the cathedral chapter of Norwich was a Benedictine monastery. The king's representatives to the pope accused Simon of a number of crimes including: "Likewise, both the elect and the electors committed the crime of simony by receiving certain persons as monks of their church with money intervening."[9] The royal objections were successful, and in 1239 Pope Gregory IX quashed the election.[10] In a case among the Cistercians in 1225, Abbot John Godard of Fontmorigny was accused of simony by a conspirator among his monks. The abbot was deposed for the breach, but ultimately he was vindicated and reinstated by the general chapter of the order.[11] Such depositions were uncommon, and in the rare situations in which prelates were punished in other ways, their fate was normally to perform a suitable penance while retaining their offices.[12]

The focus of attention in papal letters was on the guilty entrants rather than on the guilty prelates. But even in the case of entrants, the extreme penalty of penal exile to a stricter house was seldom invoked. In 1236 the bishop of Amiens was ordered by Gregory IX to send simoniac nuns of Villencort to stricter houses,[13] and in 1239 the same pope instructed the bishop of Lincoln to send guilty religious to stricter houses;[14] but in both cases the proviso "if that is possible" was added as an escape clause. The imposition of penal exile was made difficult by the resistance of many houses to their being used as places of imprisonment, a practice that they saw as expensive and burdensome.[15] Often, lesser penalties were imposed. For instance, some simoniacs were expelled from the house of entry and placed in priories of the same order, as at Quedlinburg[16] and Bec[17] in 1220, and at Klosterneuburg[18] in 1222. Canon 64 of the Fourth Lateran Council had provided that, if penal exile was not feasible, an internal punishment involving loss of seniority and the imposition of a penance was permitted. That solution was convenient both as a way to punish the guilty and to maintain order, and it was allowed at Scara in 1220,[19] in the diocese of London[20] and at the Hospital of Saint Anthony at Vienne in 1233,[21] at Villencort in 1236,[22] and in the diocese of Lincoln in 1239.[23] At other times transfer to another order was permitted. A Benedictine of Saint Nazerius of Blandrat, whose entry had been purchased for him while he was a child, was allowed by Honorius III in 1220 to enter the Austin canonry of Saint Colomban of Blandrat.[24] Another Benedictine, whose simony had also been committed in his youth, had sought the advice of his diocesan bishop, who recommended that he go to another monastery. The monk entered the Hospital of Jerusalem, and in 1220 Honorius III ratified that decision, with no mention of exile or punishment.[25] In both cases the simony had been committed while the monks were young, perhaps even minors; and the crime had occurred before the Fourth Lateran Council and so might be excused by *simplicitas*; consequently, transfer to another order probably seemed a reasonable solution.

The legal situation of simoniac religious was complicated by another factor. Canon 10 of the Third Lateran Council (1179) had imposed on simoniac entrants the penalty of *irregularitas*, that is, they were forbidden to receive and to exercise holy orders beyond those that they already possessed at entry.[26] If such simoniacs received or exercised further holy orders, they were excommunicated and were required to seek absolution from the pope himself. The penalty of *irregularitas* was not unique to simoniacal entry; it had been applied by the canon law to several other crimes, including homicide, striking a cleric, and bigamy. Defiance of the prohibition to exercise holy orders was a serious breach. Apparently, some simoniac religious did receive and exercise further holy orders and fell under excommunication for their offense. The papacy formally rescinded neither the punishment nor the need to journey to the papal curia for the lifting of the ban; however, in practice a more lenient policy was pursued. Bishops and abbots argued with success that the long, expensive journey to the curia for absolution was a danger to the spiritual welfare of the religious, because it constituted an excuse for wandering among secular men. It was not uncommon for the pope to delegate the power of absolution from excommunication to the local bishop or even to the abbot of the guilty religious.[27]

From the beginning of Innocent III's pontificate, the sheer numbers of religious involved had been a stimulus to bend the legal framework. In some religious houses simoniacal reception had apparently been an isolated event and so could be dealt with rigorously; but in others it had been used systematically, and virtually everyone was guilty. To invoke penal exile or depositions and demotions on a mass scale would have severely disrupted, perhaps annihilated, the house. Theorists like Robert de Courson might opt for destruction of a monastery in the interests of purity,[28] but church administrators were seldom if ever willing to go so far. Hence it was often expedient to permit a local bishop to use his own judgment as to how much of the law should be applied in a particular case, especially when full application of the law was too drastic to contemplate seriously.[29]

Finally, Honorius III made some *ad hoc* decisions that were intended to improve a situation rather than to punish simony. At the nunnery of Malbod, in 1217, Honorius required that the majority of the community give its assent to receptions, as a way to check the frequent simony that occurred when the abbess alone admitted new members.[30] At the nunnery of Fontevrault there were so many nuns in the priories of the house that the available resources were insufficient to support them. Poverty drove the nuns to simony and other disorders. Honorius III instructed the bishop of Soissons to fix the number of nuns in each priory with reference to the resources, so as to prevent future problems.[31]

When viewed from the papal side, the issue of simoniacal entry reflects an attempt over a period of thirty years following the Fourth Lateran Council to change the entry practices of religious houses, but an attempt thwarted to a degree by the reality of the numbers involved and by the fact that respectable religious were only too often the culprits, against whom it was difficult to invoke the full severity of the law. The papacy upheld in theory the legal prohibition on forced entry payments or pacts, while in practice it pursued a milder course consisting in some punishments, some dispensations, and some *ad hoc* decisions.

Innocent's campaign against simoniacal entry, however, had never consisted solely of punishments. He had attempted from the beginning to publicize the seriousness of the crime and to sensitize responsible officials against it. In this effort at raising consciousness about the issue, success was clearer. Simoniacal entry had not been perceived as a crime before 1130, and before 1170 it was the concern of canonists and few others. The period from the pontificate of Innocent III (1198–1216) to that of Gregory IX (1227–41) saw the issue rise in importance among the bishops, within religious orders, and in the lives of at least some individuals.

There were more than five hundred bishoprics in the Latin Church in the thirteenth century, and each bishop had the right and the responsibility to visit and to discipline the nonexempt religious houses within his diocese. Innocent and his successors had placed great hopes in the efficacy of episcopal visitation to bring about reform of religious houses, especially independent houses.[32] At the Fourth Lateran Council, Innocent III had commanded bishops to visit more regularly and to use their annual diocesan synods, which many abbots and abbesses were obliged to attend, as a forum to publicize reforms of all kinds, including opposition to simoniacal entry.[33] Many of the cases that came to the notice of the pope were referred by bishops who had uncovered them initially in the course of visitations in their dioceses.[34]

There was a long tradition of bishops issuing conciliar canons and statutes for their dioceses, but the thirteenth century witnessed a major expansion of such activity.[35] An examination of the diocesan and provincial synodal decrees and the diocesan statutes of the first half of the thirteenth century reveals that the problem of simoniacal entry was not, in fact, heavily emphasized by the bishops.[36] Simoniacal entry was treated at London in 1200,[37] at Oxford in 1222,[38] at Compiègne in 1238,[39] at Lucca in 1253,[40] at Cologne in 1260,[41] and in the diocesan statutes of Chichester (1245–52)[42] and Nîmes (1252).[43] No doubt this list could be lengthened, but it would still remain a distinct minority of the synods and statutes issued in the first half of the thirteenth century. In part such a lack of stress on the crime of simoniacal entry may be explained by the circumstances in which such canons and statutes were issued. They were directed primarily at the instruction and reform of the secular parish clergy who served the diocese and upon whose comportment so much depended. The synods and statutes gave much attention to outlining the proper life style for a priest, explaining the basic doctrines of the faith, and discussing the proper performance of the sacraments and other ecclesiastical rituals.[44] The failings and problems of monks, nuns, and other religious were legitimate concerns of synods and statutes, but they constituted a peripheral area of attention.

It was during a canonical visitation that a bishop might be expected to deal with concrete cases of simoniacal entry. Bishops were empowered to visit many of the religious houses within their dioceses, and, in special circumstances, a bishop might be invested with papal authority to visit exempt houses as well.[45] Canonical visitations were a secret affair between the visitor and the religious visited, and it was then that the scandals of a religious house would be treated, rather than during the public diocesan synod. Episcopal registers before the middle of the thirteenth century are rare, especially outside England. Consequently it is difficult to determine how frequently bishops sought out and discovered such simony. However, the surviving evidence corroborates the view gained from diocesan synodal canons and statutes that simoniacal entry into religion was not a major concern of bishops and probably was not a glaring fault in many of the houses visited. In 1233 Walter Gray, archbishop of York, visited Selby Abbey, and one of his injunctions to the monks was that the normal number of religious ought to be filled—apparently it was below normal—but he was careful to add that the new monks be received gratis.[46] The conscientious Franciscan archbishop of Rouen, Odo Rigaud, recorded only four cases of simoniacal entry in his voluminous register, kept from 1248 to 1269.[47]

A canonical visitor often had a set of questions or articles to use during visitation as a guide to the investigation. The articles of the investigation are valuable because they indicate the points that were of interest to the visitor. In an English set of questions, composed about 1259 and intended expressly for religious houses, the visitor was directed to ask "whether anyone is admitted simoniacally?" and also whether the canons of the Council of Oxford (1222), which dealt with religious, and the injunctions issued during earlier visitations were read aloud to the community several times annually.[48] Such a reading of earlier enactments would serve to keep alive prohibitions of simony, particularly those that had been issued by the Council of Oxford. Many dioceses were large and had numerous religious houses. As a consequence actual visitation might be made by delegates of the bishop or by other officials. A manual for archdeacons, attributed to the Dominican canonist Raymond of Peñaforte, gave much attention to the visitorial duties of archdeacons. The manual insisted that the archdeacon on visitation should be alert for simoniacal entry to all kinds of religious houses, including hospitals, leper houses, nunneries, canonries, and monasteries. It suggested that the archdeacon question both the head and the members of the house about the entry practices employed there.[49] The manual noted that such simony occurred now and then among monks and regular canons, "but commonly and almost all the time among Benedictine nuns,"[50] a charge that seems borne out by much of the thirteenth-century evidence. The manual's direct statement that simoniacal entry was only an occasional problem among monks and regular canons may explain why bishops gave only moderate attention to it in the 1230s, when the manual was apparently composed.

Thirteenth-century bishops were busy men, burdened with a wide range of secular and religious duties. Some attempted to implement the reform program outlined at the Fourth Lateran Council, which included opposition to simoniacal entry into religion. However, from the evidence it seems fair to surmise that most bishops focused attention on those elements of the reform program that touched the secular clergy. During visitation of religious houses, bishops probably asked about entry practices, but only as one element of the larger inquiry. For the episcopate, simoniacal entry was a peripheral issue, an occasional problem among many others.

More important for the spread of concern about simoniacal entry were the decisions taken by religious houses and orders. In the mid and late twelfth century, some religious orders had legislated against forced payments and pacts at entry. It was no coincidence that the Order of Cluny and the Order of Citeaux, along with a number of lesser groups, adopted the "modern," canonist view of entry practices during the pontificate of Innocent III. However, in the wake of the Fourth Lateran Council, the efforts by religious houses and orders to prohibit simoniacal entry for the first time or to apply already existing legislation grew even more common. For instance, the Cistercians had been slow to adopt an open condemnation of simoniacal entry gifts; and indeed, there is no evidence that the order issued a comprehensive measure against monastic simony.[51] But the Cistercians could hardly ignore the common law of the church, and beginning in the 1220s, the Cistercian general chapter took positions that reflected the fact that publicity against simoniacal entry had won the abbots over, whatever might have been the hesitations on the issue held by their twelfth-century predecessors. In 1220 the abbots of the order were specifically forbidden by the general chapter to dispense their monks from the *irregularitas* that they incurred because of simony, homicide, bigamy, and forgery of papal letters.[52] Any such cases were to be referred to the general chapter for disposition. In 1222 the abbot of Bloomkamp in Frisia confessed in the general chapter "that he received many monks and *conversi* to conversion under a condition, which is a form of simony."[53] The abbot was deposed on the spot. Subsequent events provide a significant commentary on the obstacle that *simplicitas* posed for preventing simoniacal receptions. The monks of Bloomkamp and the neighboring Cistercian abbots apparently did not take a confession of such simony too seriously, because they reelected the deposed abbot, who was removed a second time at the general chapter of 1223.[54] In 1225 the chapter was informed of a conspiracy at Fontmorigny to oust the abbot, John Godard. A monk "confessed" that he had been a simoniac in order to implicate the abbot as well in simony. The abbot of Clairvaux, who was the father-abbot and visitor of Fontmorigny, deposed Godard on the basis of the charge. Subsequently, the general chapter quashed the deposition and punished both the abbot of Clairvaux and the monk who had accused Godard.[55] For the remainder of the thirteenth century, quite in contrast to practice in the twelfth, the decisions of the Cistercian general chapters reflected an awareness of the crime of simoniacal entry and attempted to deal with it. An examination of the surviving records reveals that the practice seems to have been infrequent among the males houses of the order, but common among the nuns.[56]

But it was not only within the great orders that the anti-simoniacal legislation and propaganda had an effect. Canon 12 of the Fourth Lateran Council had ordered the numerous independent religious houses, including both Benedictines and Austin Canons, to organize themselves into provinces for triennial chapters and mutual visitations on the Cistercian model.[57] Some records of the decisions of these chapters survive, and they too reflect the effect that Innocent and his successors had in sensitizing religious officials to the problem. Simoniacal receptions were forbidden by the English Benedictines of the southern province in 1218–19 and 1249, and by those of the northern province in 1221;[58] by a Benedictine chapter meeting at Angers in July 1220;[59] by a Benedictine chapter meeting at Speyer in about 1227;[60] by a Benedictine chapter in Normandy about 1234;[61] and by English Austin Canons at Bedford in 1220.[62]

Pope Gregory IX was particularly interested in the reform and revitalization of the Benedictines, and his efforts directed to that end often included moves against simoniacal entry. He ordered visitations of Black Monk houses on a Christendom-wide scale, which were to enforce reforms based on the decisions of the Fourth Lateran Council and on his own statutes.[63] His legate, Otho, gathered all the Black Monk abbots of England to a meeting at London in 1238. Otho issued statutes for the monks, one of which commanded:

> That nothing at all be demanded from anyone who wishes to enter a monastery. But let those be admitted who ought to be admitted, purely on account of God and without any pact. Nevertheless, if anything was offered freely, without a pact, a demand or a pre-set sum, it can be received without fault.[64]

Otho also ordered each abbot to have a personal copy made of those provisions of Gregory IX's *Decretales* that related to monks, and he specified that the copy include the anti-simoniacal texts of canon 10 of Tours, canon 10 of the Third Lateran Council, and canon 64 of the Fourth Lateran Council. He further directed that ordinary monks be informed of the reforms by daily reading from the *Rule* of Benedict and from his own reform statutes.[65] In 1232 Pope Gregory directed Matthew, abbot of the Cistercian house of Foigny, and two other persons to visit the Black Monk houses of the provinces of Reims and Rouen. Matthew's statutes for Saint Vaast at Arras survive, and in chapter three he forbade the reception of boys under the age of fifteen, in part because of the illicit pacts that their parents were willing to make in order to gain a place for them in the monastery.[66]

Thus in the three decades following the Fourth Lateran Council, the independent Black Monks and Austin Canons were pressured by means of chapter meetings, papal legates and visitors, and papal statutes to pay closer attention to entry practices; and on the basis of the evidence, one can conclude that they did build prohibitions of simoniacal reception into their legislation.

Many others of the myriad forms of religious house did likewise. Hospitals were ordinarily organized as small religious congregations of men and women who served the poor, the ill, and travelers. Beginning in the 1190s, the regulations for hospitals regularly forbade simony in the reception of new staff members, and often required that a recruit swear that he had neither paid nor promised anything for his entry.[67] In 1233 Gregory IX had reacted to reports of simoniacal reception at the Hospital of Saint Anthony at Vienne by empowering the precentor, Stephen, to deal with the offenders according to the statutes of the general council.[68] In the twelfth century the military orders had been among those that had not adverted to simoniacal entry in their regulations. However, between 1229 and 1265 the Templars and the Teutonic Order legislated against it, generally in response to scandal or criticism.[69] Even the Franciscan Rule commanded the officials of that order to avoid mixing in the financial affairs of entrants and to encourage the entrants to give their property to the poor.[70] In the mid and late twelfth century, religious orders and houses that had legislated against simoniacal entry were the exception. In contrast, by the 1240s such legislation was common, normal, and probably expected as necessary to a well-run religious community. If statutes and formal enactments are a reflection of change (and I believe that they are), then the efforts at propaganda against simoniacal reception into religion had succeeded to a remarkable degree within the ranks of the religious themselves.

For simoniacal entry into religion to be checked effectively, there had to be a personal commitment on the part of officials, ordinary religious, and even entrants. Such a commitment never became universal, but there are indications that the efforts of the reformers did, in fact, win over the consciences of many individuals. One form of evidence to support such a conclusion is the testimony regarding an individual's personal crisis, which led him to seek relief. As the evidence survives, it is usually couched in the dry, unemotional legal language of a papal letter or a report on a visitation. But it is clear that behind such texts there often lie painful personal decisions. For instance, one would like to know the background to a brief entry in Odo Rigaud's register, recording his visitation of Saint Victor en Caux on 27 January 1268: "John, called of Paris, took off and cast aside his habit and returned it to the abbot in full chapter, saying that his entry had been by simoniacal wickedness."[71] Likewise, several of the letters in the papal registers were occasioned by the concern and hesitations of an individual rather than by an official investigation.[72]

The details of at least two such personal crises survive, and they are instructive about the success of the publicity against simoniacal entry. Edmund Rich, who was archbishop of Canterbury from 1233 to 1240, was canonized after his death, and the preliminary investigations for canonization involved the gathering of testimony and the writing of several *Lives* of the archbishop.[73] The chronology of Edmund's early career is not entirely certain, but it is clear that he studied and taught at Oxford and Paris between 1190 and 1204.[74] His teachers are not known, but his studies coincided with a period of academic concern about simoniacal entry, particularly at Paris.

Edmund's mother died while he was a regent master at Oxford, i.e., probably about 1198–1204.[75] She had two young daughters still at home, and on her deathbed she sought to provide for them in a way chosen by many parents before her.[76] She gave Edmund a sum of money and told him to find them places in a nunnery. However, the half-century of debate and legislation about simoniacal entry into religion had not been in vain. Edmund's biographers noted that he had moral scruples about paying for his sisters' entry, and he searched for considerable time without success for a nunnery that would receive them without any prior negotiations about an entry fee. Finally, at the nunnery of Catesby, a Gilbertine or Cistercian convent, the prioress offered to admit the girls with no pact or agreement preceding.[77] Subsequently, Edmund and his brother Reginald made gifts to Catesby. Such offerings after the fact were quite legal because no force, pact, or promise had preceeded the reception of the girls.[78] The canonists had not opposed gifts as such, but only those tainted by force or agreements, which rendered them simoniacal. Indeed, Edmund's procedure fulfilled the canonists' paradigm of an entry and a gift free from simony. Edmund Rich's concern to avoid simony was an early example of the impact that anti-simoniacal propaganda could have on an entrant or, in this case, on an entrant's kin. Edmund's actions are comprehensible because he was a part of the university environment from which concern over simony had emanated. He was the intellectual confrere of Innocent III, Robert de Courson, Raoul Ardent,[79] Emo of Huizinge, and others who promoted reform of entry practices. His action, unusual at so early a date, is explicable within the context of his education.

The second crisis over simoniacal entry was quite different. It broke out among the inner governing circle of the Templars in the east between 1229 and 1244. The Templars had a history of problems with their entry practices. In 1213 Albert of Vercelli, patriarch of Jerusalem and papal legate, had reported to Innocent III that simony was commonly committed in receiving new members into the order of the Temple.[80] Innocent dealt leniently on that occasion with the Templars because of their *simplicitas*, that is, their ignorance, which mitigated the seriousness of the crime. But for the future Innocent ordered that a stricter policy be followed. However, his admonition did not end the forbidden practices permanently, because during the mastership of Herman of Perigord (1229–44) the problem of simoniacal entry broke out again.[81] Several Templars, described in the source as "proudomes, de bone vie, de bone religion," were troubled in conscience and consulted experts, probably canon lawyers, who confirmed that their entry had indeed been simoniacal. They were mature men who held high rank within the order. They informed Master Herman of their situation, in a scene of tears and regret. The master consulted with his advisers, whom he swore to secrecy because of the scandal that such a revelation would cause. According to the canon law and to Innocent's letter of 1213, the guilty men should have been expelled from the order and sent to religious houses of stricter rule for penance. The master judged that such a course of action would result in damage internally and scandal among outsiders. He therefore wrote to an unnamed pope, either Gregory IX or Innocent IV, requesting that the pontiff entrust disposition of the situation to a friend of the order, the archbishop of Caesarea. With the pope's agreement, the matter was placed before the archbishop. In an elaborate charade the archbishop ordered the guilty Templars to give up their religious habits and, in effect, to leave the order. Several innocent Templars were present and were constituted as a commandery, or Templar community, for the occasion. They received the habits from the guilty and then withdrew to a private room where they held a chapter meeting. Each expelled Templar entered the room as if he had never belonged to the order and requested the habit as a new recruit. The commander then received each of them into the order, "at the request of the archbishop and of the brethren." These events were the working out in practice of canon 64's permission to expel a simoniac and then to receive him back with a loss of seniority and privileges.[82] It is important to note that in the canon of the Fourth Lateran Council this procedure was justified only when numbers were such that dispersal to other houses was not feasible, whereas in this case leniency was granted on the much broader rationale that high-ranking, respectable men were guilty. One of the Templars involved was said to have been chosen master of the Temple in later years. The account of the events was careful to note that this relatively mild treatment was accorded the guilty only because they were "grant piesse freres de la maison, et estoient saiges et prodomes, et de bone vie et religious."[83] If they had been objectionable on other grounds, such a favor might not have been granted them.

The actions of the Templars provide a comment on the changes in awareness wrought during the generation after the Fourth Lateran Council. In 1213 their officials and entrants had not been aware of the objectionable nature of their entry practices. Within three decades an inner group of senior Templars was troubled enough by the issue to initiate a secret process that involved high prelates from the Holy Land to Rome and back. The recurring phenomenon of respectable religious guilty of a tainted admission was present, but in this case they felt their guilt and arranged for a procedure that satisfied the law while sparing the order and the guilty any permanent or serious harm.

The final example of the success of the publicity against simoniacal entry was not a crisis, but persistent care and scrupulousness on the part of an abbot. Emo of Huizinge (ca. 1175–1237) had been a student of canon and civil law at Paris, Orleans, and Oxford in the late twelfth century. Menko, the continuator of Emo's chronicle, reported that, at Oxford, Emo and his brother had been eager collectors of law books, "*decreta*, decretals, the *Liber pauperum* and other books of canon and of civil law."[84] Emo entered a Premonstratensian house, Floridus Hortus or Bloemhof in Frisia, and in about 1214 he succeeded his cousin, also named Emo, as head of the house. In his capacity as abbot he attended the Fourth Lateran Council in 1215.[85] About 1218–19 he began to write a chronicle of his house, which included some personal reminiscences and reflections on his own motives and actions.[86] Emo's enthusiasm for canon law had obviously not waned since his student days, and his chronicle turned to the law for examples and topics. In a passage of the chronicle remarkable for its citations from the commentators on the *Decretum*, Emo recapitulated the decretists' discussion of simoniacal entry into religion.[87] The abbot's comments on his own reception practices reveal a sharp anxiety that all new members be received for religious reasons and not for the property that they might bring. Emo was a practical abbot who had no quarrel with entry gifts, provided that they were given and received without simoniacal intentions.[88] His stress on the intentions of the participants in an entry proceeding went beyond legal questions to a concern with a moral issue. He believed that the very same entry with a gift could be simoniacal or legitimate according to the intention of the entrant or the official. Emo's awareness and his insistence that an abbot must exercise vigilance in receptions point to the impact that a knowledge of the law could have on the running of a religious house.

Emo's articulate examination of his own motives in receiving new members at Bloemhof sets him apart from the more inarticulate mass of prelates. However, the monastic charters themselves, composed as they were by or at the direction of the religious, also indicate the spread of consciousness about what constituted a correct reception of a new member. In the thirteenth century the *formulae* in the charters became more circumspect in language, stressing the free-will character of the entry gift. The contents of the charters changed too. The frank and detailed charters of the eleventh and twelfth centuries, which spelled out clearly and without hesitation the conditions for entry, gave way to more prudent texts that were generally careful to avoid obvious illegality. Perhaps the illegality had been eliminated or had merely been hidden behind legally acceptable formulations. Even if the latter was true, the very attempt to conceal a practice that was formerly open is a tribute to the success of the reformers in sensitizing officials to it.

It would be incorrect to surmise that the campaign against simoniacal entry practices was so effective that the abuse disappeared in the thirteenth century. In spite of the indications that the reform propaganda had success, the means for dissemination of information and for inspection at the disposal of the church authorities were always inadequate for the task at hand. Furthermore, the notion of *simplicitas*, i.e., of mitigating ignorance, deserves closer scrutiny. Since the 1140s canonists and those influenced by them had agreed that forced payments and negotiations about entry were simoniacal. As a consequence of the impact of the canonists, by the late twelfth century a university-trained elite of theologians, bishops, lawyers, and popes was aware of, and opposed to, the grosser aspects of customary entry practices. But one must not underestimate the gap that existed even in the thirteenth century between the church of the intellectuals and that of ordinary laymen and religious. In spite of what the elite believed, many of the religious and laymen who actually arranged entry did not perceive what they did as simoniacal. When Humbert of Romans, writing about 1260, attempted to account for the many disorders visible in the religious houses of his day, he attributed them to ignorance:

> From a lack of learning, many evils have occurred in religious life and in monasteries. It is sufficient to touch on ten of those evils. . . . The seventh [disorder] is the corruption of simony, both in the reception of brethren and in the creation of officials. In many monasteries

219

the sin of simony is not reckoned [as serious], because it is not understood that by comparison to it, other crimes ought to be reckoned as
nothing.[89]

In spite of what a well-trained moralist like Humbert might wish
to be the case, many respectable religious continued in the thirteenth century to arrange for entry in the ancient but discredited
way, as the reports of Hubert Walter and Albert of Vercelli testi-
fied.

The visitation register of Archbishop Odo Rigaud of Rouen
corroborated the charges that many religious simply did not know
or understand the canon law as it affected them. Archbishop Odo
complained that the Benedictine houses that he visited in the 1240s
and 1250s too often possessed neither a copy of the Benedictine
Rule nor a copy of the reform statutes of Pope Gregory IX.[90] His
experience with one nunnery can serve as a paradigm of the deep-
rooted problem of *simplicitas*. When Odo visited the poor and indebted priory of Saint Aubin at Rouen, he recorded the following
entry in his register:

> There were sixteen nuns. The prioress was absent. In a former visita-
> tion we had forbidden them to receive or to veil anyone without our
> special mandate. They spurned our prohibition, and they received and
> veiled as a nun a certain girl of gentle birth, the daughter of the knight,
> Lord Robert who is called "Bad Neighbor."[91]

The nuns' mistake was in defying the archbishop's specific ban on
receiving new members. In an effort to determine why they had
done so, he quizzed them as to their motives. The response that he
received reflected a classic case of *simplicitas*. Naïvely the nuns
told the archbishop that they had received the girl because they
were poor and her father offered 100 shillings a year income in
return for her reception. Similar agreements could be found in
countless eleventh- and twelfth-century charters, but a new sensitivity and new legal norms were current among church administrators in the mid-thirteenth century. The nuns of Saint Aubin were
poor economically and poorly informed, and their behavior shocked
the visitor. He ordered the girl to be sent home, and he prescribed

a penance for the prioress and the community. However, he did not invoke the legal penalties of deposition or penal exile, probably because the nunnery already had serious woes that would be exacerbated by such severity. The priory of Saint Aubin had appeared in earlier entries of Odo's register as a clear example of a poor convent which suffered from the effects of poverty in a variety of ways. Odo had visited the nunnery nine times in sixteen years. Eight years before the incident noted above, he had recorded laconically that nuns were received by simony.[92] Over the course of the years, he also noted critically that they were in debt and lacked adequate stores of provisions; that the nuns took in young boys and girls as paying boarders; that they were guilty of keeping personal property and of receiving unauthorized gifts from friends; that they went outside the cloister to seek money; and that this generally lax discipline, rooted in poverty, had on occasion led to more sinister disorders like incontinence.[93] Thus simoniacal reception of members was for this house, and for others like it, a symptom of its economic difficulties and of its *simplicitas*. It is no accident that this was a house of women. Thirteenth-century opinion was virtually unanimous in seeing nunneries as the most flagrant perpetrators of simoniacal receptions, possibly because houses of women were, as a group, poorly financed and less able to survive with small entry gifts or no gifts at all than were male houses.

But ignorance of the law was not restricted to poor nunneries. Even monasteries of average or above-average prosperity were touched by it. In her study of reform in thirteenth-century England, Jane Lang found that a high percentage of monastic elections in England between 1215 and 1272 were voided by higher authorities because the religious failed, out of ignorance rather than out of malice in most cases, to comply with the complicated legal forms prescribed by canon 24 of the Fourth Lateran Council.[94] In the thirteenth century the canon law had become the province of experts, a highly developed, technical science that was too complex for the ordinary religious or monastic official. The religious were told by bishops, papal legates, and others that entry gifts had to meet certain criteria before they were legitimate, but the religious often lacked the training that would have enabled them to see the cogency of the arguments. Their *simplicitas* remained an effective impediment to full compliance with the law.

The reformers were stymied also by the fact that, in spite of their efforts, there were no mechanisms adequate to supervise on a regular basis the thousands of religious houses in Latin Christendom.[95] The bishop or other visitor might scold a monastery severely for its entry practices and mete out punishments; but his canonical inspection lasted only a day or two, and he might not be able to return for years. If the house was poor or pressed enough, it could resort to the old ways again. For instance, the abbot and community of Bec sought papal advice concerning simony in about 1210 and again in 1220.[96] One of the fundamental reasons for the relative failure of serious reform of religious houses in the thirteenth century, including reform of entry practices, was the ability of houses that wished to do so to outwait the reformers, to delay by legal maneuvers and to procrastinate until the reformers were forced to turn their attention elsewhere.

There was one final, deeper reason why simoniacal entry into religious life did not disappear entirely, and that reason was the entry gift itself. The critics of traditional entry practices had never seriously entertained the notion that gifts at entry should be eliminated entirely. Religious houses, by and large, needed the gifts, and to forbid them would have jeopardized the existence of monasticism on a large scale. In the final analysis the critics were reformers rather than revolutionaries, and they sought to purify the gift at entry by making it voluntary and free from negotiation. But the important point is that the gift survived the period from 1130 to 1250, probably cleansed of its grossest abuses but still expected and normal. If a house was poor enough, if a prelate was lax enough, or if a family was eager enough, the old pattern of negotiation, of demand and of payment, was still latent and could reemerge around the focus of the gift at entry.

Conclusion

To survey the results of seventy-five years of attention by canon lawyers and church leaders to the issue of simoniacal entry, it is appropriate to draw comparisons with the Investiture Contest of the eleventh and twelfth centuries. As in that much larger and more significant series of disputes, theoretical positions were clarified and intellectual lines of demarcation were drawn. Practices and attitudes that were endemic and respectable at the beginning of each controversy were disreputable at the end. As in the Investiture Contest, punishments for abuses were formulated and were enforced in varying degrees. In 1130 it would not have been clear what to do with a simoniacally received monk, if such a simoniac had been recognized, whereas in 1230 several clear options, graded according to seriousness of guilt and to practical restraints, were available to the prelate who had to deal with a simoniac religious. As happened in the Investiture Contest, the changes effected on a practical level were considerable, but fell short of that which purely theoretical considerations would have required. In the thirteenth century it probably remained difficult for a man or woman who gave nothing or who seemed to be unable to make a gift to gain entry to a religious house. On the other hand, the most overt forms of extortion and outright payment declined in frequency and were placed firmly outside the bounds of legality. Caesarius of Heisterbach recorded a story in his *Dialogus miraculorum* that reflected clearly the situation in the first quarter of the thirteenth century. Philip of Otterburg was an adolescent student at Paris, born of an important family, and was an absentee canon of the noble cathedral chapter at Cologne. He resolved to abandon his promising career and his social position by becoming a Cistercian monk. However, in a gesture of humility, he attempted to conceal his respectable social origins by exchanging clothes with a poor student. Dressed in shabby garb, and probably looking to contemporaries like a goliard, he approached a Cistercian house called Bonavallis, where he requested admission as a novice. His disguise succeeded only too well. Caesarius noted, "When the brethren of Bonavallis saw him dressed in a shabby, worn-out cloak, they took him for a poor wandering student and they refused to receive him." Philip was understandably shocked and responded, "If you do not receive me, you will probably regret it and when you want to receive me, you will not be able to do so." The monks ultimately changed their minds, and Philip rose to be an abbot of the order.[97] Whatever the historical basis for this tale, Caesarius' telling of it reflects his own age. The monks of Bonavallis did not openly mention a gift, and the boy did not promise one, for that was clearly simony. Yet a candidate who appeared impoverished was initially rejected for the unexpressed reason that he did not seem likely to offer a "voluntary" gift. It was probably legal, but just barely. Such subtle and debatable forms of simony were discussed by the casuists and became better known to wide circles in the church and influenced them in varying degree.

In summation, a practice that had been normal and respectable before 1130 had become a crime by 1230. It is clear that simoniacal reception persisted, but it was less common in the thirteenth century and was associated with *simplicitas* and poverty. What had originated as an interconnected group of customary practices useful to religious houses and their lay neighbors on social-economic grounds had ended as a crime that greed, carelessness, or necessity might lead a religious house to commit, but that could no longer be justified or defended.

1. For a general study of the application in England of the canons of the Fourth Lateran Council, see M. Gibbs and J. Lang, *Bishops and Reform, 1215-1272, with Special Reference to the Lateran Council of 1215* (London, 1934). There is a wealth of detail about the gradual penetration of the Fourth Lateran decrees into the statutes of the English Church in *Councils and Synods with Other Documents Relating to the English Church*, ed. F. M. Powicke and C. R. Cheney (Oxford, 1964), vol. 2, parts 1 and 2. There have been studies of the history of specific canons; for example, E. Diebold, "L'Application en France du canon 51 du IVe concile de Latran d'après les anciens statuts synodaux," *L'Année canonique* 2 (1953): 187-95; and J. Baldwin, "The Intellectual Preparation for the Canon of 1215 against Ordeals," *Speculum* 36 (1961): 613-36, which traces debates among university masters preceeding the council's condemnation of clerical participation in ordeals.

2. G. LeBras, C. Lefebvre, and J. Rambaud-Buhot, *L'Age classique, 1140-1378, sources et théorie du droit*, Histoire du droit et des institutions de l'église en occident, no. 7 (Paris, 1965), pp. 222-32; S. Kuttner, *Repertorium der Kanonistik, 1140-1234*, Studi e Testi no. 71 (Vatican City, 1937), pp. 272-385; and C. Duggan, *Twelfth-Century Decretal Collections and Their Importance in English History*, University of London Historical Studies, no. 12 (London, 1963), pp. 1-65.

3. Innocent's letter to Hubert Walter, "Dilectus filius," was incorporated into (1) the *Compilatio III*, bk. 5, title 2, canon 2, *Quinque compilationes antiquae necnon collectio canonum lipsiensis*, ed. E. Friedberg (Leipzig, 1882), p. 130; (2) the Collection of Alanus,

made about 1208, bk. 5, title 1, canon 4, R. von Heckel, "Die Dekretalensammlungen des Gilbertus und Alanus nach den weingartener Handschriften," *Zeitschrift der Savigny-Stiftung für Rechtsgeschichte*, Kanonistische Abteilung, no. 29 (1940), pp. 116–357; (3) the Collection of Bernardus Compostellanus antiquus, composed about 1208, bk. 5, title 3, canon 2, H. Singer, "Die Dekretalensammlung des Bernardus Compostellanus antiquus," *Sitzungsberichte der kaiserlichen Akademie der Wissenschaften in Wien*, Philos.-hist. Klasse, no. 171 (1914), p. 22.

4. *Corpus iuris canonici*, vol. 2: *Decretalium collectiones*, ed. E. Friedberg (Leipzig, 1879), cols. 5–927.

5. Ibid., cols. 750–65.

6. Pott 3142.

7. Pressutti 2522, 2772, 2901, 6949; Auvray 1658, 3417, 4716.

8. Henry of Segusia (Hostiensis), *Summa* (Lyons, 1542), fol. 233^r, bk. 5, tit. 2, canon 19, Veniens: "Sed quare non removentur priores vel abbates recipientes etiam per modum inquisitionis convicti: cum hec sit pena simoniacorum ordinaria. . . . Respondeo . . . vel non erat utile monasteriis veteres iam amovere prelatos."

9. Auvray 3759: "Item quod tam electus quam electores commiserunt vitium symonie, recipiendo quosdam in monachos ecclesie sue, pecunia mediante." On the career of Simon of Elham, see J. Le Neve, *Fasti ecclesiae anglicanae, 1066-1300*, vol. 2, *Monastic Cathedrals*, comp. D. E. Greenway (London, 1971), pp. 57, 60.

10. Auvray 4714.

11. Canivez, *Statuta*, vol. 2, canon 55, p. 46.

12. Odo Rigaud, *Registrum visitationum*, ed. T. Bonnin (Rouen, 1852), p. 631.

13. Auvray 3417.

14. Auvray 4716.

15. Religious houses resented especially the expense involved in keeping a troublemaker in penal exile and sought recompense from the home abbey of the exile (*Die ältesten Consuetudines der Kärtauser*, ed. J. Hogg, *Analecta cartusiana* 1 [Berlin, 1970], c. 85, p. 233; Council of Oxford (1222), canon 53, Powicke and Cheney, *Councils*, 2/1, p. 123; D. J. Laporte, "Un Règlement pour les monastères bénédictins de Normandie (xiiie-xve)," *Revue bénédictine* 58[1948]: 140, ch. 48 and 52).

16. Pressutti 2522.

17. Pressutti 2901.

18. *Opera omnia Honorii III*, ed. C.-A. Horoy, Bibliotheca patristica medii aevi, vol. 4 (Paris, 1880), no. 137, col. 114.

19. Pressutti 2772; Pott 6400.

20. Auvray 1174.

21. Auvray 1658.

22. Auvray 3417.

23. Auvray 4716.

24. Pressutti 2654.

25. Pressutti 2912.

26. On *irregularitas* see the fundamental article by F. Gillmann, "Zur Geschichte des Gebrauchs des Ausdrücke 'irregularis' und 'irregularitas'," *Archiv für katholisches Kirchenrecht* 91 (1911): 49–86; see also G. Oesterlé, "De potestate abbatum dispensandi ab irregularitatibus," *Liturgica* 2 (Montserrat, 1958): 465–81.

27. Pressutti 2772, 2901, 3154, 3743, 5844, 6100, 6238; Auvray 818, 971, 1174, 1658, 2410, 4180, 4716.

28. *Summa* of Robert de Courson, BN lat. 14524, fol. 14ᵛ.

29. Pressutti 3154, 6100, 6166; Auvray 1658.

30. Pressutti 592.

31. Pressutti 3737.

32. C. R. Cheney, *Episcopal Visitation of Monasteries in the Thirteenth Century* (Manchester, 1931), pp. 17-19; U. Berlière, "Innocent III et la réorganisation des monastères bénédictins," *Revue bénédictine* 32 (1920): 145-49.

33. Fourth Lateran Council, canons 7, 8, 33, 64, Mansi, vol. 22, cols. 991 ff.

34. Pressutti 2772, 3154, 3737, 3743, 6100, 6166, 6238; Auvray 818, 971, 1174, 2410, 4780.

35. For information on the major expansion of episcopal statute-making in the thirteenth century, see A. Artonne et al., *Répertoire des statuts synodaux des diocèses de l'ancienne France du xiii⁵ à la fin du xviii⁵ siècle*, Documents, études et répertoires publiés par l'Institut de recherche et d'histoire des textes, no. 8 (Paris, 1963).

36. I examined councils and diocesan statutes printed or signaled in Powicke and Cheney, *Councils*, 2/1 and 2; Artonne, *Répertoire*; and Mansi, vols. 22-23.

37. Canon 14, Mansi, vol. 22, cols. 720-21.

38. Powicke and Cheney, *Councils*, 2/1, canon 42, p. 119. The Council of Oxford was especially important because of its role in mediating many of the reforms of the Fourth Lateran Council to the English Church (Gibbs and Lang, *Bishops*, pp. 105-6, 113-14).

39. Canon 20, Mansi, vol. 23, col. 492c-d.

40. Mansi, vol. 23, col. 822c.

41. Canon 7, Mansi, vol. 23, col. 1025d.

42. Canon 65, Powicke and Cheney, *Councils*, 2/1, p. 464.

43. *Thesaurus novus anecdotorum*, ed. E. Martène and U. Durand (Paris, 1717), vol. 4, cols. 1029-30, canon 10.

44. Gibbs and Lang, *Bishops*, pp. 105-30.

45. Cheney, *Episcopal Visitation*, pp. 26-28; Aloisio di Palo, *Innocenzo III e gli ordini religiosi* (Vatican City, 1957), pp. 9-29.

46. *The Register, or Rolls, of Walter Gray, Lord Archbishop of York*, ed. J. Raine, Surtees Society, no. 56 (Durham, 1872), pp. 327-28: "Item quod debitus numerus monachorum gratis adimpleatur."

47. Rigaud, *Registrum*, pp. 115 and 361, records simoniacal entry at the nunnery of Saint Aubin; ibid., pp. 469 and 617, at the monastery of Saint Victor en Caux.

48. Burton Annals in *Annales monastici*, vol. 1, ed. H. R. Luard, Rolls Series 36/1 (London, 1864), pp. 484-85. See also A. Sweet, "A Set of Monastic Visitation Articles," *Catholic Historical Review*, n.s., 1 (1922): 483, for a fourteenth-century set of articles from Ely Priory that dealt with simony. On the general character of visitation articles, see Cheney, *Episcopal Visitation*, pp. 72-75.

49. *Summa pastoralis*, ed. L. Delisle, in *Catalogue général des manuscrits des bibliothèques publiques des départements* (Paris, 1849), 1: 630-31, 637-38.

50. *Summa pastoralis*, ibid., p. 631: "Hoc enim aliquando contigit fieri apud monachos et canonicos, sed quasi communiter et fere semper apud moniales nigras."

51. V. Hermans, "De novitiatu in ordine Benedictino-Cisterciensi et in iure communi usque ad annum 1335," *Analecta sacri ordinis Cisterciensis* 3 (1947): 22–25.

52. Canivez, *Statuta*, vol. 1, chap. 29, pp. 522–23: "Praecipitur ut abbates in istis casibus non dispensent: in simonia, in homicidiis, in bigamiis, in falsariis litterarum Domini Papae. . . . . In istis casibus supradictis recurratur ad consilium Capituli generalis; in aliis casibus conceditur abbatibus dispensare hoc anno, usque ad sequens Capitulum generale."

53. Ibid., vol. 2, chap. 40, p. 21: "Abbas de Florido Campo qui in Capitulo generali publice confessus est quod multos monachos et conversos sub conditione ad conversionem recipit, quod est species simoniae, deponitur in instanti."

54. Ibid., chap. 36, pp. 29–30.

55. Ibid., chap. 55, p. 46.

56. Ibid., chap. 7, 1247, p. 316; chap. 3, 1249, p. 335; vol. 3, chap. 3, 1300, p. 300. About 1225 Jacques de Vitry noted specifically that Cistercian nuns were not ordinarily guilty of simoniacal reception (*The Historia Occidentalis of Jacques de Vitry*, ed. J. F. Hinnebusch, Spicilegium Friburgense, no. 17 [Fribourg, 1972], chap. 15, p. 116). In the 1270s Gilbert of Tournai, O.F.M., singled out Cistercian nuns for criticism of their reception practices (A. Stroick, "Collectio de scandalis ecclesiae. Nova editio," *Archivum Franciscanum historicum* 24 [1931], chap. 19, p. 57).

57. U. Berlière, "Les Chapitres généraux de l'ordre de Saint Benoît," *Mélanges d'histoire bénédictine* (Maredsous, 1902), 4: 52–171; and *Documents Illustrating the Activities of the General and Provincial Chapters of the English Black Monks, 1215–1540*, ed. W.A. Pantin, Camden Third Series, nos. 45, 47, 54 (London, 1931–37). Regular canons also adopted chapters and visitations, on which see *Chapters of the Augustinian Canons*, ed. H. E. Salter, Canterbury and York Series, no. 29 (London, 1922); and G. G. Meersseman, "Die Reform der salzburger Augustinerstifte (1218) eine Folge des IV Laterankonzils," *Zeitschrift für schweizerische Kirchengeschichte* 48 (1954): 81–95.

58. *Documents*, ed. Pantin, 1: 9–10, 38, 233.

59. M. Prou, "Statuts d'un chapitre général bénédictin tenu à Angers en 1220," in *Mélanges d'archéologie et d'histoire*, École française de Rome, no. 4 (1884), chap. 7, p. 351.

60. J. Zeller, "Drei Provinzialkapitel O. S. B. aus der Kirchenprovinz Mainz aus der Tagen des Papstes Honorius III," *Studien und Mitteilungen aus der Geschichte des Benediktiner-Ordens und seiner Zweige*, n. s., 12 (1925): chap. 4, p. 79.

61. D. J. Laporte, "Un Règlement pour les monastères bénédictins de Normandie (xiiie–xve s.)," *Revue bénédictine* 58 (1948): chap. 11, p. 133.

62. Salter, *Chapters*, p. 23.

63. P. Schmitz, *Histoire de l'ordre de Saint Benoît* (Maredsous, 1948), 3:55–59.

64. Matthew Paris, *Chronica majora*, ed H. R. Luard, Rolls Series 57/3 (London, 1876), p. 500; "Item, quod ab aliquo, qui velit monasterium ingredi, nihil exigatur omnino: sed pure propter Deum, et sine aliqua pactione, qui admittendi fuerint admittantur. Recipi tamen poterit sine culpa, si quid sine pactione et exactione et taxatione aliqua, fuerit gratis oblatum."

65. Ibid., pp. 503–16.

66. M.-A. Dimier, "Les Statuts de l'abbé Matthieu de Foigny pour la réforme de l'abbaye de Saint-Vaast (1232)," *Revue bénédictine* 65 (1955): chaps. 3 and 4, p. 116.

67. *Statuts d'hôtels-Dieu et de léproseries*, ed. L. Legrand, Collection de textes pour servir à l'étude et à l'enseignement de l'histoire (Paris, 1901): (1) statutes of the leper

house of Noyon (late twelfth century), chap. 1, pp. 194–95; (2) statutes of the Hôtels-Dieu of Montdidier (1207), Amiens (1233), Noyon (1218), St. Riquier (1233), Abbeville (1243), Beauvais (1246), Rethel (1247), Montreuil-sur-mer (1250), chap. 3, p. 36; (3) statutes of the Hôtel-Dieu of Paris (c. 1220), chap. 3, p. 44. See also *Summa pastoralis*, attributed to Raymond of Peñaforte, p. 635, on the visitation of a *domus eleemosynaria*.

68. Auvray 1658.

69. *La Règle du Temple*, ed. H. de Curzon (Paris, 1886), chap. 224, p. 153; chap. 246, p. 159; chaps. 272 and 273, p. 166; chap. 417, p. 228; chap. 431, p. 234; chap. 544, p. 287–288; chap. 598, p. 311; chap. 673, p. 343; *Die Statuten des deutschen Ordens nach den 'ältesten Handschriften*, ed. M. Perlbach (Halle, 1890), pp. 86–87, 164. Pressutti 5844.

70. *Opuscula sancti patris Francisci Assisiensis*, Bibliotheca franciscana ascetica medii aevi I, 3d ed. (Quaracchi, 1949), *Regula* I, chap. 2, pp. 25-26; *Regula* II, chap. 2, pp. 64–65.

71. Rigaud, *Registrum*, p. 617: "Johannes dictus de Parisius habitum suum deposuerat et abiecerat, et reddiderat abbati in pleno capitulo, dicens se ingressum fuisse per symoniacam pravitatem."

72. Pressutti 2654, 2912, 5679.

73. C. H. Lawrence, *St. Edmund of Abingdon: A Study in Hagiography and History* (Oxford, 1960), studies the genesis of the *vitae* of Edmund Rich.

74. Ibid., pp. 110-24. J. C. Russell,"Notes on the Biography of St. Edmund of Abingdon," *Harvard Theological Review* 54 (1961): 147-58, attempts to give more chronological precision to Edmund's early career.

75. Russell, "Notes," pp. 152-53. Lawrence, *St. Edmund*, p. 116, defends the years 1195 to 1201 as the period of Edmund's regency in arts at Oxford.

76. Pott 3713; *St. Aubin*, vol. 1, no. 71, 1060-81; *St. Père*, vol. 2, no. 35, 1101-29; *Gellone*, no. 320, before 1140; Guibert of Nogent, *De vita sua*, ed. G. Bourgin, Collection de textes pour servir à l'étude et à l'enseignement de l'histoire, no. 40 (Paris, 1907), pp. 47-54.

77. "Vita beati Edmundi Cantuariensis archiepiscopi," in Martène, *Thesaurus*, vol. 3, cols. 1779-80. On the author of this *vita* see Lawrence, *St. Edmund*, pp. 46-47.

78. Lawrence, *St. Edmund*, pp. 315-17, contains the charters recording the gifts from Edmund and Reginald to Catesby. Lawrence is hard put to explain why the *vitae* insisted that Edmund refused to commit simony to gain entry for his sisters, yet the charters prove that he did make a gift. In the context of the canonistic doctrine of free gifts, the two facts are quite compatible (ibid., p. 107).

79. Raoul Ardent was a student and master at Paris in the late twelfth century and a disciple of Peter the Chanter. He wrote a *Speculum universale*, a manuscript of which is extant in BN lat. 3240. On the issue of simoniacal entry to religion, Raoul's *Speculum*, book 12, chap. 73, is an extract from Peter the Chanter's *Verbum Abbreviatum*, chap. 38, which is printed in Migne, vol. 205, cols. 130-31. See also J. Grûndel, *Das "Speculum Universale" des Radulphus Ardens*, Mitteilungen des Grabmann-Instituts des Universität München, vol. 5 (Munich, 1961); and M.-T. D'Alverny, "L'Obit de Raoul Ardent," *Archives d'histoire doctrinale et littéraire du moyen âge* 15/17 (1940-42): 403-5.

80. Pott 4783.

81. Curzon, *La Règle*, chaps. 544-48, pp. 285-88.

82. *Conciliorum oecumenicorum decreta*, ed. J. Alberigo et al. (Freiburg im Breisgau, 1961), canon 64, p. 240:"Quod si propter nimiam multitudinem alibi forte nequiverint commode collocari, ne forte damnabiliter in saeculo evagentur, recipiantur in eodem monasterio dispensative de novo mutatis prioribus locis et inferioribus assignatis."

83. Curzon, *La Règle*, p. 287.

84. *Menkonis Chronicon*, ed. L. Weiland, MGH, *SS*, 23 (Hanover, 1874): 524:"Oxonie etiam Decreta, Decretales, Librum Pauperum, nec non et alios libros canonici iuris et legalis, vigilias dividendo, scripserunt, audierunt et glossaverunt, nichil se habere credentes, quamdiu ipsis aliquis liber defuit ex utilioribus. . . . " The Chronicles of Emo and Menko were also edited by H. O. Feith and G. Acker Stratingh, *Kronijken van Emo en Menko*, Werken vitgegeven door het Historisch Genootschap, n. s. 4 (Utrecht, 1866).

85. On Emo see H. Heijman,"Emon," *DHGE*, vol. 15, cols. 434–37; and P. Gerbenzon, *Emo van Huizinge, een vroege decretalist* (Gröningen, 1965).

86. *Emonis Chronicon*, ed. L. Weiland. MGH, *SS*, 23 (Hanover, 1874): 454–523.

87. Ibid., pp. 492–94.

88. Ibid., pp. 487, 492, 494.

89. Humbert of Romans, *Expositio super regulam sancti patris Augustini*, in M. de la Bigne, *Maxima bibliotheca veterum patrum* (Lyons, 1677), vol. 25, col. 635b: "Ex defectu eruditionis multa mala secuta sunt in Religione, et in monasteriis de quibus decem tangere sufficit. . . . Septimum est corruptio symoniaca, tam in receptione fratrum, quam in institutione praelatorum. Peccatum symoniae in multis monasteriis non reputabatur, quia non agnoscebatur, quod comparatione ipsius caetera crimina pro nihil reputantur."

90. Cheney, *Episcopal Visitation*, pp. 157–58 and 169, table A.

91. Rigaud, *Registrum*, p. 361: "Ibi erant XVI moniales. Priorissa erat absens. In alia autem visitatione inhibuimus eisdem ne aliquam reciperent nec velarent, sine mandato nostro speciali; ipse tamen spreta inhibitione nostra, quandam domicellam, videlicet filiam domini Roberti dicti Mali Vicini, militis, in monialem receperunt et velarunt."

92. Rigaud, *Registrum*, p. 115.

93. Ibid., pp. 412, 115, 297, 550.

94. Gibbs and Lang, *Bishops*, pp. 138–39.

95. Berlière,"Innocent III," pp.22–23; U. Berlière,"Honorius III et les monastères bénédictins, 1216–1227," *Revue belge de philologie et d'histoire* 2 (1923): 461–84; Cheney, *Episcopal Visitation*, pp. 122–28.

96. Pott 4160; Pressutti 2901.

97. Caesarius of Heisterbach, *Dialogus Miraculorum*, ed. J. Strange (Cologne, 1851), 1:46.

Bibliography

I. PRIMARY SOURCES

A. Manuscripts

Albertus. Gloss on the *Compilatio* II. Paris, Bibliothèque Nationale (hereafter BN) ms. latin 3932, fols. 70–102ᵛ.

Benencasa. *Casus.* Paris, BN ms. latin 3922, fols. 13–54ᵛ.

Benencasa. *Casus.* Paris, BN ms. latin 14320, fols. 2–76.

Damasus. Gloss on the *Compilatio* I. Paris, BN ms. latin 3930.

Damasus. Gloss on the *Compilatio* II. Paris, BN ms. latin 3930.

"Ecce vicit leo." *Apparatus* to the *Decretum.* Paris, BN ms. nouvelles acquisitions latines 1576.

Everard of Ypres. *Summula decretalium quaestionum.* Reims ms. 689.

Guilelmus Vasco or Naso. Gloss on the *Compilatio* I. Paris, BN ms. latin 3932, fols. 1–69ᵛ, passim.

Honorius. *Summa quaestionum.* Paris, BN ms. latin 14591, fols. 50–83.

Huguccio. *Summa.* Paris BN ms. latin 3892.

Huguccio. *Summa.* Paris, BN mss. latins 15396–15397.

"Ius naturale." *Apparatus* to the *Decretum.* Paris, BN ms. latin 15393, level a.

John of Faenza. *Summa.* Paris, BN ms. latin 14606, fols. 1–166ᵛ.

Raoul Ardent. *Speculum universale,* books 9–14. Paris, BN ms. latin 3240.

Robert de Courson. *Summa.* Paris, BN ms. latin 14524.

Sicardus of Cremona. *Summa.* Paris, BN ms. latin 14996, fols. 1–146ᵛ.

Summa coloniensis. Paris, BN ms. latin 14997, fols. 1–183ʳ.

Summa "Cum in tres partes." Paris, BN ms. latin 16540.

Summa Monacensis. Munich, Clm 16084, fols. 1–9, 11–16, 18–27ᵛ.

Summa "Omnis qui iuste iudicat" or *Lipsiensis.* Rouen ms. 743.

Summa "Quoniam status ecclesiarum." Paris, BN ms. latin 16538.

Summa "Tractaturus Magister." Paris, BN ms. latin 15994.

Tancred. Gloss on the *Compilatio* I. Paris, BN ms. latin 15399.

B. Printed Cartularies

"Cartulaire d'Assé-le-Riboul." Ed. Arthur Bertrand de Broussillon. *Archives historiques du Maine* 3 (1903): 1-48.

"Cartulaire d'Azé et du Genêteil." Ed. E. du Brossay. *Archives historiques du Maine* 3 (1903): 49-168.

Cartulaire de Berdoues. Ed. Jean Marie Cazauran. La Haye, 1905.

Cartulaire de l'abbaye cardinale de la Trinité de Vendôme. Ed. Charles Métais. Paris, 1893-97. 4 vols. La Société archéologique de Vendômois.

Cartulaire de l'abbaye cistercienne de Perseigne. Ed. Gabriel Fleury. Mamers, 1880.

Cartulaire de l'abbaye de Conques en Rouergue. Ed. Gustave Desjardins. Paris, 1879. Documents historiques publiés par la Société de l'Ecole des chartes.

Cartulaire de l'abbaye de Gimont. Ed. l'abbé Clergeac. Paris and Auch, 1905. Archives historiques de la Gascogne, 2d ser., no. 9.

Cartulaire de l'abbaye de la Luzerne. Ed. François Dubosc. Saint-Lô, 1878. Archives départementales de la Manche, vol. 1.

Cartulaire de l'abbaye de Montiêramey. Ed. Charles Lalore. Paris and Troyes, 1890. Collections des principaux cartulaires du diocèse de Troyes, vol. 7.

Cartulaire de l'abbaye de Notre-Dame des Vaux de Cernay. Ed. L. Merlet and A. Moutié. Paris, 1857-58. 3 vols. Société archéologique de Rambouillet: documents pour servir à l'histoire du département de Seine et Oise.

Cartulaire de l'abbaye de Notre-Dame d'Ouscamp. Ed. Achille Peigné-Delacourt. Amiens, 1865. Mémoires de la Société des antiquaires de Picardie: documents inédits concernant la province, vol. 6.

Cartulaire de l'abbaye de Redon en Bretagne. Ed. Aurélian de Courson. Paris, 1863. Collection de documents inédits sur l'histoire de France, première série: histoire politique.

Cartulaire de l'abbaye de Saint-Corneille de Compiègne. Ed. Emile-Epiphanius Morel. Montdidier, 1904-9. 2 vols. Société historique de Compiègne.

Cartulaire de l'abbaye de Saint-Aubin d'Angers. Ed. Arthur Bertrand de Broussillon. Paris, 1903. 3 vols. Documents historiques sur Anjou, vols. 1–3.

Cartulaire de l'abbaye de Sainte-Croix de Quimperlé. Ed. Léon Maitre and Paul de Berthou. 2d ed., Paris and Rennes, 1904. Bibliothèque bretonne armoricaine, vol. 4.

Cartulaire de l'abbaye de Saint-Etienne de Baigne en Saintonge. Ed. Paul Cholet. Niort, 1868.

Cartulaire de l'abbaye de Saint-Loup de Troyes. Ed. Charles Lalore. Paris, 1875. Collection des principaux cartulaires du diocèse de Troyes, vol. 1.

Cartulaire de l'abbaye de Saint-Père de Chartres. Ed. Benjamin Guérard. Paris, 1840. 2 vols. Collection de documents inédits sur l'histoire de France, première série: histoire politique.

Cartulaire de l'abbaye de Saint-Sernin de Toulouse (844–1200). Ed. C. Douais. Paris and Toulouse, 1887.

Cartulaire de l'abbaye de Saint-Vaast d'Arras rédigé au xiie siècle par Guimann. Ed. E. Van Drival. Arras, 1875. Documents inédits concernant l'Artois, vol. 6.

Cartulaire de l'abbaye de Saint Victor de Marseilles. Ed. Benjamin Guérard avec collaboration de MM. Marion et Delisle. Paris, 1857. 2 vols. Collection de documents inédits sur l'histoire de France, première série: histoire politique.

Cartulaire de l'abbaye de Vigeois en Limousin (954–1167). Ed. H. de Montégut. Limoges, 1907.

Cartulaire de l'abbaye du Paraclet. Ed. Charles Lalore. Paris and Troyes, 1878. Collection des principaux cartulaires du diocèse de Troyes, vol. 2.

"Cartulaire de la Haie-aux-Bonshommes." Ed. Paul de Farcy. *Bulletin de la Commission historique et archéologique de la Mayenne,* 2d ser., 21 (1905): 165–99, 295–324.

"Cartulaire de l'ancienne Chartreuse des Ecouges." Ed. Alexis Auvergne. *Documents inédits relatifs au Dauphiné.* Grenoble, 1865. 1:81–294.

Cartulaire de l'église de la Sainte-Trinité de Beaumont-le-Roger. Ed. Etienne Deville. Paris, 1912.

"Le Cartulaire de Saint-Maur-sur-Loire." Ed. Paul Marchegay. *Archives d'Anjou* (Angers, 1843), 1:293–429.

"Cartulaire saintongeais de la Trinité de Vendôme." Ed. Charles Métais. *Archives historiques de la Saintonge et de l'Aunis* 22 (1893): 1–431.

Cartulaires de la Chartreuse d'Oujon et de l'abbaye de Hautcrêt. Ed. Jean-Joseph Hisely. Lausanne, 1854. Mémoires et documents publiées par la Société d'histoire de la Suisse Romande, vol. 12.

Cartulaires des abbayes d'Aniane et de Gellone: Cartulaire d'Aniane. Ed. l'abbé Cassan and E. Meynial. Montpellier, 1900. Société archéologique de Montpellier.

Cartulaires des abbayes d'Aniane et de Gellone: Cartulaire de Gellone. Ed. Paul Alaus, l'abbé Cassan, and E. Meynial. Montpellier, 1898. Société archéologique de Montpellier.

"Cartularium monasterii beatae Mariae Caritatis Andegavensis." Ed. Paul Marchegay. *Archives d'Anjou*, vol. 3. Angers, 1854.

Chartes de Durbon. Ed. Paul Guillaume. Montreuil-sur-mer, 1893. Société d'études des hautes alpes, vol. 2.

Les Chartes de l'ordre de Chalais, 1101-1400. Ed. J. Ch. Roman. Paris and Ligugé, 1923. 3 vols. Archives de la France monastique, vols. 23-25.

Chartes de Notre-Dame de Bertaud. Ed. Paul Guillaume. Gap and Paris, 1888. Société d'études des hautes alpes, vol. 1.

Chartes et documents concernant l'abbaye de Cîteaux, 1098-1182. Ed. J. Marilier. Rome, 1961. Bibliotheca Cisterciensis, vol. 1.

La Chartreuse de Saint-Hugon en Savoie. Ed. Eugène Burnier. Chambery, 1869. Mémoires de l'Académie imperiale de Savoie. 2d. ser., vol. 11, part 2.

Essai historique sur l'abbaye de Saint Martin d'Autun. Ed. Jacques-Gabriel Bulliot. Autun, 1849. 2 vols.

Petit cartulaire de l'abbaye de Saint-Sulpice en Bugey. Ed. Marie-Claude Guigue. Lyons, 1884. Collection de documents inédits pour servir à l'histoire des anciennes provinces de Lyonnais, Forez, Beaujolais, Bresse, Dombes, et Bugey.

"Recueil de chartes concernant l'abbaye de Saint-Victor-en-Caux." Ed. Charles de Robillard de Beaurepaire. *Mélanges publiées par la Société de l'histoire de la Normandie.* 5th ser. Paris and Rouen, 1898. Pp. 332-453.

Recueil des chartes de l'abbaye de Clairvaux. Ed. Jean Waquet. Troyes, 1950. Archives départementales de l'Aube, fasc. 1.

Saint-Denis de Nogent-le-Rotrou (1031-1789): Histoire et cartulaire. Ed. Charles Métais and le vicomte de Souancé. 2d ed. Vannes, 1899. Archives du diocèse de Chartres, vol. 1.

C. *Other Printed Sources*

Les Actes de Pierre. Ed. L. Vouaux. Paris, 1922.

Adam of Eynsham. *The Life of Saint Hugh of Lincoln.* Ed. Decima Douie and Hugh Farmer. London, 1961-62. 2 vols. Nelson Medieval Texts.

Alan. *Decretal Collection.* In Rudolf von Heckel. "Die Dekretalensammlungen des Gilbertus und Alanus nach den Weingartener Handschriften." *Zeitschrift der Savigny-Stiftung für Rechtsgeschichte,* Kanonistische Abteilung, no. 29 (1940), pp. 116–357.

Albert de Mora (Gregory VIII). *Institutiones.* In Paul Kehr, "Papst Gregor VIII als Ordensgründer." *Miscellanea Francesco Ehrle.* Rome, 1924. 2:248–75. Studi e testi, no. 38.

Analecta cartusiana, vol. 1: *Die ältesten Consuetudines der Kärtauser.* Ed. James Hogg. Berlin, 1970.

Annales ordinis sancti Benedicti occidentalium monachorum patriarchae. Ed. J. Mabillon. Paris, 1703–39. 6 vols.

Anselm of Canterbury. *Liber Anselmi de humanis moribus per similitudines.* In *Memorials of St. Anselm.* Ed. R. W. Southern and F. S. Schmitt. London, 1969. Pp. 37–93. Auctores Britannici medii aevi, vol. 1.

―――. *Sancti Anselmi cantuariensis archiepiscopi opera omnia.* Ed. F. S. Schmitt. Edinburgh, 1946–61. 6 vols.

Anselm of Lucca. *Collectio canonum.* Migne, vol. 149, cols. 486–534.

Assomption, Antonin de l'. *Les Origines de l'ordre de la Très-Sainte-Trinité d'après les documents.* Rome, 1925.

Augustine of Hippo. *Sermo LXXXVI.* Migne, vol. 38, cols. 523–30.

Aurelian. *Regula Sancti Aureliani ad monachos.* Migne, vol. 68, cols. 385–98.

Bartholomew of Brescia. *Glossa ordinaria.* In *Decretum Gratiani.* Lyons, 1501.

Basil. *Consuetudines.* In *Analecta cartusiana,* vol. 1: *Die ältesten Consuetudines der Kartäuser.* Ed. James Hogg. Berlin, 1970. Pp. 142–218.

Becquet, Jean. "Les Chapitres généraux de l'ordre de l'Artige." *Revue Mabillon* 45 (1955): 181–99.

―――. "L'Institution: premier coutumier de l'ordre de Grandmont." *Revue Mabillon* 46 (1956): 15–32.

Benedict the Abbot. *Gesta regis Henrici secundi.* Ed. William Stubbs. London, 1867, Rolls Series, no. 49, vols. 1–2.

Benedict the Levite. *Capitularia falsa.* Ed. F. Knust. In MGH, *Leges* II/2. Hanover, 1837. Pp. 17–158.

Benedict of Nursia. *Sancti Benedicti regula monachorum.* Ed. Philibert Schmitz. 2d ed. Maredsous, 1955.

Bernard of Clairvaux. *Epistolae.* Ed. J. Leclercq and H. Rochais. In *Sancti Bernardi opera,* vol. 7. Rome, 1974.

Bernard of Compostella. *Collectio.* In Heinrich Singer. "Die Dekretalensammlung des Bernardus Compostellanus antiquus." *Sitzungsberichte der kaiserlichen Akademie der Wissenschaften*, Philosophisch-historische Klasse, no. 171 (1914), pp. 37–115.

Bernard of Parma. *Casus.* In *Decretales Domini Gregorii Papae Noni.* . . . Paris, 1527.

Bernard of Pavia. *Bernardi Papiensis Faventini episcopi summa decretalium.* Ed. E. T. Laspeyres. Ratisbon, 1860.

Bernold of Constance. *Apologeticus.* Ed. F. Thaner. In MGH, *Libelli de lite.* Hanover, 1892. 2:59–88.

Bonaventure. *Opera omnia.* Quaracchi, 1882–1902. 10 vols.

Burchard of Worms. *Libri viginti decretorum.* In Migne, vol. 140, cols. 537–1058.

Caesarius of Arles. *Sancti Caesarii* . . . *opera omnia.* Ed. Germain Morin. Maredsous, 1937–42. 2 vols.

Caesarius of Heisterbach. *Caesarii Heisterbacensis* . . . *dialogus miraculorum.* Ed. Joseph Strange. Cologne, 1851–57. 3 vols.

Capitularia regum francorum. Ed. A. Boretius and V. Krause. In MGH, *Legum sectio* 2. Hanover, 1883–97. 2 vols.

Cassian, John. *Institutions cénobitiques.* Ed. Jean-Claude Guy. Paris, 1965. Sources chrétiennes 109. Série des textes monastiques d'occident, no. 17.

Chapters of the Augustinian Canons. Ed. Herbert E. Salter. London, 1922. Canterbury and York Series, no. 29.

Chevalier, Jules. "Formule d'oblation d'enfant tirée des archives de l'ordre de St. Ruf. XIIIe siècle." *Bulletin d'histoire ecclésiastique et d'archéologie religieuse des diocèses de Valence, Digne, Gap, Grenoble, et Viviers* 7 (1886–87): 86–88.

Chronicon universale anonymi laudunensis. Ed. G. Waitz. In MGH, *SS* 26:442–57. Hanover, 1882.

Chronique de l'abbaye de Saint-Trond. Ed. Camille de Borman. Liège, 1872–77. 2 vols. Société des bibliophiles liègeois.

La Chronique de Saint-Hubert dite Cantatorium. Ed. Karl Hanquet. Brussels, 1906. Commission royale d'histoire: recueil de textes pour servir à l'étude de l'histoire de Belgique.

Chroniques de Saint-Martial de Limoges. Ed. Henri Duplès-Agier. Paris, 1874.

Codex regularum monasticarum et canonicarum. Ed. Lukas Holste, 2d ed. Augsburg, 1759, 6 vols.

Collectio bonnevallensis. In H. Mordek,"Die Rechtssammlungen der Handschrift von Bonneval—ein Werk der karolingischen Reform." *Deutsches Archiv für Erforschung des Mittelalters* 24 (1968): 339-434.

Collectio claustroneoburgensis. In Ferdinand Schönsteiner,"Die *Collectio Claustroneoburgensis,* eine neu entdeckte Kanonsammlung." *Jahrbuch des Stiftes Klosterneuburg* 2 (1909): 1-154.

Concilia aevi karolini. Ed. A. Werminghoff. In MGH, *Legum sectio* 3. Hanover, 1904-8. 2 vols.

Concilia Magnae Britanniae et Hiberniae. Ed. David Wilkins. London, 1737. 4 vols.

Concilia salisburgensia. Ed. F.L. Dalham. Augsburg, 1888.

Conciliorum oecumenicorum decreta. Ed. J. Alberigo et al. Freiburg im Breisgau, 1962.

Constitutiones canonicorum regularium ordinis arroasiensis. Ed. L. Milis. Turnhout, 1970. Corpus christianorum: Continuatio mediaevalis, no. 20.

Corpus juris canonici. Ed. Emil Friedberg. Leipzig, 1879-81. 2 vols.

Cosnier, Michel. *Fontis Ebraldi exordium.* La Flèche, 1641.

Councils and Synods with Other Documents Relating to the English Church. Ed. C.R. Cheney and F. M. Powicke. Oxford, 1964. Vol. 2 in 2 parts.

Creytens, R. "Les Constitutions primitives des soeurs dominicaines de Montargis (1250)."*Archivum fratrum praedicatorum* 17 (1947): 41-84.

De antiquis ecclesiae ritibus. Ed. Edmond Martène. 2d ed. Antwerp, 1736-38. 4 vols.

Decretales pseudo-isidorianae et capitula Angilramni. Ed. P. Hinschius. Leipzig, 1863.

Dimier, M.-Anselme. "Les Statuts de l'abbé Matthieu de Foigny pour la réforme de l'abbaye de Saint Vaast (1232)." *Revue bénédictine* 65 (1955): 110-25.

———. "Un Témoin tardif peu connu du conflit entre Cisterciens et Clunisiens." In *Petrus Venerabilis, 1156-1956.* Ed. Giles Constable and James Kritzeck. Rome, 1956. Pp. 81-94. Studia Anselmiana, vol. 40.

Documents Illustrating the Activities of the General and Provincial Chapters of the English Black Monks, 1215-1540. London, 1931-37. 3 vols. Camden Third Series, vols. 45, 47, 54.

Donatus. *Regula Sancti Donati vesontionensis episcopi ad virgines.* Migne, vol. 87, cols. 273-98.

Ducange, C. *Glossarium ad scriptores mediae et infimae latinitatis.* Ed. G. A. L. Henschel. Paris, 1840-50. 7 vols.

237

Dugdale, William. *Monasticon anglicanum.* Ed. John Caley, Henry Ellis, and Bulkeley Bandinel. London, 1817-30. 6 vols. in 8 parts.

Emo of Huizinge. *Chronicon.* Ed. L. Weiland. MGH, *SS* 23:454-523. Hanover, 1874; and *Kronijken van Emo en Menko.* Ed. H. O. Feith and G. Acker Stratingh. Utrecht, 1866. Werken vitgegeven door het Historisch Genootschap, n.s., vol. 4.

Epistolae pontificum romanorum ineditae. Ed. Samuel Loewenfeld. Leipzig, 1885.

Exordium parvum. In Joseph Turk, "Cistercii statuta antiquissima." *Analecta sacri ordinis cisterciensis* 4 (1948): 32-108.

Ferreolus. *Regula Sancti Ferreoli uceticensis episcopi ad monachos.* Migne, vol. 66, cols. 959-76.

Fournier, Paul. "Notice sur le ms. H 137 de l'école de medicine de Montpellier." *Annales de l'Université de Grenoble* 9 (1897): 357-89.

Fransen, G. "Les 'questiones' des canonistes: essai de dépouillement et de classement." *Traditio* 12 (1956): 566-92; 13 (1957): 481-501; 23 (1967): 516-34.

Fructuosus of Braga (attributed). *Regula monastica communis.* Migne, vol. 87, cols. 1111-27.

Geoffrey of Vendôme. *Epistolae.* Migne, vol. 157, cols. 33-212.

———. *Libelli.* Ed. E. Sackur. MGH, *Libelli de lite* 2:676-700. Hanover, 1892.

Gerald of Wales. *Gemma ecclesiastica.* Ed. J. S. Brewer. London, 1862. Rolls Series, no. 21/2.

———. *Speculum ecclesiae.* Ed. J. S. Brewer. London, 1873. Rolls Series, no. 21/4.

Gerhoh of Reichersberg. *Epistola ad Innocentem papam.* Ed. E. Sackur. MGH, *Libelli de lite* 3:202-39. Hanover, 1897.

———. *Liber de simoniacis.* Ed. E. Sackur. MGH, *Libelli de lite* 3:239-72. Hanover, 1897.

Germania pontificia. Ed. Albert Brackmann. Berlin, 1910-11. Vol. 1, parts 1 and 2. Regesta pontificum romanorum. Ed. Paul Kehr.

Gesta abbatum trudonensium. Ed. Rudolph Koepke. MGH, *SS* 10:213-448. Hanover, 1852.

Gesta pontificum cameracensium. Ed. Charles de Smedt. Paris, 1880. Société de l'histoire de France.

Gilbert: see Alan.

Gilbert Foliot. *The Letters and Charters of Gilbert Foliot, Abbot of Gloucester (1139-1148), Bishop of Hereford (1148-1163), and London (1163-1187).* Ed. Adrian Morey and Christopher Brooke. London, 1967.

Gilbert of Sempringham. *Un Procès de canonisation à l'aube du xiiie siècle, 1201-1202. Le Livre de saint Gilbert de Sempringham.* Ed. Raymonde Foreville. Paris, 1943.

Gilbert of Tournai, *Collectio de scandalis.* In Autbertus Stroick, "Collectio de scandalis ecclesiae. Nova editio." *Archivum franciscanum historicum* 24 (1931): 33-62.

Gratian. *Decretum.* Ed. Emil Friedberg. In *Corpus juris canonici,* vol. 1. Leipzig, 1879.

Gregory I. *Gregorii I papae registrum epistolarum.* Ed. P. Ewald and L. Hartmann. MGH, *Epistolarum tomi,* vol. 2 in 2 parts. Berlin, 1891-93.

————. *XL Homiliarum in Evangelia libri duo.* Migne, vol. 76, cols. 1075-1312.

Gregory IX. *Les Registres de Grégoire IX.* Ed. Lucien Auvray. Paris, 1890-1907. 3 vols. Bibliothèque des écoles françaises d'Athènes et de Rome.

Guibert of Nogent. *De vita sua.* Ed. G. Bourgin. Paris, 1907. Collection de textes pour servir à l'étude et à l'enseignement de l'histoire, vol. 40.

Guigo. *Consuetudines carthusienses.* Migne, Vol. 153, cols. 631-760.

————. *De vita solitaria.* Ed. "un chartreux." In *Lettres des premiers chartreux.* Paris, 1962. Pp. 135-49. Sources chrétiennes 88: série des textes monastiques d'occident, vol. 10.

Guilloreau, Léon. "Chapitres généraux et statuts de Guillaume de Sabran." *Revue Mabillon* 6 (1910): 300-328; 7 (1911): 224-43.

Henry of Segusio (Hostiensis). *Summa aurea.* Lyons, 1542.

Hermann von Minden. Letters. In Gabriel Löhr, "Drei Briefe Hermanns von Minden O. P. über die Seelsorge and die Leitung der deutschen Dominikanerinnenklöster." *Römische Quartalschrift für christliche Altertumskunde und für Kirchengeschichte* 33 (1926): 159-67.

Honorius of Autun. *De apostatis.* Ed. I. Dieterich. MGH, *Libelli de lite* 3:57-63. Hanover, 1897.

Honorius III. *Opera omnia Honorii III.* Ed. César-August Horoy. Paris, 1879-80. Bibliotheca patristica medii aevi, vols. 1-4.

————. *Regesta Honorii papae III.* Ed. Pietro Pressutti. Rome, 1888-95. 2 vols.

Hrabanus Maurus. *Liber de oblatione puerorum.* Migne, vol. 107, cols. 419-40.

Hugo Francigena. *Tractatus de conversione Pontii de Lazario, et exordio Salvaniensis monasterii.* In *Miscellaneorum liber tertius.* Ed. Etienne Baluze. Paris, 1680. Pp. 205-26.

Humbert of Romans. *Speculum religiosorum.* In *Maxima bibliotheca veterum patrum,* 25:665-753. Lyons, 1677.

Humbert of Silva Candida. *Libri III adversus simoniacos.* Ed. F. Thaner. MGH, *Libelli de lite* 1:95–253. Hanover, 1891.

Idungus of Prufening. *Dialogus duorum monachorum.* Ed. R. B. C. Huygens. In "Le Moine Idung et ses deux ouvrages: *Argumentum super quatuor questionibus* et *Dialogus duorum monachorum.*" *Studi medievali,* 3d ser., 13 (1972): 291–470.

Initia consuetudinis benedictinae. Ed. J. Semmler et al. In *Corpus consuetudinum monasticarum,* vol. 1. Siegberg, 1963.

Innocent III. *The Letters of Pope Innocent III (1198–1216) concerning England and Wales.* Ed. C. R. and M. G. Cheney. Oxford, 1967.

———. *Opera omnia.* Migne, vols. 214–17.

Ivo of Chartres. *Correspondance,* vol. 1. Ed. Jean Leclercq. Paris, 1949. Les Classiques de l'histoire de France au moyen âge, vol. 22.

———. *Decretum.* Migne, vol. 161, cols. 47–1036.

———. *Panormia.* Migne. vol. 161, cols. 1041–1344.

Jacques de Vitry. *Die Exempla des Jacob von Vitry.* Ed. Goswin Frenken. *Quellen und Untersuchungen zur lateinischen Philologie des Mittelalters,* vol. 5, no. 1. Munich, 1914.

———. *The Historia Occidentalis of Jacques de Vitry. A Critical Edition.* Ed. John F. Hinnebusch. Fribourg, 1972. Spicilegium friburgense, no. 17.

Jean de Joinville. *Histoire de Saint Louis.* Ed. Natalis de Wailly. Paris, 1868.

John Godard. *Opuscula.* In C. H. Talbot. "Two Opuscula of John Godard, First Abbot of Newenham." *Analecta sacri ordinis Cisterciensis* 10 (1954): 208–67.

John of Worcester. *The Chronicle of John of Worcester, 1118–1140.* Ed. J. R. H. Weaver. Oxford, 1908. Anecdota Oxoniensia, 4th ser., no. 13.

John Zemeke (Johannes Teutonicus). *Apparatus* to *Compilatio IV* "Quoniam simoniaca." In Antonius Augustinus, *Antiquae collectiones decretalium.* Paris, 1609. P. 834.

Julianus Pomerius. *De vita contemplativa.* Migne, vol. 59, cols. 415–520.

Justinian. *Corpus iuris civilis: Novellae.* Ed. Rudolph Schoell and William Kroll. Berlin, 1895. Vol. 3.

Laporte, J. "Un Règlement pour les monastères bénédictins de Normandie (xiiie-xive siècles)." *Revue bénédictine* 58 (1948): 125–44.

Laurent, M.-H. "La Lettre 'Quae honorem conditoris' (1 octobre 1247)—note de diplomatique pontificale." *Ephemerides Carmeliticae* 2 (1948): 5–16.

Leclercq, Jean. "Documents pour l'histoire des chanoines réguliers." *Revue d'histoire ecclésiastique* 44 (1949): 556–69.

————. "Documents sur la mort des moines." *Revue Mabillon* 45 (1955): 165–80; 46 (1956): 65–81.

————. "Nouvelle réponse de l'ancien monachisme aux critiques des cisterciens." *Revue bénédictine* 67 (1957): 77–94.

Lettres des premiers chartreux, vol. 1. Ed. "un Chartreux." Paris, 1962. Sources chrétiennes 88: série des textes monastiques d'occident, vol. 10.

Libri Carolini. Ed. H. Bastgen. MGH, *Legum sectio III, Concilia III, Supplementum*. Hanover, 1924.

Marcarius. *Regula sancti Macarii*. Migne, vol. 103, cols. 447–52.

Mansi, Giovanni Domenico. *Sacrorum conciliorum nova et amplissima collectio*. . . . Florence, 1759–98. 31 vols.

Marbod of Rennes. *Epistolae*. Migne, vol. 171, cols. 1465–92.

Marchegay, Paul. *Archives d'Anjou*. Angers, 1843–54. 3 vols.

Meersseman, G. G. "Die Reform der Salzburger Augustinerstifte (1218) eine Folge des IV Laterankonzils." *Zeitschrift für schweizerische Kirchengeschichte* 48 (1954): 81–95.

Menko. *Menkonis Chronicon*. Ed. L. Weiland. MGH, *SS* 23:523–61. Hanover, 1874.

Nörr, Knut Wolfgang. "Die Summen 'De iure naturali' und 'De multiplici iuris divisione'." *Zeitschrift der Savigny-Stiftung für Rechtsgeschichte*, Kanonistische Abteilung, no. 48 (1962), pp. 138–63.

Odo of Canterbury. Letter to his brother Adam. In *Vetera Analecta*. Ed. Jean Mabillon. 2d ed., pp. 477–78. Paris, 1723.

————. Jean Leclercq. "Profession monastique, baptême et pénitence d'après Odon de Cantorbery." *Studia Anselmiana* 31 (1953): 124–40.

Odo Rigaud. *Registrum visitationum*. Ed. T. Bonnin. Rouen, 1852.

Papsturkunden in Benevent und in der Capitanata. Ed. Paul Kehr. *Nachrichten der Göttinger Gesellschaft der Wissenschaften*. Phil.-hist. Klasse no. 1, (1898).

Paucapalea. *Die Summa des Paucapalea über das Decretum Gratiani*. Ed. J. F. von Schulte. Giessen, 1890.

Paul Warnefrid. *Pauli Warnefridi commentarium in sanctam regulam*. Monte Cassino, 1880.

Peter Abelard. *Institutio seu Regula Sanctimonialium*. In Terence P. McLaughlin, "Abelard's Rule for Religious Women." *Mediaeval Studies* 18 (1956): 241–92.

————. *Petri Abaelardi opera hactenus seorsim edita*. . . . Ed. Victor Cousin, C. Jourdain, and E. Despois. Paris, 1849–59. 2 vols.

————. *Sermones*. Migne, vol. 178, cols. 379–610.

Peter of Blois. *Petri Blesensis . . . opera omnia.* Ed. J. A. Giles. Oxford, 1846. 4 vols. Patres ecclesiae anglicanae.

Peter of Blois the Younger. *Petri Blesensis opusculum de distinctionibus in canonum interpretatione adhibendis, sive . . . Speculum juris canonici.* Ed. Theophilus Reimarus. Berlin, 1837.

Peter the Chanter. *Summa de sacramentis et consiliis animae.* Ed. Jean-Albert Dugauquier. Louvain, 1954-67. 3 vols. in 5 parts. Analecta mediaevalia namurcensia, nos. 4, 7, 11, 16, 21.

————. *Verbum abbreviatum.* Migne, vol. 205, cols. 21-554.

Peter Damian. *Liber gratissimus.* Ed. L. de Heinemann. MGH, *Libelli de lite* 1:15-75. Hanover, 1891.

————. *Rhetoricae declamationis invectio in episcopum monachos ad saeculum revocantem.* Migne, vol. 145, cols. 366-80.

————. "Vita B. Domenici Loricati." *AASS,* October, vol. 6 (Paris, 1868), pp. 621-28.

Peter the Deacon. *Chronicon monasterii casinensis,* books 3-4. Ed. W. Wattenbach. MGH, *SS* 7:727-844; and in Migne, vol. 173, cols. 763-978.

Peter de Honestis. *Regula clericorum.* Migne, vol. 163, cols. 691-748.

Petit, Jacques. *Theodori . . . poenitentiale.* Paris, 1677.

Prou, Maurice. "Statuts d'un chapitre général bénédictin tenu à Angers en 1220." *Mélanges d'archéologie et d'histoire. Ecole française de Rome* 4 (1884): 345-56.

Quinque compilationes antiquae nec non collectio canonum lipsiensis. Ed. Emil Friedberg. Leipzig, 1882.

Ralph, *De peccatore et ratione.* In Jean Leclercq. "La Vêture 'ad succurrendum' d'après le moine Raoul." *Studia Anselmiana* 37 (1955): 158-68.

Rambaud-Buhot, J. "Un Corpus inédit de droit canonique de la réforme carolingienne à la réforme grégorienne." In *Humanisme actif. Mélanges d'art et de littérature offerts à Julien Cain.* Paris, 1968. 2:271-81.

Ranulph de Glanville. *De legibus et consuetudinibus regni Angliae.* Ed. G. E. Woodbine. New Haven, Conn., 1932. Yale Historical Publications, Manuscripts and Edited Texts, no. 13.

Raymond of Pennaforte (attributed). *Summa pastoralis.* Ed. L. Delisle. In *Catalogue général des manuscrits des bibliothèques publiques des départements.* Paris, 1849. 1:592-649.

Regesta pontificum Romanorum ab condita ecclesia ad annum post Christum natum MCXCVIII. Ed. Philip Jaffé. 2d ed., G. Wattenbach, F. Kaltenbrunner, P. Ewald, and S. Loewenfeld, eds. Leipzig, 1885-88. 2 vols.

Regesta pontificum Romanorum inde ab anno post Christi natum MCXCVIII ad annum MCCCIV. Ed. A. Potthast. Berlin, 1875. 2 vols.

Regula ad virgines. Migne, vol. 88, cols. 1053-70.

Regula magistri, La Règle du maître. Ed. Adalbert de Vogüé. Paris, 1964-65. 3 vols. Sources chrétiennes, vols. 105-7. Série des textes monastiques d'occident, vols. 14-16.

Regula monasterii Tarnatensis. Migne, vol. 66, cols. 977-86.

Regula Templi. La Règle du Temple. Ed. Henri de Curzon. Paris, 1886. Société de l'histoire de France. See also Gustav Schnürer, "Die ürsprungliche Templerregel." *Studien und Darstellungen aus dem Gebiete der Geschichte.* Freiburg im Breisgau, 1903. Vol. III, Parts 1 and 2.

Robert of Bridlington. *The Bridlington Dialogue.* Ed. and trans. a Religious of the C.S.M.V. London, 1960.

Robert Courson. V. L. Kennedy, "Robert Courson on Penance." *Mediaeval Studies* 7 (1945): 291-336.

Robert of Torigni. *The Chronicle of Robert of Torigni.* Ed. R. S. Howlett. London, 1889. Rolls Series, no. 82/4.

Roger Bacon. "Compendium studii philosophiae." In *Fr. Rogeri Bacon opera quaedam hactenus inedita.* Ed. J. S. Brewer. London, 1859. 1:393-519. Rolls Series, no. 15.

Roland Bandinelli. *Die Summa Magistri Rolandi nachmals Papstes Alexander III. nebst einem Anhange Incerti Auctoris Quaestiones.* Ed. F. Thaner. Innsbruck, 1874.

Roman, J. "Visites faites dans les prieurés de l'ordre de Cluny du Dauphiné." *Bulletin d'histoire ecclésiastique et d'archéologie religieuse des diocèses de Valence, Digne, Gap, Grenoble et Viviers* 4 (1883-84): 86-94.

Rudolph of Saint Trond. *Epistola missa de coenobio Sancti Panteleonis* and *Rescriptum.* Ed. R. Koepke. MGH, *SS* 10:319-24. Hanover, 1852; or *Chronique de l'abbaye de Saint-Trond.* Ed. Camille de Borman. Liège, 1872. 1:243-64.

———. Wilhelm Levison. "A Rhythmical Poem of about 1100 (by Rodulf of Saint-Trond?) against Abuses, in Particular Simony and Dancing in Churchyards." *Medievalia et Humanistica* 4 (1946): 3-25.

Rufinus. *Die summa decretorum des Magister Rufinus.* Ed. Heinrich Singer. Paderborn, 1902.

Rymer, Thomas. *Foedera, conventiones, litterae et cujuscunque generis acta publica. . . .* Ed. Adam Clarke, John Caley, and Frederick Holbrooke. London, 1816-69. 7 vols.

Scriptores ordinis Grandimontensis. Ed. Jean Becquet. Turnhout, 1968. Corpus Christianorum, Continuatio Mediaevalis, vol. 8.

Select Pleas of the Crown. Ed. F. W. Maitland. London, 1888. Selden Society, vol. 1.

Sigebert of Gembloux. *Apologia contra eos qui calumniantur missas conjugatorum sacerdotum.* Ed. E. Sackur, MGH, *Libelli de lite* 2:436–48. Hanover, 1892.

Smaragdus. *Commentaria in Regulam Sancti Benedicti.* Migne, vol. 102, cols. 689–932.

Statuta capitulorum generalium ordinis Cisterciensis. Ed. Joseph Marie Canivez. Louvain, 1933–41, 8 vols. Bibliothèque de la Revue d'histoire ecclésiastique, fasc. 9–14b.

Statuta ordinis Cartusiensis a Domino Guigone priore Cartusie edita. Basel, 1510.

Die Statuten des Deutschen Ordens nach den ältesten Handschriften. Ed. Max Perlbach. Halle, 1890.

Statuts, chapitres généraux et visites de l'ordre de Cluny. Ed. Gaston Charvin. Paris, 1965–, 7 vols. to date.

Les Statuts de Prémontré reformés sur les ordres de Grégoire IX et d'Innocent IV au xiiie siècle. Ed. Placide Lefevre. Louvain, 1946. Bibliothèque de la Revue d'histoire ecclésiastique, fasc. 23.

Statuts d'hôtels-dieu et de léproseries. Ed. Léon Legrand. Paris, 1901. Collection de textes pour servir à l'étude et à l'enseignement de l'histoire, vol. 32.

Stephan of Tournai. *Les Lettres d'Etienne de Tournai.* Ed. Jules Desilve. Paris and Valenciennes, 1893.

―――. *Die Summa des Stephanus Tornacensis über das Decretum Gratiani.* Ed. J. F. von Schulte. Giessen, 1891.

Summa "Elegantius in iure divino" seu Coloniensis. Vol. 1. Ed. G. Fransen. New York, 1969. Monumenta iuris canonici, Series A; Corpus glossatorum I/1.

The Summa Parisiensis on the decretum Gratiani. Ed. Terence P. McLaughlin. Toronto, 1952.

Thesaurus novus anecdotorum. Ed. Edmond Martène and Ursin Durand. Paris, 1717. 5 vols.

Tractatus pro clericorum conubio. Ed. E. Dümmler. MGH, *Libelli de lite* 3: 588–96. Hanover, 1897.

Ulrich of Cluny. *Antiquiores consuetudines Cluniacensis monasterii.* Migne, vol. 149, cols. 635–778.

Valvekens, J.B. "Acta et decreta capitulorum generalium ordinis Praemonstratensis." *Analecta Praemonstratensia* 42 (1966): i–ix, 1–22; 43 (1967): 23–102.

Vetera analecta. Ed. Jean Mabillon. 2d ed., Paris, 1723.

Vetera monumenta Slavorum meridionalium historiam illustrantia. Ed. Augustin Theiner. Rome-Zagreb, 1863–75. 2 vols.

Vetus disciplina monastica. Ed. Marquard Herrgott. Paris, 1726.

Vita beati Edmundi cantuariensis archiepiscopi. In *Thesaurus novus anecdotorum.* Ed. Edmund Martène and Ursin Durand. Paris, 1717. Vol. 3, cols. 1775–1826.

Vita sancti Arialdi. AASS, June, 5:279–303.

"Vitae B. Petri Abrincensis et B. Hamonis monachorum coenobii saviniacensis." Ed. E. P. Sauvage. *Analecta Bollandiana* 2 (1883): 475–560.

Vitae patrum. Migne, vol. 73.

Waefelghem, Raphäel van. "Les premiers statuts de l'ordre de Prémontré: le clm 17.174 (xiiᵉ siècle)." *Analectes de l'ordre de Prémontré* 9 (1913): 1–74.

Waldebert. *Regula ad virgines.* Migne, vol. 88, cols. 1053–70.

Wallace, Wilfrid. *Life of St. Edmund of Canterbury from Original Sources.* London, 1893.

Walter, J. von. *Die ersten Wanderprediger Frankreichs. Studien zur Geschichte des Monchtums.* Leipzig, 1903. Studien zur Geschichte der Theologie und der Kirche, vol. 9, part 3.

Walter Daniel. *The Life of Ailred of Rievaulx.* Ed. and trans. F. Powicke. London, 1950. Nelson Medieval Classics.

Warinus of Saint Arnulf. *Epistola ad Joannem fiscamnensem.* In *Vetera analecta.* Ed. Jean Mabillon. Paris, 1723. 2d ed., pp. 450 ff.

William of Andrès. *Chronica Willelmi Andrensis.* Ed. J. Heller. MGH, *SS* 24:684–773. Hanover, 1879.

William of Auvergne. *Guilelmi Alverni . . . opera omnia.* Ed. B. Le Feron. Paris, 1674. 2 vols.

William of Newburgh. *Historia rerum Anglicarum.* Ed. R. S. Howlett. London, 1884–85. Rolls Series, no. 82/1–2.

William Perault. *Sermones.* In *Guilelmi Alverni . . . opera omnia.* Ed. B. Le Feron. Paris, 1674. 2:1–476.

Wilmart, André. "Les Ouvrages d'un moine de Bec: un débat sur la profession monastique au xiiᵉ siècle." *Revue bénédictine* 44 (1932): 21–46.

Zeller, Josef. "Drei Provinzialkapitel O. S. B. in der Kirchenprovinz Mainz aus den Tagen des Papstes Honorius III." *Studien und Mitteilungen zur Geschichte des Benediktinerordens und seiner Zweige,* n.s., 12 (1925): 73–97.

II. SECONDARY WORKS

Alverny, Marie-Thérèse d'. "L'Obit de Raoul Ardent." *Archives d'histoire doctrinale et littéraire du moyen âge* 15/17 (1940–42): 403–5.

Amann, Emile, and Auguste Dumas. *L'Eglise au pouvoir des laïques (888–1057)*. Paris, 1942. Histoire de l'église depuis les origines jusqu'à nos jours, vol. 7.

Amann, Emile. "Simon le magicien." *Dictionnaire de théologie catholique*, vol. 14, cols. 2130–40.

Ansillon, Johannes. *De Simonia et munerum ac retributionum gratificatione in re beneficiaria*. Liège, 1677.

Baix, F. "Brogne." *Dictionnaire d'histoire et de géographie ecclésiastiques*, vol. 10, cols. 818–32.

Baldwin, John. "The Intellectual Preparation for the Canon of 1215 against Ordeals." *Speculum* 36 (1961): 613–36.

Baldwin, John. *Masters, Princes, and Merchants: The Social Views of Peter the Chanter and his Circle*. Princeton, N.J., 1970. 2 vols.

Baldwin, Marshall. *Alexander III and the Twelfth Century*. Glen Rock, N.J., 1968. The Popes through History, vol. 3.

Barraclough, Geoffrey. *Papal Provisions: Aspects of Church History Constitutional, Legal, and Administrative in the Later Middle Ages*. Oxford, 1935.

Bauer, Hans. *Das Recht der Ersten Bitte bei den deutschen Königen bis auf Karl IV*. Kirchenrechtliche Abhandlungen, vol. 94. Stuttgart, 1919.

Becker, Alfons. *Papst Urban II (1088–1099)*. Stuttgart, 1964. Schriften der Monumenta Germaniae Historica (Deutsches Institut für Erforschung des Mittelalters), vol. 19, part 1.

Becquet, Jean. "Bibliothèque des écrivains de l'ordre de Grandmont." *Revue Mabillon* 53 (1963): 59–79.

———. "Grandmont." *Catholicisme*, vol. 5, cols. 192–93.

———. "La Règle de Grandmont." *Bulletin de la Société archéologique et historique du Limousin* 87 (1958): 9–36.

———. "Les premiers écrivains de l'ordre de Grandmont." *Revue Mabillon* 43 (1953): 121–37.

Berardi, Carlo Sebastiano. *Gratiani canones genuini ab apocryphis discreti*. . . . Venice, 1777. 2 vols. in 3 parts.

Berlière, Ursmer. *La "familia" dans les monastères bénédictins du moyen âge*. Académie royale de Belgique, Classe des lettres et des sciences morales et politiques: Mémoires. 2d ser., vol. 29, fasc. 2. Brussels, 1931.

———. "Honorius III et les monastères bénédictins, 1216–1227." *Revue belge de philologie et d'histoire* 2 (1923): 237–65, 461–84.

———. "Innocent III et la réorganisation des monastères bénédictins." *Revue bénédictine* 32 (1920): 22–42, 145–49.

———. "Le Nombre des moines dan les anciens monastères." *Revue bénédictine* 41 (1929): 231–61; 42 (1930): 19–42.

———. *Le Recrutement dans les monastères bénédictins aux xiiie et xive siècles.* Académie royale de Belgique, Classe des lettres et des sciences morales et politiques: Mémoires. Vol. 18, fasc. 6. Brussels, 1924.

———. "Les Chapitres généraux de l'ordre de Saint Benoît." *Mélanges d'histoire bénédictine* 4 (Maredsous, 1902): 52–171.

Bernard, Antoine. *La Sépulture en droit canonique du décret de Gratien au concile de Trente.* Paris, 1933.

Besse, J. M. "Du droit d'oblat dans les anciens monastères français." *Revue Mabillon* 3 (1907): 1–21, 116–33.

Bishko, C. J. "Gallegan Pactual Monasticism in the Repopulation of Castile." In *Estudios dedicados a Menéndez Pidal.* Madrid, 1951. 2:513–31.

Blanc, C. "Les Pratiques de piété des laïcs dans les pays du Bas-Rhône au xie et xiie siècles." *Annales du Midi* 72 (1960): 137–47.

Bloch, Marc. *Feudal Society.* Trans. L. A. Manyon. London, 1961.

Boussard, Jacques. *The Civilization of Charlemagne.* Trans. F. Partridge. London, 1968.

Boyd, Catherine. *Tithes and Parishes in Medieval Italy: The Historical Roots of a Modern Problem.* Ithaca, N.Y., 1952.

Brooke, Christopher N. L. "The Composition of the Chapter of Saint Paul's, 1086–1163." *Cambridge Historical Journal* 10 (1950–52): 111–32.

———. "Gregorian Reform in Action: Clerical Marriage in England 1050–1200." *Cambridge Historical Journal* 12 (1956): 1–21.

Brückner, W. "Sterben im Mönchsgewand. Zum Funktionswandel einer Totenkleidsitte." In *Kontakte und Grenzen: Probleme der Volks-, Kultur- and Sozialforschung. Festschrift für Gerhard Heilfurth zum 60 Geburtstag.* Göttingen, 1969. Pp. 259–77.

Cambridge Economic History of Europe, vol. 1. 2d ed. M. M. Postan, ed. Cambridge, 1966.

Catalogue général des manuscrits des bibliothèques publiques des départements. Paris, 1849–85. 7 vols.

Catholicisme: hier, aujourd'hui, demain. Ed. G. Jacquemet. Paris, 1948-. 7 vols. to date.

Cheney, Christopher R. *English Synodalia of the Thirteenth Century.* London, 1941.

————. *Episcopal Visitation of Monasteries in the Thirteenth Century.* Manchester, 1931. Manchester University Publications, Historical Series, no. 58.

————. *Hubert Walter.* London, 1967.

————. "Legislation of the Medieval English Church." *English Historical Review* 50 (1935): 193-224, 385-417.

Chénon, Emile. *Histoire générale du droit français public et privé des origines à 1815.* Ed. F. Olivier-Martin. Paris, 1926-29. 2 vols.

Chibnall, Marjorie. "Richard of Canterbury." *New Catholic Encyclopedia* 12:477-78.

Classen, Peter. *Gerhoch von Reichersberg: eine Biographie mit einem Anhange über die Quellen, ihre handschriftliche Überlieferung und ihre Chronologie.* Wiesbaden, 1960.

Clavis patrum latinorum. 2d ed. Eligius Dekkers, ed. *Sacris Eruditi* 3. Steenbrugen, 1961.

Clercq, Charles de. *La Législation religieuse franque de Clovis à Charlemagne.* Université de Louvain: Recueil de travaux publiés par les membres des conférences d'histoire et de philologie. 2d ser., fasc. 38. Louvain, 1938.

————. *La Législation religieuse franque de Louis le Pieux à la fin du ixe siècle.* Antwerp, 1958.

Compain, Luc. *Etude sur Geoffroi de Vendôme.* Bibliothèque de l'école des hautes études: Sciences philologiques et historiques, vol. 86. Paris, 1891.

Constable, Giles. *Monastic Tithes from Their Origins to the Twelfth Century.* Cambridge, 1964. Cambridge Studies in Medieval Life and Thought, n.s., no. 10.

Coulton, George G. *Five Centuries of Religion.* Cambridge, 1923-50. 4 vols. Cambridge Studies in Medieval Life and Thought.

Demelius, H. "Erbrecht der Klosterleute im alten Wien." In *Speculum Iuris et Ecclesiarum: Festschrift für Willibald M. Plöchl.* Vienna, 1967. Pp. 31-41.

Deroux, M.-P. "Les Origines de l'oblature bénédictine." *Revue Mabillon* 17 (1927): 1-16, 81-113, 193-217, 305-51.

Deshusses, J. "Chape (droit de)." *Dictionnaire de droit canonique*, vol. 3, cols. 519-21.

Deshusses, J., and R. Naz. "Dot des religieuses." *Dictionnaire de droit canonique*, vol. 4, cols. 1431-36.

Deslandres, Paul. *L'Ordre des Trinitaires pour le rachat des captifs.* Rome and Toulouse, 1903. 2 vols.

Devailly, G. "Une Enquête en cours: l'application de la réforme grégorienne en Bretagne." *Annales de Bretagne* 75 (1968): 293-316.

Dickinson, J. C. *The Origins of the Austin Canons and Their Introduction into England.* London, 1950.

Dickson, Marcel, and Christiane Dickson, "Le Cardinal Robert de Courson: sa vie." *Archives d'histoire doctrinale et littéraire du moyen âge* 9 (1934): 53-142.

Diebold, E. "L'Application en France du canon 51 du IVe concile de Latran d'après les anciens statuts synodaux." *L'Année canonique* 2 (1953): 187-95.

Dillay, M. "Le Régime de l'église privée du xie au xiiie siècle dans l'Anjou, le Maine, la Touraine. Les réstitutions d'églises par les laïques." *Revue historique de droit français et étranger.* 4th ser., 4 (1925): 253-94.

Dimier, Marie-Anselme. "S. Bernard et le droit en matière de *transitus.*" *Revue Mabillon* 43 (1953): 48-82.

———. "Saint Bernard et le recrutement de Clairvaux." *Revue Mabillon* 42 (1952): 17-30, 56-78.

Douglas, David C. *William the Conqueror: The Norman Impact upon England.* Berkeley and Los Angeles, 1964.

Drehmann, Johannes. *Papst Leo IX und die Simonie. Ein Beitrag zur Untersuchung der Vorgeschichte des Investiturstreites.* Leipzig, 1908. Beiträge zur Kulturgeschichte des Mittelalters und der Renaissance, vol. 2.

Dubois, J. "Quelques problèmes de l'histoire de l'ordre des Chartreux à propos de livres récents." *Revue d'histoire ecclésiastique* 63 (1968): 27-54.

Duby, Georges. "Dans la France du Nord-Ouest au xiie siècle: les 'jeunes' dans la société aristocratique." *Annales. Economies, sociétés, civilisations* 19 (1964): 835-46.

———. *Rural Economy and Country Life in the Medieval West.* Trans. C. Postan. Columbia, S. C., 1968.

DuCange, Charles. *Glossarium mediae et infimae Latinitatis.* Ed. G. A. L. Henschel. Paris, 1840-50. 7 vols.

Duggan, Charles. *Twelfth-Century Decretal Collections and Their Importance in English History.* London, 1963. University of London Historical Studies, no. 12.

Dulcy, S. *La Règle de saint Benoît d'Aniane et la réforme monastique a l'époque carolingienne.* Nimes, 1935.

Duméril, Alfred. "De l'état du clergé régulier en Normandie sous le pontificat d'Eude Rigaud." *Mémoires de la Société des antiquaires de Normandie* 17 (1847): 107–25.

Durtelle de Saint-Sauveur, Edmond. *Recherches sur l'histoire de la théorie de la mort civile des religieux des origines au seizième siècle.* Rennes, 1910.

Eynde, D. van den. *L'Oeuvre littéraire de Géroch de Reichersberg.* Rome, 1957. Spicilegium Pontificii Athenaei Antoniani, vol. 11.

———. "Le Recueil des sermons de Pierre Abélard." *Antonianum* 37 (1962): 17–54.

Fechter, J. *Cluny, Adel und Volk. Studien über das Verhältnis des Klosters zu den Ständen (910–1156).* Stuttgart, 1966.

Figueras, C. M. "Acerca del rito de la profésion monástica medieval 'ad succurrendum'." *Liturgica* 2 (Montserrat, 1958): 359–400.

———. *De impedimentis admissionis in religionem usque ad Decretum Gratiani.* Montserrat, 1957. Scripta et documenta, no. 9.

Fina, K. "Ovem Suam Require. Eine Studie zur Geschichte des Ordenswechsels im 12. Jahrhundert." *Augustiniana* 7 (1957): 33–56.

Fliche, Augustin. "Innocent III et la réforme de l'église." *Revue d'histoire ecclésiastique* 44 (1949): 87–152.

Fontette, Micheline de. *Les Religieuses à l'âge classique du droit canonique.* Paris, 1967. Bibliothèque de la Société d'histoire ecclésiastique de la France.

Foreville, Raymonde. "Clément III." *Dictionnaire d'histoire et de géographie ecclésiastiques,* vol. 12, cols. 1096–1109.

———. *Latran I, II, III et Latran IV.* Paris, 1965. Histoire des conciles oecumeniques, no. 6.

Fournier, Paul. "Deux controverses sur les origines du Décret de Gratien." *Revue d'histoire et de littérature religieuse* 3 (1898): 253–80.

Fournier, Paul, and Gabriel Lebras, *Histoire des collections canoniques en occident depuis les Fausses Décretales jusqu'au Décret de Gratien.* Paris, 1931–32. 2 vols. Bibliothèque de l'histoire du droit, vols. 4, 5.

Fransen, G. "La Date du Décret de Gratien." *Revue d'histoire ecclésiastique* 51 (1956): 521–31.

Friedberg, Emil. *Die Canones-Sammlungen zwischen Gratian und Bernhard von Pavia.* Leipzig, 1897.

Gams, Pius. *Series episcoporum ecclesiae catholicae.* Ratisbon, 1873–86. In three parts.

Ganshof, François. *Qu'est-ce la féodalité?* 3d ed. Brussels, 1957.

Ganshof, François, and Adriaan Verhulst. "Medieval Agrarian Society in Its Prime: France, the Low Countries, and Western Germany." In *The Cambridge Economic History of Europe,* vol. 1. 2d ed., Cambridge, 1966. Pp. 290–339.

Gaudemet, Jean; Jean-François Lemarignier; and Guillaume Mollat. *Institutions ecclésiastiques.* Paris, 1962. Histoire des institutions français au moyen âge, vol. 3.

Génestal, R. *Histoire de la légitimation des enfants naturels en droit canonique.* Paris, 1905. Bibliothèque de l'école pratique des hautes études: Sciences religieuses, vol. 18.

———. *Rôle des monastères comme établissements de crédit, étudié en Normandie du xie à la fin du xiiie siècle.* Paris, 1901.

Génestout, A. "La Régle du maître et la Régle de S. Benoît." *Revue d'ascetique et de mystique* 21 (1940): 51–112.

Genicot, L. "Aristocratie et dignités ecclésiastiques en Picardie aux xiie et xiiie siècles." *Revue d'histoire ecclésiastique* 67 (1972): 436–42.

———. "L'Evolution des dons aux abbayes dans le comté de Namur du xe au xive siècle." In *XXXe congrès de la fédération archéologique et historique de Belgique: annales.* Brussels, 1936. Pp. 133–48.

———. "La Noblesse dans la société médiévale, à propos des dernières études relatives aux terres d'Empire." *Le moyen âge* 71 (1965): 539–60.

Gerbenzon, Peter. "Bertram of Metz, the Author of 'Elegantius in iure divino' (Summa Coloniensis)?" *Traditio* 21 (1965): 510–11.

———. *Emo van Huizinge, een vroege Decretalist.* Groningen, 1965.

Gibbs, Marion, and Jane Lang. *Bishops and Reform, 1215-1272, with Special Reference to the Lateran Council of 1215.* London, 1934. Oxford Historical Series.

Gilchrist, John T. *"Simoniaca Haeresis* and the Problem of Orders from Leo IX to Gratian." In *Proceedings of the Second International Congress of Medieval Canon Law.* Ed. S. Kuttner and J. J. Ryan. Vatican City, 1965. Pp. 209–35. Monumenta iuris canonici, Series C, Subsidia I.

Gillmann, Franz. *Des Laurentius Hispanus Apparat zur Compilatio III auf der staatlichen Bibliothek zu Bamberg.* Mainz, 1935.

————. "Magister Albertus Glossator der Compilatio II." *Archiv für katholisches Kirchenrecht* 105 (1925): 122–91.

————. "Zur Geschichte des Gebrauchs des Ausdrücke 'irregularis' und 'irregularitas'." *Archiv für katholisches Kirchenrecht* 91 (1911): 49–86.

Gossmann, Francis J. *Pope Urban II and Canon Law.* Washington, D.C., 1960. Catholic University of America Canon Law Studies, no. 403.

Graham, Rose. *St. Gilbert of Sempringham and the Gilbertines.* London, 1901.

Gründel, Johannes. *Das "Speculum Universale" des Radulfus Ardens* Munich, 1961. Mitteilungen des Grabmann-Instituts der Universität München, no. 5.

Grundmann, Herbert. *Religiöse Bewegungen im Mittelalter.* Berlin, 1935. Historische Studien, no. 267.

Guillemain, Bernard. "Chiffres et statistiques pour l'histoire ecclésiastique du moyen âge." *Le moyen âge* 59 (1953): 341–65.

Haendler, G. *Epochen karolingischer Theologie. Eine Untersuchung über die karolingische Gutächten zum byzantinischen Bilderstreit.* Berlin, 1958. Theologische Arbeiten, no. 10.

Haenens, A. d'. *Les Invasions normandes en Belgique au ixᵉ siècle. Le phénomène et sa répercussion dans l'historiographie médiévale.* Louvain, 1967. Université de Louvain: Recueil de travaux d'histoire et de philologie, 4th ser., fasc. 38.

Hafner, Wolfgang. *Der Basiliuskommentar zur Regula S. Benedicti.* Münster, 1959. Beiträge zur Geschichte des alten Mönchtums und des Benediktinerordens, no. 23.

Hallinger, Kassius. *Gorze-Kluny, Studien zu den monastischen Lebensformen und Gegensätzen des Hochmittelalters.* Rome, 1950–51. 2 vols. Studia Anselmiana, nos. 22–23 and 24–25.

Hammond, E. A. "Physicians in Medieval English Religious Houses." *Bulletin of the History of Medicine* 32 (1958): 105–20.

Hansay, Alfred. *Etude sur la formation et l'organisation économique du domaine de l'abbaye de Saint-Trond depuis les origines jusqu'à la fin du xiiiᵉ siècle.* Ghent, 1899. Université de Gand: Recueil de travaux publiés par la faculté de philosophie et de lettres, no. 22.

Hanssens, S. "De legatiereis van Robert van Courson in Vlaanderen en Henegouwen." In *Miscellanea historica in honorem Alberti de Meyer.* Louvain and Brussels, 1946. 1:528–38.

Hauviller, Ernst. *Ulrich von Cluny: ein biographischer Beitrag zur Geschichte der Cluniacenser im 11. Jahrhundert.* Münster, 1896. Kirchengeschichtliche Studien, vol. 3, part 3.

Heijmann, H. "Emon." *Dictionnaire d'histoire et de géographie ecclési-astiques*, vol. 15, cols. 434-37.

Heintschel, Donald, *The Medieval Concept of an Ecclesiastical Office* Washington, D.C., 1956. Catholic University of America Canon Law Studies, no. 363.

Herlihy, David. "Church Property on the European Continent, 701-1200." *Speculum* 36 (1961): 81-105.

Hermans, Vincentius. "De novitiatu in ordine Benedictino-Cisterciensi et in iure communi usque ad annum 1335." *Analecta sacri ordinis Cister-ciensis* 3 (1947): 1-110.

Hirsch, E. "Der Simoniebegriff und eine angebliche Erweiterung dessel-ben im elften Jahrhundert." *Archiv für katholisches Kirchenrecht* 86 (1906): 3-19.

Holtzmann, Walter. "Die Benutzung Gratians in der päpstlichen Kanzlei im 12. Jahrhundert." *Studia Gratiana* 1 (1953): 323-49.

Holzherr, Georg. "Die *Regula Ferioli*: das älteste literarische Zeugnis der Benediktinerregel?" *Studia Anselmiana* 42 (1957): 223-29.

Horn, Hans-Jürgen. "Giezie und Simonie." *Jahrbuch für Antike und Christentum* 8/9 (1965-66): 189-202.

Huizing, Peter. "The Earliest Development of Excommunication *Latae Sententiae* by Gratian and the Earliest Decretists." *Studia Gratiana* 3 (1955): 277-320.

H(unt), W(illiam). "Richard." *Dictionary of National Biography* 48 (London, 1896): 191-94.

Imbert, Jean. "Le Droit romain dans les textes juridiques carolingiens." In *Studi in onore di Pietro de Francisci*. Milan, 1956. 3:61-67.

————. *Les Hôpitaux en droit canonique du décret de Gratien à la sécularisa-tion de l'administration de l'Hôtel-Dieu de Paris en 1505*. Paris, 1947. L'Eglise et l'Etat au moyen âge, no. 8.

Iung, N. "Pierre le Chantre." *Dictionnaire de théologie catholique*, vol. 12, pt. 2, cols. 1901-6.

Kealy, Thomas. *Dowry of Women Religious*. Washington, D.C. 1941. Catholic University of America Canon Law Studies, no. 134.

Kemp, B. R. "Hereditary Benefices in the Medieval English Church: A Herefordshire Example." *Bulletin of the Institute of Historical Research* 43 (1970): 1-15.

Kemp, E. W. *Canonization and Authority in the Western Church*. Oxford, 1948.

————. "Pope Alexander III and the Canonization of Saints." *Transactions of the Royal Historical Society*, 4th ser., 27 (1945): 13-28.

Knowles, David, and R. Neville Hadcock. *Medieval Religious Houses: England and Wales.* London, 1953.

Knowles, David. *The Monastic Order in England: A History of Its Development from the Times of Saint Dunstan to the Fourth Lateran Council, 943-1216.* 2d ed. Cambridge, 1963.

———. "The Primitive Documents of the Cistercian Order." In *Great Historical Enterprises: Problems in Monastic History.* London, 1963. Pp. 197-224.

———. "The *Regula Magistri* and the *Rule* of Saint Benedict." In *Great Historical Enterprises: Problems in Monastic History.* London, 1963. Pp. 135-95.

———. "The Reforming Decrees of Peter the Venerable, with a Note by M. M. Postan." In *Petrus Venerabilis, 1156-1956.* Ed. Giles Constable and James Kritzeck. Rome, 1956. Studia Anselmiana, no. 40. Pp. 1-20.

Kowalski, Romuald. *Sustenance of Religious Houses of Regulars.* Washington, D.C. 1944. Catholic University of America Canon Law Studies, no. 199.

Kurze, W. "Der Adel und das Kloster S. Salvatore all'Isola im XI. und XII. Jahrhundert." *Quellen und Forschungen aus italienischen Archiven und Bibliotheken* 47 (1967): 446-573.

Kuttner, Stephan, and Eleanor Rathbone. "Anglo-Norman Canonists of the Twelfth Century: An Introductory Study." *Traditio* 7 (1949-57): 279-358.

Kuttner, Stephan. "Gratian." *Encyclopaedia Brittanica.* Chicago, 1968. 10:707-8.

———. *Harmony from Dissonance: An Interpretation of Medieval Canon Law.* Latrobe, Pa., 1960. Wimmer Lecture, no. 10.

———. *Repertorium der Kanonistik, 1140-1234.* Prodomus Glossatorum I. Vatican City, 1937. Studi e testi, no. 71.

Ladner, Gerhard. "Reformatio." In *Ecumenical Dialogue at Harvard.* Ed. S. H. Miller and G. E. Wright. Cambridge, Mass., 1964. Pp. 172-90.

Landry, Charles. *La Mort civile des religieux dans l'ancien droit français, étude historique et critique.* Paris, 1900.

Lawrence, Clifford Hugh. *Saint Edmund of Abingdon: A Study in Hagiography and History.* Oxford, 1960.

LeBras, Gabriel; Charles Lefebvre; and Jacqueline Rambaud-Buhot. *L'Age classique, 1140-1378: sources et théorie du droit.* Paris, 1965. Histoire du droit et des institutions de l'Eglise en occident, no. 7.

LeCacheux, Marie-Josephe. *Histoire de l'abbaye de Saint-Amand de Rouen, des origines à la fin du xvie siècle.* Caen, 1937.

Leclercq, Jean. "La Crise du monachisme aux xie et xiie siècles." *Bulletino dell'Istituto Storico Italiano per il Medio Evo e Archivio Muratoriano* 70 (1958): 19-41.

―――. "Simoniaca Heresis." *Studi Gregoriani* 1 (1947): 523-30.

―――. *La Vie parfaite*. Paris, 1948. Tradition monastique, no. 1.

Leinz, A. *Die Simonie. Eine kanonistische Studie*. Freiburg im Breisgau, 1902.

Lentini, Anselmo. "Note sull'oblazione dei fanciulli nella Regola di S. Benedetto." *Studia Anselmiana* 18/19 (1947): 195-225.

Lesne, Emile. "Une Source de la fortune monastique: les donations à charge de pension alimentaire du viiie au xe siècle." *Mélanges de philosophie et histoire publiés à l'occasion du cinquantenaire de la faculté des lettres de l'Université de Lille. Mémoires et travaux . . . des facultés catholiques de Lille* 32 (1927): 33-47.

Lewis, Charles E. "Ricardus Anglicus: A *familiaris* of Archbishop Hubert Walter." *Traditio* 22 (1966): 469-71.

Lucchesi, Giovanni. "La 'Vita S. Rodulphi et S. Dominici Loricati' di S. Pier Damiano." *Rivista di storia della Chiesa in Italia* 11 (1965): 166-77.

Luchaire, Achille. "Innocent III et le quatrième concile de Latran." *Revue historique* 97 (1908): 225-63; 98 (1909): 1-21.

―――. *La Société française au temps de Philipe-Auguste*. Paris, 1909.

Lynch, Joseph. "Cistercians and Underage Novices." *Cîteaux* 24 (1973): 283-97.

Maccarrone, Michele. "Innocenzo III primo del suo pontificato." *Archivio della r. deputazione romana di storia patria* 66 (1943): 59-134.

―――. "Riforma e sviluppo della vita religiosa con Innocenzo III." *Rivista di storia della chiesa in Italia* 16 (1962): 29-72.

McLaughlin, Terence P. *Le très ancien droit monastique de l'occident*. Ligugé and Paris, 1935. Archives de la France monastique, no. 38.

Mahn, Jean B. *L'Ordre cistercien et son gouvernement des origines au milieu du xiiie siècle, 1098-1265*. 2d ed. Paris, 1951.

Marchal, Jean. *Le "droit d'oblat": essai sur une variété de pensionnés monastiques*. Poitiers, 1955. Archives de la France monastique, no. 49.

Marié, G. "Convers." *Catholicisme*, vol. 3, cols. 159-60.

Marie-Joseph, P. "Albert de Verceil." *Dictionnaire d'histoire et de géographie ecclésiastiques*, vol. 1, cols. 1564-67.

Meier-Welcker, Hans. "Die Simonie im frühen Mittelalter." *Zeitschrift für Kirchengeschichte* 64 (1952): 61-93.

Michel, Anton. *Die Sentenzen des Kardinals Humbert, das erste Rechtsbuch der päpstlichen Reform.* Leipzig, 1943. Schriften des Reichsinstituts für ältere deutsche Geschichtskunde, no. 7.

Miller, Edward. "England in the Twelfth and Thirteenth Centuries: An Economic Contrast?" *Economic History Review,* 2d ser., 24 (1971): 1–14.

Mirbt, Carl. *Die Publizistik im Zeitalter Gregors VII.* Leipzig, 1894.

Mollat, G. "La Restitution des églises privées au patrimoine ecclésiastique en France du ixe au xie siècle." *Revue historique de droit français et étranger,* 4th ser., 27 (1949): 399–423.

Moorman, John R. H. *Church Life in England in the Thirteenth Century.* Cambridge, 1946.

Mor, Carlo G. "Le Droit romain dans les collections canoniques des xe et xie siècles." *Revue historique de droit français et étranger,* 4th ser., 6 (1927): 512–24.

Musset, Lucien. *Les Invasions: le second assaut contre l'Europe Chrétienne, viie-xie siècles.* Paris, 1965. 2d ed. La nouvelle Clio, 12.

Naz, R. "Compilationes (Quinque Antiquae)." *Dictionnaire de droit canonique,* vol. 3, cols. 1239–41.

———. "Somme." *Dictionnaire de droit canonique,* vol. 7, cols. 1073–74.

Oesterlé, G. "De potestate abbatum dispensandi ab irregularitatibus." *Liturgica 2* (Montserrat, 1958): 465–81.

———. "Irregularités." *Dictionnaire de droit canonique,* vol. 6, cols. 42–66.

Oliger, Livarius. "De pueris oblatis in ordine Minorum (cum textu hucusque inedito Fr. Johannis Peckam)." *Archivum Franciscanum historicum* 8 (1915): 389–447; 10 (1917): 271–88.

Orestano, R. "Beni dei monaci e monasteri nella legislazione Giustinianea." In *Studi in onore di Pietro de Francisci.* Milan, 1956. 3:561–94.

Orlandis, José. "Notas sobre la 'Oblatio puerorum' en los siglos xi y xii." *Anuario de historia del derecho español* 31 (1961): 163–73.

Pacaut, Marcel. *Alexandre III: étude sur la conception du pouvoir pontifical dans sa pensée et dans son oeuvre.* Paris, 1956. L'Eglise et l'Etat au moyen âge, no. 11.

———. "Roland Bandinelli." *Dictionnaire de droit canonique,* vol. 7, cols. 702–26.

Palo, Aloisio di. *Innocenzo III e gli ordini religiosi.* Vatican City, 1957.

Parisella, Innocentius. "Ecclesiae Romanae dimicatio contra simoniam a Leone IX usque ad Concilium Lateranense I (1049–1123)." *Apollinaris* 15 (1942): 95–140.

Peltier, H. "Raban Maur." *Dictionnaire de théologie catholique*, Vol. 13, pt. 2, cols. 1601-20.

Porée, A. A. *Histoire de l'abbaye de Bec*. Evreux, 1901.

Poupardin, René. "Les grandes familles comtales à l'époque carolingienne." *Revue historique* 72 (1900): 72-95.

Rambaud-Buhot, Jacqueline. "Les *Paleae* dans le décret de Gratien." In *Proceedings of the Second International Congress of Medieval Canon Law*. Ed. S. Kuttner and J. J. Ryan. Vatican City, 1965. Monumenta iuris canonici, Series C, Subsidia I. Pp. 23-44.

Riepenhoff, J. R. *Zur Frage des Ursprungs der Verbindlichkeit des Oblateninstituts. Ein Beitrag zur Geschichte des mittelalterlichen Bildungswesen*. Münster, 1939. Münstersche Beiträge zur Geschichtsforschung, no. 74/75.

Russell, Josiah Cox. "Notes on the Biography of St. Edmund of Abingdon." *Harvard Theological Review* 54 (1961): 147-58.

Ryan, J. Joseph. *Saint Peter Damiani and His Canonical Sources: A Preliminary Study in the Antecedents of the Gregorian Reform*. Toronto, 1956. Pontifical Institute of Medieval Studies, Studies and Texts, no. 2.

Ryder, R. A. *Simony: An Historical Synopsis and Commentary*. Washington, D.C., 1931. Catholic University of America Canon Law Studies, no. 65.

Saltet, Louis. *Les Réordinations: étude sur le sacrement de l'ordre*. Paris, 1907. Etudes d'histoire des dogmes et d'ancienne littérature ecclésiastique.

Schmitz, Philibert. *Histoire de l'ordre de Saint Benoît*. Maredsous, 1942-56. 7 vols.

Schulte, Johann F. von. "Die Paleae im Dekret Gratians." *Sitzungsberichte der kaiserlichen Akademie der Wissenschaften*. Philos.-historische Klasse, no. 78 (1874), pp. 287-312.

Seckel, Emil. "Canonistische Quellenstudien I. Die Westminster Synode 1175, eine Quelle falscher oder verfälschter Canonen in den nachgratianischen Sammlungen." *Deutsche Zeitschrift für Kirchenrecht*, 3d ser., 9 (1899): 159-89.

Seidl, Johann. *Die Gott-Verlobung von Kindern in Mönchs- und Nonnen-Klöstern oder De pueris oblatis*. Munich, 1872.

Semmler, Josef. "Zur Uberlieferung der monastischen Gesetzgebung Ludwigs des Frommen." *Deutsches Archiv für Erforschung des Mittelalters* 16 (1960): 309-88.

Sinopoli, Mario. "Influenza di Graziano nell'evoluzione del diritto monastico." *Studia Gratiana* 3 (1955): 321-48.

Smith, Arthur Lionel. *Church and State in the Middle Ages.* Oxford, 1913.

Snape, Robert Hugh. *English Monastic Finances in the Later Middle Ages.* Cambridge, 1926. Cambridge Studies in Medieval Life and Thought.

Stickler, A. M. "L'Evolution de la discipline du célibat dans l'Eglise en occident, de la fin de l'âge patristique au concile de Trente." In *Sacerdoce et célibat. Etudes historiques et théologiques.* Gembloux and Louvain, 1971. Pp. 373–442.

Stuckert, Howard Morris. *Corrodies in the English Monasteries: A Study in English Social History of the Middle Ages.* Philadelphia, 1923.

Stutz, Ulrich. "Die Cistercienser wider Gratians Dekret." *Zeitschrift der Savigny-Stiftung für Rechtsgeschichte.* Kanonistische Abteilung, no. 9 (1919), pp. 63–98.

———. *Geschichte des kirchlichen Benefizialwesens von seinen Anfängen bis auf die Zeit Alexanders III.* 2d ed., Hans Erich Feine, ed. Aalen, 1961. Vol. 1.

———. "The Proprietary Church as an Element of Medieval Germanic Ecclesiastical Law." In *Medieval Germany, 911–1250.* Trans. Geoffrey Barraclough. Oxford, 1939, 2:35–70.

Tellenbach, Gerd. *Church, State, and Christian Society at the Time of the Investiture Contest.* Trans. R. F. Bennett. Oxford, 1958. Studies in Medieval History, no. 3.

Tillmann, Helene. *Papst Innocenz III.* Bonn, 1954. Bonner historische Forschungen, no. 3.

Torquebiau, P. "Corpus Juris Canonici." *Dictionnaire de droit canonique,* vol. 4, cols. 610–43.

Ullmann, Walter. *The Growth of Papal Government in the Middle Ages.* 3d ed. London, 1970.

Vacandard, E. "Célibat ecclésiastique." *Dictionnaire de théologie catholique,* vol. 2, cols. 2068–88.

Valous, Guy de. "Cluny." *Dictionnaire d'histoire et de géographie ecclésiastiques,* vol. 13, cols. 35–174.

———. *Le Monachisme clunisien des origines au xve siècle.* Paris, 1935. 2 vols. Archives de la France monastique, nos. 39–40.

Valvekens, J. B. "Fratres et sorores 'ad succurrendum'." *Analecta Praemonstratensia* 37 (1961): 323–28.

Vetulani, Adam. "Nouvelles vues sur le Décret de Gratien." In *La Pologne au xe congrès international des sciences historiques à Rome.* Warsaw, 1955. Pp. 83–105.

Vielhaber, Klaus. *Gottschalk der Sachse.* Bonn, 1956. Bonner historische Forschungen, no. 5.

Vogüé, Adalbert de. *La Communauté et l'abbé dans la règle de saint Benoît.* Paris, 1961. Textes et études theologiques.

Vooght, P. de. "La *Simoniaca haeresis* selon les auteurs scholastiques." *Ephemerides theologicae lovanienses* 30 (1954): 64–80.

Walter, Johannes von. *Die ersten Wanderprediger Frankreichs.* Leipzig, 1903. Studien zur Geschichte der Theologie und der Kirche, vol. 9, pt. 3.

Weber, N. A. *A History of Simony in the Christian Church to 814.* Baltimore, 1909.

Weitzel, Joseph. *Begriff und Erscheinungsformen der Simonie bei Gratian und den Dekretisten.* Munich, 1967. Munchener Theologische Studien, Kanonistische Abteilung, no. 25.

Wilmart, André. "La Collection chronologique des écrits de Geoffroi, abbé de Vendôme." *Revue bénédictine* 43 (1931): 239–45.

Wood, Susan. *English Monasteries and Their Patrons in the Thirteenth Century.* Oxford, 1955. Oxford Historical Series, British Series.

Young, Charles R. *Hubert Walter, Lord of Canterbury and Lord of England.* Durham, N.C., 1968. Duke Historical Publications.

Index

Abraham, 40

Ad succurrendum entry, 13, 27–36, 54 n.40 and n.41; canonical requirements for, 53 n.17; defense of, 51 n.16; and litigation, 33–34

Age of recruits, 38, 39, 55 n.46; and Carthusians, 56 n.56; and Cistercians, 57 n.62; and Cluniacs, 39; and Grand-montines, 56 n.56.

Alan, canonist, 131, 132

Albert, canonist, 132

Albert de Mora. *See* Gregory VIII, pope

Albert of Vercelli, patriarch of Jerusalem, 190–92, 194, 216, 220; and Carmelite rule, 201 n.47

Alexander III (Roland Bandinelli), pope, 109, 114, 147–54, 155, 156, 157, 179, 193; and canon *Monachi non pretio*, 149–50, 183; and canon *Non satis*, 148–49, 204; and decretal letter *Veniens*, 127, 130–31, 150–51, 204

Amann, Emile, 64

Amiens, bishop of, 205

Anagni, 153

Ananias and Saphira, example of, 74, 92, 93, 94–95

Andrès, monastery of, 45

Angers, 49; Benedictine chapter meeting in 1220, 212

Aniane, monastery of, 47

Anna and Samuel, example of, 40, 94–95

Anselm, archbishop of Canterbury, 27

Auctoritates, 87, 93, 95, 96, 122, 123;

Gerhoh of Reichersberg and, 103 n.35; Gratian and, 93–94, 97, 118–19

Augustine, bishop of Hippo, 89; rule of, 155; sermon 86 on almsgiving, 100 n.19

Baldwin, John W., 180

Bamberg, 91

Basil, prior of La Grande Chartreuse, 160

Bec, monastery of, 198 n.23; simoniac monks at, 184, 186, 191, 206, 222

Becquet, Jean, 165

Bedford, chapter of English Austin canons at, 212

Benedict of Aniane, 62

Benedict the Levite, 63

Benedict of Nursia, *Rule* of, 213, 220; and children, 86–87; and entry gifts, 62, 74, 86–87, 162; interpretation of, 86–87, 89, 92; and recruitment, xii–xvi

Berdoues, monastery of, 16–17, 34, 141 n.65, 161

Bernard of Clairvaux: and entry gifts, 75, 161; and Gerhoh of Reichersberg, 91; recruitment efforts of, 22 n.49

Bibliothèque nationale (Paris), 189

Bloemhof (Floridus Hortus), monastery of, 218

Bloomkamp, monastery of, 163, 211, 212

Bonavallis, monastery of, 223–24

Bonaventure, 202 n.61

Boniface, pope. *See* Pseudo-Boniface, pope

Braga (572), Council of, 96

Burchard, bishop of Worms, 94

Caesarea, archbishop of, 216

Caesarius of Heisterbach, 29, 123, 223–24

Carmelites, rule of, 201 n.47

Carthusians, 158, 189; and economic policy, 8, 17; and entry payments, 160–61, 165

Cassian, John, 73, 74

Catesby, nunnery of, 215

Celestine III, pope, 157, 163

Chalcedon (451), Council of: and monastic recruitment, xiv; and simony, 66, 125, 126

Chalons (813), Council of, 70–71

Charlemagne, 3, 61, 62; and Byzantine Empire, 62–63

Charles the Bald, 3

Chichester (1245–52), diocesan statutes of, 209

Cistercians, 28, 165, 189, 196 n.2, 197 n.19; and age of recruits, 39–40; and economic policy, 7–8, 17; and entry *ad succurrendum*, 33–34; and entry payments, 161–63, 194, 205, 211–12, 223; and Gratian, 161–62, 174 n.57; and oblation, 39–40; and promises of future entry, 174 n.55 and n.62

Citeaux, monastery of, 161

Clairvaux, monastery of, 50 n.1, 212

Clement III, pope, 111, 127, 156–57, 182, 192, 193, 204

Cluniacs, 165; and age of recruits, 39; and entry payments, 163–65, 194, 211; and numbers, 50 n.2; and oblation, 44–45; and recruitment, 22 n.49

Cluny, monastery of, 11, 41, 69

Cologne, 223; council in 1260, 209

Compiègne (1238), Council of, 209

Compilatio II, 127

Compilatio III, 116, 157

Conques, monastery of, 35

Conversi, 17, 163; and *nutriti*, 36, 37, 55 n.54. *See also Laicus conversus*

Coulton, G. G., 60 n.93

Decretum. See Gratian

Deeds of the Abbots of Saint Trond, 31

De regularibus. See Clement III, pope

Dickson, Marcel and Christiane, 188

Dilectus filius, 182–83; in canonical collections, 204, 224 n.3

Dowry, monastic, xvii, 194, 202 n.2

Duggan, Charles, 153

Duplex legationis edictum of 789, 61

Edmund Rich, archbishop of Canterbury, 228 n.74 and n.75; and entry payments, 215–16, 228 n.78; and oblation, 46

Elisha, 66

Emo of Huizinge, abbot of Bloemhof, 216 218–19

Eugene II, pope, 3

Everard of Ypres, 124

Fontevrault, nunnery of, 48, 207

Franciscans, rule of, 214

Frankfort (794), council of, 61

Fraterna societas, 109–11

Fructuosus of Braga, 73–74

Fulda, monastery of, 37

Gellone, monastery of, 6, 46

Génestout, Augustin, xii

Geoffrey, abbot of the Holy Trinity at Vendôme, 52 n.24, 71

Gerald of Wales, 28

Gerhoh of Reichersberg, 90–93, 94, 95

Giezi, 66

Gift at entry, xvi–xvii, 3; Benedict's *Rule* and, xiv; legitimacy of, 112–17; and negotiations, 11–18; and poor monasteries, 117–22; reluctance to accept, 72–75, 81 n.72; timing of, 116, 137 n.38, n.39, and n.40

Gilbert of Sempringham, 167

Gilbertines. *See* Sempringham

Gimont, monastery of, 34, 162

Godfrey, duke of Lorraine, 33

Gottschalk of Orbais, 37

Grandmontines, 8, 165–67; and entry payments, 166–67; customary of the, 166

Gratian, 40, 93–98, 112; and Cistercians,

161-62; and his commentators, 107-8; *dicta* of, 93, 95; *paleae* in *Decretum* of, 97-98, 105 n.51; and poor religious houses, 118-19

Gratian, bishop of Todi, 170 n.12, 171 n.19

Gregory I, pope, xv, 96, 130; and concept of simony, 66, 78 n.28, 79 n.45

Gregory VII, pope, 127

Gregory VIII (Albert de Mora), pope, 155

Gregory IX, pope, 205, 208, 214, 216; *Decretales* of, 204, 213; and reform of Benedictines, 212-13, 220

Guibert, abbot of Nogent, 38-39, 46, 48

Guigo I, prior of La Grande Chartreuse, 160

Guigo II, prior of La Grande Chartreuse, 160

Henry III, king of England, 205

Herman of Perigord, grand master of the Templars, 216-17

Hincmar, archbishop of Reims, 37

Hirsau, monastery of, 41

Holy Trinity, monastery of the, 8-9, 14, 29-30, 44

Holy Trinity, order of the, 8, 168

Honorius III, pope, 204, 205, 206, 207

Hospital of Jerusalem, 206

Hospitals, 111, 168, 213-14

Hostiensis (Henry of Segusio), 205

Hrabanus Maurus, 37

Hubert Walter, archbishop of Canterbury, 180-83, 186, 187-88, 191, 220; and canonists, 196 n.8

Hugh IV, abbot of Cluny, 163-64

Hugh V, abbot of Cluny, 164

Hugh, bishop of Lincoln, 181; and entry feast at Saint Neot's, 173 n.41; and Nun-Coton, 158-59, 193

Huguccio, 119-20, 121, 180

Humbert of Romans, 219-20

Ingressus, purchase of, 108-12

Innocent III, pope, 11, 125, 147, 157, 163, 165, 168-69, 179-95 passim, 203, 204, 205, 208, 211; and the order of the Holy Trinity, 168; and the Templars, 111, 216

Innocent IV, pope, 216

Irregularitas as punishment for simoniacs, 149-50, 152, 206-7; at Bec, 184-85; among Cistercians, 211

Ivo, bishop of Chartres, 52 n.24, 70, 94

Jancelinus, prior of La Grande Chartreuse, 160

John, king of England, 187

John, abbot of Fécamp, 71

John Godard, abbot of Fontmorigny, 163, 205, 212

John of Matha, 168

John of Wales, 157

Justinian, xv, 87; and property of entrants, xvi-xvii; and punishment of simoniacs, 128, 129

Klosterneuburg, canonry of, 206

Laicus conversus, 110, 134 n.12

Lang, Jane, 221-22

Lateran (1139), second council of the, 184

Lateran (1179), third council of the, 152; and canon *Monachi non pretio*, 149-50, 180, 184, 213; and *Irregularitas*, 185, 206

Lateran (1215), fourth council of the, 193-95, 203, 204, 218; impact of, 211, 213, 224 n.1; and treatment of simoniacal religious, 125, 127, 194-95, 217

Lateran monastery, 183

Leo IX, pope, 79 n.42

Liber de simoniacis, 91, 92-93

Libri carolini, 76 n.9

Lincoln, bishop of, 205, 206

London, bishop of, 206

London (1127), Council of, 98, 154

London (1175), Council of, 111

London (1200), Council of, 180, 209

London (1238), Benedictine meeting at, 213

Lothario dei Segni. *See* Innocent III

Louis the Pious, 61, 62

Lucca (1253), Council of, 209

Mabillon, Jean, 83, 90
McLaughlin, Terence P., 109
Malbod, nunnery of, 207
Matthew, abbot of Foigny, 213
Melfi (1089), Council of, 64, 69; and canon law, 98, 154; and Gratian's *Decretum*, 97-98
Menko, 218
Monachi non pretio, 149, 152, 180, 183, 197 n.21; and canonical collections 171 n.21
Montpellier (1215), council of, 188
Mortgage, 10-11

Nicaea (787), second Council of, 62-63
Nîmes (1252), diocesan statutes of, 209
Non satis, 149, 152, 171 n.21
Normandy, Benedictine chapter meeting in 1234, 212
Norwich, bishop of, 205
Numbers in religious houses, 3-4, 22 n.51, 25-26; Cluniacs and, 22 n.51; Cistercians and, 22 n.51; and resources, 50 n.1, 158-59; and simony, 181, 186, 194-95, 207
Nun-Coton, nunnery of, 158-59, 193
Nutriti. See Conversi

Oblation of children, 36-50, 83-84; and Benedict's *Rule*, 36; and Bernard of Clairvaux, 56 n.61; and clerical marriage, 42-43; and entry gift, 89; permanence of, 55 n.47, n.50 and n.51
Odo of Canterbury, 28
Odo of Sully, bishop of Paris, 168
Odo Rigaud, archbishop of Rouen, 210, 214, 220-21
Orleans, 218
Otho, papal legate, 213
Ourscamp, monastery of, 161
Oxford, 215, 218; council in 1222, 209, 210, 226 n.38

Paris, 180, 215, 218, 223; council in 1213, 187-88
Paucapalea, 109, 128

Pauperes christi, monks as, 86, 100 n.11
Penal exile for simoniacal entrants, 126, 130, 142 n.76; resistance to, 225 n.15; to a stricter order, 156-57, 172 n.35, 192, 205
Peter, saint, 66-67, 92
Peter Abelard, 48, 72-73, 74-75
Peter of Benevento, 188
Peter the Chanter, 111, 121, 122-23; and Bernard of Clairvaux, 75, 161; and Innocent III, 180; *Summa de sacramentis* of, 75, 188; *Verbum abbreviatum* of, 121
Peter Collevacino, 183
Peter Damian, 32, 71
Peter the Venerable, abbot of Cluny, 39, 44-45, 164-65
Peter Waldo, 48
Philip of Otterburg, 223
Pippin, king of Italy, 3
Poor Clares, entry payments among, 202 n.61
Potthast, A., 184
Premonstratensians, 8, 123, 218; and entry payments, 145 n.104; and promise of future enry, 174 n.62; and simoniacal reception, 160
Privatio officii, 151
Propositum religionis, 109
Pseudo-Boniface, pope: letter of (*Quam pio*), 95-96, 97, 115-16, 122-23; origin of, 104 n.46
Punishment of simoniacal entrants, 124-27, 182-83, 204-5

Quam pio. See Pseudo-Boniface, pope
Quedlinburg, nunnery of, 206

Ralph, Norman monk, 28
Raoul Ardent (Radulphus Ardens), 216, 228 n.79
Raymond of Peñaforte, 210
Reading, monastery of, 164
Redon, monastery of, 15, 35
Reginald Rich, 215
Regula monasterii tarnatensis, 74
Reims, 213

Religious habit as second baptism, 27–28, 31, 51 n.14

Richard, archbishop of Canterbury, 153–55

Robert de Courson, 180, 187–90, 207, 216; and visitation of Vezelay, 183–84

Robert, abbot of Saint Victor, 168

Roland Bandinelli. *See* Alexander III

Rome: council in 595, 96, 98; council in 1099, 69

Ronceray, nunnery of Le, 6, 12, 48

Rouen, 213; council in 1214, 187–88

Rudolph of Saint Trond, 83–90, 94, 95, 112, 114

Rufinus, 11–12, 116–17, 117–18, 128–29; and *irregularitas*, 170 n.10; and penal exile, 126, 151–52; and poor religious houses, 117–18, 120–21

Rule of the Master, xii

Sackur, Ernst, 91

Saint Andrew, canonry of, 155

Saint Anthony, hospital of, 206, 214

Saint Aubin (Angers), monastery of, 13, 15, 48, 49

Saint Aubin (Rouen), priory of, 220–21

Saint Bavo, monastery of, 40

Saint Colomban, canonry of, 206

Saint Denys de Nogent-le-Rotrou, monastery of, 17, 49, 115

Saint Maur-sur-Loire, monastery of, 32

Saint Nazerius, monastery of, 206

Saint Panteleon, monastery of, 83, 84, 87, 89, 113, 114

Saint Peter of Chartres, monastery of, 47

Saint Trond, monastery of, 31

Saint Vaast, monastery of, 213

Saint Victor-en-Caux, monastery of, 214

Saint Victor (Marseilles), monastery of, 67

Saint Victor (Paris), canon of, 27, 29

Samuel. *See* Anna

Saphira. *See* Ananias

Saragossa, bishop of, 156, 157

Selby Abbey, 209

Sempringham, order of, 167–68; rule of, 177 n.90

Sens, archbishop of, 183

Sibertus, prior of Saint Panteleon, 83–85

Sicardus of Cremona, 112–13, 129

Simon Magus, 66–67, 149, 167

Simon of Elham, 205

Simoniacal entry, 68–70, 84–85, 88; among Cluniacs, 164; after 1150s, 159–60; before 1150s, 159; *exactio*, 91–92, 112–17, 136 n.32; nuns and, 193–94, 202 n.59, 212, 221, 227 n.56; and *pactio*, 114; and payment, 127–32; and university masters, 200 n.39

Simony, 64–70, 78 n.26, 91–92, 134 n.11

Simplicitas, 191–92, 211–12; as mitigating circumstance, 194–95, 204, 206, 216, 219–22

Souther, Richard, 37

Speyer, Benedictine chapter meeting in about 1227, 212

Stephan, bishop of Tournai, 40, 112, 119, 129

Stephen of Liciac, prior of Grandmont, 165, 166

Stephen of Muret, 165, 166

Stutz, Ulrich, 161–62

Summa coloniensis, 113, 117, 119, 121, 126

Summa "De iure naturali", 111, 129–30

Summa lipsiensis, 130

Summa parisiensis, 109–11, 116

Summa "Tractaturus magister", 129

Templars, 111, 190–92, 214, 216–17

Teutonic Knights, 214

Thierry, abbot of Saint Trond, 98 n.1

Toledo (633), fourth Council of, 37

Tours (1163), Council of, 149–49, 152, 213

Transitus, xv, 56 n.55, 141 n.74, 189

Turpe lucrum, 70–71, 72

Ulrich of Cluny, 41–44

Urban II, pope, 69, 98. *See also* Melfi (1089), Council of; and Rome (1099), Council of

Urban III, pope, 155

Valvekens, J. B.

Van den Eynde, Damian, 91

Veniens, 150–52, 157, 170 n.18, 171 n.21, 204; addressee of, 170 n.12, 171 n.19

Vezelay, monastery of, 183–84, 189

Vigeois, monastery of, 123

Villencort, nunnery of, 205, 206

Visitation, 209–10, 222; by archdeacon, 210; secrecy of, 197 n.15

Vita apostolica, 48–49

Vitae patrum, 27

Walter Gray, archbishop of York, 209

Warin, abbot of Saint Arnulph, 71

Werimbald of Cambrai, 48

Westminster: Council in 1173, 154; Council in 1175, 154–55

Wilkins, David, 154

William of Auvergne, bishop of Paris, 42

William, abbot of Hirsau, 41

Worms (868), Council of, 37